PEOPLE, MARKETS, GOODS:
ECONOMIES AND SOCIETIES IN HISTORY
Volume 10

Cameralism in Practice

PEOPLE, MARKETS, GOODS:
ECONOMIES AND SOCIETIES IN HISTORY

ISSN: 2051-7467

Series editors
Barry Doyle – University of Huddersfield
Steve Hindle – The Huntington Library
Jane Humphries – University of Oxford
Willem M. Jongman – University of Groningen
Catherine Schenk – University of Glasgow

The interactions of economy and society, people and goods, transactions and actions are at the root of most human behaviours. Economic and social historians are participants in the same conversation about how markets have developed historically and how they have been constituted by economic actors and agencies in various social, institutional and geographical contexts. New debates now underpin much research in economic and social, cultural, demographic, urban and political history. Their themes have enduring resonance – financial stability and instability, the costs of health and welfare, the implications of poverty and riches, flows of trade and the centrality of communications. This paperback series aims to attract historians interested in economics and economists with an interest in history by publishing high quality, cutting edge academic research in the broad field of economic and social history from the late medieval/ early modern period to the present day. It encourages the interaction of qualitative and quantitative methods through both excellent monographs and collections offering path-breaking overviews of key research concerns. Taking as its benchmark international relevance and excellence it is open to scholars and subjects of any geographical areas from the case study to the multi-nation comparison.

PREVIOUSLY PUBLISHED TITLES IN THE SERIES ARE
LISTED AT THE END OF THE VOLUME

Cameralism in Practice

State Administration and Economy in Early Modern Europe

Edited by

Marten Seppel and Keith Tribe

THE BOYDELL PRESS

This book was supported by a grant from the Estonian Research Council (PUT119).

First published 2017
The Boydell Press, Woodbridge

ISBN 978-1-78327-228-0

The Boydell Press is an imprint of Boydell & Brewer Ltd
PO Box 9, Woodbridge, Suffolk IP12 3DF, UK
and of Boydell & Brewer Inc.
668 Mt Hope Avenue, Rochester, NY 14620–2731, USA
website: www.boydellandbrewer.com

A catalogue record for this book is available
from the British Library

The publisher has no responsibility for the continued existence or accuracy of URLs for
external or third-party internet websites referred to in this book, and does not guarantee
that any content on such websites is, or will remain, accurate or appropriate.

This publication is printed on acid-free paper

Contents

List of Illustrations   vii
List of Contributors   viii

Introduction: Cameralism in Practice   1
    Marten Seppel

1. Comparing Cameralisms: The Case of Sweden and Prussia   17
    Lars Magnusson

2. Baltic Cameralism?   39
    Keith Tribe

3. Cameralism in Russia: Empress Catherine II and Population Policy   65
    Roger Bartlett

4. Cameralist Population Policy and the Problem of Serfdom,
    1680–1720   91
    Marten Seppel

5. Cameralist Writing in the Mirror of Practice: The Long
    Development of Forestry in Germany   111
    Paul Warde

6. Cameralist Theoretical Writings on Manufacturing and
    Administrative Practice in the German Principalities:
    Conflict and Coherence   133
    Guillaume Garner

7. Administrative Centralisation, Police Regulations and Mining
    Sciences as Channels for the Dissemination of Cameralist
    Ideas in the Iberian World   155
    Alexandre Mendes Cunha

8. Balancing the Divine with the Private: The Practices of
    Hushållning in Eighteenth-Century Sweden   179
    Göran Rydén

9. Johan Ludvig Reventlow's Master Plan at the Brahetrolleborg
     Estate: Cameralism in Denmark in the 1780s and 1790s   203
     Ingrid Markussen

10. *Maasreguln wider die Unglücksfaelle*: Cameralism and its
     Influence on the Establishment of Insurance Schemes   221
     Frank Oberholzner

11. The Decline of Cameralism in Germany at the Turn of the
     Nineteenth Century   239
     Hans Frambach

12. Concluding Remarks   263
     Keith Tribe

Bibliography   269
Index   305

Illustrations

Figures

1. British imports of great masts, 1764–85 (Source: Roger Knight, 'New England Forests and British Seapower: Albion Revised', *The American Neptune* XLVI, No. 4 (1986), p. 228)   55

2. J. B. von Rohr, *Compendieuse Haußhaltungs-Bibliothek* (Leipzig, 1716) (Source: Niedersächsiche Staats- und Universitätsbibliothek, Göttingen)   60

Tables

1. Imports of timber products by weight and quantity, England and Wales, 1700–80 (Source: Elizabeth Boody Schumpeter, *English Overseas Trade Statistics 1697–1808* (London, 1960), Table XVI)   52

2. Navy Board contracts for pitch and tar, 1700–21 (Source: Joseph J. Malone, 'England and the Baltic Naval Stores Trade in the Seventeenth and Eighteenth Centuries', *The Mariner's Mirror* 58 (1972), 388)   54

Contributors

Roger Bartlett, D.Phil., FRHistS, Professor Emeritus of Russian History, University College London, UK. He studied at Cambridge, Oxford and Moscow Universities, taught for fifteen years at the University of Keele, and has held visiting positions at Harvard, Cornell, Marburg and the University of Latvia. Publications include: *Human Capital. The Settlement of Foreigners in Russia 1762–1804* (Cambridge, 1979, digital reprint 2008); *A History of Russia* (Basingstoke/New York, 2005); editor, *Land Commune and Peasant Community in Russia. Communal Forms in Imperial and Early Soviet Society* (Basingstoke/London, 1990); *Johann Georg Eisen (1717–1779). Ausgewählte Schriften. Deutsche Volksaufklärung und Leibeigenschaft im russischen Reich* (with E. Donnert, Marburg, 1998).

Alexandre Mendes Cunha, Ph.D., Associate Professor of History of Economic Thought of the Department of Economics of the Universidade Federal de Minas Gerais, Brazil. He is also currently a Jean Monnet Professor and the head of the Center for European Studies of the Universidade Federal de Minas Gerais. He is editor (with C. E. Suprinyak) of the collection *The Political Economy of Latin American Independence* (London, 2016). His main publications in the field of studies on cameralism are published in the journals *History of Political Economy* (2012 and 2017) and *Portuguese History* (2010), and in the collection of essays *The Dissemination of Economic Ideas* (Cheltenham, 2011).

Hans Frambach, Ph.D., Professor of Microeconomic Theory, University of Wuppertal, Germany. He earned his Ph.D. in economics in 1992, and his habilitation thesis *Arbeit im ökonomischen Denken* [*Work in Economic Thought*] (1999) quickly became one of the standard works of reference in the field. His research is focused on the history of economic thought, new institutional economics, microeconomics and the economic theory of enterprises. Since 2012 he has been the head of the working group 'Microeconomics and the History of Economic Thought' at the Schumpeter School of Business and Economics.

Guillaume Garner, Ph.D., Assistant Professor in Early Modern History, École normale supérieure Lyon, France. He completed his doctorate at the University Paris 7 in 2001 with a thesis on the question of space and territory in German cameralism and political economy (1740–1820). He has published over thirty articles, and a book *État, économie, territoire en Allemagne. L'espace dans le caméralisme et l'économie politique, 1740–1820* (Paris, 2005). From 2012 to 2015 he led the section 'Holy Roman Empire' for a project funded by the Agence Nationale de la Recherche on economic privileges in Western Europe (16th–18th century).

Lars Magnusson, Ph.D., Professor in Economic History, Uppsala University, Sweden. Dean of Faculty of Social Sciences, Uppsala University; Member of the Royal Academy of Sciences, Sweden; Member of the prize committee for the Swedish Rijksbank economic prize in honour of Alfred Nobel; President of the Scandinavian Economic History Society. Honorary doctoral degree at Kyoto Sanyo University. Books include *Mercantilism: the Shaping of an Economic Language* (London, 1994); *Economic History of Sweden* (Abingdon/New York, 2000); *Free Trade and Protectionism in America 1822–1890, I–IV* (Abingdon/New York, 2000); *Tradition of Free Trade* (Abingdon/New York, 2004, Japanese edition 2009); *Nation, State and the Industrial Revolution* (Abingdon/New York, 2009, Japanese edition 2011); *The Political Economy of Mercantilism* (Abingdon/New York, 2015); and *A Brief History of Political Economy. Tales of Marx, Keynes and Hayek* (Cheltenham, 2016).

Ingrid Markussen, Dr.phil, Professor Emeritus in History of Ideas, University of Oslo (Norway). She studied history at the University of Uppsala (Sweden) 1958–60 and the University of Copenhagen (Denmark) 1960–66. In 1991 she defended her thesis on the religious (Pietist) and economic (cameral) ideas behind the development of public compulsory schools in the rural districts of Denmark. Author of: *Visdommens lænker* [*The Chains of Wisdom*] (Sønderborg, 1988); *Til Skaberens Ære, Statens Tjeneste og Vor Egen Nytte* [*To the Honour of the Creator, the Service of the State and to our own Good*] (Odense, 1995).

Frank Oberholzner, Ph.D., works for Allianz SE. His research interests include insurance history and the perception of natural hazards in early modern Europe. He is the author of several publications on the history of German crop insurance and the perception of hailstorms in journals such as *Environment and History* and *Zeitschrift für Agrargeschichte und Agrarsoziologie*. He is the author of the monograph *Institutionalisierte Sicherheit im Agrarsektor. Die Entwicklung der Hagelversicherung in Deutschland seit der Frühen Neuzeit* (Berlin, 2015).

Göran Rydén, Ph.D., Professor of Economic History, Institute for Housing and Urban Research (IBF), Uppsala University, Sweden. His main research interests revolve around the forming and creation of modern society, in Sweden and Europe as well as on a more global scale. He has studied different aspects of industrialisation, technological change and work. In more recent times he has expanded his field of research by exploring questions about the Enlightenment and urbanisation. Publications include *Baltic Iron in the Atlantic World in the Eighteenth Century* (with Chris Evans, Leiden, 2007); editor, *Sweden in the Eighteenth-Century World: Provincial Cosmopolitans* (Farnham, 2013).

Marten Seppel, Ph.D., is Associate Professor of Early Modern History at the University of Tartu, Estonia. He did his M.Phil. at the University of Cambridge (UK). In 2010, he worked as a postdoctoral scholar at the School of Slavonic and East European Studies, UCL and in 2013–14 at the University of Uppsala, Sweden. He has published over 40 papers, including articles in the journals *Social History* and the *Scandinavian Economic History Review*. In 2013–16 he led the research project 'The Cameralist Turn in State Administration in the 17th–18th centuries' funded by the Estonian Research Council.

Keith Tribe, Ph.D., taught at University of Keele (UK) 1976–2002, retiring as Reader in Economics. He now works as a professional translator and independent scholar. He studied sociology at the University of Essex 1968–71, completing his postgraduate studies in Social and Political Sciences, University of Cambridge 1972–75, and postdoctoral studies in Germany 1979–85. Forthcoming work: a new translation of Max Weber, *Economy and Society Part One* (Cambridge, MA, 2018). Previously published: *Land, Labour and Economic Discourse* (London, 1978); *Governing Economy. The Reformation of German Economic Discourse* (Cambridge, 1988); *Strategies of Economic Order* (Cambridge, 1995/2005); *The Economy of the Word. Language, History and Economics* (New York, 2015).

Paul Warde, Ph.D., is Lecturer in Environmental History at the University of Cambridge, UK. He has previously held a research fellowship and lectureship at the University of Cambridge (1999–2007), and was Professor of Environmental History at the University of East Anglia until 2015. Paul Warde has written extensively on the economic and environmental history of Europe in the early and modern periods. Books include *Economy, Ecology and State Formation in Early Modern Germany* (Cambridge, 2006); *Power to the People. Energy in Europe over the Last Five Centuries* (with P. Malanima and A. Kander, Princeton, NJ, 2013); and edited volumes *The Future of*

Nature. Documents of Global Change (with S. Sörlin and L. Robin, New Haven, CT, 2013), and *Nature's End. History and the Environment* (with S. Sörlin, Basingstoke, 2009). He has published numerous articles in journals such as *Economic History Review*, *Past and Present*, *Continuity and Change*, *Modern Intellectual History*, *History Workshop Journal*, *Environmental History* and *Environment and History*.

Introduction

Cameralism in Practice

MARTEN SEPPEL

The primary aim of this book is to clarify the impact of cameralism in early modern Europe, and to make a tighter connection between cameralist teaching on the one hand, and administrative and economic practices on the other. It was the latter that came first: officials working in the seventeenth-century *Kammer* of the German territorial states were known as *Kameralisten*. 'Cameralism'[1] later became the name by which both teaching and practice were known, although more closely associated with the teaching than the practice. Cameralist teaching was directed to the state's interest in its resources, in better administration and in the common good, the purpose being in order to increase the prince's incomes, establish a sustainable development of economy, and create a well-ordered state.

The essays collected here explore the practices and spheres in which cameralist teaching left its mark in early modern Europe. It is exactly this linking of cameralist ideas to contemporary politics and practice which offers an important historical dimension for understanding cameralist literature. For too long the approach to cameralism has treated it as a body of thought, analysing one or another cameralist author's standpoints and works.[2]

---

1 The term 'cameralism' (*Kameralismus*) became popular only in twentieth-century historiography but derived from the eighteenth-century university discourse of *Kameralwissenschaft* – or more usually, because of the initial lack of any unitary demarcation, in the plural as the *Kameralwissenschaften*, the cameralistic sciences.

2 This tradition goes back to the best-known historiographical works on cameralism by Albion Small, Kurt Zielenziger and Anton Tautscher. However, during the last ten years or so some of the main cameralist writers like J. H. G. Justi have received greater attention: Ulrich Adam, *The Political Economy of J. H. G. Justi* (Bern, 2006); Birger P. Priddat, 'Kameralismus als paradoxe Konzeption der gleichzeitigen Stärkung von Markt und Staat. Komplexe Theorielagen im deutschen 18. Jahrhundert', *Berichte zur Wissenschaftsgeschichte* 31 (2008),

Another approach has been to study cameralist literature through the prism of a certain issue (e.g. cameralist perceptions of the role of the court, of the functioning of the grain trade, of population policy, the role of guilds, the importance of mining, policy doctrines and the state, the centrality of happiness, of work, or of gender).[3] The focus has been directed not so much to the application of cameralist ideas, but rather to the alleged 'theoretical foundations' of cameralism.

Of course, the question of whether economic ideas were reflected in any real practice is not new, and is a widely discussed topic.[4] Research on cameralist teaching has in fact for some time taken an interest in the actual practice of cameralist principles in the early modern state.[5] The subtitle

---

249–63; Hans-Christoph Schmidt am Busch, 'Cameralism as "Political Metaphysics": Human nature, the State, and Natural Law in the Thought of Johann Heinrich Gottlob von Justi', *The European Journal of the History of Economic Thought* 16 (2009), 409–30; J. G. Backhaus (ed.), *The Beginnings of Political Economy. Johann Heinrich Gottlob von Justi* (New York, 2009); Ere Pertti Nokkala, 'The Machine of State in Germany – The Case of Johann Heinrich Gottlob von Justi (1717–1771)', *Contributions to the History of Concepts* 5 (2009), 71–93; Hartmuth Becker, 'Justi's Concrete Utopia', *The State as Utopia. Continental Approaches*, ed. J. G. Backhaus (New York, 2011), pp. 41–56.

3   Volker Bauer, *Hofökonomie. Der Diskurs über den Fürstenhof in Zeremonialwissenschaft, Hausväterliteratur und Kameralismus* (Wien/Köln/Weimar, 1997); Marion W. Gray, 'Kameralismus: Die säkulare Ökonomie und die getrennten Geschlechtersphären', *WerkstattGeschichte* 19 (1998), 41–57; Lars Atorf, *Der König und das Korn. Die Getreidehandelspolitik als Fundament der brandenburg-preussischen Aufstiegs zur europäischen Grossmacht* (Berlin, 1999); Axel Rüdiger, *Staatslehre und Staatsbildung. Die Staatswissenschaft an der Universität Halle im 18. Jahrhundert* (Tübingen, 2005); Jörg Cortekar, *Glückskonzepte des Kameralismus und Utilitarismus: Implikationen für die moderne Umweltökonomik und Umweltpolitik* (Marburg, 2007); Hans-Christof Kraus, 'Kriegsfolgenbewältigung und "Peuplierung" im Denken deutscher Kameralisten des 17. und 18. Jahrhunderts', *Krieg, Militär und Migration in der Frühen Neuzeit*, ed. M. Asche, M. Herrmann, U. Ludwig and A. Schindling (Berlin, 2008), pp. 265–79; Thomas Buchner, 'Perceptions of Work in Early Modern Economic Thought: Dutch Mercantilism and Central European Cameralism in Comparative Perspective', *The Idea of Work in Europe from Antiquity to Modern Times*, ed. J. Ehmer and C. Lis (Farnham, 2009), pp. 191–213; Justus Nipperdey, 'Regulierung zur Sicherung der Nahrung. Zur Übereinstimmung von Menschenbild und Marktmodell bei Zünften und Kameralisten', *Regulierte Märkte: Zünfte und Kartelle/ Marchés régulés: Corporations et cartels*, ed. M. Müller, H. R. Schmidt and L. Tissot (Zürich, 2011), pp. 165–82; Justus Nipperdey, *Die Erfindung der Bevölkerungspolitik. Staat, politische Theorie und Population in der Frühen Neuzeit* (Göttingen, 2012).

4   For these debates, see e.g. Lars Magnusson, *The Political Economy of Mercantilism* (London/New York, 2015).

5   E.g. Karl-Heinz Osterloh, *Joseph von Sonnenfels und die österreichische Reformbewegung im Zeitalter des aufgeklärten Absolutismus. Eine Studie zum Zusammenhang von Kameralwissenschaft und Verwaltungspraxis* (Lübeck/Hamburg, 1970); Hans-Joachim Braun, 'Economic Theory and Policy in Germany, 1750–1800', *Journal of European Economic History* 4 (1975), 301–22; Karl Heinrich Kaufhold, 'Preußische Staatswirtschaft – Konzept und Realität – 1640–1806', *Jahrbuch für Wirtschaftsgeschichte* (1994), pp. 33–70; Karl Heinrich Kaufhold, '"Wirtschaftswissenschaften" und Wirtschaftspolitik in Preußen von um 1650 bis um 1800',

of Andre Wakefield's book of 2009 is 'German Cameralism as Science and Practice'. He suggests that cameralism, *qua Kameralwissenschaft*, was a kind of fantasy fiction and utopian theory, rather than any plan that could be put to use in administrative practice. He argues that 'Cameralists liked to publish "practical" treatises about how to brew beer or raise cattle, for example, and they often made it sound easy. But practical success in agriculture or manufacturing was never easy, which is why failure was the rule when it came to new state ventures. In this respect, cameralists were utopian pragmatists …'.[6] However, those contributing to the present collection believe that cameralist teaching did not remain merely theoretical. Its link with the practice of governing and economy must not be ignored; this has to be studied and explained (see the chapters by Guillaume Garner and Frank Oberholzner). It is also worth studying quite how administrative and economic practices in their turn had an impact on cameralist discourse (Lars Magnusson, Keith Tribe, Marten Seppel, Paul Warde).

Secondly, this book will argue that, besides the German principalities and Austria, cameralist teaching on state and economy had great influence also in Sweden, Denmark, Russia and even in Portugal, together with other parts of Europe. In a word, cameralism found echoes not only in the Germanic world, but throughout early modern Europe. This wider geographic perspective on cameralism has also been a point of departure for more recent research.[7] The

---

Wirtschaft, Wissenschaft und Bildung in Preussen: Zur Wirtschafts- und Sozialgeschichte Preussens vom 18. bis zum 20. Jahrhundert, ed. K. H. Kaufhold and B. Sösemann (Stuttgart, 1998), pp. 51–72; Eva Ondrušová, 'Staatswirtschaftslehre des Kameralismus: Theorie und Praxis am Beispiel von den Kameralherrschaften im Mittelslowakischen Bergbaugebiet. Einführung in das Thema', *Economy and Society in Central and Eastern Europe. Territory, Population, Consumption, Papers of the International Conference Held in Alba Iulia, April 25th–27th 2013*, ed. D. Dumitran and V. Moga (Wien, 2013), pp. 63–76.

6   Andre Wakefield, *The Disordered Police State. German Cameralism as Science and Practice* (Chicago/London, 2009); the quote, p. 136. A tendency of this kind has been also admitted by Kaufhold, '"Wirtschaftswissenschaften"', p. 52. See also Becker, 'Justi's Concrete Utopia'.

7   Erik S. Reinert and Hugo Reinert, 'A Bibliography of J. H. G. von Justi', *The Beginnings of Political Economy. Johann Heinrich Gottlob von Justi*, ed. J. G. Backhaus (New York, 2009), p. 21; Sophus A. Reinert, *Translating Empire. Emulation and the Origins of Political Economy* (Cambridge, MA, 2011); Philipp R. Rössner, 'New Inroads into Well-known Territory? On the Virtues of Re-discovering pre-classical Political Economy', *Economic Growth and the Origins of Modern Political Economy. Economic Reasons of State, 1500–2000*, ed. P. R. Rössner (London/New York, 2016), p. 12; Stellan Dahlgren, 'Karl XI:s envälde – kameralistik absolutism?', *Makt och vardag: Hur man styrde, levde och tänkte under svensk stormaktstid*, ed. S. Dahlgren, A. Florén and Å. Karlsson (Stockholm, 1993; 3rd edn, 1998), pp. 115–32; Ernest Lluch, 'Cameralism beyond the Germanic world: A Note on Tribe', *History of Economic Ideas* 5 (1997), 85–99; Alexandre Mendes Cunha, '*Polizei* and the System of Public Finance: Tracing the Impact of Cameralism in Eighteenth-century Portugal', *The Dissemination of Economic Ideas*, ed. H. D. Kurz, T. Nishizawa and K. Tribe (Cheltenham, 2011), pp. 65–83; 'Obsuzhdenie: Istoricheskij kurs "Novaja imperskaja istorija Severnoj Evrazii"', *Ab Imperio*

present collection seeks to bring together these national studies in a single volume so that we might establish a synthetic understanding of the spread of cameralist ideas outside Germany and Austria. We still do not know in which countries cameralism had the greatest influence. The cases of Russia and Portugal (Roger Bartlett, Alexandre Cunha) are especially interesting since cameralism, as a rule, did not deal with issues of colonial or imperial power. Cameralism was not particular to the German landlocked German principalities, but can be found in Denmark, Sweden and other maritime countries (Göran Rydén, Ingrid Markussen).[8] However, while cameralism had no clear reception in England, France and the Netherlands, it is noteworthy that over last thirty years there has been growing interest in cameralism in anglophone and French historical literature.[9] One theme running through the collection is that the current historiography rather underestimates the influence, popularity and the diffusion of eighteenth-century German cameralist teaching in early modern Europe.

The discourse of cameralism

Emerging in the second half of the seventeenth century, cameralist discourse sought solutions for the recurring problem of the state's financial needs arising from the expanding activities and costs of early modern states – devastation caused by war, the expansion of the state apparatus, the

(2015), no. 1, 323–86; no. 2, 253–337; Fredrik Albritton Jonsson, *Enlightenment's Frontier: The Scottish Highlands and the Origins of Environmentalism* (New Haven, CT, 2013).

8   For the colonial past of the cameralist states, see Reinert, *Translating Empire*, pp. 239–42.

9   Keith Tribe, *Governing Economy. The Reformation of German Economic Discourse 1750–1840* (Cambridge, 1988; 2nd edn, Newbury, 2017); David A. R. Forrester, 'Rational Administration, Finance and Control Accounting: The Experience of Cameralism', *Critical Perspectives on Accounting* (1990), pp. 285–317; Keith Tribe, *Strategies of Economic Order. German Economic Discourse, 1750–1950* (Cambridge, 1995/2007); David F. Lindenfeld, *The Practical Imagination: the German Sciences of State in the Nineteenth Century* (Chicago, 1997); Michael W. Spicer, 'Cameralist Thought and Public Administration', *Journal of Management History* 4 (1998), 149–59; Andre Wakefield, 'Books, Bureaus, and the Historiography of Cameralism', *European Journal of Law and Economics* 19 (2005), 311–20; Jürgen G. Backhaus (ed.), *Physiocracy, Antiphysiocracy and Pfeiffer* (New York, 2011); *The Dissemination of Economic Ideas*, ed. H. D. Kurz, T. Nishizawa and K. Tribe (Cheltenham, 2011); Richard E. Wagner, 'The Cameralists: Fertile Sources for a New Science of Public Finance', *Handbook of the History of Economic Thought. Insights on the Founders of Modern Economics*, ed. J. G. Backhaus (New York, 2012), pp. 12–35; P. R. Rössner (ed.), *Economic Growth and the Origins of Modern Political Economy. Economic Reasons of State, 1500–2000* (London/New York, 2016); Guillaume Garner, *État, économie, territoire en Allemagne. L'espace dans le caméralisme et l'économie politique 1740–1820* (Paris, 2005); P. Laborier, F. Audren, P. Napoli and J. Vogel (eds), *Les sciences camérales. Activités pratiques et histoire des dispositifs publics* (Paris, 2011).

introduction of standing armies, and the growth of the court.[10] However, cameralism did not concern itself only with the planned development of a state's economic potential and revenues, but viewed the needs of the state in a broader context: of the administrative and economic management appropriate for the welfare of the country, its people and economic prosperity. Cameralists presumed that the happiness and welfare of the population was part of the sphere of state governance. The ruler should care not only for the state's fiscal interests, but even more so for the general welfare of his subjects. This linkage of the interests of the ruler with those of his subjects was one of the principal concerns of seventeenth-century authors (such as Veit Ludwig von Seckendorff, Johann Joachim Becher and Wilhelm Schröder) – for 'the welfare and well-being of subjects is the foundation upon which all happiness of a ruler of such subjects must be based'.[11] Cameralists considered that the development of society and economy, not to mention politics, was dependent on the (right) actions of the ruler. It was cameralists who first discussed what these right actions were and how strategies might be devised for their implementation.[12] Wise management became the ideal that would secure a sustainable basis for the finances of the state and thereafter all its other ambitions.[13] Therefore, in its essence cameralism was the teaching of *Oeconomie* transferred to the level of the state. Cameralists saw the state as a large household (*Super-oekonomie*) that was governed by a wise *Hausvater* (= *Landesvater*).[14] This formed one of the central ideological principles of cameralism.

The cameralist attitude can primarily be identified through the logic of suggested solutions, and the existence of a common terminology. It can be argued that there was little, if anything, about cameralist policy and practice that was unique to cameralism. Cameralism in practice cannot be identified simply by looking at the actions associated with it; instead, we can claim that such actions were cameralist by examining how these actions were explained. Thus, cameralism was first and foremost a way of thinking and a common

10   Bauer, *Hofökonomie*, p. 164.
11   Keith Tribe, 'Cameralism and the Sciences of the State', *The Cambridge History of Eighteenth-Century Political Thought*, ed. M. Goldie and R. Wokler (Cambridge, 2006), pp. 528–9; the quote, p. 529; Tribe, *Strategies*, p. 8; Gustav Marchet, *Studien über die Entwickelung der Verwaltungslehre in Deutschland von der zweiten Hälfte des 17. bis zum Ende des 18. Jahrhunderts* (Munich, 1885), p. 118.
12   Thomas Simon, *"Gute Policey": Ordnungsleitbilder und Zielvorstellungen politischen Handelns in der Frühen Neuzeit* (Frankfurt a.M., 2004), pp. 387–8.
13   For the concept of 'sustainability' and its connection with cameralism, see e.g. Paul Warde, 'The Invention of Sustainability', *Modern Intellectual History* 8 (2011), 153–70.
14   Simon, *"Gute Policey"*, pp. 452, 455, 462; Keith Tribe, 'Die Wirtschaftssemantik der frühen Neuzeit', in Herbert Matis, Erich W. Streissler, Monika Streissler and Keith Tribe, *Philipp Wilhelm von Hörnigks 'Oesterreich über alles'* (Düsseldorf, 1997), p. 269; Gray, 'Kameralismus'; Reinert, *Translating Empire*, p. 235. See also Göran Rydén's chapter in this volume.

language (rhetoric).[15] There is little consensus over the specific and definite character of 'cameralism'. Cameralism is generally considered to have dealt with domestic issues – the crown's domain management, state finances and administration – rather than with commerce, foreign trade, colonial policy or military power. Cameralists set their sights neither on international trade nor on colonial conquest, but instead on geopolitical realities, together with the natural and mineral resources of particular states or regions. For cameralists, the key to sustainable wealth and happiness lay neither in conquest nor expansive economic development, but instead in the conservation and effective exploitation of local resources (agriculture, mining, forestry, fisheries and manufacturing).[16]

While cameralism was often treated as a 'German version of mercantilism' in the earlier literature, recent studies have sought to make a clear distinction between mercantilism and cameralism.[17] Of course, any such distinction has always depended on how these terms are currently defined in the historiography, for while the *Kameralwissenschaften* were conceived and described as such, 'mercantilism' was always a label applied retrospectively to seventeenth- and eighteenth-century literature.[18] For instance, Thomas Simon argues that mercantilist writers focused manifestly on commerce and trade as a base for the acquisition of riches and their economic approach was very limited; while, by contrast, eighteenth-century cameralists concentrated on the organisation of domestic production (riches can be produced through one's own efforts) and were interested in all spheres of economy and society (though paying only peripheral interest to foreign trade).[19] In addition, more than a century ago Albion Small laid emphasis upon the great importance of

15   Cf. Magnusson, *Political Economy*, p. 9.
16   Walter Braeuer, 'Kameralismus und Merkantilismus. Ein kritischer Vergleich', *Jahrbuch für Wirtschaftsgeschichte* (1990), 107–8; Lisbet Koerner, *Linnaeus: Nature and Nation* (Cambridge, MA/London, 1999), p. 6; Reinert, *Translating Empire*, pp. 238, 242–3, 255.
17   See especially: Keith Tribe, 'Mercantilism and the Economics of State Formation', *Mercantilist Economics*, ed. L. Magnusson (Boston, MA, 1993), pp. 175–86; Braeuer, 'Kameralismus', pp. 107–11; Andre Wakefield, 'Cameralism: A German Alternative to Mercantilism', *Mercantilism Reimagined. Political Economy in Early Modern Britain and its Empire*, ed. P. J. Stern and C. Wennerlind (New York, 2014), pp. 134–50; Thomas Simon, 'Merkantilismus und Kameralismus. Zur Tragfähigkeit des Merkantilismusbegriffs und seiner Abgrenzung zum deutschen "Kameralismus"', *Merkantilismus. Wiederaufnahme einer Debatte*, ed. M. Isenmann (Stuttgart, 2014), pp. 76–8; Magnusson, *Political Economy*; Lars Magnusson, 'Was Cameralism Really the German Version of Mercantilism?', *Economic Growth and the Origins of Modern Political Economy. Economic Reasons of State, 1500–2000*, ed. P. R. Rössner (London/New York, 2016), pp. 57–71; Jürgen Backhaus, 'Mercantilism and Cameralism: Two Very Different Variations on the Same Theme', *Economic Growth and the Origins of Modern Political Economy. Economic Reasons of State, 1500–2000*, ed. P. R. Rössner (London/New York, 2016), pp. 72–8.
18   Lars Magnusson discusses this in his chapter below.
19   Simon, *"Gute Policey"*, pp. 461–3.

administrative technology in the doctrine of cameralism, an issue that was missing in anything that might be considered mercantilist discourse.[20] Nor is there anything to be said for the alternative option of contrasting mercantilism to cameralism. They still shared much common ground (as in a similar understanding regarding population policy and trade policy, although the latter was not at the centre of cameralist teaching). More recently Sophus A. Reinert has pointed out that, even if cameralism focused on 'technologies of effective administration rather than on imperialist gambits or sophisticated moral and political theory', its ends coincided with those of mercantilist economic thinking, seeking to ensure wealth and a strong economy.[21] There has long been debate over whether mercantilism has any analytic content, and whether it would be better to abandon the term altogether.[22] By contrast, the appropriateness of the term cameralism for the genre of cameralist literature and the academic cameralism of the eighteenth century remains undisputed.[23]

The essays in this volume deal with the period from the sixteenth to the turn of the nineteenth century, with an emphasis on the eighteenth century. It can be argued that this is when cameralism 'in its fullest sense' first emerged.[24] Johann Heinrich Gottlob von Justi has been treated as the main representative and 'perfecter' of the cameralistic science during this period.[25] Nonetheless, it is perhaps more appropriate to speak of a gradual development of cameralist thought. Kurt Zielenziger separated 'new' eighteenth-century cameral science (as established in 1727) from the earlier sixteenth-/seventeenth-century 'old'

20   Albion W. Small, *The Cameralists. The Pioneers of German Social Polity* (Chicago/ London, 1909), preface; Wakefield, 'Cameralism', pp. 134–5; Wakefield, *The Disordered*, p. 3. Hans-Joachim Braun defines cameralism as 'a combination of theorems of political economy, public finance and administrative principles and ends of population policy', and therefore 'cameralism is not to be identified with mercantilism' since only 'the theorems of political economy are more or less identical with mercantilist economics': Braun, 'Economic Theory', p. 301.

21   Reinert, *Translating Empire*, p. 237. Similarly: Backhaus, 'Mercantilism and Cameralism', pp. 72–8; Kaufhold, '"Wirtschaftswissenschaften"', p. 51; Braun, 'Economic Theory', p. 303.

22   Donald C. Coleman, *Revisions in Mercantilism* (London, 1969); Lars Magnusson, *Mercantilism. The Shaping of an Economic Language* (London/New York, 1994); Magnusson, *The Political Economy*; *Merkantilismus. Wiederaufnahme einer Debatte*, ed. M. Isenmann (Stuttgart, 2014).

23   However, Philipp R. Rössner more recently prefers the term 'economic reason of state' instead of referring to mercantilism or cameralism: Rössner, 'New Inroads'.

24   More recently, e.g. Magnusson, *Mercantilism*, p. 189; Magnusson, *The Political Economy*, pp. 80, 83; Simon, *"Gute Policey"*, pp. 306, 389.

25   E.g. Anton Tautscher, *Staatswirtschaftslehre des Kameralismus* (Bern, 1947), p. 411; Schmidt am Busch, 'Cameralism', p. 410. Marcus Sandl has pointed out that such an interpretation is still problematic: Marcus Sandl, *Ökonomie des Raumes: der kameralwissenschaftliche Entwurf der Staatswirtschaft im 18. Jahrhundert* (Köln/Weimar/Wien, 1999), pp. 46–7.

cameralists.[26] Anton Tautscher saw three phases of cameralism that developed over three centuries, from the sixteenth to the turn of the nineteenth century. Cameralist forerunners ('*Vorläufer*' and '*Vorbereiter*') dealt mainly with the juridical and financial political issues arising in cameral administration. To this group belonged Melchior Osse, Georg Obrecht, Christoph Besold and Kaspar Klock. Then from the mid-seventeenth century the 'scientists of cameralism' (*Wissenschaftler des Kameralismus*)[27] worked out political economy as a politico-economic theory. The representatives of this stage were Seckendorff, Becher, Hörnigk, Schröder, Jakob Bornitz, Johann Georg Leib, Theodor Lau and Justus Christoph Dithmar. Finally, the 'systematic perfecters of cameralism' (*die systematischen Vollender des Kameralismus*) were mainly: Georg Heinrich Zincke, Justi, Joachim Georg Darjes, Johann Friedrich von Pfeiffer, Sonnenfels, Johann Heinrich Jung (Jung-Stilling), Karl Gottlob Rössig, Theodor Anton, Heinrich Schmalz and others.[28] Keith Tribe has labelled these two last periods of the cameralist literature as the courtly form of the seventeenth century (*die höfische Form des 17. Jahrhunderts*); and the academic form of the eighteenth century (*die akademische Fassung des 18. Jahrhunderts*).[29]

Cameralism and practice

Studying cameralism in practice involves three dimensions. First, cameralist authors themselves emphasised the very practical output of their teaching. Cameralism was seen as a practical science, one which can be studied as an intellectual issue. Secondly, it can be approached through asking how cameralist solutions worked out in actual practice. Thirdly, the more indirect and broader influence of cameralism upon the functioning and practices of state governance, economy and society can be clarified.

Practical cameralism
Seventeenth-century cameralist authors emphasised that their writing had practical value and was therefore significant. Their general purpose was not

26   Kurt Zielenziger, *Die alten deutschen Kameralisten. Ein Beitrag zur Geschichte der Nationalökonomie und zum Problem des Merkantilismus* (Jena, 1914), pp. 98–9, 104, 414.
27   More commonly, the cameralist phase of the second half of the seventeenth century has been called the 'older' or 'earlier' cameralism, e.g.: Kaufhold, '"Wirtschaftswissenschaften"', p. 54; Sandl, *Ökonomie*, pp. 44, 52.
28   Anton Tautscher, 'Kameralismus', *Handwörterbuch der Sozialwissenschaften*, vol. 5 (Göttingen, 1956), pp. 465–6; Erhard Dittrich, *Die deutschen und österreichischen Kameralisten* (Darmstadt, 1974), p. 37.
29   Tribe, 'Die Wirtschaftssemantik', p. 265.

only to present general theoretical constructs, but also practical advice to the Prince. As Becher wrote in 1668, pure theory cannot abandon practice, 'Because all the work without the theory is uncertain, and the theory without practice lies in this fever as well. Nevertheless the theory must come before the exercise and practice.'[30] Cameralism was indeed meant to be first and foremost a practical science, or at least cameralist theory sought application in practice.[31] With this in mind Frederick William I founded cameralist professorships at Halle and at Frankfurt an der Oder in 1727. The academic cameral sciences that subsequently developed in the eighteenth century were justified in terms of their practical nature. As Johann Heinrich Gottlob von Justi wrote in his *Staatswirthschaft*, cameralist science had a specific place in the university, something that could not be said about metaphysics, astronomy, literature and philology, all of which were enchanting and entertaining sciences, but not practical.[32]

Actual applicability

It is by virtue of this claim that cameralist literature has been evaluated in terms of the applicability of the ideas it presents, since cameralists themselves emphasised the practicality of their theory. However, cameralist projects that saw the light of day tended to have mixed success, with a tendency to prove themselves ultimately impractical. There are many examples of the failure of cameralist practice. Emperor Joseph II's infamous recyclable drop-door coffin was very practical and economical, but in spite of an imperial order it was doomed to fail.[33] However much cameralist literature one reads, the question of the link between cameralism and practice remains obscure. To establish that link we need to turn to other sources.

The impact of cameralism

Although there is the question of quite how practical cameralist solutions really were, another question concerns the broader impact of cameralism on governance and economy. Even if most of the practical solutions suggested by cameralists were not original or were ineffective, this does not mean that early modern government could not follow a particular cameralist logic, together with principles and goals. One may agree with Karl Heinrich Kaufhold's

---

30   Dittrich, *Die deutschen*, p. 58; Tautscher, *Staatswirtschaftslehre*, p. 9.

31   Tautscher, *Staatswirtschaftslehre*, p. 8; Osterloh, *Joseph von Sonnenfels*; Sandl, *Ökonomie*, p. 48; Pierangelo Schiera, *Dell'arte di governo alle scienze dello stato: Il Cameralismo e l'assolutismo tedesco* (Milan, 1968), pp. 315, 321; Braun, 'Economic Theory', p. 302; Kaufhold, '"Wirtschaftswissenschaften"', p. 52.

32   Wakefield, 'Cameralism', p. 140.

33   Karl Vocelka, 'Enlightenment in the Habsburg Monarchy: History of a Belated and Short-Lived Phenomenon', *Toleration in Enlightenment Europe*, ed. O. P. Grell and R. Porter (Cambridge, 2000), p. 204.

conclusion that answering the question of whether cameralism was a success or a failure is a complicated matter, that it has been much debated and is obviously one without a single clear answer. It would be easy to compile a long list of bungled plans, failures, unrealised projects, cases of mismanagement and corruption. Some cameralist undertakings surely failed. However, this failure should not be evaluated from a present-day perspective, for one must bear in mind the limited capacity of early modern states. On the other hand, there were an impressive number of successes, start-ups, expansions and improvements. The impact of cameralism on the development of state and economy should not be underestimated. Kaufhold shows that between 1650 and 1800 Prussia became a powerful European power with an effective administration and strong economy; and Prussian state policy owed a great deal to cameralist principles.[34] At the same time it is plain that 'economic ideas constitute only one of many factors behind the formulation of concrete policies'.[35]

If the direct influence of specific authors is for the most part very difficult to evaluate, then detecting the indirect influence of their economic ideas is sometimes easier. Naturally this takes us quickly to the well-known historico-methodological puzzle of how to clearly verify the existence of a theory or a norm behind a manifest practice.[36] Recently Paul Slack has argued that in the case of improvement, cultural change came first and that this had an effect on economic behaviour: 'The ways in which people think about their economic status, future prospects, and general well-being affect their behaviour as economic and political actors.'[37] It can therefore be claimed that it does not necessarily matter to what extent cameralists were utopian or idealists. More important is the kind of influence their propaganda and values actually had on governance and development in society. There seems to be no doubt that they created a new understanding of state administration and its objectives. The political ideologies of the nineteenth century all had some kind of idealist basis, but one cannot deny the influence of nationalism, liberalism or

34   Karl Heinrich Kaufhold, 'Deutschland 1650–1850', Handbuch der europäischen Wirtschafts- und Sozialgeschichte, vol. 4, ed. I. Mieck, H. Kellenbenz, W. Fischer and J. A. van Houtte (Stuttgart, 1993), pp. 583–4; Kaufhold, 'Preußische Staatswirtschaft', pp. 33–70.
35   Magnusson, 'Mercantilism', p. 17.
36   This has been always a debated issue: see Karl Heinrich Kaufhold, 'Einführung', Wirtschaft, Wissenschaft und Bildung in Preussen: Zur Wirtschafts- und Sozialgeschichte Preussens vom 18. bis zum 20. Jahrhundert, ed. K. H. Kaufhold and B. Sösemann (Stuttgart, 1998), p. 11. Kaufhold has also discussed the methodological possibilities for analysing the connection between the cameralistic sciences and state economic policy, pointing out that in most cases one is only able to conclude indirectly that cameralist ideas or thinking were behind the practice: Kaufhold, '"Wirtschaftswissenschaften"', pp. 51–3, 71.
37   Paul Slack, The Invention of Improvement. Information and Material Progress in Seventeenth-Century England (Oxford, 2015).

socialism on the development of the modern understanding of the world. Or as Hans Frambach puts it in his chapter, many of the human failings observed in this context are in no way cameralism-specific: they apply throughout the academic disciplines.

Cameralism inside and outside of Germany

Cameralism has been seen as something of a German *Sonderweg* of the early modern period.[38] Jürgen Backhaus emphasises that a German *Sonderweg* in the evolution of political economy did not however mean 'a separate track', but a 'separate set of questions they tried to answer with the most appropriate technique'.[39] It cannot be denied that, as a doctrine, cameralism developed primarily in German-language literature; and that one can see at work its reflection, imitation and adaptation in other parts of Europe. Cameralism became attractive to some European governments, but found no reception in other countries. One of the prime motivations of interest in cameralist teaching was a recognition by rulers or economic writers of their own country's economic backwardness, and an ambition to catch up with what were perceived to be more progressive states.[40] This was the case in Russia, Portugal, Sweden and Denmark.

The diffusion of cameralism is also evident in the chairs for cameralism founded outside the German universities in the eighteenth century. After the foundation of cameralist chairs in 1727 at the Prussian universities of Halle and Frankfurt an der Oder, but before other German professorships in the

38   This is discussed by Lars Magnusson in the following chapter. See also Magnusson, 'Was Cameralism'; Magnusson, *Political Economy*, pp. 79–80; Pierangelo Schiera, 'Il cameralismo e il pensiero politico tedesco: un "Sonderweg" anticipato!', *Römische historische Mitteilungen* 31 (1989), 299–317; Jürgen G. Backhaus, 'The German Economic Tradition: From Cameralism to the Verein für Sozialpolitik', *Political Economy and National Realities*, ed. M. Albertone and A. Masoero (Torino, 1994), pp. 329–56; Ernest Lluch, 'Der Kameralismus, ein vieldimensionales Lehrgebäude: Seine Rezeption bei Adam Smith und im Spanien des 18. Jahrhunderts', *Jahrbuch für Wirtschaftsgeschichte* (2000), pp. 133–54; Simon, *"Gute Policey"*, pp. 452–3; Simon, 'Merkantilismus', p. 77; Philipp R. Rössner, 'Kameralismus, Kapitalismus und die Ursprünge des modernen Wirtschaftswachstums – aus Sicht der Geldtheorie', *Vierteljahrschrift für Sozial- und Wirtschaftsgeschichte* 102 (2015), 437–71.
39   Backhaus, 'The German Economic Tradition', p. 330.
40   Susan Richter, 'German "Minor" Thinkers? The Perception of Moser's and Justi's Works in an Enlightened European Context', *Administrative Theory & Praxis* 36 (2014), 51–72. For the idea that cameralism was as an early tradition of development economics, see: Erik S. Reinert, 'German Economics as Development Economics: From the Thirty Years' War to World War II', *The Origins of Development Economics. How Schools of Economic Thought Have Addressed Development*, ed. K. S. Jomo and E. S. Reinert (London/New York, 2005), pp. 53–9; Buchner, 'Perceptions of Work', pp. 195–7.

cameral sciences, chairs were created at Uppsala (Sweden) in 1741, at Turku (Sweden/Finland) in 1747, and at Lund (Sweden) in 1750.[41] In Denmark the cameral sciences were taught at the Academy of Sorø from the 1750s.[42] The reception of cameralism is also in evidence at the University of Moscow.[43] During the first half of the 1760s two unsuccessful attempts were made by professors (who were mostly German in origin) in the Philosophy Faculty to include cameral sciences in their curriculum. Then in 1765 a direct proposal was submitted to the authorities to establish a professorship of economy, cameral sciences and mining affairs in the Philosophy Faculty. Official approval was however not forthcoming.[44]

Tracing the spread of cameralist ideas in early modern Europe provides us with a basis for comparative studies on the different developments of state administration and economy in the eighteenth century. The first chapter of the collection, by Lars Magnusson, shows that what cameralism came to mean in German-speaking parts of Europe was not directly transferred to other parts of Europe where cameralism found a reception; instead, modifications were made according to local conditions and interests. Magnusson compares cameralist teachings in Prussia and Sweden; or more specifically, the cases of Justus Christoph Dithmar who was the first cameralist professor in Prussia, and Anders Berch who was the first professor of this kind at the University of Uppsala. There were many similarities between those two professors other than the similar titles of their textbooks. However, in Sweden Berch focused much more on foreign trade and commerce; an especially important topic for the Swedish economy.

Similarly, in Chapter 2 Keith Tribe looks at the perspective upon cameralism from Sweden and other Baltic countries. Tribe has already emphasised the geographical reach of cameralism throughout the Baltic region (Åbo/Turku, Uppsala and elsewhere) during the eighteenth century,[45] while mainly focusing on German territories. In the present contribution Tribe asks whether cameralism in the Baltic region, a major trading area of

---

41   Magnusson, 'Economics', p. 249; Lisbet Koerner, 'Daedalus Hyperboreus: Baltic Natural History and Mineralogy in the Enlightenment', *The Sciences in Enlightened Europe*, ed. W. Clark, J. Golinski and S. Schaffer (Chicago/London, 1999), p. 398. See also Lars Magnusson's chapter in the present volume.

42   See Ingrid Markussen's chapter.

43   Erich Donnert, *Politische Ideologie der Russischen Gesellschaft zu Beginn der Regierungszeit Katharinas II. Gesellschaftstheorien und Staatslehren in der Ära des aufgeklärten Absolutismus* (Berlin, 1976), pp. 33–4; Michael Schippan, *Die Aufklärung in Russland im 18. Jahrhundert* (Wiesbaden, 2012), pp. 304–5; Nikolai K. Karataev, *Ekonomicheskie nauki v Moskovskom universitete (1755–1955)* (Moscow, 1956), p. 33; Nikolai K. Karataev, *Ocherki po istorii ekonomicheskikh nauk v Rossii XVIII veka* (Moscow, 1960), pp. 228, 245.

44   Karataev, *Ekonomicheskie nauki*, pp. 13–17.

45   Tribe, 'Cameralism and the Sciences of the State', pp. 525–46 (the chapter was written in 1990).

international significance at the time, gave more attention to foreign markets and export trading, matters that were not usually the main interest of German cameralism. Tribe examines more specifically the significance of the Baltic timber trade, activity that had close connections with domain administration. However, Tribe concludes that we cannot speak of a more specific and market-oriented 'Baltic cameralism'. The eighteenth-century cameralist literature from this region remained largely unconcerned by the organisation of the timber trade, despite its intensity and profitability.

The issue of population became one of the main issues for cameralists, considering the size of its population to be an objective criterion for the development of a state. Growth of the population was a guarantee of the growth of the economy and the happiness of the state.[46] Population policy (called *Peuplierungspolitik* in German literature) in the early modern states clearly shows a relationship between the theory and practice of cameralism. In Chapter 3 Roger Bartlett develops this point through the case of eighteenth-century Russia. The Empress Catherine II was heavily influenced by German cameralist thought, and this was reflected in her population policy, including foreign immigration, social legislation, medical provision, the status of the peasantry, interest in the recording of population numbers, as well as internal policing, private life, urbanisation and economic development.

To promote population growth governments began to consider the abolition of serfdom as a possible measure for this purpose. Marten Seppel argues in Chapter 4 that cameralist thinking and government interest in 'peopling policy' led to the identification of serfdom as an issue by the second half of the seventeenth century. Although we cannot find any discussion of serfdom in central cameralist discourse before the works of Justi in the 1750s, it is possible to detect cameralist principles and arguments behind the first attempts to abolish serfdom in Brandenburg-Prussia, the Swedish Baltic provinces and Pomerania, Mecklenburg and elsewhere between 1680 and 1720.

Similarly, Paul Warde's essay (Chapter 5) raises the question of the extent to which cameralist arguments simply formalised and described practices and policies that states were already putting into effect. This is a perspective upon cameralism that has so far not been considered in any detail, and it connects to a wider literature on early modern state formation. Warde argues that cameralist writing on forest management was not particularly prescriptive, but was mostly confined to repeating principles that had already been promulgated in forest legislation. He shows that Hans Carl von Carlowitz's *Silvicultura oeconomica* of 1713, which is considered to be the first major work of modern forestry, is not as original in its treatment of timber supply as is often assumed.

---

46 Nipperdey, *Die Erfindung*, p. 617.

Cameralists were among the first to acknowledge the role of technology in the growth of the economy. In the eighteenth century Justi and Sonnenfels contributed a great deal to the promotion of manufacturing. In Chapter 6 Guillaume Garner discusses the relationship between cameralist writings on manufacturing and related administrative policy in the German principalities in the eighteenth century. While he concludes that any direct influence of cameralist science on the manufacturing policy in the German principalities is practically impossible to verify, and that in some questions (like the role of monopolies and the final aims of the industrial policy) there were clear differences between discourse and practice, many common concerns are still visible.

The state functions through its officeholders; and so the efficiency, organisation and authority of state administration depended to a large degree on the education, experience and personality of its officials.[47] In the case of eighteenth-century Portugal, Alexandre Mendes Cunha (Chapter 7) demonstrates how administrative reforms inspired by cameralist policy could be introduced because officials had met and been influenced by Austro-German cameralists. In the aftermath of the Lisbon earthquake of 1755 there were three spheres where the influence of cameralism was particularly visible: the process of administrative centralisation, an increasing attention to police matters, and growing interest in sciences related to mining. Cunha concludes that it was especially the introduction of new principles into mining activity that reflects the reception of cameralist teaching in the Iberian world.

In Chapter 8 Göran Rydén examines cameralist influence on the running of an eighteenth-century iron-making enterprise (*bruk*) in Sweden. He notes that in Sweden cameralist thinking (including Anders Berch's main work) was mostly integrated with the so-called *oeconomia* (*hushållning*) literature, analogous to German *Hausväterliteratur* and which had a very strong tradition in Sweden from the seventeenth century onwards.[48] Rydén presents a study of the household management instructions employed by the private *brukshushållning* of Leufsta in Uppsala county, an enterprise belonging to the heirs of an influential Dutch–Swedish seventeenth-century mine owner and industrialist, Louis De Geer. Rydén looks therefore at both the theoretical and the practical side of household management teaching.

Ingrid Markussen's contribution (Chapter 9) is a case study of a Danish nobleman, Johan Ludvig Reventlow, who promoted industry, reformed agriculture, established new schools and created a system of poor relief for his Danish estate during the last quarter of the eighteenth century. Here again

47 See André Holenstein, 'Introduction: Empowering Interactions: Looking at Statebuilding from Below', *Empowering Interactions: Political Cultures and the Emergence of the State in Europe, 1300–1900*, ed. W. Blockmans, A. Holenstein and J. Mathieu (Farnham, 2009), p. 21.
48 See Leif Runefelt, *Hushållningens dygder. Affektlära, hushållningslära och ekonomiskt tänkande under svensk stormaktstid* (Stockholm, 2001).

we see an example of practical cameralist reforms that demonstrate the broad range of issues with which cameralists involved themselves. Many of the proposals made by Justi and others relating to agricultural reform are reflected in the agrarian reforms that Reventlow introduced on his estate.[49] Markussen has shown in her earlier studies the impact of cameralist thought on the development of school system in Denmark (as similarly in Germany and Austria).[50]

Frank Oberholzner's contribution (Chapter 10) examines another common topic of eighteenth century cameralist writing, one that was closely connected with cameralist aims – the institution of insurance. Insurance was not of course invented by cameralists, but already existed in the High Middle Ages; and Gottfried Wilhelm Leibniz had prepared a detailed proposal on public insurance. However, the cameralists Justi and Ferdinand Friedrich Pfeiffer advocated a whole range of applications for insurance: the death of farm animals, damage caused by fire, water, hail, locusts and cloudbursts, together with other natural hazards.[51] Oberholzner looks at the example of crop insurance in particular. He concludes that many cameralist writers supported the establishment of insurance companies, seeing them as a means for satisfying the general need for security. Oberholzner does not limit his study to a theoretical overview, but shows in conclusion how and when the first crop insurance companies were actually established in Germany. Many projects failed before the first enterprise was finally founded in 1791, although this did not prove an immediate success.

While there is no agreement about the beginning of cameralism, there is greater consensus about its demise during the early years of the nineteenth century. Christian Daniel Voß's *Handbuch der allgemeinen Staatswissenschaft nach Schlözers Grundriß* (6 vols, 1796–1802) has been widely seen as the last traditional cameralist opus. In Chapter 11 Hans Frambach reviews the principal explanations for this decline in the final empirical contribution to the book. He shows convincingly that financial policy and administrative circumstances developed to the disadvantage of cameralism. Cameralist financial expertise was no longer required to the extent that it had been. Their teaching had become diversified, and some of its areas had been appropriated by other fields of study, jurisprudence for example. Cameralism ceased to be practical, and in the universities was increasingly replaced by *Nationalökonomie* and the *Staatswissenschaften*.

---

49 Cf. Adam, *The Political Economy*, pp. 221–2.
50 Ingrid Markussen, *Til Skaberens Ære, Statens Tjeneste og vor egen Nytte. Pietistiske og kameralistiske ideer bag fremvæksten af en obligatorisk skole i landdistrikterne i Danmark* (Odense, 1995), p. 55. See also James Van Horn Melton, *Absolutism and the Eighteenth-century Origins of Compulsory Schooling in Prussia and Austria* (Cambridge, 1988), pp. 112–14.
51 See also Anton Felix Napp-Zinn, *Johann Friedrich von Pfeiffer und die Kameralwissenschaften an der Universität Mainz* (Wiesbaden, 1955), pp. 55–7.

In conclusion Keith Tribe (Chapter 12) reviews the issues raised by contributors and presents a synthesis of their findings that seeks to move beyond a simple contrast of theory and practice, and explores the ways in which we can register the influence of cameralism beyond the territories in which it initially developed.

There are further topics that could have been included here and that need more detailed treatment, but which are not directly treated here; examples would be taxation policy,[52] and private life and sexuality.[53] The implementation of cameralist norms was in the hands of *(Gute) Policey*,[54] and this is an issue that would require separate treatment in this context. One distinctive form of *Policey* was 'medical police', creating a political model for the protection of public health.[55] Here the prime aim was 'the growth of the population, the safety of life and the well-being of the subjects,' as Joseph II put it in one of his circulars in 1765.[56] Roger Bartlett touches on this issue in his chapter on Catherinean cameralist policy in Russia, but more work certainly needs to be done on this issue and its direct linkage to cameralism.[57]

The present collection cannot be comprehensive; the intention is rather to make a contribution to an understanding of cameralism and its impact in early modern Europe. Cameralist language and teaching led to initiatives in policy and actions that introduced a new way of thinking for the administration of early modern territorial states. Cameralism posed new questions for the development of the modern state: the abolition of serfdom, concern for public health, schooling, the regulation of internal security and 'good police', actualisation of popular welfare, and the establishment of insurance companies. It provided a medium for the rationalisation of state and society. It is however much easier to describe the development of cameralist discourse than to measure its real impact on policy and economy. Nonetheless, cameralist argument did not fall on deaf ears.

52   Johannes Jenetzky, *System und Entwicklung des materiellen Steuerrechts in der wissenschaftlichen Literatur des Kameralismus von 1680–1840* (Berlin, 1979).
53   For cameralists' ideas about sex, see Hull, *Sexuality*, pp. 172–97. I thank Mati Laur for bringing my attention to this topic.
54   See e.g. Hans Maier, *Die ältere deutsche Staats- und Verwaltungslehre* (München, 2009; 1st edn, 1966); Marc Raeff, *The Well-Ordered Police State. Social and Institutional Change through Law in the Germanies and Russia, 1600–1800* (New Haven/London, 1983); Thomas Simon, 'Policey im kameralistischen Verwaltungsstaat: Das Beispiel Preußen', *Policey und frühneuzeitliche Gesellschaft*, ed. K. Härter (Frankfurt a.M., 2000), pp. 473–96.
55   Slack, *The Invention*, p. 251; George Rosen, 'Cameralism and the Concept of Medical Police', *Bulletin of the History of Medicine* 27 (1953), 21–42; Caren Möller, *Medizinalpolizei. Die Theorie des staatlichen Gesundheitswesens im 18. und 19. Jahrhundert* (Frankfurt a.M., 2005).
56   Martin Dinges, 'Medicinische Policey zwischen Heilkundigen und "Patienten" (1750–1830)', in *Policey und frühneuzeitliche Gesellschaft*, ed. K. Härter (Frankfurt a.M., 2000), p. 265.
57   See also Nipperdey, *Die Erfindung*.

Comparing Cameralisms:
The Case of Sweden and Prussia

LARS MAGNUSSON

The *nestor* of Swedish economic history, Eli F. Heckscher, rightly drew attention to the important influence of Justus Christoph Dithmar's 1731 *Einleitung in die Oeconomische- Policey- Cameral-Wissenschaften* on the first Swedish-language textbook, written by Anders Berch and published in 1747 as *Inledning til almänna hushålningen, innefattande grunden til politie, oeconomie och cameral wetenskaperne*. Berch had become professor in *Jurisprudentia, oeconomiae et commercium* at Uppsala University in 1741, the first ever Swedish chair for economic subjects.[1] Dithmar had likewise become professor in the newly created chair for *Kameral-Ökonomie und Polizeiwissenschaft* in Frankfurt an der Oder in 1727, also the first chair of its kind at this university. It must however be said that Heckscher's comparison of the two manuals was sketchy, and by no means systematic. All the same, he emphasised their similar structure, dividing up their subject matter into three parts: oeconomy, police (*Policey*) and cameralistic sciences. He also pointed out that anything that might resemble 'analysis' in the modern sense of the word was absent from both texts. Instead, they might better be described as manuals prescribing or giving advice on how to become an economic (and moral) householder. Dithmar primarily addressed future landowners or state administrators, while Berch also included students from mercantile and manufacturing families among his potential readers.

Heckscher was mainly interested in the differences between the two textbooks, perhaps thinking that they indicated something about the socio-economic contexts of the two countries. First he pointed out that Berch's book was more advanced than Dithmar's, being placed intellectually 'on a much

---

1 Eli F. Heckscher, *Sveriges ekonomiska historia sedan Gustav Vasa*, II:2 (Stockholm, 1949), pp. 827–8.

higher plane'.[2] Berch had divided up his subject, *almänna hushålningen*, into two parts, *enskild* (individual) and *almänn* (general) householding. General householding was a synthesis including oeconomy, *Policey* and Cameralism. By contrast, Heckscher considered that Dithmar's division between a *Stadt* (town) and *Land* (agriculture) economy was more traditional. At the same time he did distinguish between the individual and general levels, the former detailing technicalities of husbandry and related matters, while the economy as a whole was dealt with in a broader fashion. Secondly, he pointed out that, while both Berch and Dithmar should be considered as conservative proponents of a highly regulated economy, they differed on one vital point: that of the wider aim of regulation. Dithmar focused on the interest of the state or the ruler, while Berch pointed to the *lycksalighet* (happiness in English, *Glückseligkeit* in German) of the whole people.

Heckscher was nevertheless certain that the different socio-economic fundamentals of the two countries were of major significance. Berch was certainly inspired by Dithmar when he set out to write a text for his Swedish students, and then published *Inledning til almänna hushålningen*. However the contexts were very different, and it was perhaps not coincidental that Heckscher preferred to call Berch a Swedish 'mercantilist', while referring to Dithmar as a 'cameralist'. Moreover, Heckscher regarded the 'Cameralistic attitude' as part and parcel of a wider Mercantilistic system of theory and practice dominating the European mind in the early modern period. Hence he generally accepted the *Sonderweg* interpretation of Cameralism as a German version of Mercantilism.[3]

Wilhelm Roscher, in his monumental *Geschichte der National-Oekonomik in Deutschland*, had introduced the idea that Cameralism was a German *Sonderweg*, or a native version of a broader mercantilistic discourse named so by Adam Smith in 1776.[4] Roscher in fact called the whole period from 1648 up to end of the eighteenth century the 'politico-cameralist epoch of German political economy'. This was succeeded by the 'epoch of scientific economic thinking', but not even Roscher – who in fact tried very hard to find in Germany a break-point of the kind represented by Smith's *Wealth of Nations* – could conceal that much of the Cameralist approach survived into the nineteenth century and beyond.[5] This approach was even more clearly

---

2 Heckscher, *Sveriges ekonomiska historia*, II.2, p. 828.
3 On this theme, see Lars Magnusson, 'Was Cameralism Really the German Version of Mercantilism?', *Economic Growth and the Origins of Modern Political Economy*, ed. Ph. R. Rössner (London, 2016), pp. 57–71.
4 Wilhelm Roscher, *Geschichte der National-Ökonomik in Deutschland* (Munich, 1874), p. 219. Smith in Book IV of *Wealth of Nations* had criticised the 'mercantile system', i.e. a system of regulation, not directly writings about this system.
5 Keith Tribe, *Governing Economy. The Reformation of German Economic Discourse 1750–1840* (Cambridge, 1988). See also the introduction to this volume.

emphasised by Gustav Schmoller. Building on Roscher, Friedrich List and others, he stated that the German mercantilist *Sonderweg* mirrored the late formation of German territorial states, Prussia being the prime instance of a territorial state with limited access to the sea and no navy.[6] Schmoller argued that, in a German context, mercantilist theories 'meant, practically, nothing but the energetic struggle for the creation of a sound state and a sound national economy, and for the overthrow of local and provincial economic institutions.'[7]

This approach has survived until quite recently; the entry for 'Cameralism' in the *New Palgrave Dictionary of Economics* states that Cameralism was 'a version of mercantilism, taught and practised in the German principalities (*Kleinstaaten*) in the seventeenth and eighteenth centuries'.[8] Heckscher adopted a similar interpretation from German historical economists in his seminal work *Mercantilism*, published first in Swedish in 1931.[9]

Today the serious problems arising from the conception of a *Sonderweg* are familiar. Most problematic is that it presupposes the existence of a historical 'blueprint' from which another particular path diverges. The difficulty with all such narratives is that this original model is itself an ideal construction only loosely related to its referent. Since the features of the *Sonderweg* are themselves constructed as differences from this (idealised) original model, both the original model and the supposedly diverging path of development are at best idealisations, at worst fabrications. The industrial and political development of Britain during the nineteenth century was the original model from which Germany was supposed to have 'diverged', but this perspective always rested on a very questionable historical understanding of British and German political and economic developments. Today it is accepted that it is not a matter of ranking the development of states according to the degree to which they might match some original model; instead, it is important to examine varying responses to historical circumstance. In this sense there were many *Sonderwege* (or none at all). As at all other times, during the eighteenth century ideas and discourse diffused through processes of emulation, interpretation and translation.

Here I seek to continue where Heckscher left off: to examine the similarities between Prussian and Swedish discourse on economics and householding before 1750, the time when chairs in this new subject were inaugurated in both

---

6 Schmoller published his most important works during the 1880s and 1890s when naval competition with Great Britain became a major political issue in Germany, following the foundation of the Second Empire in 1871.

7 Gustav Schmoller, *The Mercantile System and its Historical Significance* (New York, 1897), p. 76.

8 See Horst Reckenwald's entry on Cameralism in *The New Palgrave Dictionary of Economics*, 2008.

9 For this see Lars Magnusson, *The Political Economy of Mercantilism* (London, 2015), ch. 2.

countries. I will focus on the two texts already introduced; and in particular, discuss Heckscher's claim that, despite their many similarities, there is a principal difference: the aim to which the highly regulated economy which they both advocated was directed.

Sweden and Prussia

In the mid-eighteenth century Prussia was an emerging European power, while Sweden was a declining one. The Peace of Nystad in 1721 brought an end to the Great Northern War (1700–21), and with it Sweden not only lost most of its Baltic provinces (with the exception of Finland, which remained a part of Sweden until 1809), but it also took a new political direction. The absolutist rule of Charles XI and the warrior king Charles XII was replaced by a form of constitutionalism. Based on contemporary conceptions of a political contract, the new constitution placed most power in the hand of a Diet formed of four Estates – the nobility, the clergy, the burghers, and (uniquely in Europe at the time) the peasantry. The King was to rule with the consent of the Estates. Legislation proposed by the king and his government (the *Riksråd*) had to be passed by a majority in the four different Estates at a common Diet held around every five years. The Estates quickly turned into two loosely organised oligarchies, a two-party system formed of the Hats and the Caps. The former had its base among the nobility and burghers; the latter did include some noblemen, but found its main support in the Estates of the clergy and the peasants. From the 1730s onwards the Hats pursued an aggressive interest-based policy in favour of the major exporting merchants (*Skeppsbroadeln*) based principally in Stockholm and Gothenburg, strongly advocating the establishment of manufactures (in cloth, but also of exotic items such as porcelain, tobacco and silk) and the protection of iron-mining interests. For this purpose the Hats – who held power from the end of the 1730s to the mid-1760s – established a policy of protection that included strict regulation of both industry and trade (both domestic and foreign trade, with an emphasis on the latter). This served to protect nascent manufacturing industry from foreign competition, and also discouraged the export of raw material through navigation acts intended to promote a native commercial export fleet.[10]

There has been some discussion of the extent to which such policies of forced economic modernisation were successful. Without doubt, at their peak during the 1750s such policies contributed to the rise of a manufacturing sector, especially in Stockholm, and supporting more than 20,000 workers

---

10   For an overview, see Michael Roberts, *The Age of Liberty: Sweden 1719–1772* (Cambridge, 1986).

in the textile industry alone. On the other hand, it is also argued that these policies implied a neglect of agriculture, and that favouring the city limited rural development. There were especially restrictive policies related to rural proto-industry and trade – at least in theory. At this time Sweden was reliant on the import of foodstuffs from abroad. The loss in 1721 of corn provinces on the eastern shores of the Baltic was a pivotal moment. The establishment of a strictly protectionist regime in the 1730s was officially attributed to an imbalance in the Swedish balance of trade. No doubt the adoption of this regime can for the most part be attributed to food shortages. All the same, the policy promoted industrial protection, involving what we would today call import substitution.

However, in the mid-1760s these policies were heavily modified. At the Diet of 1765/66 the Caps took power, replacing the predominance of the Hats. Major subsidies to manufacturing, and some of the associated privileges, were abolished. Military defeat lay behind the change of government. Since the Nystad peace there had been widespread revanchist sentiment against Russia, and this had formed a major element in Swedish foreign policy. An unsuccessful war to recover the lost Baltic territories in 1743 increased economic burdens on the population and led to a peasant revolt in the countryside. Sweden's involvement in the Seven Years' War (1756–63) against Prussia, seeking to regain Pomerania, was also unsuccessful. Increasing debt and inflation followed, with political agitation directed against the nobility and in particular the rich *Skeppsbroadel* who was accused of corruption and the pursuit of economic policies for their own gain. The Caps would rule for less than a decade, however. In 1772 Gustavus III staged a *coup d'état*, overthrowing the power of the Diet and returning to a modified version of absolute rule. In Swedish history the period between 1721 and 1773 is known as the 'Age of Freedom', emphasising the weak position of the monarch and rule by the Diet.

Prussia, on the other hand, was a rising power during the eighteenth century.[11] Brandenburg and Prussia – the latter still a Polish fiefdom – were united in 1618, together with the Rhineland provinces of Cleves and Mark. The aftermath of the Thirty Years' War had also been a catastrophe for Sweden. The Great Elector Frederick William I (a Hohenzollern) engaged in various alliances during the 1650s, and in the process detached his territories from Polish and Swedish fiefdom. In 1701 Frederick William's son, Frederick III, was able to upgrade Prussia from a duchy to a kingdom within the Holy German Empire, and crowned himself King Frederick I. Mirabeau was perhaps the first to say that from its early years Brandenburg-Prussia was not a state with an army, but rather an army with a state; Frederick I's

---

11 For the following, see Christopher Clark, *Iron Kingdom: The Rise and Downfall of Prussia, 1600–1947* (London, 2006) and H. W. Koch, *History of Prussia* (London, 1987).

successor Frederick William I was called 'the soldier king'. His successful operations during the Great Northern War resulted in Sweden ceding most of Pomerania to Prussia. Frederick I's son, Frederick II ('the Great') fought no fewer than three wars in the 1740s against Habsburg Austria (part of the War of Austrian Succession), resulting in the incorporation of the great lands of Silesia. Success in the battlefield against Austria and other powers demonstrated Prussia's status as one of the great powers of Europe. This was lent even more emphasis when Prussia in 1772, with the first partition of Poland, was able to join geographically Brandenburg and Prussia, formerly separated by Polish territory.

There is no doubt that in the mid-eighteenth century the Prussian economy was a machine for preparing and conducting war. From Machiavelli onwards rulers of territorial European states understood that a primary means to increase state revenue was to extend its territory. Through increased revenue a state could augment its power and pay for large armies. Control of territory did not necessarily imply the alteration of frontiers in the modern sense. It often involved the establishment of fiefdoms, including some regal rights to property and a right to tax. Income extraction through the extension of territory predominated with respect to another method, which would become more important over time: the increase of revenue through economic deepening, by better householding, but also greater concentrations of population and by the development of agriculture and industry. Some have argued that this shift of emphasis can be traced back to the Italians, particularly to Giovanni Botero who in his *Della ragion di Stato* of 1589 argued that a prince's power had to be based on some form of consent on the part of his subjects. Rulers should seek to win the people to their side. From this idea there developed the notion of a well-planned, orderly economy – where there was a focus on the well-being of the population.[12] For example, it has been argued that Botero was a direct influence upon Veit Ludwig von Seckendorff's *Teutscher Fürsten-Stat* (1656).[13] However, this transformation took time. The incorporation of Silesia by Prussia in the 1740s can be clearly identified as an example of this path to increased income. Silesia had abundant resources: rich agricultural lands, minerals in the mountains, and a flourishing domestic textile industry. It included several important trading cities, such as present-day Wrocław and Katowice.

---

12   On this, see Magnusson, *Political Economy of Mercantilism*, pp. 55f.

13   See Erik S. Reinert with Kenneth E. Carpenter, 'German Language Economic Bestsellers before 1850', *Economic Growth and the Origins of Modern Political Economy*, ed. Ph. R. Rössner (London, 2016), pp. 26f. Reinert rather exaggerates when he speaks of Botero and the Boteriens as a leading influence on everything from Mun and Misselden in 1620s England to Seckendorff in mid-seventeenth century Germany, and even up to the middle of the eighteenth century in Sweden. There is however no doubt that Botero's book reached a wide audience.

However, the other 'intensive' method gained ground at the same time. During the winter of 1739–40 the heir to the throne (the later Frederick the Great) drafted his critique of Machiavelli's *The Prince*.[14] He argued against the extractive method, particularly if it meant destruction and the subjection of people in newly acquired lands. Instead the good ruler should implement rule by laws, which took into consideration how the land had previously been ruled. The ruler must also respect constitutions and the role of Estates and corporations. Moreover, he should introduce proper administration, stimulate population growth and promote the economy.[15] It has been said that Frederick here shows himself to be seriously interested in the welfare of his subjects, that we here can find the embryo of the modern welfare state. It is true that welfare – *Glückseligkeit* in the contemporary idiom – was emphasised. But it was only in the patriarchal sense of wishing good fortune, *Glück*, to the humble subjects of the state. In fact as Justus Christoph Dithmar, appointed to a new cameralistic chair at Frankfurt an der Oder in 1727 emphasised, ruler and subjects (*Unterthanen*) were one and the same body. The interests of the subjects were identical to those of the ruler. They could not be separated.

'Translation'

I have already argued against the notion of blueprints or models in intellectual history, while these days no-one knowingly subscribes to the 'Whig interpretation of history', in which the past is no more than a lengthy anticipation of the present.[16] Such perspectives do not merely assume progress, they also underrate the role of interpretation, emulation and translation. If we wish to understand past texts we need to identify the intentions of their authors, a view associated since the 1970s with what has become known as Cambridge School of intellectual history. Accordingly, we need to pay more attention to the performative nature of texts and acknowledge, as James Tully argues, that 'the author will be doing something in speaking and writing the words, sentences, arguments'.[17] By recapturing the intention of the author Quentin Skinner suggests that:

---

14   See, for a discussion of this, Tribe, *Governing Economy*, pp. 19f.
15   Frederick II, *Refutation of Machiavelli's Prince; or Anti-Machiavel by Frederick of Prussia* (Athens, OH, 1981).
16   See further Lars Magnusson, 'Is Mercantilism a Useful Concept Still?', *Merkantilismus. Wiederaufnahme einer Debatte*, ed. M. Isenmann (Stuttgart, 2014), and Lars Magnusson, *The Tradition of Free Trade* (London, 2004).
17   James Tully, *Meaning and Contexts: Quentin Skinner and his Critics* (Oxford, 1988), p. 8. Cf. Magnusson, *Tradition of Free Trade*, pp. 12f.

We need ... to be able to give an account of what they were doing in
presenting their arguments: what conclusion or what or course of action
they were supporting or defending, attacking or repudiating, ridiculing
with irony, scorning with polemical silence, and so on, and on through the
entire gamut of speech acts embodied in the vastly complex act of intended
communication that any work of discursive reasoning will compromise.[18]

Since we have to understand the specific political, social, economic and
historical context within which texts are produced there are complex issues of
the manner in which interpretation, emulation and translation arise historically. Texts are not passively received, but are actively interpreted within a
particular discourse rooted in specific historical (and institutional) contexts.[19]
Such a process of interpretation – or we might call it 'translation' – affects the
way texts are interpreted and sensed at different times or in different settings.
Hence 'translation' should not be understood simply as a passive transformation of one natural language into another. When a text is translated from
one language into another we often observe omissions great and small, the
insertion of explanatory passages or the rewriting to a greater or less degree.
Such changes are seldom *ad hoc*, or simply a chance outcome. Instead, they
they tell us something of how texts, including the concepts and idioms that
they employ, might be understood in different contexts. Perhaps the most
obvious example in economic discourse is recent discussion concerning the
'true' meaning of Physiocracy – which diffused from France as far as Russia,
Poland and Sweden.[20] Further, it is often noted that Smith's writing as well as
British political economy was read differently outside the British intellectual
and discursive context. In a country like Sweden, where manufacturing and
iron-making were established early but then took time to fully develop, Adam
Smith was primarily seen as an exponent of a new political economy that
laid emphasis upon industrial production, rather than trade or agriculture,
as a path to economic growth and political power – a view shared with
German and American protectionists, the central figure in both cases being
Friedrich List. In the early nineteenth century there was consequently no
inherent contradiction in defending Smith *in principle*, while at the same time
advocating the need for tariffs to protect infant-industries.[21]

18   Quentin Skinner, 'The Idea of Negative Liberty: Machiavellian and Modern Perspectives',
Quentin Skinner, *Visions of Politics: Renaissance Virtues* (Cambridge 2002), p. 194.
19   See Lars Magnusson, 'The Reception of a Political Economy of Free Trade: the Case of
Sweden', *Free Trade and its Reception 1815–1860*, vol. I, ed. A. Marrison (London, 1998),
pp. 145–60. For a more recent contribution, see Sophus Reinert, *Translating Empire. Emulation
and the Origins of Political Economy* (Cambridge, MA, 2011), ch. 1.
20   Lars Magnusson, 'Physiocracy in Sweden 1760–1780', *La Diffusion Internationale de la
Physiocratie*, ed. B. Delmas, T. Demals and Ph. Steiner (Grenoble, 1995), pp. 381–99.
21   Magnusson, 'The Reception of a Political Economy of Free Trade', pp. 145f.

Sophus Reinert has recently identified the process of what he calls 'emulation',[22] examining the various translations of the late-seventeenth-century Bristol merchant-writer John Cary's *Essay on the State of England*, first published in 1695. This was republished several times in his lifetime (he died around 1720); translated first into French in 1755, then to Italian in 1757–58, and lastly to German in 1788. In its journey around Europe what had originally been a small book of one hundred pages not only gained many more pages (the Italian 'translation' by Antonio Genovesi, professor of commerce in Naples, contained more than 1,000 pages). The 'translators' took great liberties with the original and made changes they considered appropriate for their own native readers. Hence the result was not simply a translation, but also a process in which many of Cary's views and proposals became distorted and took on new meanings. Most pertinently, Cary's little book was altered from its advocacy of English protectionism and colonialism into a general 'science of trade' that sought to determine how the wealth of a nation could be achieved. What Reinert calls 'emulation' is close to what I above refer to as translation; although 'emulation' does capture the performative character of this process. Cary's book was open to this reworking because it appeared to provide advice about the way in which German and Italian states might become as rich as England. The perception that England had enjoyed a period of economic growth, combined with the ruthlessness of its protectionist institutions (such as the Navigation Acts), and also its success in building a colonial system – these all paved the way for the successful export of its discourse of political economy, founded upon the conception of reason of state and the strategies of national wealth and power that David Hume called 'jealousy of trade'.[23]

University science

Keith Tribe has presented cameralism as a university science that first emerged after 1720 in Prussian universities.[24] Frederick I took an active part in the introduction of economic teaching to his country, seeking to reorganise the Prussian state, enlarge its population and increase the flow of income to his coffers. The new sciences built on older discourse of householding, including what was known as *Hausväter* literature. A clear influence was Veit Ludwig von Seckendorff (1626–92) who in his *Teutscher Fürsten-Stat* (1656)

---

22   Reinert, *Translating Empire*.
23   On jealousy of trade – the concept David Hume made famous – see Istvan Hont, *Jealousy of Trade. International Competition and the Nation-State in Historical Perspective* (Cambridge, MA, 2005).
24   Tribe, *Governing Economy*.

filled his pages with advice and principles – most probably on the basis of his lengthy service with Duke Ernst von Gotha – in which good husbandry and *Hofverwaltung* were central.[25] Inspired by the Prussian initiative, similar academic appointments were made elsewhere. Tribe states that by 1770 cameralism had 'an established place within the teaching programmes of many of the thirty-one German universities that functioned at the time'.[26] Simon Peter Gasser (1676–1745) was appointed to the first chair in *Oeconomie, Policey and Cammersachen*, created in Halle in 1727. He had already been appointed professor of Jurisprudence at Halle in 1720. A specialist in domain administration, in his new position he lectured on the basis of Ludwig von Seckendorff's *Teutscher Fürsten-Stat*.[27] From his own published textbook of 1729, *Einleitung zu den Oeconomischen, Politischen und Cameral-Wissenschaften*, we can conclude that he mainly taught technical agriculture – how to build robust farmhouses, the best way to treat cattle and fields, the techniques of milling, forestry, hunting and taxation.[28] Before his appointment as a professor he had been a *Kammerrat*, and had in 1716 been sent to Cleves (part of the Prussian territories) to reform domain administration.[29]

The second appointment in Prussia was the historian Justus Christoph Dithmar (1678–1737).[30] He had been first appointed professor of History in 1710 at Frankfurt an der Oder. Little is known about his teaching as professor of *Kameral-, Ökonomie- und Polizeiwissenschaften*, the new chair to which he was appointed in 1727. From his textbook *Einleitung in die Oeconomische-Policey- Cameral-Wissenschaften* (1731) we can gather that he was broader in his teaching than Gasser, including crafts and manufactures in towns. He also wrote more extensively on taxation.

The third university to make a similar appointment was the University of Rinteln, founded in 1610 and which in 1730 inaugurated a chair in *Landwirtschaftliche oeconomiae*. Rinteln was in Hessen-Kassel, not Prussia, and the appointee was Johann Hermann Fürstenau, a veterinarian by training. In 1736 he published *Gründliche Anleitung Zu der Hauhaltungs-Kunst*, which as the title suggests was devoted to an exposition of 'householding', beginning with Aristotle and dealing extensively with technical agricultural

25   Roscher called him a conservative *Nationalökonom*: see Roscher, *Geschichte der National-Ökonomik*, pp. 238f.

26   Tribe, *Governing Economy*, p. 11.

27   Erhard Dittrich, *Die deutschen und österreichischen Kameralisten* (Darmstadt, 1974), pp. 82f. See also Roscher, *Geschichte der National-Ökonomik*, pp. 372f.

28   Tribe, *Governing Economy*, p. 43.

29   More on Gasser in Wilhelm Stieda, *Die Nationalökonomie als Universitätswissenschaft* (Leipzig, 1906), pp. 18f. Also Tribe, *Governing Economy*, pp. 42f.

30   Dittrich, *Die deutschen und österreichischen Kameralisten*, p. 85f; Tribe, *Governing Economy*, pp. 43f.

matters, concluding with a third section dealing with public economy, a category that included landed estates, the domains of the ruler, and also towns and the usefulness of universities.[31] There were parallel developments in Sweden. In 1741 a new chair for the economic sciences was established in the old University of Uppsala (founded in 1477), and two other followed shortly: in Åbo (Turku) in 1747, and in Lund in 1750.[32]

The chair in Uppsala had a prehistory. It was first proposed in 1731, in a dissertation entitled *De felicitate patrise per oeco-nomiam promovenda*, most probably written by the professor of astronomy in Uppsala, Anders Celsius, who had studied in Halle and was highly influenced by Christian Wolff. The response to the dissertation was delivered by Anders Berch, an ambitious young bureaucrat from Stockholm closely connected with the Hat party. When the Hat party gained power in the Diet of 1738–39 the new government determined to establish a chair for the economic sciences in Uppsala – under the condition that Berch received it. The professors and faculties at Uppsala University were reluctant, to say the least. Economic matters were regarded as far too practical for a learned university. The botanist Carl von Linné was rather more positive, but only if the chair was placed in the Faculty of Medicine. Resistance was especially strong when it was instead suggested that the chair should be placed in the Faculty of Law, replacing an older chair in Roman Jurisprudence.[33] There is therefore a political context to the establishment of the Uppsala chair. Its supporters and instigators were the rich merchants, iron-industry manufacturers and nobility who made up the Hat party, and not the king or his administrators.[34] Nor were they much concerned with the increase of tax revenue through good administration in town and country. It was the deficit in the balance of trade between Sweden and Europe that was the most important issue. The agitation to achieve a balance was especially aggressive in the Chamber of Commerce. This body has been established in 1654 and, in a sometimes contradictory manner, sought to balance commercial interests (especially those of the Stockholm *Skeppsbroadeln*) with those of the provincial iron *bruk* (iron manufactures). Moreover, it vacillated over the question of whether protection or free trade should prevail, and whether priority should be given to exporters or importers.[35]

The deficit in the balance of trade was discussed at every Diet from the mid-1720s onwards, and became one of the most important reasons for

31   Tribe, *Governing Economy*, pp. 44f.
32   This was well ahead of the Naples chair in *commercio e meccanica* to which Antonio Genovesi was appointed in 1755.
33   On this, Claes Annerstedt, *Uppsala Universitets historia*, vol. II (Uppsala, 1908–09).
34   Sven-Eric Liedman, *Den synliga handen* (Stockholm, 1986).
35   Sven Gerentz, *Kommerskollegiet och näringslivet* (Stockholm, 1951); and Lars Magnusson, 'Handeln, Näringarna och den Ekonomiska Politiken', *Det svenska urverket. Kommerskollegium 350 år*, ed. B. G. Hall (Stockholm, 2001).

the establishment of Hat rule in 1738/39.[36] Hence it also became the main argument for the introduction of policies lending protection manufactures, as noted earlier. For those who argue that such policies always and everywhere were intended to create a positive balance of trade, the Swedish case is a disappointment.[37] It was instead a deficit that the politicians feared. They argued that under a deficit bullion flowed out of the country, made money scarce, depressed economic activity and increased rents. The Uppsala chair must be seen in this context. Teaching economics was a remedy for the deficit and was also linked to new policies promoting agriculture and population; but it was also aimed at the growth of foreign commerce and manufactures, the displacement of foreign (mainly Dutch) shipping and imported finished goods. This explains why *commercium* was part of the title of the new Uppsala chair, linked to *Jurisprudentia* and *oeconomiae*. It was in fact the first chair in Europe to refer to commerce, which underlines the importance given by the Hat party to foreign trade and domestic production.

Justus Christoph Dithmar

Born in Rothenburg in 1678, Dithmar had first studied in Marburg and then at the university of Leiden – according to Wilhelm Stieda, accompanying a young member of the von Danckelmann family.[38] His appointment to Frankfurt an der Oder as an *außerordentlicher Professor* in History in 1710 seems, according to the same source, to have been owed to his patron, Eberhard von Danckelmann, who had been released from his Berlin prison in 1707. Moreover in 1711 Dithmar became *Ordinarius* at Viadrina (Frankfurt an der Oder). In 1710 he published a work on the life of the eleventh-century Pope Gregorius VII, but his most well-known work was his extensive commentary on Tacitus' *Germania*, *Taciti de situ moribus et populis Germaniae libellus cum … commentario*. This was first published in 1724 and went through at least three further editions up to 1766. As already noted, in 1727 he was appointed to the new chair at Halle in *Kameral-, Ökonomie- und Polizeiwissenschaften*, and subsequently wrote the *Einleitung in die Oeconomische- Policey- Cameral-Wissenschaften* (1731) as his textbook. This was not however the only economic text written by Dithmar; since 1729 he had been involved with the journal *Ökonomischen Fama*, the first periodical in Germany to deal with economic and administrative issues, especially

36   J. W. Arnberg, *Anteckningar om Frihetstidens Politiska Ekonomi* (Uppsala, 1868).

37   For a more general critique of the favourable balance of trade theory and its place in Mercantilism, see Magnusson, *Political Economy of Mercantilism*.

38   On Dithmar, see Roscher, *Geschichte der National-Ökonomik*, p. 431, and Stieda, *Die Nationalökonomie*, pp. 9, 21f.

agriculture and the administration of great landed domains. His knowledge of such matters (especially given his role as Counsellor for Sonnenburg in Neumark) is very relevant to his *Einleitung*. In his introduction Dithmar divided his subject into three parts, as had become usual: the sciences of *Oeconomie*, *Policey* and *Cammersachen*. Dealing with *Oeconomie*, the first authority he mentioned in passing is Aristotle, but he defines this subject as primarily practical. Having then defined *Policey-Wissenschaft* he suggests that it deals with *Politiensachen*, 'the maintenance of the internal and external nature of a state in good order for the common happiness of each and all'.[39] He also states that the science of *Policey* is part of *Staatsklugheit*. Finally, cameral science deals with the prince's domains and dues, and how he might be enriched by his subjects – through the *Prästationen der Unterthanen*.[40]

The second part of the text covers 83 pages and deals with *Landoeconomie*. The first chapters discuss *Landgüter* in general, the rights and titles of landownership, and the boundaries between lands. There then follows a number of chapters dealing with different aspects of agriculture in northern Germany: the building of farmhouses, cattle (it is better to plough with oxen than horses), arable practices (especially the role of manure), the utility of different seeds, a short note on vineyards (in these northerly parts not such a significant issue), forests, hunting, and fishing in rivers and lakes. Also in this part we are provided with an overview of ownership rules and rights over mine-workings. We learn about villages and how they should be maintained in an orderly state. The administration of land is discussed, as are matters relating to distilling and beer-making. In the final part of this section the importance of obedience to the *Gutsherr* is emphasised.

The third part covers 43 pages dealing with *Stadtökonomie*. Dithmar first gives a historical outline of towns in Germany (which is surprisingly short) and their laws. Then he considers the citizenry in general and their various privileges, moving on to a number of different town trades and occupations: brewers and innkeepers are given pride of place, then dealing with artisans of different trades, and the role of guilds. In Chapter Six he describes urban commerce and the different kinds of merchants, distinguishing those trading in raw materials from those handling finished goods. He then briefly describes what a bill of exchange is, outlines various manufactures, and even the ordeals of the despised *Bankerottirer*. It is clear that some of these passages are borrowed from Savary's *Dictionnaire universel du Commerce* (1723), and not drawn from Dithmar's own knowledge of commerce and trade.

---

39 Justus Christoph Dithmar, *Einleitung in die öconomischen, Policey- und cameral-Wissenschaften* – this is the title of the fifth edition, with some additions by Daniel Gottfried Schreber (Frankfurt an der Oder, 1755), p. 153. Since this is available as a reprint I refer to this version.
40 Dithmar, *Einleitung*, p. 25.

The fourth part deals with *Policeywissenschaft* in 89 pages. It consists for the most part of a long list of different policies, regulations and prescriptions that are intended to improve both *Land-* and *Stadtoeconomie*. We once again go through different branches, trades and occupations so that suggestions and remedies can be made. However, Dithmar opens with a first chapter where he again defines the science of *Policey* as *Gute Ordnung und Glückseligkeit*. Moreover, the internal nature of a state is said to be determined by (1) the number of inhabitants, (2) Christian worship, (3) a well-regulated life, (4) health, (5) decorum, and lastly (6) the wealth and subsistence of its inhabitants.[41] Dithmar emphasises that a large population is a precondition for a powerful state – a view often articulated during this period.[42] Also notable is his emphasis on health – the importance of clean water, clean air, fresh food and hospitals for the sick; but also the importance of maintaining rules on quarantine in times of pestilence.

In Chapters 16 to 18 he discusses the way in which urban commerce, craft production and manufactures should be properly organised. He maintains that the last are the true source of a nation's wealth – but only if properly regulated. Here he cites from other writers, such as the Austrians Johann Joachim Becher and Wilhelm von Schröder.[43] He repeats their argument that it should be forbidden to export raw materials and import foreign goods. Following Becher, he distinguishes 'monopoly', 'propoly' (the accumulation of goods for speculative ends) and 'polypoly' (unconstrained competition) as three equally evil practices that can ruin a country's trades. In Chapter 17 he argues for the strict treatment of paupers, and proposes that Jews should not be permitted to levy interest above twelve per cent. Finally, in Chapter 19 he considers the causes for a state losing its wealth. These are presented in the following order: (1) the decline of Christian faith; (2) workers taking Mondays off; (3) a superfluity of beggars; (4) excessive consumption of food, drink and clothing; (5) gambling; (6) excessive foreign travel; (7) lotteries and trading in shares; (8) alchemy; (9) giving those without capacity money; (10) debt; (11) ruin through the pursuit of court cases; and lastly (12) debasement of the currency, reducing the value of money and leading to bankruptcies. *Cameralwissenschaft* is finally defined and outlined in the final part. This science is said to be directed to the increase of the ruler's income. He then enumerates the means by which a prince can enrich himself: through his own his land, his dues, taxation, tolls on transportation by river and highway, his exclusive rights to postal services, duties, hunting and forestry, and so on. He

---

41   Dithmar, *Einleitung*, p. 154.
42   For a recent overview, see Ted McCormick, 'Population: Modes of Seventeenth-Century Demographic Thought', *Mercantilism Reimagined. Political Economy in Early Modern Britain and Its Empire*, ed. P. J. Stern and C. Wennerlind (Oxford, 2014), pp. 25–45.
43   For a presentation, see Magnusson, *Political Economy of Mercantilism*, pp. 78–92.

also emphasises that the ruler has a monopoly on minting coin, and rejects the idea that a ruler should adopt any measure that might reduce its value.

What did Dithmar really mean when he spoke about the wealth of a country and of the happiness of its people? Here Eli Heckscher made a clear distinction between the cameralism of Dithmar and Berch's work in Sweden. For Dithmar, the common people of town and country are subjects. This becomes even clearer in Chapter 7 of the third part on *Policey*, where he clearly states that it is the duty of the territorial ruler to see that his subjects are well provided for according to their rank. Hence he must see to their well-being – in cities and villages – while ensuring that their productive capacity increases, so that they might be able to pay more tax. This is also the duty of the nobility, whose privileges had been conferred so that they might protect the common people from oppressive taxes, rents, contributions, billeting and tolls.

Nor does Dithmar see any contradiction between the interest of the territorial ruler, the nobility and subjects. At the end of the book he once more emphasises the way in which rulers were to provide for their subjects. He should look to his own interests at the same time as he enriches his country – increasing the wealth of the territory. In a country where subjects thrive it is impossible for a ruler to become poor. Dithmar insists that their interests are in fact the same.

Anders Berch

Anders Berch was thirty years old when he was appointed to the chair in Uppsala.[44] His teaching at the so-called *Theatrum Oeconomicum*, close to the river Fyris in the very centre of medieval Uppsala, appears to have followed the text of Dithmar and other contemporary German works. It contained three parts: policy, economy and cameralism. In contrast to Dithmar and Gasser, Berch was not a historian or a lawyer, nor had he held a chair in another subject. His expertise was rather in commerce, industry and manufactures, material with which he had dealt during his time as *auskultant* at the Collegium of Commerce in Stockholm. He had been employed here since the presentation of his Uppsala dissertation in 1731, when he had argued for the establishment of economic teaching in Sweden. Besides this, he took a keen interest in agricultural innovation: the introduction of new and more productive tools, together with practices such as enclosures, the more intensive use of manure and the introduction of crop rotation. On his

---

44 His biography is provided in Liedman, *Den synliga handen*; Annerstedt, *Uppsala Universitets historia*, vol. II.

premises at the *Theatrum Oeconomicum* he kept a set of miniature agricultural tools and equipment, especially ploughs and harrows.

Inledning til almänna hushålningen ('An Introduction to General Householding') begins with a short introductory chapter[45] that notes his reliance upon foreign authorities: Dithmar's *Einleitung* (Berch calls him Ditmer), and also Theodor Ludwig Lau's *Entwurff einer wohl-eingerichteten Policey* (1717). The third German authority he mentions is Johann Ehrenfried Zschackwitz, professor of Imperial History and Public Law at Halle who in 1739 had published his *Gründliche Abhandlung der vollständigen Oeconomicae, Politicae und Cameralis*. Two Frenchmen, Nicholas De La Mare and du Brillet, are also mentioned, both involved in the well-known publication *Traité de la Police* (1705–38 in four volumes, du Brillet being responsible for volume IV). In the introduction Berch also introduced the concept of *Borgerlig sällhet*, which in English is probably best translated as 'civic happiness'. He states that the prime aim of the three different sciences of *Policey*, *Oeconomy* and *Cameralis* is to find the best means of achieving this. Later on he uses the concept *Människans lycksalighet* (human happiness) for much of the same thing. The trinity of sciences is defined in the usual manner. *Policey* serves to provide order in society, *oeconomy* to administer but also to enlarge the national economy, and *cameralis* to put the state on a sound financial footing.

There is also a second and longer introductory paragraph, where he defines his subject in greater detail and provides some general definitions. He begins by pointing out that good and proper householding is the cornerstone of a country's strength. The aim is to create 'prosperity and wealth' (*wälstånd och förmögenhet*). Here he also introduces the concept of 'utility' (*nytta*). This was a word often used in contemporary Swedish discussions of economic issues: everything should be directed to this goal, including the sciences, teaching at the University, the creation of learned societies and policies of reform.[46] We might also note that he was familiar with the contemporary discussion of natural rights, since he briefly discusses the basis of human societies: to form a society to protect himself man has had to give up some natural rights. Society must be orderly and, above all, no favours should be granted to any particular person or groups of persons. Such favour only gives rise to disturbances and *rubbningar* (social disorder). Later on he refers to the view of Hobbes and his followers, who thought society was created by fear and violence, and to those of Pufendorf, who argued that a *socialis appetitus* could be a basis for social order.[47]

---

45 Anders Berch, *Inledning til almänna hushålningen, innefattande grunden til politie, oeconomie och cameral wetenskaperne* (Stockholm, 1747).
46 Sten Lindroth, *Sveriges lärdomshistoria*, vol. II (Stockholm, 1997).
47 Berch, *Inledning*, pp. 23f.

Moreover, it is here that he makes the distinction upon which Heckscher laid such emphasis, that between 'individual' and 'general' householding. Berch was in his book and his teaching concerned with the latter. In this section he also argues against the use of *Oeconomiae* by von Seckendorff and others as a general description of the field to which Berch addressed himself, using instead 'General Householding'. This is no small thing, for it implies that he refuses to identify his subject matter with *Staatsklugheit* and the proper rule of the *Hausvater*, distancing himself from a purely Aristotelian conception of his subject-matter.

He subdivides General Householding into the three different sciences that we have already encountered. The first is the science of Police (*Politiewetenskapen*), declaring this the most important of the three. Then he turns to the important role of a large population.[48] We do not know if Berch had read Peter Süßmilch's *Die göttliche Ordnung*, published only six years before Berch's book. However, the arguments are quite similar, and are commonly encountered during this period. According to Berch, a less populous country was at the same time a realm lacking in industry and industrious workers, who are the most useful of all to society. Population growth can be achieved, he suggests, by stimulating early marriage, establishing orphanages, educating midwives, stimulating immigration and hindering emigration. A population shortage can also be compensated for by introducing labour-saving methods, including simple mechanical devices. Like so many others at the time, his argument for the attraction of foreign workers presumed an increased religious tolerance.

Most of the section on *Policey* is – perhaps unsurprisingly – devoted to measures that could be useful in creating greater wealth and prosperity. He presents a whole list of reforms and innovations that should be introduced, as was usual for the time. For an orderly society in which industry can thrive, perhaps the most important for Berch were: religious toleration and harmony, schooling, the suppression of seditious practices, sobriety, putting paupers in workhouses, introducing proper medical care, cleanliness, and the education of wet-nurses and midwives. Berch is ambivalent over the question of whether the consumption of luxury goods should be restricted or not. Such consumption could stimulate increased production; hence something in itself vicious could in fact lead to a common good. However, if luxury consumption led to the import of such items it should be regulated, if not altogether prohibited.

In the second part Berch deals with the science of *Oeconomy*. He divides this into several parts, like Dithmar, but in a different manner. First he considers agriculture. Here his main advice for increasing population and

---

48 Discussed most recently by MacCormick, 'Population'.

production is the introduction of enclosure (*skiften*) and village ordinances (*byordningar*). The more hands in agriculture the better, he argues, as this leads to industry rather than idleness. New tools and even some machinery must be introduced, as well as new methods of tillage. Forest management should be improved. A balance should be struck between keeping animals (who produce manure) and arable land: too few cattle leads to smaller harvests and declining productivity.

Then he turns to mining, which he puts in second place to agriculture. Opening new mines increases the wealth of the country, increases national capital and also the stock of money – if its products are sold to aliens. To support this industry the forests must be properly administered and water-courses kept in good order. Then he deals with handicrafts and manufactures (*handaslögder*), which work up natural resources. The most useful branches in the economy are argued to be those that employ most hands, and so both traditional artisans organised in guilds and new manufactures should be confined to towns – he is opposed to what he calls *kladdande* (casual ventures) with such trades in the countryside. He used, like Dithmar, the distinction between 'monopoly', 'propoly' and 'polypoly', being opposed to all these ways of conducting industry and trade. The last (unconstrained competition) in particular leads to disorder, the neglect of agriculture and a production of lower quality goods. Hence he was also – as emphasised by Heckscher – a keen adherent of the extremely protectionist policy for manufactures introduced by the Hats at the Diet of 1738/39; it was of course the Hats who had installed Berch in Uppsala in the first place.

Berch also here defines what he calls 'the national gain'. This is created by added value produced in handicrafts and (most importantly) new manufactures (Berch even uses the word 'fabrique').[49] Adding value can be achieved through the use of domestic natural goods, but also through the import of such goods. It is doubtful whether Berch really believed that re-exporting finished goods could be of any importance for Sweden – something that everybody at the time knew had made the Dutch provinces so rich. All the same, this fitted with his view that the more hands set to work, the richer the country.

Lastly, the fourth section of *Oeconomy* deals with 'Trade'. This too should be conducted in an orderly manner. If properly regulated trade 'was the most precious jewel (*ögonsten*) of the country'.[50] He presumed that trade should be a speciality of the towns. Moreover, a distinction should be made between those towns that were *uppstäder*, which only had the right to trade with the countryside and between themselves, and those that were *stapelstäder* and permitted to conduct trade with foreigners. Berch lays great emphasis upon

49 Berch, *Inledning*, p. 262.
50 Berch, *Inledning*, p. 270.

the importance of these and other regulations: they should aim at creating the maximum wealth for the country, preventing the import of finished goods and encouraging the export of goods that had had value added to them through human labour. We can see little in Berch's text of what has become known as the 'mercantilist theory' of a favourable balance of trade. Instead he writes about the danger of the deficit in Swedish foreign trade. He also seems to be aware, at least in principle, of the general idea behind the specie-flow argument later made famous by David Hume. He acknowledged an early form of a quantity theory of money, stating that an inflow of gold and silver would cause inflation. This would disrupt exports when prices rose, since foreigners might retaliate by imposing a higher and less favourable exchange rate – leading in this way to a deficit in the balance of trade. Hence a favourable trade balance (or an unfavourable one, even though he does not mention this) could not be enduring.[51] This is very far from the argument advanced by Adam Smith, that the 'mercantile system' was founded upon a confusion of bullion with wealth.[52]

In the final part of the book Berch deals briefly with the science of the *Camera*, its brevity suggesting his lack of direct familiarity with this field. He also hesitates to suggest that a rulers dues and imposts (the regalian rights) should be used to increase the income of the state. On the one hand, he is certainly aware of that the king needed money in order to conduct *Policey*. On the other hand, he gives much more space to the argument that taxes or rents should not be too high, since this could endanger industry and general prosperity. Moreover, he considers that it is of the greatest importance that the state's income should not be left in the exchequer. It must be set to work: it is as important to spend as it is to collect. Hence taxes must be used in order to create the greatest happiness, *borgerlig sällhet* and *lycksalighet*, in the country.

Let us return to the issue of Berch's moral philosophy, and particularly the question Heckscher raised concerning the difference between Dithmar and Berch. We have already noted the strong influence of Wolff on Berch's thinking. In this he was not alone in Sweden during the 1740s. Most prominently perhaps the Commissar for Manufactures, Johan Fredrik Kryger, argued in his *Naturlig Theologie* (1744–53) for highly regulatory economic policies – not least in favour of already highly-favoured manufactures – on the basis of Wolffian moral philosophy. For Kryger, 'concord' was at the core of a civilised state. Indeed 'perfection' (*perfectio*) presupposed 'concord in multiplicity'.[53] According to Kryger, God had created a natural order in which

51   On this, see Berch, *Inledning*, pp. 343f.
52   Magnusson, *Political Economy of Mercantilism*, pp. 2–7.
53   See Tore Frängsmyr, 'Den gudomliga ekonomin: Religion och hushållning I 1700-talets Sverige', *Lychnos. Lärdomshistorika samfundets årsbrok* (1971–72), pp. 217–44; and Lars

conflicting desires and interest could be balanced: 'that in the whole system of nature they make such splendid order and concord, that they are linked as in a chain'.[54]

Berch was a follower of what has been called by Swedish scholars *Oeconomiae divina*.[55] Referring to the great debates in moral philosophy of the time, he defined society in his *Inledning* as a bond in which the individual had to surrender some of his natural freedoms in order to find society and protection. This message is even more clearly spelled out in a speech that he gave to the students in Uppsala and later had printed, *Tal om den proportion som de studerande ärfodra till de ledige beställningar i riket* (1749). Here he argued for that the number of students in different subjects should be proportional to the need for different crafts and occupations in the kingdom, a form of planned and strictly regulated labour market. Among other things he here states that 'A civic society surely does not place any upon our arms: but we have nevertheless, through harmonious agreement and union, exchanged our unfettered natural freedom for one that is circumscribed and regular.' And he continues: 'And if the civic enactments shall have any semblance of compulsion, then it is founded only upon this rule: the prosperity of the inhabitants shall be the essential aim of civil society.'[56]

Conclusions

There are certainly similarities between Dithmar's *Einleitung* and Berch's *Inledning*. Dithmar had been appointed to his chair in Frankfurt twelve years before Berch, and had written a textbook for his new subject. What was more natural than for Berch to be inspired, to emulate or 'translate' it for his own purposes? Moreover, the books by Berch and Dithmar books have very similar titles and divide up their subject-matter into the same three parts: oeconomy, police and cameralism. They also share a *dirigiste* attitude to economic policy, as noted by Eli Heckscher, always and everywhere defending existing regulations, especially in trade and commerce, and at the same time seeking to extend them. Nonetheless, they seem to be worlds apart. Why is this?

First and most obviously, it was no accident that Berch's chair had a different title from Dithmar's and included the term *Commercium*. It is also evident that Berch devoted much more space in his book to discussion of

Magnusson, 'Corruption and Civic Order – Natural Law and Economic Discourse in Sweden during the Age of Freedom', *Scandinavian Economic History Review* 37 (1989), 78–105.

54   Tore Frängsmyr, *Wolffianismens genombrott i Sverige* (Uppsala, 1972), p. 230.
55   Frängsmyr, 'Den gudomliga ekonomin'.
56   Anders Berch, *Tal om den proportion som de studerande ärfodra till de ledige beställningar i riket* (Stockholm, 1749), p. 11.

trade and commerce, especially foreign commerce and its role in the wealth of a country. This should not surprise us given the different socio-economic characters of Sweden and Prussia, and the more obvious interest in foreign commerce for Sweden in the first part of the eighteenth century.

Secondly, both Berch and Dithmar write of the necessity of concord between different interests in a well-ordered state. Berch is much more explicit about the source of his inspiration: from contemporary arguments on natural rights in general, and from Wolff's version in particular. Dithmar's moral philosophy is less obvious, nor are his inspirations clear. He explicitly mentions in his text Christian Thomasius several times – Halle's radical Rector and Professor of Law from 1710, who had been forced to flee from Frankfurt an der Oder and seek protection in Berlin from the Great Elector Frederick. He also refers, perhaps unsuprisingly given the influence on Thomasius, to Grotius (but not once to Pufendorf). Thomasius taught Natural and Roman Law, and for his work on Tacitus Dithmar must have at least consulted his *Institutiones iurisprudentiae divinae* (1688) or *Fundamenta juris naturae et gentium* (1705).[57] However, we see little trace of any influence in Dithmar's textbook. Perhaps he considered his subject too practical to involve himself in the subtleties of contemporary natural rights discourse.

Thirdly, from this it seems paradoxical perhaps that Berch's reading of Wolff (and of others) seems to lead in a very different direction than that taken by Dithmar regarding social happiness or welfare. As Keith Tribe has pointed out, something we might call 'welfare', or perhaps better in German *Glückseligkeit*, was a cornerstone of Cameralist university science from the early beginnings in Halle and Frankfurt an der Oder in the 1720s.[58] However, our comparison between Berch and Dithmar makes it clear that 'welfare' could mean quite different things. As I have argued, Dithmar gives it a highly patriarchal twist. Here it is the idea of the *ganze Haus*, identified by Otto Brunner many years ago, that shines through.[59] According to Dithmar, the *Landesfürst* and the *Unterthanen* have identical interests. Moreover, the *Fürst* is like a father (*Hausvater*) to his children, his wife and his servants. They are one and the same body and cannot be separated. With Berch it is strikingly different. His household is distinct from Dithmar's neo-Aristotelian conceptualisation of the patriarchal family. Berch concedes that there are different interests in society, but that in an ordered society could these should be mitigated for the sake of a common good. Concord can be established, but

---

57 On Thomasius, see Hans-Erich Bödeker (ed.), *Strukturen der deutschen Frühaufklärung* (Göttingen, 2008).

58 Tribe, *Governing Economy*, pp. 30ff.

59 This is of course noted by Tribe, *Governing Economy*, p. 24. The seminal text by Otto Brunner is 'Das "ganze Haus" und die alteuropäische "Ökonomik"', *Zeitschrift für National-ökonomie* 13 (1952), 114–39.

it had to be based upon a compromise. It had to be founded in a contract that could satisfy men's aptitude for sociability, but also provide protection. Like so many at this time, Berch seeks an alternative to Hobbes' cruel and unbending world that seemed so close to blasphemy in its denial of human sociability, too radical for Christians of whatever confession. Berch is the prudent servant of the state. He seeks to strike a compromise between regulation and sociability.[60]

Given that Berch and Dithmar share some similarities, but also differences, can we draw the conclusion that Berch was a mercantilist and Dithmar a cameralist? This of course depends on how we make our distinctions. What Heckscher saw as Berch's 'more developed' discussion of commerce, of the balance of trade and similar matters might perhaps lead us to such a conclusion. But what might be the benefit of so doing? Perhaps it would be more interesting – as we suggest here – to consider how emulation and translation takes place in different societal contexts.

---

60   On this, see Istvan Hont, 'The Language of Sociability and Commerce: Samuel Pufendorf and the Theoretical Foundations of the "Four Stages Theory"', *The Language of Political Theory in Early Modern Europe*, ed. A. Pagden (Cambridge, 1987), pp. 253–76.

2

Baltic Cameralism?

KEITH TRIBE

Throughout the eighteenth century, *Kameralwissenschaft* was understood primarily as a body of writing and teaching related to the economic management of the territorial state. It sought to delineate the practices that would foster the well-being of the population, and hence the strength of the state. As I argue in *Governing Economy*,[1] the project to establish Cameralism as a science in northern German universities shaped a body of writing that reflects not how the economy of town and country actually functioned, but that was instead more normative: it articulated a conception of good order in state and economy. What we learn from studying the textbooks produced in the course of the eighteenth century illuminates therefore these conceptions of 'good order', not whether economic administration and practice was in fact orderly.

Cameralist teaching was developed primarily in North German Protestant universities; as a discourse of Reform and Enlightenment it also found a place in universities of the Austrian territories of the later eighteenth century, as also in Russia and in Sweden. This northern connection to Russia and Sweden ran through the Baltic Sea, which was a major northern trading area both for its coastal states, and for those areas with major rivers flowing into it. This formed a distinct and extensive common Northern European economic space which not only fostered mutual trade, but which was already firmly linked into the Atlantic trading area through the significant presence of Dutch merchants in the seventeenth century, and British in the eighteenth. The British in particular were primarily seeking timber and timber products: pitch and tar, potash, and also the Swedish iron whose production was linked not only to deposits of iron ore, but to vast forests that could provide the charcoal needed

---

1 Keith Tribe, *Governing Economy. The Reformation of German Economic Discourse 1750–1840* (Cambridge, 1988; 2nd edition, Newbury, 2017).

to smelt it.[2] Also of significance was flax for rope and cordage, and linen for sailcloth. The significant expansion of the British Navy in the course of the eighteenth century was predicated upon access to the Baltic trades, despite all efforts in the earlier part of the century to source timber and timber products from the American colonies.

During the eighteenth century, therefore, long-distance trading relations linked the Baltic to the Atlantic. The extensive forests of this area were domain land or part of large private estates requiring long-term management; and so there is on the face of it a possible connection between the emergent cameralist discourse of state administration and the literature of commerce, trade and power that linked the interests of merchants to those of the state. Did anything like a "Baltic Cameralism" emerge from this nexus that might reflect the world of overseas trade and international markets, transcending the more usual cameralist emphasis upon the good order of a closed, domestic economy? A kind of export-oriented Cameralism? Raising this question also provides a useful test of the normative characteristic of cameralist writing – that it discourses at length on good order and practice, only indirectly indicating the way in which these conceptions related to actual economic relationships, practices and products.

We can no longer reconstruct in any detail the rhythm of economic activity in the territorial states of Northern Europe: what was produced where and in what quantities, where it was consumed and by whom, the movement of prices, taxes, fees and duties paid.[3] The materials now available to us provide at best an image of the structure of such activity, not its ongoing process. However, where goods are traded between states by sea we sometimes have data on products, quantities and prices together with dates, permitting the flow of economic activity to be reconstructed at least in part. Throughout the eighteenth century British customs officers recorded goods shipped in and out of British ports; Swedish district officials did likewise;[4] while Danish customs officials recorded the ships and cargoes passing through the Danish straits ('the Sound'). The Baltic trade in timber and timber products was therefore recorded in transit and on its arrival in Britain, whose merchantmen were

---

2   During the eighteenth century Swedish blast furnaces and forges consumed charcoal equivalent to 3 million cubic metres of timber a year; charcoal-burning accounted for half of the national consumption of timber – Svante Lindqvist, 'Labs in the Woods: The Quantification of Technology during the Late Enlightenment', Tore Frängsmyr, *The Quantifying Spirit in the Eighteenth Century*, ed. J. L. Heilbron and Robin E. Rider (Berkeley, 1990), p. 302.

3   The volumes of the *Acta Borussica* published from 1894, and the new series that has appeared since 1994, are of course a rich source in this regard – see, for a useful synthesis of the older material, Gustavo Corni, *Stato assoluto e società agraria in Prussia nell'età di Federico II* (Bologna, 1982).

4   See the account of this data in John Rice, 'Patterns of Swedish Foreign Trade in the Late Eighteenth Century', *Geografiska Annaler. Series B, Human Geography* 47 (1965), 86–7.

by the eighteenth century the largest trading presence in the Baltic.[5] These records make up a rich resource with which we can assess flows of trade; if combined with the records of the Royal Navy we also have a significant record of the consumption of these products. While we lack much in the way of systematic records on the output side – the sale of timber, or of leases for the exploitation of timber, to merchants often based in the major seaports – it is nonetheless possible to assess the nature and scale of the engagement of northern state domain land and estates in international trade.

This chapter therefore reverses the approach that I took in *Governing Economy*. Rather than construct a perspective upon conceptions of economic order through a study of cameralist teaching and practical writings, I here examine one demonstrably significant area of economic activity and consider in what way, if at all, this was represented in contemporary writing on economic administration. To anticipate my conclusion: such reflection is only partial and indirect – there is no 'Baltic Cameralism'. But this negative conclusion is not really the point of what follows, for in reaching this conclusion I raise the question: why not? Why, if the activity of economic administration had such significant commercial consequences, were these consequences apparently overlooked in cameralist literature? More generally, this touches upon the supposition that the economic literature of the eighteenth century, or of any period, more or less directly reflects the state of contemporary economic and commercial activity, its progress and its constraints.

This supposition is generally presumed to have originated in Book IV of Adam Smith's *Wealth of Nations*,[6] in which he mounts a critique of two contemporary 'systems of political œconomy': the 'mercantile or commercial system' and the 'agricultural system'. Smith considered the latter, associated with François Quesnay and those who later became known as Physiocrats, as ingenious, but of no practical import, and so devoted only one chapter to it. Book IV Ch. IX is therefore devoted to a critique of *ideas*, rather than of actual policies. By contrast, the critique of the 'system of commerce', or 'the modern system' as he calls it in the eight foregoing chapters of *Wealth of Nations*, relates to *policies* designed to artificially promote wealth: pretending to one ultimate object:

5   As Sven-Erik Åström notes, English economic historians have tended to focus upon exports, rather than imports, in dealing with industrial development. Sven-Erik Åström, 'English Timber Imports from Northern Europe in the Eighteenth Century', *Scandinavian Economic History Review* 18 (1970), 12.
6   Book IV was entitled 'Of Systems of Political Œconomy'. Adam Smith, *An Inquiry into the Nature and Causes of the Wealth of Nations* (London, 1976) (henceforth WN. This edition is based on the third edition of 1784; the first edition was published in 1776.). Smith was critical of 'men of system', and so the title reflects this antipathy.

to enrich the country by an advantageous balance of trade. It discourages the exportation of the materials of manufacture, and of the instruments of trade, in order to give our own workmen an advantage, and to enable them to undersell those of other nations in all foreign markets: and by restraining, in this manner, the exportation of a few commodities, of no great price, it proposes to occasion a greater and more valuable exportation of others.[7]

This general stance much later became known as 'mercantilism', a term characterising both ideas *and* policies, which has since become widely used as a general term for early writings directed to the augmentation of a state's wealth and power.

Two points need to be made here. First of all, as already suggested, Smith directed his criticism of the 'mercantile system' to actual policies, not the arguments embodied in pamphlets arguing for one policy or another. Second, while Smith was here criticising a mode of economic regulation, he did not contrast it directly to his 'system of natural liberty'. Instead, he developed his arguments concerning natural liberty in WN IV.ix, contrasting his own conception of natural liberty to the approach of Quesnay and his followers. Thus we do not find in Book IV a direct contrast between regulation and economic liberty; what we can find, rather, is the idea that:

> If a nation could not prosper without the enjoyment of perfect liberty and perfect justice, there is not in the world a nation which could ever have prospered.[8]

This stance significantly moderates Smith's presumed general hostility to the system of commerce as a unitary system of regulation. Nonetheless, the idea that 'mercantilism' denotes the idea of regulation, and that its counter-concept is free trade, is one now routinely used to characterise the historical option that Smith advanced, pitting his 'natural system of liberty' against the prevailing 'system of commerce'.

Moreover, in the process all pre-Smithian writing that is not Physiocratic became by default 'mercantilist'. Bruno Hildebrand was influential in establishing this reading, expounding it as part the introductory article to the first German periodical dedicated to political economy:

> The oeconomists of the absolutist state, the so-called mercantilists, regarded the economic life of peoples as the product of human government, a life whose purpose was attained by decree. The Physiocrats and Adam Smith, by contrast, claimed that the human world was governed by natural

7   WN IV.viii.1. Ch.viii was added in the third edition.
8   WN IV.ix.28.

laws as immutable as those which ruled the world of plants and minerals; hence they considered all such government regulations to be disadvantageous restraints imposed upon the healthy development of economic life according to its own natural laws. Against the mercantilist system of prohibition and protection they set the principle of free trade; against the established orders of guilds and industrial monopolies they set free competition; against the remnants of the medieval agrarian constitution they set the necessity of completely free and partible landed property; against the system of commercial police they set that of unconditional commercial freedom.[9]

Hildebrand is here broadly quite right in his judgement that political oeconomy treated the regularities of economic life as a construction of government, rather than the product of autonomous human activity; this aspect of the contrast he was drawing subsequently vanished, however, so that 'mercantilism' became little more than a system of regulation and prohibition. By extension, cameralism then became associated with mercantilism as the German variant of a regulatory system, compounding the problem. But if there is any merit in this association, why do we search cameralist writing in vain for discussion of the commercial relationships so typical of the Baltic region? If we are to consider the relationship of cameralist discourse to trading relationships, we must first deal with this confusion.

The problem of 'mercantilism'

In 1931 Eli Heckscher, Professor of Economic History at the Stockholm School of Economics from 1929, published what would become his seminal study of early modern commerce, adopting as his title a term developed in the 1880s by Gustav Schmoller: *Merkantilismus*.[10] Schmoller had taken up Adam Smith's terminology[11] in reviewing the various economic measures adopted in the nascent Prussian state that had promoted state formation. The regulatory policies that had been the object of Smith's criticism were now reinterpreted positively, as contributing to the formation and consolidation of the Prussian state. While this inflection of 'mercantilism' involved a teleology of state

9 B. Hildebrand, 'Die gegenwärtige Aufgabe der Wissenschaft der Nationalökonomie', *Jahrbücher für Nationalökonomie und Statistik* 1 (1863), 6.
10 Eli Heckscher, *Merkantilisment; ett led I den ekonomiska politikens historia* (Stockholm, 1931); translated into German as *Der Merkantilismus* (Jena, 1932); and into English as *Mercantilism* (London, 1935; 2nd edn in two vols, 1955), cited here from the Routledge 1994 reprint.
11 Although Schmoller was an increasingly strident critic of what he considered to be Smith's formal and ahistorical approach to economic activity.

formation, it is also worth noting that Schmoller laid emphasis here on the role of the 'territorial economy': rather than seeing the emergent state as part of a larger process in which control was increasingly centralised,[12] attention was instead directed to the co-ordination of territorial power, extending across areas where urban settlements were few and far between.[13] And he summarised 'mercantilism' in the following terms:

> The essence of this system lay not in an emphasis upon the accumulation of money or on the balance of trade, nor simply in customs frontiers, protective tariffs and the regulation of shipping, but rather in something more: in the total reorganisation of society and its organisation, together with the state and its institutions, replacing a local and rural economic policy with one based upon state and nation.[14]

Heckscher likewise emphasised the importance of policies in creating a 'uniform economic sphere' subordinate to state direction, suggesting that the chief objective here was the strengthening of the power of a state with respect to its neighbours and competitors.[15]

However, as Heckscher's book unfolds we discover that his primary source of material comes not, as with Schmoller, from the territorial states of Northern Europe, but from the rather different polities of England and France, both unitary states throughout the period. Consequently, the sources which Heckscher examines – tolls, weights and measures, coinage, guild regulation, capital, corporations and companies – are factors which are not so much instruments of state formation, but of the consolidation of an existing state. Schmoller's purpose, tracking the emergence of state co-ordination from the diversity of territorial economic organisation, was instead diverted by Heckscher back into a more Smithian path, in which the various regulatory instruments were envisaged as so many obstacles to the realisation of free trade. For Heckscher, the option was either mercantilism or *laissez-faire*, the

12   Recent literature on early modern political economy that has directed attention to markets and state regulation invariably presumes a modern, centralised state; but 'the modern state' was a creation of the nineteenth, not of the eighteenth century. This unhistorical presumption can be seen at work in Philipp Robinson Rössner, 'Heckscher Reloaded? Mercantilism, the State, and Europe's Transition to Industrialization, 1600–1900', *Historical Journal* 58 (2015), 663–83.

13   This approach is also reflected in Guillaume Garnier's *État, économie, territoire en Allemagne. L'espace dan le caméralisme et l'économie politique 1740–1820* (Paris, 2005).

14   Gustav Schmoller, 'Das Merkantilsystem in seiner historischen Bedeutung [1884]', *Umrisse und Untersuchungen zur Verfassungs-, Verwaltungs- und Wirtschaftsgeschichte* (Berlin, 1898), p. 37.

15   '[M]ercantilism is primarily an *agent of unification*'. Heckscher, *Mercantilism* I, 2nd edn, p. 22.

former representing state intervention, and the latter opposed to any state activity other than the maintenance of law and order.[16]

Heckscher's subsequent principal reputation has been as a contributor to the Heckscher–Ohlin model of comparative advantage, of the distribution of the advantages from trade according to the factor endowments of the trading economies concerned.[17] It is usually supposed that in *Principles of Political Economy and Taxation* Ch. 7 (1817) David Ricardo originated the argument that comparative, rather than absolute, advantage underpinned the development of international trade, the basic conception that is articulated in all modern trade theory.[18] Here we might note that when Ricardo imagined two economies exchanging wine and wool, he was simply recalling the terms of England's 1703 Methuen Treaty with Portugal as printed in its entirety in Adam Smith's *Wealth of Nations* Book IV Ch. 6, and so presumably recycling something he had read. Later James Mill, when tidying up Ricardo's rather confused account of international trade in his own *Elements of Political Economy*, replaced wine and wool with corn and cloth, the two specimen countries now being England and Poland;[19] hence reflecting the real significance of the Baltic trades for eighteenth- and early nineteenth-century Britain. While this aspect of British trading relations and policy is absent from *Mercantilism*, Heckscher did go on to write a history of the Swedish economy from 1520 to 1815 whose later parts dealt in some detail with Swedish external trade in the eighteenth century.[20] And while German secondary works are not completely ignored in *Mercantilism*,[21] there are in the index just two references to the vast contemporary German literature: "Cameralism: German" is represented individually by Becher, Hörnigk and Schröder, all of them seventeenth-century writers connected in one way or

16   Heckscher, *Mercantilism* II, 2nd edn, p. 316.
17   Heckscher first sketched this model in Eli Heckscher, 'Utrikeshandelns verkan på inkomstfördelningen. Några teoretiska grundlinjer', *Ekonomisk Tidskrift* 21 (1919), 1–32, translated as 'The Effect of Foreign Trade on the Distribution of Income', *Readings in the Theory of International Trade*, ed. H. S. Ellis and L. A. Metzler (Philadelphia, 1949), pp. 272–300; and this model was first fully elaborated by his student Bertil Ohlin in his *Interregional and International Trade* (Cambridge, MA, 1933).
18   See my discussion of this: Keith Tribe, *The Economy of the Word. Language, History, and Economics* (New York, 2015), ch. 4.
19   James Mill, *Elements of Political Economy*, in *James Mill. Selected Economic Writings*, ed. D. Winch (Edinburgh, 1966), p. 271. *Elements* was first published in 1821; Winch reproduces the third edition of 1826.
20   Eli Heckscher, *Sveriges Ekonomiska Historia från Gustav Vasa*, two volumes in four parts (Stockholm, 1935, 1936, 1949). Volume 1.1 (1935) deals with the sixteenth century, 1.2 (1936) deals with the period from then until 1720, while volume 2 (1949) concerns the period 1720–1815, ch. X of 2.1 being devoted to trade and shipping. See Lars Magnusson's brief discussion in his 'Introduction' to Heckscher, *Mercantilism* I, pp. xx–xxi.
21   See, for example, Heckscher, *Mercantilism* II, pp. 262–3.

another with the Austrian court, Becher and Schröder also spending time in England. Heckscher did later include a chapter on "Economic Discussion" in his economic history of Sweden, linking domestic Swedish debate to the emergence of cameralist chairs in Germany, the influence of Becher, Hörnigk and Schröder in Sweden, together with the reception in Sweden of the Physiocrats and Adam Smith.[22] But none of this material, nor anything related to his knowledge of Baltic trades, found its way into his account of 'mercantilism'. The existence of an extensive eighteenth-century German-language literature is there reflected only in his reference to three seventeenth-century writers who are treated as 'mercantilists'.

The entire Baltic region was one dominated by territorial states in which domain administration played a significant part in local economic activity. The British economy relied on this region for supplies of shipbuilding timber, masts, spars, tar, pitch, hemp and potash, the last critical to the English woollen industry, and the remainder vital to the British merchant marine and the Royal Navy. In the seventeenth century the Dutch had predominated, its ships carrying three-quarters of the grain that passed through the Sound in that century.[23] Here, one would think, was a region within which emergent state economic administration linked up with an Atlantic economy in which trade might not be entirely free, but which was conducted by independent merchants. But Heckscher's attention in *Mercantilism* is resolutely turned away from the trading region of which Sweden was then still a part, towards the more distant engagements of French and British merchants in the Atlantic and beyond in which the Baltic seems to play no part. Despite the work's manifestly international focus, it is limited both geographically and substantively by its focus upon administration and policy, rather than starting from the actual trading relations that existed and how these might or might not have shaped policy and debate. And so, despite the monumental character of Heckscher's work, its own focus has in turn distracted our attention from the actual significance of the Baltic trades in international commerce.

Britain and the Baltic trades

Throughout the eighteenth century Northern Europe[24] was the most significant international trading region by value for England and Wales; between 1710 and 1758 imports were in almost every year higher than from the next

---

22   Heckscher, *Sveriges Ekonomiska Historia* II.2, pp. 827, 839, 871ff, 877ff.

23   David Kirby, *Northern Europe in the Early Modern Period. The Baltic World 1492–1772* (London, 1990), p. 229.

24   European ports north of Antwerp – Note 4 to External Trade Table 14 in B. R. Mitchell, *British Historical Statistics* (Cambridge, 1988), p. 492.

two most significant regions (Southern Europe, followed by the British West Indies),[25] in most years the total of imports and exports eclipsing those of Asia, Africa and the American Colonies combined. Using figures calculated by Deane and Cole, Mitchell shows that for Great Britain during the last quarter of the eighteenth century, imports from 'The North' (Denmark, Norway, East Country, Poland, Prussia, Russia and Sweden – i.e. the Baltic trades) generally exceeded those from Northwest Europe (France, the Low Countries, and the German states excluding Prussia).[26] From this we might infer that Baltic trading made up a substantial proportion of 'Northern Europe' for British traders. Central to these trade flows was the exchange of timber and timber products for British cloth; both the Royal Navy and the merchant marine relied heavily upon Baltic timber, and more or less exclusively upon the region for its supplies of pitch, tar and hemp. Both the construction of new ships, and the maintenance of existing ones, required large quantities of imported material; by the later part of the century British ships were the principal trading presence in Baltic waters.[27] The Baltic was also extremely significant as a source of potash, essential for various stages in the manufacture of cloth during the eighteenth century, and a heavy consumer of hardwood – one cubic metre of oak yielded just over one pound of potash according to one estimate.[28] And by the early eighteenth century the annual consumption of iron in Britain was roughly twice the amount supplied by domestic forges, the shortfall being made up by Baltic imports – by 1700 Britain took 60% of Swedish iron exports, and by mid-century there were around 2,500 forgemen employed in Sweden, as against around 1,000 in Britain. While Sweden enjoyed ample sources of iron ore, of greater significance was the ample supply of charcoal upon which its around 420 ironworks depended.[29]

Van Creveld pointed out a long time ago that for all the attention Napoleon's campaigns have attracted from historians and strategists, the

25 Imports from Southern Europe were marginally higher in 1717, 1723; while Northern Europe was throughout this period the principal destination of English and Welsh exports.

26 Phyllis Deane and W. A. Cole, *British Economic Growth, 1688–1955* (London, 1962); Mitchell, *British Historical Statistics*, External Trade Table 15, p. 496. As with other data, values here are those entered in the ledger, and therefore unadjusted.

27 By the 1790s some 10,000 ships, the great majority British, passed through the Sound annually, travelling eastward mainly in ballast, and returning predominantly with timber: Sven-Erik Åström, *From Tar to Timber. Studies in Northeast European Forest Exploitation and Foreign Trade 1660–1860* (Helsinki, 1988), p. 111.

28 Michael North, 'The Export of Timber and Timber By-products from the Baltic Region to Western Europe, 1575–1775', in Michael North, *From the North Sea to the Baltic, Essays in Commercial, Monetary and Agrarian History, 1500–1800* (Aldershot, 1996), p. I.9.

29 See Åsa Eklund, Chris Evans and Göran Rydén, 'Baltic Iron and the Organisation of the British Iron Market in the Eighteenth Century', *Britain and the Baltic. Studies in Commercial, Political and Cultural Relations 1500–2000*, ed. P. Salmon and T. Barrow (Sunderland, 2003), pp. 131, 132, 134.

one area in which he is acknowledged to have been an innovator – logistics – remains the least studied.[30] While van Creveld's attention is purely on land-based warfare, an analogous argument can be extended to seaborne trade and warfare: just as the forward movement of Rommel's Afrika Corps was limited by the ever-increasing number of petrol-consuming lorries needed to ferry the fuel needed to keep the front moving forward,[31] without a constant flow of imported booms, masts, hawsers, nails, hemp, flax, pitch and tar the Royal Navy could not have remained at sea at all, let alone for the extended periods customary by the later eighteenth century. The same went for coastal and long-distance seaborne trades – the ships upon which it all depended required constant maintenance and regular refits, consuming large quantities of material whose source lay primarily in the Baltic.[32] Then there was the replacement of ships lost to storm and enemy action, quite apart from any addition to the naval and merchant fleet to keep pace with increases in the flows of international trade. For the Royal Navy, the Seven Years' War marked a turning point: for the next fifty years the North Atlantic was added to the Mediterranean and the Baltic as a space in which European hostilities were conducted, adding considerably to the numbers of ships needed, and the amount of maintenance that each ship required to remain seaworthy.

The Baltic was thus central to British trade, both as a source of the materials needed for merchant ships to ply their trade, and as a destination for voyages. But the contemporary English commercial literature focused primarily on the export trade, while discussion of imports primarily focused on the pernicious effects of 'French goods'. Where the significance of the Baltic trades was raised, this was usually where arguments were advanced relating to the advantages of the colonies as alternative sources, although Defoe, for instance, did recognise the higher freight costs involved.[33] This

30   Martin van Creveld, *Supplying War. Logistics from Wallenstein to Patten* (Cambridge, 1977), p. 2: 'Similarly, no one has yet made a detailed study of the arrangements that made it possible to feed an ambulant city with a population of 200,000 while simultaneously propelling it forward at a rate of fifteen miles a day.'

31   Van Creveld demonstrates that Rommel's eventual defeat in North Africa in 1942 was primarily due to his reliance on motor vehicles to move supplies and fuel forward; it was the combined effect of limited port capacity, fuel-dependency and very large distances that ensured his defeat. British and allied forces were supplied mainly by rail, and the further they retreated, the closer they got to their supply bases – the exact opposite of Rommel's problem. Creveld, *Supplying War*, pp. 198–200.

32   The reliance of the Royal Navy on materials imported from the Baltic is emphasised in Daniel A. Baugh, *British Naval Administration in the Age of Walpole* (Princeton, NJ, 1965), pp. 276, 280.

33   See Ryan Walter, *A Critical History of the Economy. On the Birth of the National and International Economies* (Abingdon, 2011), pp. 54–7. See also the discussion of Baltic trade in Ryan Walter, 'Slingsby Bethel's Analysis of State Interests', *History of European Ideas* 41 (2015), 498–9. In 1695 the expulsion of English factors from Sweden disrupted trade and emphasised

goes some way to explain why it is that Heckscher, a Swede writing about the literature of trade and commerce in the seventeenth and eighteenth century, could end up writing only about France and Britain – and not drawing any connection with the very extensive contemporary Swedish, German, Dutch or Italian literature. Heckscher's problem was that his treatment of early modern commercial discourse failed to consider why it was that the geographical extent of the material he examined was so circumscribed. German contemporary literature dealing with economic administration and regulation was perhaps the most extensive of all, and yet, as noted above, Heckscher refers to a very limited number of sources in a vast literature.[34] Among the 1,000 pages or more of Humpert's 1937 *Bibliographie*[35] there are almost forty pages devoted to forestry, almost one hundred and forty to *Technologie*, and one hundred and forty to trade and commercial sciences – but none of these texts appear to address an obvious point: that the principal source of the staples traded internationally through the Baltic was domain and estate forest, managed for the most part by the stewards and officers at whom the new cameralistic sciences of the eighteenth century were directed, and hence involving a direct linkage between the practice of estate management and the conduct of international trade. By assuming that the published writings on commerce and regulation that he used were more or less direct mediations of actual economic activity, in *Mercantilism* Heckscher produced an account of the early modern economy that got things back to front: he ignored all evidence of Sweden's active connection with an international economy, and wrote instead about the impediments to the development of an international economy recorded in English and French writing.

This chapter cannot resolve this puzzle – the existence of the Baltic as a trading area of international significance – but where the source of staples lay in economies which were apparently remote from the international economy, and where the interface between local economic administration and the international economy attracted so little contemporary attention, nor has since then been subject to much discussion. The purpose here is more to review possible reasons for this apparent disconnection between the significance of existing flows of trade, and the lack of any substantial reflection of this in

England's dependence upon Sweden for naval stores; David Kirby, 'The Royal Navy's Quest for Pitch and Tar during the Reign of Queen Anne', *Scandinavian Economic History Review* 22 (1974), 98 cites discussion of this in Charles Davenant, *Discourses on the Publick Revenue*, vol. 2 (London, 1698), pp. 86–7, 189.

34   In his introductory chapter, 'The Argument', Heckscher contrasts *laissez-faire* and mercantilism through the counterposition of Smith's *Wealth of Nations* (1776) to Becher's *Politische Discurs* (1667) – *Mercantilism* I, 2nd edn, p. 25. For detail on Johann Joachim Becher's (1635–82) time in England in the last two years of his life, see Pamela H. Smith, *The Business of Alchemy. Science and Culture in the Holy Roman Empire* (Princeton, NJ, 1994), pp. 258–9.

35   Magdalene Humpert, *Bibliographie der Kameralwissenschaften* (Cologne, 1937).

contemporary literature addressed to the good management of the territorial economy. More broadly, this essay points to a substantial gap in our under-standing of the early modern economy: that we in fact know very little about the way in which production became integrated with consumption through market relations. This essay provides strong evidence for the existence of this integration by virtue of demonstrating the existence of major trade flows – but highlights how little we actually know about the organisation of early modern markets. Heckscher's apparent neglect in *Mercantilism* of the part his own country played in British trade is not therefore so much a personal oversight, but more an effect of the literature with which he worked.

Baltic products and their distribution

First some remarks about the staples that are our concern here. Leaving aside the importance of imported potash to the British woollen industry, but for which we have no accessible figures for consumption, the goods under particular examination here all relate primarily to the construction and maintenance of ships:[36] the various kinds of timber that went into them, the pitch and tar used to make them watertight, and the hemp used to make miles of ropework. Tar was produced from birch or pinewood in a dry distillation oven, and was used to waterproof hulls; pitch was produced by a similar process, differing from tar in its greater viscosity, and was used mainly for caulking. In each case, substantial volumes of timber were required as raw material, neither pine nor birch ever forming a significant part of British forest and woodland. The main source of masts and booms was likewise pine, while some structural oak in merchantman or warship had to be imported, for lack of adequate domestic supplies. It used to be thought that the expansion of the Royal Navy in the seventeenth century was predicated on the destruction of large tracts of domestic woodland, but it is now argued that any reduction in British woodland can be traced back to the early medieval period, if not indeed the Iron Age.[37]

The classic study of the importance of timber and timber products to British maritime power is Albion's *Forests and Sea Power*, which identified a growing crisis in the supply of raw materials for the construction and maintenance of ships in the later seventeenth century which, Albion argued, contributed

36 Although it should be said that the domestic building trades also relied heavily upon imported timber; the advantage of the focus upon the Navy is the existence of extensive records of naval contracting.
37 See Oliver Rackham, *Trees and Woodland in the British Landscape* (London, 2001), pp. 94ff.

to failures of naval strategy.[38] While it was true that the Commissioners for Trade and Plantations were established in 1696 for the express purpose of finding alternatives to Baltic sources of supply, their principal success lay in establishing a system that recorded imports and exports, not in finding significant alternative suppliers of naval stores. Even in the early eighteenth century the Navy was importing annually from 2,000 to 5,300 lasts[39] of Swedish pitch and tar, as compared with an average of 25 from the colonies. In the course of the eighteenth century imports of pitch and tar did fluctuate, but continued to hit ever higher peaks, as with the 18,698 lasts recorded as imported in 1768, almost entirely from the Baltic area.[40]

The figures gleaned from the records by Elizabeth Boody Schumpeter clearly indicate the volume and fluctuation of trade; since much of the data she assembled was by value and unweighted it is difficult to draw direct inferences about changes in the volume of trade, whereas Table XVI gives amount of imports by piece for items originating for the most part in the Baltic. Schumpeter's figures remain of value because of the way that Mitchell's more recent *British Historical Statistics* aggregates the timber items listed simply as 'timber', merging material imported for maritime use with that used in the building trades (Table 1). The supply of pitch and tar clearly fluctuated from year to year quite widely, as did in the earlier years the supply of all kinds of masts; but notable here is a general increase in the number of 'great masts' from around 1760, whose significance is discussed below.

The Great Northern War of 1700–21 did disrupt trade in the Baltic to the advantage of colonial trade, but the major long-term significance was a decline in Dutch influence, and a commensurate rise in a British commercial presence. The value of Navy Board contracts for pitch and tar during the period of the Great Northern War also bears witness to the slight significance of colonial trade even at this time (see Table 2). Later in the century Swedish figures show that England accounted for 28% by value of Swedish exports, as compared with 24% for the entire Baltic region.[41]

The story was similar with respect to masts, as can be seen from Schumpeter's statistical summary. 'Great masts' (anything larger than 18 inches in diameter) had at one time been sourced from New England, rather than the Baltic (and hence Albion's emphasis on colonial administration);

38 Robert Greenhalgh Albion, *Forests and Sea Power. The Timber Problem of the Royal Navy 1652–1862* (Cambridge, MA, 1926).
39 1 last of tar = 12 barrels, one large hoop tar barrel = 125 litres, so 2,000 lasts = 3 million litres. Åström, *From Tar to Timber*, p. 12. See Table 1 below.
40 Elizabeth Boody Schumpeter, *English Overseas Trade Statistics 1697–1808* (London, 1960). Most of the data recorded in this collection is by value, and as T. S. Ashton notes in his 'Introduction' (p. 4), the absence of a satisfactory system of weights meant that the series of values presented in the collection can be indicative only.
41 Rice, 'Patterns of Swedish Foreign Trade', Table III, p. 94.

Table 1. Imports of timber products by weight and quantity, England and Wales 1700–80

	Hemp Rough cwt.	Pitch & Tar Lasts	Masts			Oak Planks Loads	Timber Oak Loads
			Great	Middle	Small		
1700	81982	2705	995	982	1279		917
1701	138135	2906	113	335	945	1903	
1702	109215	879	154	323	450	1604	
1703	175413	3835	710	156	1209	3100	24
1704	267171	5127	537	653	842	1268	
1705							
1706	41456	3507	1015	711	1298	569	119
1707	149398	3403	1643	2004	2876	2707	55
1708	178536	3242	1222	1168	2026	3057	104
1709	167007	3088	1176	1264	2267	1296	384
1710	91346	3395	1847	1426	977	2269	722
1711	153660	3456	1021	984	707	1230	6
1712							
1713	80812	2703	2243	2181	3565	1102	4
1714	56307	3392	933	1865	5744	1438	
1715	197984	4269	747	1687	2888	938	
1716	157020	6601	512	835	1632	744	
1717	173355	7694	478	673	1862	2578	
1718	146243	7850	1021	1080	2754	1096	
1719	98638	6380	753	888	1871	1107	364
1720	137777	4848	1442	1490	3414	3536	308
1721	139809	3863	919	633	1272	2040	421
1722	72467	4971	652	916	1376	1286	113
1723	109586	6224	419	721	1929	1570	269
1724	144238	7466	644	1224	2256	3558	
1725	157830	9378	899	1054	2348	1703	20
1726	165622	8814	629	686	2043	1206	
1727	163340	3680	601	752	1694	1083	
1728	154241	2250	749	857	1726	2761	
1729	157822	3926	684	1132	2153	1251	
1730	181849	4399	904	896	2612	2245	924
1731	76704	4652	685	844	1723	1981	603
1732	140903	7083	1252	978	2014	4762	1144
1733	201786	7348	774	1024	1613	5735	954
1734	153325	9675	931	799	2129	2863	693
1735	147749	7127	714	587	1370	3915	1793
1736	150179	11794	928	683	2127	3114	1801
1737	218858	5941	727	651	2221	2163	1111
1738	178062	5468	882	840	1877	3450	707
1739	237477	3972	506	844	1734	1695	539

	Hemp Rough cwt.	Pitch & Tar Lasts	Masts			Oak Planks Loads	Timber Oak Loads
			Great	Middle	Small		
1740	188902	4795	752	954	2619	2242	522
1741	228550	5796	1632	1665	2558	4323	437
1742	229633	7425	1777	1780	2898	7207	380
1743	111031	6194	2244	1086	1689	2142	279
1744	243957	6881	1355	821	1136	2213	372
1745	239119	5564	2014	999	1155	2607	143
1746	212678	5955	1807	1793	2885	2674	196
1747	241920	6719	1641	1447	1540	1874	210
1748	313456	5857	1502	3369	4049	3297	3387
1749	169534	5512	1470	1865	1594	2269	336
1750	299177	7748	1861	1926	2176	5077	558
1751	136656	9472	1838	1786	2426	4125	525
1752	297017	9797	1548	1577	2281	4644	1313
1753	211937	9591	1299	1839	2348	4485	303
1754	240199	4901	1434	1909	2117	4886	1282
1755	416307	6988	2290	1580	3059	3679	2027
1756	455944	7751	2648	2745	4745	3518	244
1757	258871	5335	2137	2289	2924	5694	323
1758	207345	6602	1698	2688	2794	4522	174
1759	544287	6066	2256	2685	3986	5707	234
1760	68029	5361	1913	2011	2708	3463	298
1761	285611	7947	3339	1950	1844	4491	427
1762	272822	5499	2578	1711	3289	3605	4267
1763	275920	8280	2573	2293	3817	8327	283
1764	344623	10231	2814	1194	2092	6217	748
1765	336852	11551	2716	3085	5516	8395	1448
1766	206793	9786	2594	2246	5201	8095	1665
1767	152677	16236	1677	2068	3668		2455
1768	266197	18698	1484	3254	4015		2248
1769	241105	7280	2504	2431	3682		2450
1770	360692	7035	1652	2905	3945		7032
1771	501868	9177	4246	4046	7007		6160
1772							
1773							
1774							
1775	298376	13183	1459	3261	5102		4468
1776							
1777							
1778							
1779							
1780	376071	7328	4045	5488	5125	4332	698

Source: Elizabeth Boody Schumpeter, *English Overseas Trade Statistics 1697–1808* (London, 1960), Table XVI.

Table 2. Navy Board contracts for pitch and tar, 1700–21

Sweden	£61,257
Russia	£44,133
Carolina	£9,719
New England	£5,466
Norway	£1,550
East Country	£1,152
Virginia–Maryland	£675
Plantation	£56

Source: Joseph J. Malone, 'England and the Baltic Naval Stores Trade in the Seventeenth and Eighteenth Centuries', *The Mariner's Mirror* 58 (1972), 388.

but as warships grew in size during the course of the eighteenth century mainmasts could no longer feasibly be made from single sticks, and in fact the practice of constructing composites was well-established by the later seventeenth century.[42] The problems in the supply of finished masts to which Albion pointed were not in fact related to a lack of materials, as he supposed, but instead to a shortage of the skilled labour required to build composite masts. Knight notes that even during the Seven Years' War naval dockyards were using no more than a dozen very large sticks of over 32 inches in diameter.[43] Moreover, the predominance of imports great masts from Riga became even more marked following the onset of the American War of Independence. Åström, using Schumpeter's figures, draws attention to the rapid increase of imports of masts in the 1770s, reflecting the increased activity related to the War of Independence.[44] Knight's presentation of the fluctuations in imports of great masts, and their sources, clearly emphasises both these aspects (see Figure 1).

As for boards and planks, the diffusion of the Dutch fine-blade saw in the later seventeenth and early eighteenth centuries altered the supply of timber, making it possible to part-process timber before export. Åström

42 Roger Knight, 'New England Forests and British Seapower: Albion Revised', *The American Neptune* 46 (1986), 222–3.

43 Knight quotes the Commissioner of the Halifax Yard noting in 1788 that while very large sticks certainly existed, they were variable in quality and remote from the watercourses necessary for their transport; Knight, 'New England Forests', p. 223.

44 Åström, 'English Timber Imports', Diagram 1, p. 15. Table 1, p. 16 indicates that the prime source for 'great masts' at this time was Russia, presumably the port of Riga. See also his Table 2, Imports of Masts into England and Wales 1766–85, p. 19.

Figure 1. British imports of great masts, 1764–85

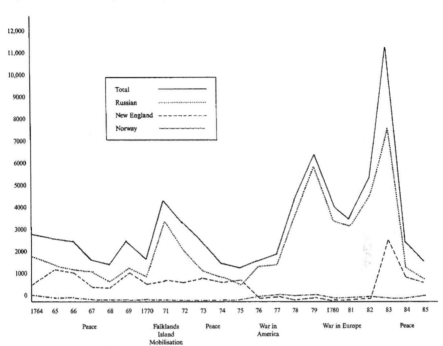

Source: Roger Knight, 'New England Forests and British Seapower: Albion Revised', *The American Neptune* XLVI, No. 4 (1986), 228.

employs a Thünen model to determine the transport zones for staples in the Ostrobothnia region of Finland, with shipbuilding and sawmills on the coast, a tar-burning zone further inland, and then deeper inland still slash-and-burn agriculture.[45] Ash was exported through Danzig and Königsberg, while pitch and tar production shifted by the eighteenth century to Sweden and Finland; tar produced around Vasa, Uleåborg and Gamlakarleby was known as 'Stockholm tar' since that was the port from which it was shipped, Karelian tar being shipped through Viborg.[46]

North suggests that the shift to Sweden and Finland for both timber and timber products was related to the over-exploitation of Polish and Prussian forests, related to the earlier practice of leasing domain land to merchant entrepreneurs for a fixed sum. In the southern Baltic region there was a shift

45   Åström, *From Tar to Timber*, pp. 56ff.
46   Michael North, *The Baltic. A History* (Cambridge, MA, 2015), p. 130.

back to the exploitation of forest land by the local administration at the same time as the principal sources moved north; although Åström also notes that by the 1790s Memel specialised in the export of fir timber, being the point of departure for 20% of the westbound ships passing through the Sound.[47]

The above can do no more than outline some features of the Baltic trades of the later seventeenth and eighteenth centuries. The secondary literature typically falls into two halves: on the one hand, the shifting sources of timber and timber products for the Baltic export trade are reviewed; on the other, there is a relatively new literature based upon Royal Navy contracts that record volumes of timber, pitch and tar, and hemp used in the construction and maintenance of a growing number of ships through to the end of the eighteenth century. Åström in particular carries the story up to the 1860s, when the shift away from timber and towards iron as a basic shipbuilding material became decisive.

One possibility regarding the secondary literature might therefore be related to the chronology of the writing of economic history. Just at that point in the later nineteenth century where scholars and students in the Baltic would have come increasingly under the influence of a nascent German economic history, the market for pitch, tar, spars and masts went into dramatic decline. Maritime demand for these products collapsed with the shift to iron for shipbuilding and, eventually, steel ropework for those sailing ships that continued to be built. Instead, new industrial products and markets came to predominate in a Baltic that was no longer dominated by Dutch or British merchantmen. This might again account for the relative neglect of Baltic trade in the earlier writings of Heckscher, whose own doctoral dissertation defended at Uppsala in 1907 was on the role of railways in Swedish industrial development.[48] A focus upon the industrialisation of the Baltic economies by younger scholars in the early twentieth century would therefore have detached forest-based industries from their older orientation to shipping and commerce, and realigned them with new industrial uses for timber products.

This then would be one explanation for the lack of any sustained examination in the secondary literature of the way in which during the entire early modern period the Baltic trades were central to the development of long-distance European trading and market relationships. Another development was the way that, from the 1960s onward, the agrarian history of the Southern Baltic (Mecklenburg, Pomerania, Prussia, the East Country, Russia) was analysed by Polish and East German historians in terms of the re-feudalisation

---

47   North, 'The Export of Timber', p. 9. See also the more detailed study by Enn Küng, 'The Timber Trade in Pärnu in the Second Half of the Seventeenth Century', *Ajalooline Ajakiri* (2011), nos 137/138, 243–63.
48   See Lars Magnusson, 'Introduction' to Heckscher, *Mercantilism*, new edition (London, 1995), p. xiv.

of the estate economy, shifting the focus inward to the organisation of labour, rather than outward to the market relationships with which this process was associated. Then, more recently, attention has shifted away from the internal organisation of the estate economy to its engagement in broader economic cycles, focusing on grain production and long-run price cycles.[49] As with the broader problem already identified with the disjoint treatment of production for an international market and the demand that sustained that market, a coherent account of the development of trading networks would have to link the conduct of the estate economy to the opportunities for selling the goods produced by these estates through these trading networks.

Taking account of the developing historiography of the region might therefore go some way to account for the apparent failure in the older secondary literature to see the Baltic as just one part of a world economy. But this perspective sheds no light on the apparent reticence of contemporary commercial or oeconomic writing with respect to the exploitation of timber and the connections that it forged.

Oeconomic writing

Instead, the focus of the established German and Swedish literature of the period was on internal administration, upon 'householding', as in the text published in 1747 by Anders Berch, 'Professor of Laws, and the Science of Householding and Commerce' at Uppsala.[50] Here the principal branches of the *Wirtschaftswesen* were listed as arable cultivation, mining, manufacture and trade.[51] The first main section of the book was not devoted to any of these topics, however, but to an exposition of *Policeywissenschaft*, the wide range of measures for the promotion of good order and sound morals. Not until one-third through the book do we come to the second part, and deal directly with agriculture, examining in turn arable cultivation, meadows, woods, plantations, cattle-raising, hunting, fisheries and finally insects and pests. Having also dealt with mining, craft production and trade, this last is described as the means through which the former three are united and set in motion – but, Berch goes on, it is best limited to the towns.[52] The third main section deals with *Cameralwissenschaft*, the science and practice of domainal

---

49 See Michael North, 'Die Entstehung der Gutswirtschaft im südlichen Ostseeraum', *Zeitschrift für Historische Forschung* 26 (1999), 50ff.
50 See the preceding chapter.
51 Anders Berch, *Einleitung zur allgemeinen Haushaltung*, ed. D. G. Schreber (Halle, 1763), p. 12.
52 Berch, *Einleitung*, pp. 179ff, 320.

administration, the levying of taxes, and keeping accounts of incomings and outgoings:

> For *oeconomia cameralis* is the sole mode of acquisition of which the ruler can make use; and some publicists have come to understand by this the entire *oeconomia publica*. If one wished to allow that the intention of general householding was only concerned with the enrichment of the ruler's treasury, that would be the end of the matter; but since general householding involves more than the collection of revenues; but has to do with the ways and means through which the inhabitant can be put in a position to be able to contribute to the revenue of the ruler, and assess the suitability of other means of rendering the inhabitants prosperous and rich, which was the objective of the entire second section; while other measures are to be taken if one wishes to levy payments upon them that do not weigh too heavily, or lay waste the the means of subsistence that are described in this section; by which the difference between the *Oeconomia publica* and *camerali*, the latter being a part of the former, as outlined in Ch. 3 §10.[53]

Cameralistic science was in this account then the study of the sources of the ruler's revenues, in part from the good management of domainal land, in part from the levying of taxes upon subjects in such a way that the activity was not diminished or distorted in any way.[54] There is of course an extensive literature on these matters reaching from the early years of the eighteenth century to the 1760s;[55] the consistency of the arguments and themes can be seen from the writings of von Rohr, who in 1716 outlined arguments about *oeconomia publica* and *Cameral-Wissenschaft* in strikingly similar terms to Berch some thirty years later – according to von Rohr, 'Land Oeconomica' includes arable cultivation, cattle raising, market gardening, vineyards, fisheries, hunting and forestry matters, the brewing of beer and so on.[56] The casual association of forestry with hunting here was also usual for the literature. The frontispiece of von Rohr's book (Figure 2) involves a conventional perspective of the rural economy, with fields, meadows, orchards and fisheries – far removed from the endless tracts of forest that surrounded the Baltic and upon which trade drew so heavily. So how might the management of these tracts be reflected in the contemporary literature on forestry?

A historical survey of forestry literature published by Widenmann in the nineteenth century clearly identified the linkage between forest management and state administration, arguing that the:

53   Berch, *Einleitung*, pp. 427–8.
54   See the discussion of Berch's book in Pierangelo Schiera, *Dall' Arte di Governo alle Scienze dello Stato. Il Cameralismo e l'Assolutismo Tedesco* (Milan, 1968), pp. 396–402.
55   See 'Cameralism as a "Science"', ch. 3 of my *Governing Economy*.
56   J. B. von Rohr, *Compendieuse Haußhaltungs-Bibliothek* (Leipzig, 1716), p. 84.

creation and extraction of the useful materials of woodland is treated by the science of forestry not merely as a part of human economic activity, but also as an object of concern of the state, for while it is a matter of great importance for the state to promote all kinds of economic activity, it is primarily securing the satisfaction of the general need for forest products that is of great importance. From the first standpoint the creation and extraction of useful woodland material is a particular economic branch – forest economy; while from the second standpoint it appears to be an object of state concern, and forms together with state economy, influence of the state upon the economic circumstances of its members, the state forest economy; or together with what can be called the commercial policy of the state, forest policy; or together with economic welfare, the welfare of the forest economy.[57]

Widenmann emphasised that while in many countries the forests were an important branch of activity, only in Germany had a science of forestry developed, owing to the fact that forestry was here the object of systematic teaching. While forest and woodland had been private property since the time of Tacitus, he notes the imposition of regulations in the fifteenth century by rulers seeking to control the exploitation of forests and foster good practice in the use of woodland on the part of a growing population. From the sixteenth century onwards collections of these regulations were published, but not until the eighteenth century did forest management become an explicit object of such writing. Among notable early writers Widenmann singles out von Hohberg as a writer on rural economy who presented a worthwhile summary of matters relating to the management of forest and woodland.[58] But the first specialised work is identified as Carl von Carlowitz's *Sylvicultura Oeconomica* of 1713, a work of over five hundred pages that included advice on the care of woodlands as well as the most suitable means for their exploitation. However, in the course of the eighteenth century the forest was increasingly viewed from the perspective of hunting, so that the descriptive literature itself progressively ran woodland management together with the customs and practices of hunting, while foresters charged with maintaining extensive tracts of forest were increasingly drawn from the ranks of those appointed in relation to the pursuit of hunting, rather than those more generally involved in estate administration.[59]

Widenmann notes approvingly the publication in 1757 of Wilhelm Gottfried Moser's *Grundsäze der Forst-Oeconomie*, but goes on to suggest that Moser was neither a forester, nor someone well-acquainted with natural

57   Kreisforstrath Wilhelm von Widenmann, *Geschichtliche Einleitung in die Forstwissenschaft* (Tübingen, 1837), pp. 1–2.
58   von Widenmann, *Geschichtliche Einleitung*, pp. 22–3, p. 39.
59   von Widenmann, *Geschichtliche Einleitung*, p. 43.

Figure 2. J. B. von Rohr, *Compendieuse Haußhaltungs-Bibliothek* (Leipzig, 1716)
Source: Niedersächsiche Staats- und Universitätsbibliothek, Göttingen.

Julii Bernhards von Röhr
Compendieuſe
Haußhaltungs-
Bibliotheck

Darinnen nicht allein
Die neueſten und beſten Autores,
Die ſo wohl

Von der Haußhaltung
überhaupt,
Als vom Ackerbau, Viehzucht, Jägerey,
Gärtnerey, Kochen, Bierbrauen, Weinbergen,
Wäldern, Bergwercken u. ſ. w. geſchrieben, recenſiret
und beurtheilet,
Sondern auch überall
Des Autoris eigene Meditationes,
Nebſt andern curieuſen Obſervationen aus den Anti-
quitæten, der Phyſic und Mathematic ein-
gemiſchet werden.

Leipzig, 1716.
Verlegts Johann Chriſtian Martini,
Buchhändler in der Nicolai-Straſſe.

history, but a cameralist, and so not capable of assessing the principles of forest economy that he assembled – a judgement that clearly draws a line between teaching and practice. However, at the same time there also appeared a work by Johann Gottlieb Beckmann, who was himself a forester and, according to Widenmann, the first to write in detail not only about the practical aspects of woodland management from his own experience, but who was the first to outline principles of rotation and sustainability on the basis of stands of woodland to be felled in successive years.[60] Following on from this, there was a marked increase during the second half of the eighteenth century in the composition of texts on forest management by practitioners, although Widenmann notes the empirical cast of these writings, and their lack of any foundation in 'natural laws' – they were 'unscientific' because empirical and unsystematic. Nonetheless, the need to teach the principles of forest management fostered systematisation, and according to Widenmann it was Gleditsch, appointed to teach forestry at the institute founded in 1770 at Tegel, who published the first 'scientific' account of forest economy;[61] and this was then followed by other texts on forestry linked to teaching institutions throughout Germany. Not until the 1820s did von Thünen begin to make calculations about the optimum rotation period, moving away from the practice of forestry to a new forestry economics.[62]

It was only in the second half of the eighteenth century that it became possible to relate the exploitation of forest products to existing commercial relationships, in part through the introduction of techniques that could convert a forested area into a quantity of (saleable) timber.[63] Indeed, reports of the over-exploitation of Prussian forests in the mid-eighteenth century add plausibility to the idea that systematic management of forest resources lagged a long way behind developing market opportunities, and also behind systematic consideration of the constraints upon commercial exploitation of products whose source lay in forests whose life-cycle took at least two human generations. In this context, the annual cycle of field and vineyard were much more manageable objects, although we might also note that here too

60   Johann Gottlieb Beckmann, *Versuche und Erfahrungen bei der Holzsaat nebst einigen Beiträgen zur Verbesserung der Forstwirthschaft*, 2 parts (Chemnitz, 1756, 1759).

61   Johann Gottlieb Gleditsch, *Systematische Einleitung in die neuere aus ihren eigenthümlichen physikalisch-ökonomischen Gründen hergeleitete Forstwissenschaft*, 2 vols (Berlin, 1774–75).

62   Johann Heinrich Thünen, *The Isolated State in Relation to Agriculture and Political Economy. Part III: Principles for the Determination of Rent, the Most Advantageous Rotation Period and the Value of Stands of Varying Age in Pinewoods* (Basingstoke, 2009).

63   Henry E. Lowood, 'The Calculating Forester: Quantification, Cameral Science, and the Emergence of Scientific Forestry Management in Germany', *The Quantifying Spirit in the Eighteenth Century*, ed. T. Frängsmyr, J. L. Heilbron and R. E. Rider (Berkeley, 1990), pp. 325f.

agronomical writing only began to displace *Hausväterliteratur* towards the very end of the eighteenth century.

Agrarian production and Baltic markets

It is notable that the indigenous development of a 'forest science' linked to the commercial exploitation of timber resources found little or no resonance in the contemporary literature of the *Cameralwissenschaften*. This is part of our answer to the conundrum of a possible 'Baltic Cameralism': the mainstream literature simply disregarded this aspect of estate management that had such significant commercial implications. A 'practical science' developed that required mathematical skill and botanical knowledge, but which was embodied in a specialist literature and taught in dedicated forestry schools. A *Wissenschaft* came into being, but was the preserve of vocational training, not university education. The same would be true of mining, or agronomy. The *Kameralwissenschaft* taught in North German universities conceived agricultural activity largely in terms of what might be encountered on the plains of Northern Germany and Central Europe. Stieda's survey of German universities does include mention of Kiel, Rostock, Greifswald, Uppsala and Åbo (Turku)[64] – but none of the contemporary literature addresses the maritime trading that was so typical of the Baltic, and of its extensive hinterlands that were linked to such commercial trade through rivers such as the Oder, the Vistula, the Daugava or the Niemen. Nor, for that matter, would one gather from cameralist writing that grain was the most significant export from the ports of the Southern Baltic; and so the failure of a substantial international trade in forest products to find any distinct resonance in cameralist writing is indicative not so much of the neglect of this particular market, but instead the absence from cameralistic writing of *any* direct consideration of the emerging markets for the products of field and forest.

This in turn points up a disjunction in eighteenth-century writing on economic activity – between farming activities and commercial activities. English, French, Italian, Dutch and German commercial literature was directed to merchants; despite the development within universities of new areas of interest – not only agrarian administration, but also population, currency and precious metals, geography, *Reisebeschreibungen* and *Statistik* – commerce did not here attract any great attention. As I have argued

---

64 Wilhelm Stieda, *Die Nationalökonomie als Universitätswissenschaft* (Leipzig, 1906), pp. 108, 107, 23, 65. Indeed, Stieda here estimates that of 32 German, Scandinavian, Dutch, Swiss and Austrian universities in 1755, only three – Åbo, Göttingen and Rinteln – had established chairs of *Ökonomie*.

elsewhere,[65] the European political economy of the early nineteenth century developed not from a literature of commerce and market relationships, but instead from a literature of agrarian order. Insofar as the Baltic region can be characterised as a significant and autonomous trading region with links to Atlantic economies – England, France, Holland, Spain and beyond – this extensive activity found little or no resonance in the political oeconomy of the eighteenth century.

65   See Tribe, *Economy of the Word*, pp. 46–7.

3

Cameralism in Russia:
Empress Catherine II and Population Policy

ROGER BARTLETT

If anyone should ask me whether the chief concern of a genuine and wise cameralist [...] could be expressed in a single word and concept, I would not hesitate for a moment to cry out the word POPULATION. Yes! Truly! POPULATION must be this chief focus of all the measures he takes.

J. H. G. von Justi[1]

Social and economic thought in eighteenth-century Russia

The eighteenth century for Russia was a period perhaps more than any other when the country and its best minds were open to the intellectual currents of contemporary Europe. Emperor Peter I, the Great (ruled 1696–1725), in Aleksandr Pushkin's famous phrase, 'cut a window through to Europe'.[2] Russia's subsequent emergence as a great power and her opening to European science and culture coincided with the Enlightenment and the extraordinary supranational fluidity of its ideas and thought. During the century that followed Peter's reign, European ideas found increasing access and were taken up by the educated elites. French thought and literature were prominent – Voltaire had a following already in the 1730s – but German ideas also circulated in increasing measure. Christian Wolff had been invited repeatedly

---

1 Johann Heinrich Gottlob von Justi, *Gesammlete Politische und Finanzschriften über wichtige Gegenstände der Staatskunst, der Kriegswissenschaften und des Cameral- und Finanzwesens*, 3 vols (Copenhagen/Leipzig, 1761–64), III, Zweyte Abtheilung no. VIII, 'Von der Bevölkerung als dem Haupt-Augenmerke weiser Finanz-Collegiorum', p. 379; cf. Albion W. Small, *The Cameralists: The Pioneers of German Social Polity* (Chicago/London, 1909, reprint 1969), p. 477.
2 On Peter I, see Lindsey Hughes, *Russia in the Age of Peter the Great* (New Haven, CT, 1998).

by Peter I and his successor Empress Catherine I to relocate to St Petersburg: he refused, but co-operated actively in the search for staff (mainly Germans) for the new Academy of Sciences. As in Germany, Wolff's became the dominant school philosophy in Russia during most of the eighteenth century, until supplanted by Kant; it was taught to succeeding generations of Russian students mainly through the textbooks of Wolff's populariser Friedrich-Christian Baumeister, repeatedly published in Russian translation.[3]

Cameralist ideas also became important. As Marc Raeff emphasised in his pioneering account of cameralism in Russia, Peter's reign 'was marked by the introduction of contemporary Western European norms in the political, cultural and institutional spheres – in short, a conscious taking over of the basic ideas of the well-ordered police state and of mercantilism and an effort to implement them in practice'.[4] By the time of Empress Catherine II, the Great (ruled 1762–96), the full range of ideas of the period of the Enlightenment was available to educated members of the government and elites. As knowledge of foreign languages and cultures spread among the post-Petrine literate classes, cameralist and other Western writings could be read in their original languages or in French; translations into Russian appeared later in the century.[5]

Catherine was unusual among monarchs of Imperial Russia in her avid interest in ideas.[6] She is often seen as a disciple of French thinkers and the *philosophes*, with her enthusiasm for Montesquieu, her correspondence with Voltaire, her patronage of Grimm and Diderot. Catherine was, however, eclectic in her philosophy of government: over time her interest ranged widely through authorities from many countries and cultures, whether the Italian Beccaria, the German Bielfeld, the French already noted, or the Englishman

3   Four titles in seven editions, 1760–89. See Tatiana V. Artem'eva (ed.), *Khristian Vol'f i russkoe vol'fianstvo*, *Filosofskii Vek* 3 (St Petersburg, 1998); Tatiana V. Artem'eva, 'Wolffianism as a Philosophical Foundation of Encyclopedism in Russia', *Christian Wolff und die europäische Aufklärung*, I (*Christian Wolff, Gesammelte Werke*, III Abtg, Bd. 101), ed. J. Stolzenberg and O.-P. Rudolph (Hildesheim, 2007), pp. 165–79; Wolfgang Drechsler, 'Christian Wolff (1679–1754): A Biographical Essay', *European Journal of Law and Economics* 4 (1997), 111–28.

4   Marc Raeff, *The Well-Ordered Police State. Social and Institutional Change through Law in the Germanies and Russia, 1600–1800* (New Haven, CT, 1983), p. 182. Raeff's ideal model of the 'well-ordered police state' has been brilliantly assailed by Andre Wakefield, *The Disordered Police State: German Cameralism as Science and Practice* (Chicago, 2009). However, Wakefield fails to appreciate positive aspects of cameralism and cameralist writers.

5   Some examples in Philip H. Clendenning, 'Eighteenth-Century Russian Translations of Western Economic Works', *Journal of European Economic History* 1 (1972), 745–53.

6   On Catherine II the writings of Isabel de Madariaga remain unsurpassed: *Russia in the Age of Catherine the Great* (London, 1981, latest edition 2002). See also O. A. Omel'chenko, '*Zakonnaia monarkhiia' Ekateriny II. Prosveshchennyi absoliutizm v Rossii* (Moscow, 1993); Claus Scharf, *Katharina II, Deutschland und die Deutschen* (Mainz, 1996); Simon Dixon, *Catherine the Great* (London, 2009).

Blackstone. The theoretical framework that most strongly influenced her practice, however, was that of the German cameralists and similar writers, whose ideas underlay the government of all the contemporary European absolutist monarchies.

Catherine II's first – and only public – systematic statement of political philosophy was her 'Great Instruction' (*Nakaz*), composed to guide the Commission for the Composition of the Project of a New Law Code, which she convened in 1767 to address the disorder in Russian legislation. It was an attempt to provide principles for the modern and enlightened ordering of Russian reality, textually based extensively on Montesquieu's *De l'Esprit des Lois* – Catherine made a public virtue of her plagiarism, while adapting her original.[7] But the Empress also drew on other recent European works, including Cesare Beccaria's *On Crimes and Punishments* (*Dei Delitti e delle Pene*, 1764) and German writers on 'police science'. The Prussian cameralist Jacob Friedrich Freiherr von Bielfeld had sent his new *Institutions Politiques* (1760) to the Empress personally. Catherine rewarded Bielfeld with the Imperial Order of St Anna, had his work translated into Russian, and based some thirty-eight clauses of the *Nakaz* upon it.[8] She also borrowed from Johann Heinrich Gottlob von Justi. His major work *The Foundations of the Power and Happiness of States, or Comprehensive Exposition of the Entire Science of Police* appeared in 1760–61, and was translated into Russian in 1772–78.[9] Catherine had also probably met Justi's work in Denis Fonvizin's 1766 translation of the principal texts of the contemporary European

7 A. N. Medushevskii, *Proekty agrarnykh reform v Rossii XVIII–nachalo XXI veka* (Moscow, 2005), p. 47, stresses continuities with the Imperial Law Commission of 1754–61. Catherine, Montesquieu and the *Nakaz*: Nadezhda Plavinskaia, 'Catherine II (1729–1796)', *Dictionnaire Montesquieu*, dir. Catherine Volpilhac-Auger, ENS Lyon, 2013, http://dictionnaire -montesquieu.ens-lyon.fr/fr/article/1377669577/en, accessed 10 Sept. 2015.

8 Jakob Friedrich von Bielfeld, *Institutions politiques*, 2 vols (La Haye, 1760), vol. 3 Leiden 1772; vols 1–2 translated as *Nastavleniia politicheskie Barona Bil'felda*, 2 vols (Moscow, 1768–75). Order of St Anna: M. M. Shpilevskii, 'Politika narodonaseleniia v tsarstvovanie Ekateriny II', *Zapiski Imperatorskogo Novorosiiskogo Universiteta* (Odessa) 6 (1871), p. 5 (1–178). Catherine's borrowings: N. D. Chechulin, ed., *Nakaz Imperatritsy Ekateriny II, dannyi Kommissii o sochinenii proekta novogo ulozheniia* (St Petersburg, 1907), pp. cxxix–cxlvii (Bielfeld: cxxxiv–cxxxviii).

9 J. H. G. von Justi, *Die Grundfeste zu der Macht und Glückseligkeit der Staaten; oder ausführliche Vorstellung der gesamten Policey-Wissenschaft*, 2 vols (Königsberg/Leipzig, 1760–61); Russian: *Osnovanie sily i blagosostoianiia gosudarstv, ili Podrobnoe nachertanie vsekh znanii kasaiushchikhsia do gosudarstvennogo blagochiniia*, 4 parts (Moscow, 1772–78). On Justi, besides the writings of Keith Tribe, see Ulrich Adam, *The Political Economy of J. H. G. Justi* (Bern 2006); J. G. Backhaus (ed.), *The Beginnings of Political Economy / Johann Heinrich Gottlob von Justi* (New York, 2009); a negative view: Wakefield, *The Disordered Police State*.

'trading nobility' controversy, which she discussed in the *Nakaz*.[10] She was evidently not perturbed by (or may not have known) the fact that Justi had incurred Russian wrath in 1759–60 by publicly criticising Russian and Austrian behaviour during the Seven Years' War, which he alleged 'disgraced the gender' of the Empresses Elizabeth Petrovna and Maria Theresa: so that when the Russians briefly occupied Berlin in 1760, Justi's offending work was among those publicly burnt by the hangman.[11] Twenty-four paragraphs of the *Nakaz*, on towns, police and finance, can be attributed to Justi's *Foundations*.[12]

Populationism in Europe and Russia

Catherine shared the cameralists' concern for population and population growth. The idea that these were essential to the well-being, power and 'happiness' of states was not only central to cameralist thought, but also reflected a conviction that went much wider, forming one of the prominent topics of eighteenth-century writing on economic matters. The extent of population of a state became the yard-stick by which its success and the morality of its government were measured in mainstream Enlightenment discourse. It featured prominently in contemporary European debates over forms of government, and in the argument between the 'ancients' and the 'moderns'.[13] The unreliability of available population data, whether for the contemporary or the classical world, enabled conclusions to be drawn in line with writers' ideological predilections; really reliable censuses came after this period. As Frederick Whelan noted, 'the population polemics of the eighteenth century thrived (unlike those of today) on a shortage of accurate data, but their ideological character arose even more fundamentally (just as today) from the meanings – hopeful or threatening – that were ascribed to (alleged) demographic facts as such'. Beliefs and theories about population

10   D. Fonvizin, *Torguiushchee dvorianstvo protivu polozhennoe dvorianstvu voennomu* (St Petersburg, 1766) contained texts of Justi, Coyer and D'Arc: Ulrich Adam, 'Justi and the Post-Montesquieu Debate on Commercial Nobility in 1756', *The Beginnings of Political Economy / Johann Heinrich Gottlob von Justi*, ed. J. Backhaus (New York, 2009), p. 76 (75–98); Chechulin, *Nakaz*, p. cxxxviii; *Nakaz*, §§272, 275, 331.

11   E. S. Reinert, 'Johann Heinrich Gottlob von Justi – the Life and Times of an Economist Adventurer', *The Beginnings of Political Economy / Johann Heinrich Gottlob von Justi*, ed. J. Backhaus (New York, 2009), p. 41 (33–74).

12   Chechulin, *Nakaz*, pp. cxxxviii–cxl.

13   Sylvana Tomaselli, 'Moral Philosophy and Population Questions in Eighteenth-Century Europe', *Population and Development Review* 14 (1988), Supplement: Population and Resources in Western Intellectual Traditions, pp. 7–29. Thanks to Simon Dixon for this and other references.

traced a remarkable trajectory during the later eighteenth century: the conviction that modern Europe's supposed depopulation proved its inferiority to antiquity gave way to the contrary view that modern populousness could either be deduced from, or demonstrated, the superiority of modern institutions, followed by a renewed but opposite form of pessimism in the face of apparently inevitable overpopulation.[14]

Montesquieu had devoted a whole book of *De l'Esprit des lois* (XXIII) to population. The cameralist writers shared Montesquieu's interest – he was revered as a classic thinker[15] – but they went further: in seeking to realise their goal of maximising the state's potential, its 'might and happiness', they considered that people were its first resource. These ideas were most fully worked out in the fifteen years after 1750.[16] Justi devoted the entire Second Book of his treatise on 'police science' to the increase of population: he identified good agriculture and large population as the two primary foundations of state power and prosperity, and saw them as inextricably linked:

> Cultivation of the land and population will increase [and decline] in direct relationship to each other [...] And they have a similarly direct and equal relationship to the happiness of the state. Without power and strength no state can be happy [...]; and without a large population no power or strength can be imagined. [...] population and cultivation of the land are both equally essential to the happiness of the state.[17]

Cameralist writers saw adequate population levels as crucial for all major areas of government activity – political affairs (manpower and military might);[18] 'police' (dense population facilitates internal control and good social organisation); commerce (consumption and circulation of goods) and finance (taxation and revenue). Non-cameralists, for instance Montesquieu and the later Physiocrat Mirabeau the elder (author of the phenomenally popular populationist work *L'Ami des Hommes* [1756–58]), echoed the concern of such seventeenth-century writers as J. J. Becher about the necessary balance between population and the resources that could sustain it; but they too coupled population increase with agriculture and commerce as a true basis

---

14   F. G. Whelan, 'Population and Ideology in the Enlightenment', *History of Political Thought* 12 (1991), 72 (35–72).

15   Bielfeld, *Institutions Politiques*, I, pp. 14–15, §9: Concerning the law of nations, Grotius, Pufendorf and Montesquieu are 'classiques dans cette Science'; for natural law, 'on ne connoit rien qui soit comparable au grand Ouvrage du célèbre Baron de Wolff'.

16   Justus Nipperdey, *Die Erfindung der Bevölkerungspolitik. Staat, politische Theorie und Population in der frühen Neuzeit* (Göttingen, 2012), pp. 397–400.

17   Justi, *Die Grundfeste*, I, pp. 173–4, §§207–8.

18   On the practicalities of state power and international relations, see Christopher Storr, ed., *The Fiscal–Military State in Europe in the Long Eighteenth Century. Essays in Honour of P. G. M. Dickson* (Farnham/Burlington, VA, 2009), esp. pp. 41–2 and ch. 4.

of national wealth. Apart therefore from the improvement of agriculture, which both fed and provided work for an expanding population, 'populationism' or *Peuplierungspolitik* led administrators into numerous other fields of government action. It implied renewed attention to matters of medicine and hygiene, a new concern with birth- and death-rates and means to record them. It required measures to diminish poverty, emigration, food shortage, infanticide, and to increase marriage, children, commerce and immigration.

These ideas went hand in hand with the policies of Central European states, above all Friedrich II's Prussia. The Prussian Johann Peter Süßmilch dedicated the second and later editions of his famous statistical work, *The Divine Order in the Alterations of the Human Race* (1741, 1761, 1765), to Friedrich because 'the whole government of Your Royal Highness serves as proof, that you consider sensible population of the state to be a principal concern of a ruler'.[19] The work of Joseph von Sonnenfels, *Principles of Police, Commerce and Financial Science* (Vienna, 1765–67),[20] a standard textbook for many years, was largely a systematisation of Austrian bureaucratic practice. Russian rulers' populationism was part of a general European concern.

In eighteenth-century Russia populationist ideas were increasingly current. They are not prominently cited in the legislation and policies of Peter the Great at the start of the century, despite his adoption of the model of the 'well-ordered' or 'regular' state (*reguliarnoe gosudarstvo*); but they were familiar to the geographer, historian and administrator Vasilii Tatishchev (1686–1750), a 'fledgling from Peter's nest', who placed 'increase of the people' first in a list of six sources of national wealth.[21] In 1754 the Imperial Senate considered a memorandum drafted by the aristocrat and military specialist Count Petr Shuvalov entitled 'Concerning various means to the benefit of the state', alternatively known as 'Concerning the preservation of the people', which stressed the primary importance of population.[22] When Mikhail Lomonosov (1711–65), outstanding man of letters, scientist and Academician (and former student of Christian Wolff at Marburg), composed a eulogy to Peter I in 1755, praising Peter's daughter the reigning Empress Elizabeth, he enumerated population growth among the blessings of her

19   Johann Peter Süßmilch, *Die göttliche Ordnung in den Veränderungen des menschlichen Geschlechts, aus der Geburt, dem Tode und der Fortpflanzung desselben*, 3rd edn (Berlin, 1765), II, p. 2a. Cp. Bielfeld's praise for Friedrich's administration: *Institutions Politiques*, I, iii.

20   Joseph von Sonnenfels, *Grundsätze der Polizei, Handlung und Finanzwissenschaft* (Vienna, 1765–67): the primacy of population increase is emphasised in §24. Russian translation: *Nachal'nye osnovaniia politsii ili blagochiniia* (Moscow, 1787).

21   In an early memorandum, 'Napomnenie na prislannoe rospisanie vysokikh i nizhnikh gosudarstvennykh i zemskikh pravitel'stv', quoted by P. A. Alefirenko, *Krest'ianskoe dvizhenie i krest'ianskii vopros v 30–50 gg. XVIII veka* ([Moscow], 1958), p. 336.

22   Sigurd Ottovich Shmidt, 'Proekt P. I. Shuvalova 1754 g. "O raznykh gosudarstvennoi pol'zy sposobakh"', *Istoricheskii arkhiv* 6 (1962), 100–18.

reign; and in 1761 he addressed a project-letter to his patron, the favourite Ivan Shuvalov (Petr's cousin) on the same subject, known as 'On the preservation and increase of the Russian people' – the first systematic Russian treatise on the subject. Lomonosov thought that this was the 'most important matter' for Russia's prosperity since 'in [it] consists the greatness, power and wealth of the whole state, and not in its great extent, useless without inhabitants'. Other Academicians and Moscow University staff subsequently also wrote and lectured on the subject.[23]

By 1762 and Catherine's accession such 'populationism' was well established in Russia, and not only in academic or scholarly circles. Catherine herself as Grand Duchess had already recorded her personal interest, in notes in a commonplace collection: 'Peace is necessary for this vast empire, we need people, not devastations: let's make our enormous deserts swarm with them, if possible,' she wrote. She likewise approved non-conversion to Christianity of polygamous ethnic groups in the Empire – 'plurality of wives is more useful for population [growth]' – and deplored high infant mortality – 'what a loss for the state'. Others of these notes, in more bellicose vein, articulated the fundamental aspiration of all cameralists and populationists, to maximise state wealth and power: territorial and commercial expansion of the realm, wrote the Grand Duchess, 'would raise this Empire to a degree of might above that of the other empires of Asia and Europe. And who could resist the limitless power of an absolute prince who rules over a warlike people?' This would redound to her personal prestige, she added – 'The glory of the country makes my own glory.'[24]

The Empress's concern over population was shared in Russian high society. Abandoned children must be preserved – the Foundling Homes proposed by Count Ivan Betskoi, in high favour with Catherine in the first years of her reign, attracted generous private donations, and some nobles and aristocrats even took in foundlings personally – 'Many have agreed of their own accord, while waiting for the Foundling Home to open, to feed some,' the Empress

23 'O sokhranenii i razmnozhenii rossiiskogo naroda', M. V. Lomonosov, *Polnoe sobranie sochinenii*, ed. S. I. Vavilov (Moscow/Leningrad, 1950–59), VI, pp. 382–403. Discussion: J. M. Letiche, trans. and ed., *A History of Russian Economic Thought: Ninth through Eighteenth Centuries* (Berkeley/Los Angeles, 1964, translation of a Soviet handbook), pp. 387–96; Roger P. Bartlett, *Human Capital. The Settlement of Foreigners in Russia 1762–1804* (Cambridge, 1979), pp. 27–9. See also Shpilevskii, 'Politika narodonaseleniia', pp. 42–9; Michael Schippan, *Die Aufklärung in Russland im 18. Jahrhundert* (Wiesbaden, 2012), pp. 304–6; I. I. Eliseeva, A. L. Timkovskii, S. F. Svin'in, E. A. Ivanova and L. G. Shumeiko (eds), *M. V. Lomonosov i sotrudnichestvo rossiiskikh i nemetskikh uchenykh. Sb. nauchnykh trudov rossiisko-nemetskogo nauchnogo seminara* (St Petersburg, 2012), pp. 99–133.

24 *Sbornik Imperatorskogo Russkogo Istoricheskogo Obshchestva* (St Petersburg, hereafter *SIRIO*), VII, pp. 85–6, 99–100, c.1761. In these notes Catherine also declared a love of Liberty, and opposition to the enslavement of man by man.

wrote to a correspondent in 1763. 'Stroganov has taken two and Countess Bruce one [...] They have all taken one or two, some more.'[25] Almost all commentators on Russian society and economy in the later eighteenth century held the same view, and equally considered the vast Russian empire underpopulated. Proponents of social reform – for instance Johann Georg Eisen[26] – were at one in this with social conservatives such as Mikhail Shcherbatov,[27] while the hostile French commentator Jean-Baptiste Chappe d'Auteroche claimed that Russian government policies were depopulating the Empire.[28] During Catherine's reign foreign-trained scholars and scientists working within Russia also pursued the theme – the historian August Ludwig Schlözer and the astronomer Wolfgang Ludwig Krafft, for example, were both involved in the development of population statistics. Medical professionals were well aware of the value of their work for preserving population: Dr Johann Kerstens, first professor of medicine at Moscow University, wrote *Medical instructions and rules for rural dwellers, serving to the increase of the inadequate number of people in Russia*.[29] The populationist case also prompted concern for peasant welfare: it was made succinctly in 1766 by Ivan Elagin, prominent courtier, secretary to the Empress and member of the Court Chancellery (*Dvortsovaia Kantseliariia*) in charge of Court lands in the empire, in a memorandum proposing agrarian reform, which he presented to Catherine:

> The growth of the number of inhabitants is the source of enrichment of the state: for the more subjects there are, the more land is made fertile, manufactures and factories flourish, revenues multiply, and plenty abounds everywhere. This proposition is irrefutably proven by the case of Holland, whose entire wealth derives from her large population: for neither her size nor the quality of her land is such as to enrich her. Therefore in all wise government, care is taken over nothing so much as over the increase of population.[30]

25   P. M. Maikov, *Ivan Ivanovich Betskoi. Opyt ego biografii* (St Petersburg, 1904), p. 143 and footnote, also quoted: Bartlett, *Human Capital*, p. 33.

26   Roger Bartlett, 'Russia's First Abolitionist: The Political Philosophy of J. G. Eisen', *Jahrbücher für Geschichte Osteuropas* 39 (1991), 161–76; *Johann Georg Eisen. Ausgewählte Schriften. Volksaufklärung und Leibeigenschaft im russischen Reich*, ed. R. Bartlett and E. Donnert (Marburg, 1998).

27   Such statements occur repeatedly in Shcherbatov's writings, e.g. 'Mnenie o poselennykh voiskakh', in: id., *Neizdannye sochineniia* (Moscow, 1935), pp. 64–5.

28   Chappe d'Auteroche, *Voyage en Sibérie, fait par ordre du roi en 1761 [...]*, 2 vols (Paris, 1768), I, pp. 238–43.

29   I. Kh. Kerstens, *Nastavleniia i pravila vrachebnye dlia derevenskikh zhitelei, sluzhashchiia k umnozheniiu nedovol'nogo chisla liudei v Rossii* (Moscow, 1769).

30   'Proekt D. S. S. i chlena Dvortsovoi Kantseliarii Ivana Elagina ob opredelenii v neot"emlemoe vladenie dvortsovym krest'ianam zemli i o razdache kazennykh dereven', za izvestnuiu platu,

The rhetoric of populationism found its way into apparently unrelated administrative texts. In 1775, for instance, after victory in Catherine's first Turkish war, the Russian government moved to tighten central control of the southern steppes. One measure was the suppression of the unruly Zaporozhian Cossack 'host' and destruction of their headquarters on the Dnieper. In preparatory official discussions the traditionally male Zaporozhian community was accused of 'wifelessness' (*bezzhenstvo*), which prevented population increase, and the Manifesto published to justify their suppression denounced the Zaporozhians among other things for attracting fugitive peasants and thereby depopulating the surrounding region.[31]

Once established on the throne, in June 1762, Catherine showed herself an enthusiast for populationist policies. 'No prince in modern times has ever made the subject of population so intimate a concern of government as the late empress,' observed the British chronicler of Catherine's reign, William Tooke.[32] Russia's vast extent meant that the country had a lower population density than its European neighbours, and Siberia was notoriously empty. Under the new Empress the Russian government for the first time made the well-being and increase of its population a primary concern. Chapter XII of Catherine's *Nakaz*, entitled 'Of Population'[33] (and much of it derived directly from Montesquieu), begins with the declarative assertion that:

> Russia not only has not Inhabitants enough but it contains immense Tracts of Land, neither peopled nor cultivated. And therefore it is impossible to devise sufficient means of Encouragement for increasing the Number of People in the State. [§265]

The chapter noted the beneficent effect on population of 'public Tranquillity

---

na vremennoe i opredelennoe vladenie vol'nym soderzhateliam', *Zhurnal zemlevladel'tsev* 6 (1859), no. 21, 1–32, no. 22, 135–84 (§4). Elagin further proposed giving peasants property rights in land, to improve agriculture and increase population. Another encomium to agriculture, Ivan Komov's *On Agriculture* (1788): Colum Leckey, *Patrons of Enlightenment. The Free Economic Society in Eighteenth-Century Russia* (Newark, DE/Lanham, MD, 2011), pp. 158–61.

31 *Polnoe Sobranie Zakonov Rossiiskoi Imperii* [Complete Collection of Laws of the Russian Empire, first series], 45 vols (St Petersburg, 1830, hereafter *PSZ*), no. 14354 (3 August 1775); N. Polonska-Vasylenko, 'Manifest 3 serpnia roku 1775 v svitli togochasnykh idei', *Zapiski istoriko-filol. viddilu Ukrains'koi Akad. Nauk* 12 (1927), 165–80.

32 William Tooke, *View of the Russian Empire during the Reign of Catherine the Second and to the Close of the Present Century*, 3 vols (London, 1799), II, p. 241.

33 Chechulin, *Nakaz*, pp. 77–85, §§264–92. Quotations here in the English 'Macartney–Dukes' translation, pub. Paul Dukes (ed.), *Russia under Catherine the Great*, 2 vols (Newtonville, MA, 1977), vol. 2, and in: Imperatritsa Ekaterina Vtoraia, *Nakaz, dannyi Komissii o sochinenii proekta novogo Ulozheniia*, ed. V. A. Tomsinov (Moscow, 2008), pp. 446–520 (English version: W. E. Butler and V. A. Tomsinov (eds), *The Nakaz of Catherine the Great: Collected Texts* [Clark, NJ, 2010]). In quoted passages capitalisation follows the original.

and Happiness' and ease of living, and by contrast the adverse effect of harsh laws and unjust land-tenure. It castigated modern Russian nobles' demand for money rents from their serfs, which drove the peasants from the plough to earn cash across the Empire, remaining absent sometimes as long as fifteen years: a law to curb such noble thoughtlessness would greatly favour both agriculture and population. It deplored high infant mortality among peasants; the ravages of syphilis; the popular misery caused (in any country) by the oppression of poverty, hard laws or excessive taxes. Where a country has suffered for a long time from 'some interior Evil and bad Policy', and is 'stripped of its Inhabitants', recovery of population is very difficult: the Empress recommended the Roman remedy of actively allocating land to any who would cultivate it. Roman laws and testamentary arrangements favouring marriage and numerous children were considered, though some 'were inconsistent with our orthodox Religion'. Conditions and age for marriage should be carefully defined, and parents encouraged to marry off their children. Premiums for large families might reward fertility, but were still more valuable 'to render their Lives as comfortable to them as possible' and 'to furnish the careful and industrious with Means to provide for themselves'. Temperance was recommended. The chapter ended with consideration of relations with foreigners. Some states naturalise foreigners, bastards or children of foreign men and native women, but only until their population is sufficient; Canadian 'Wild People' burn captives, but take them into their tribe if there are empty houses; conquerors sometimes intermarry with the conquered, 'whereby they attain two great Ends, the Securing to themselves of the conquered People, and an Increase of their own'.

This partial and eclectic set of thoughts and recommendations did not amount to a coherent population policy, but it did encourage consideration of a broad spectrum of different factors affecting population numbers. Later the Empress had further thoughts and penned 'Additions to the Great Instruction'. Here she was more specific: the 'main foundations' of the nation's economy are 'nothing but people'; consequently it is necessary (1) to encourage 'the increase of the people', (2) to 'use them to advantage', assisting 'the various arts and professions' according to their usefulness, and giving pride of place to agriculture.[34]

The *Nakaz* was an advisory statement of principle: actual policy and the legislation to implement it were supposed to be worked out by the Legislative Commission itself – its structure included specialist sub-commissions, of which the ninth had as its first sphere of competence 'the increase of the people'. In the event, the Commission was prorogued on the outbreak in 1768 of war with Turkey and never reconvened, so that no new Law Code

34   *Nakaz*, §§602–6.

was drafted (the problem of clarifying and codifying Imperial Russian law was only resolved in the 1830s). But Catherine learnt a great deal from the Commission's documents and deliberations; and the *Nakaz*, although not legally binding, retained great weight and authority in official circles.[35]

The populationist policies of Catherine II

Catherine brought with her to the throne a strong sense of duty to govern well, in the spirit of the Enlightenment, and she found the Russian government in great need of improvement. Her reign was marked therefore from the outset by wide-ranging change and reform. Even before the summoning of her Legislative Commission, Catherine had begun to implement measures within the sphere of population policy; and the intention to safeguard and support the population played a central role throughout her domestic policy. These concerns can also be seen in areas that cannot be fully explored here for lack of space – economic policies, questions of grain trade and luxury, education, local administration.

Perhaps the most wide-ranging of all Catherine's populationist measures were her attempts to improve medical services.[36] Here as in other areas of social provision, Peter the Great had introduced some improvements, primarily for military purposes, setting up military hospitals and surgery schools and a central Medical Chancellery; the new Academy of Sciences had some medical functions; and Peter's successors had taken some further steps. But there was no effective medical presence in the countryside except for native healers, and provision in towns apart from the capitals was slight. Almost all qualified doctors were foreigners. The new Empress interested herself immediately in medical matters, and was supported by an increasing sense of Enlightened duty and purpose among the medical profession. According to Andreas Renner, her policy in this field had greater coherence than that of her predecessors, and her personal engagement drove matters forward. 'As an annual average more laws regarding medical matters were passed in her reign than ever before.'[37]

Taking advice from senior officials conversant with medical affairs, Catherine replaced the Medical Chancellery in 1763 with a new Medical

35   Chechulin, *Nakaz*, pp. cxlvii–cliv, considers the *Nakaz* as a source of law.
36   The best modern accounts are John T. Alexander, *Bubonic Plague in Early Modern Russia: Public Health and Urban Disaster* (Baltimore/London, 1980, reprint Oxford, 2003), and Andreas Renner, *Russische Autokratie und europäische Medizin. Organisierte Wissenstransfer im 18. Jahrhundert* (Stuttgart, 2010): the following section is based upon them and Shpilevskii, 'Politika narodonaseleniia', unless otherwise indicated.
37   Renner, *Autokratie*, p. 127.

College, equivalent in status and function to existing government Colleges. Its remit was to promote public health and medical care for the Empire's population; to oversee apothecaries' shops; and to take responsibility for training native doctors – in 1764 it was given the power to award MD degrees, previously obtainable only by study abroad. Its responsibilities included assigning medical staff to posts in the provinces. It had 92 staff, but received insufficient funding and resources to match Catherine's ambitions: in Renner's words, its duty to supply medical provision across the Empire was 'more a public statement of will than a realistic programme'.[38] In 1764 Moscow University, founded in 1755, finally opened its chartered Medical Faculty; but it too lacked laboratory and clinical facilities, and until 1791 could not award medical degrees. In 1763 Catherine personally funded a hospital for the poor in Moscow; shortly thereafter Moscow and St Petersburg each acquired a city hospital; decrees of 1764 also provided for additional military hospitals in the provinces, and in subsequent years Catherine supported isolation hospitals for venereal disease and smallpox, and the development of rudimentary mental hospitals (*dollgauzy*, from German *Tollhaus*). Between them these bodies promised a base for further development; but the promise was poorly fulfilled, for lack of funding, efficient administration and personnel.

High rates of mortality were a concern widely shared among government and elite: the need for increased general medical and public health provision was canvassed at the Legislative Commission. Infant mortality was a particular scourge, especially condemned in cameralist writing as both an outright and a future loss of population. Part of the problem was the danger of child-birth. Already in 1757 the Medical Chancellery had taken first meagre steps to begin training for midwives. In 1763 Catherine approved the project of her childcare expert Ivan Betskoi for a lying-in hospital and foundling home in Moscow; a similar maternity hospital opened in St Petersburg in 1771. Midwives for the Moscow hospital had to be engaged from abroad – like doctors, trained midwives at this time were few and largely foreign – and the Foundling Home trustees proposed to Betskoi the creation of an Institute of Midwifery attached to the Home itself. This finally opened in 1784, attached to the St Petersburg rather than the Moscow Home, which only gained its own Institute in 1800. In 1789 a Midwives' Statute was promulgated regulating the profession.[39] From 1769 the Medical College had made some provision for obstetrics training, which became centred in the Imperial Surgical Institute. The Midwifery Institutes attached to the Foundling Homes became the main training bodies for women studying midwifery, and also gave education more widely on women's diseases. Qualification was by examination in the Medical College, and conferred a certificate of right to practise.

38   Renner, *Autokratie*, p. 62.
39   *PSZ*, nos 16804, 16805 (20 September 1789), based on German *Hebammenordnungen*.

Betskoi's Foundling House itself opened in Moscow in 1764, its St Petersburg equivalent in 1770, and foundling homes were established in many other cities across the Empire.[40] They catered for illegitimate births as well as orphans. Admissions policy was the most liberal of all European foundling homes. Children were accepted and mothers helped with no questions asked, to avoid stigmatising or frightening off young women who might otherwise commit infanticide or suicide. Apart from the direct populationist aim of saving the lives of infants (and mothers), Betskoi had educational aspirations, hoping that the foundlings could be reared as a 'new breed of people', model citizens for the Empire and subjects of the Empress. The laudable aims of these institutions were frustrated by practical difficulties, by their costs and especially by the huge mortality, which they too suffered and were never able satisfactorily to overcome.[41]

Apart from the Foundling Houses and development of midwifery provision, a variety of other measures was taken to ensure infants' and children's welfare, and also that of unwed mothers. In 1764 the Holy Synod enjoined priests (inclined to severity) to show compassion to single mothers, and dioceses to set up orphanages and follow the prescriptions of the Foundling Houses.[42] In 1766 Catherine ordered the printing and distribution to all government offices of an official 'Short instruction, taken from the best authors, with physical remarks concerning the upbringing of children from birth to youthful age'.[43] Its first clause denounced harm to pregnant women. It covered different age ranges, dealt with care of children, feeding and nursing, food and drink, inoculation, teaching, punishments, medicines, games, use of baths – a general hygiene of childhood. It was evidently intended not only for educational institutions, but for use in private families as well. The reign saw a significant rise in the publication of handbooks of popular advice, addressed to the public, on matters of health, medicine and disease.

One major threat to children's lives was smallpox, one of the most virulent diseases of the eighteenth century and especially dangerous to infants. When Catherine came to the throne, inoculation against smallpox had only begun to make its way into the Russian Empire: it was already practised in the Baltic provinces,[44] and was gradually taken up among medics during the 1760s. Elsewhere in Europe it was well-known, and highly controversial: objections

---

40   David Ransel, *Mothers of Misery. Child Abandonment in Imperial Russia* (Princeton, NJ, 1988; reprint 2014), p. 43.
41   Maikov, *Ivan Ivanovich Betskoi*, ch. 4–5; Ransel, *Mothers of Misery*, ch. 3.
42   *PSZ*, no. 12033 (January 1764).
43   *PSZ*, no. 12785 (16 November 1766).
44   *Johann Georg Eisen, Ausgewählte Schriften*, pp. 51–5; F. Amelung, 'Die Schutzpockenimpfung in Livland im 18. Jahrhundert', *Rigasche Stadtblätter*, no. 28, 15 July 1904, pp. 223–7, no. 29, 23 July, pp. 231–5, is imperfect but has useful data. Thanks to Marten Seppel for this reference and other help.

ranged from fear of infection to concern for divine law. Catherine's personal decision in 1768 to have herself and her son inoculated, by the English doctor Thomas Dimsdale, was a deliberate and self-conscious act of Enlightened rationality. At one stroke the Empress pre-empted any of the controversies raging in other countries, and made smallpox inoculation acceptable and fashionable among the elite.[45] The practice was introduced into the Foundling Homes, and isolation hospitals for smallpox sufferers set up in St Petersburg, Kazan', Irkutsk and elsewhere. In time smallpox inoculation became almost a routine event in Russia, although serf peasants inoculated at their lords' command habitually offered whatever resistance they could; but it remained a voluntary proceeding, and government plans for a travelling inoculation service were abandoned. The medical effectiveness of the procedure is still open to discussion. Inoculation for smallpox as developed in the eighteenth century was eventually overtaken by Jennerian vaccination, which led to its banning in Russia in 1804.

Besides smallpox, Catherine and her officials had to confront other epidemic diseases, notably syphilis and plague. Epidemics could raise questions not only of population loss, but of public order and economic disruption, and of medical control and official competence. Syphilis was associated both with prostitution, personal immorality and intimate matters unsuitable to public discussion: the 'French sickness' as it was commonly known was not named prominently in published literature, and Catherine herself denounced it namelessly in her *Nakaz* (§267), simply as 'a Disease unknown to our Ancestors [which] was brought from America to these Northern parts and diffused itself to the Destruction of the human Race'. Treatments, usually with mercury, were developed, but the new isolation hospitals were largely used in fruitless attempts to control prostitution. They had little effect upon the incidence of the disease. Plague was much rarer, but much more frightening and deadly: the notorious outbreak of 1771 in Moscow killed over 50,000, some one-fifth of the inhabitants, in that year alone, and sparked riots in which Archbishop Amvrosii was murdered. While the methods used for dealing with these epidemics gave only modest success, the actions of Catherine and her officials suggest, according to Renner, 'a systematization and institutionalization of an epidemic-political catalogue of measures and professional medical expertise', which was a marked advance on previous practice.[46]

---

45   W. J. Bishop, 'Thomas Dimsdale, MD, FRS and the Inoculation of Catherine the Great of Russia', *Annals of Medical History* 4 (1932), 321–38; P. H. Clendenning, 'Dr Thomas Dimsdale and Smallpox Inoculation in Russia', *Journal of the History of Medicine and Allied Sciences* 29 (1974), 399–421; Roger Bartlett, 'Russia in the 18th-Century European Adoption of Inoculation for Smallpox', *Russia and the World of the Eighteenth Century*, ed. R. Bartlett, A. G. Cross and K. Rasmussen (Columbus, OH, 1988), pp. 193–213, 681–4.
46   Renner, *Autokratie*, p. 140.

Efforts to improve medical care and public health continued throughout the reign. Catherine's 1775 Provincial Statute, which radically reformed the Empire's provincial administration, reflected her continuing wish to provide and enforce medical provision: it envisaged new levels of local medical staffing and offices of public welfare able to run local hospitals and supervise public health measures such as inoculation and quarantines. The 1775 statute expressed her wish as autocrat to extend 'medical police' out from the centre, to the benefit both of the state and the people themselves. At the same time it embodied her intention, emphasised by Marc Raeff,[47] to enlist and co-opt local forces to supply the deficit in central autocratic capacity, and her recognition of the desirability of devolving central power to localities more closely concerned with their own needs. However, the autocratic action lacked resources to make 'medical police' a reality on the ground; the local nobility often received unenthusiastically the invitation to invest its time, energy and money in what appeared to be alien state requirements.

The practical results of Catherine's efforts to extend and upgrade the medical and public health provision available to her subjects, in order to increase their number and make them more productive, fell far below her wishes and intentions. By the end of her reign many posts remained unfilled and institutions in abeyance, and traditional folk practices were largely unaffected by 'scientific' medicine. Renner sums up the Russian achievement of this period as an 'incomplete system of medical "police"',[48] and significant improvement was only achieved in the later nineteenth century. At the same time however the principle of state-provided public health provision for the population had been clearly asserted, the relatively tiny number of medically qualified practitioners had notably increased, native Russians were becoming involved in the higher ranks of the profession, and at the highest social and professional level Russia was integrated into European practice.

Another major populationist programme upon which Catherine embarked almost immediately on coming to the throne was the development of immigration. Within four months of her accession, the new Empress took up already existing government plans to encourage foreigners to immigrate and settle in Russia.[49] This was a ubiquitous practice among the principal European powers in the eighteenth century, who broadly disregarded theorists' warnings

47   Raeff, *Well-Ordered Police State*, p. 237.
48   Renner, *Autokratie*, p. 128.
49   G. G. Pisarevskii, *Iz istorii inostrannoi kolonizatsii v Rossii v XVIII veke* (Moscow, 1909); Bartlett, *Human Capital*; Detlef Brandes, *Von den Zaren adoptiert: die deutschen Kolonisten und die Balkansiedler in Neurussland und Bessarabien 1751–1914* (München, 1993); I. R. Pleve, *Nemetskie kolonii na Volge vo vtoroi polovine XVIII veka*, 2nd edn (Moscow, 2002; American translation 2001); H. Lehmann, H. Wellenreuther and R. Wilson (eds), *In Search of Peace and Prosperity. New German Settlements in Eighteenth-Century Europe and America* (University Park, PA, 2000).

of expense, economic disruption and difficulties of social integration. In
December 1762 a brief Imperial Russian Manifesto invited settlement in the
Empire by any foreigners except Jews. A second Manifesto of July 1763 laid
out a full set of conditions for immigrants, together with a register of available
lands; and a brand-new government office was created, the Chancellery of
Guardianship of Foreigners (*Kantseliariia opekunstva inostrannykh*), with
collegiate status and under the presidency of the favourite, Count Grigorii
Orlov, to guide the settlement programme and ensure the well-being of the
newcomers. This initiative, taken in competition with other European states
that also had populationist agendas, proved initially very successful. In fact
in 1766 immigration had to be suspended, partly to allay the hostility of
other states – in 1768 Joseph II as Holy Roman Emperor banned any further
emigration from Imperial territories – partly because the administration was
overwhelmed, and could not cope with the some 30,000 foreigners who had
arrived. Most of these were settled in compact 'colonies' around Saratov on
the middle Volga; a number formed colonist villages elsewhere in European
Russia. When recruitment resumed after the end of the first Turkish war
(1768–74), it was directed south, where Prince Grigorii Potemkin was engaged
in developing the northern Black Sea littoral and was eager to gain all the new
population he could – he even attempted to acquire British convicts whom the
British government wished to get rid of.[50] The colonists shared the common
fate of frontier settlers and often experienced great difficulties in establishing
themselves in undeveloped areas, with difficult climatic and soil conditions
and sometimes hostile neighbours; their settlement was controversial – they
were blamed for local Russian peasant land shortage and for driving away the
nomadic Kalmyk population of the Trans-Volga steppe. But by the end of the
century some 100,000 new persons had been added to the population, and in
the nineteenth century the foreign colonies prospered and grew.[51]

The same impulse lay behind simultaneous efforts to recover Russian
subjects who had fled their homes and, very frequently, the country. In the
eighteenth century lower-class flight was a constant problem[52] – in 1726 Peter

50   Bartlett, *Human Capital*, p. 128.
51   See for example David Moon, *The Plough that Broke the Steppes. Agriculture and Environment on Russia's Grasslands, 1700–1914* (Oxford, 2013). Raeff, *Well-Ordered Police State*, pp. 230–1, confuses the motivation of government policy, supposing that the authorities were seeking technically skilled foreign 'culture bearers' (*Kulturträger*) to improve agriculture and crafts. This view was occasionally voiced in contemporary discussions, and the Russian government was happy to welcome craftsmen bringing new skills. But the fundamental impulse, especially in the early stages, was essentially populationist: the authorities wished simply to maximise population, of whatever character and origin (Bartlett, *Human Capital*, pp. 34, 52–4).
52   V. I. Semevskii, *Krest'iane v tsarstvovanie Ekateriny II*, 2 vols (St Petersburg, 1901–03); N. V. Kozlova, *Pobegi krest'ian v Rossii v pervoi treti XVIII veka: iz istorii sotsial'no-ekonomicheskoi zhizni strany* (Moscow, 1983).

the Great's favourite Aleksandr Menshikov complained 'We are supplying not just Poland with our peasants, but our enemies as well,'[53] and the situation got no better over the century. The reasons for flight were various – oppression at home or the blandishments of new landlords, as well as hope for greener grass abroad or on remote peripheries. Lomonosov in his 1761 letter to Shuvalov blamed flight 'mostly on landlord oppressions and military conscriptions', and recommended lenient treatment. Besides serf peasants fleeing landlord exactions and conscripts running from military service, townsmen fled taxes, Old Believer religious dissidents fled religious persecution.

Under Catherine as early as July 1762 a decree was issued summoning fugitives of all categories to return home, promising immunity from punishment for flight and even for crimes committed.[54] This decree, which built on measures of the previous reign, had limited success. The December 1762 colonist manifesto included provision for Old Believers to return, and was shortly amplified by a special decree, concerted with the Holy Synod, offering the schismatics positive incentives, immunities and material benefits:[55] the desire to regain lost population led the authorities to promise a degree of religious toleration not just to non-Orthodox foreign colonists and immigrants (an established policy since before Peter I), but to Orthodox deviants who hitherto had been subject to persecution. This appeal and others later did result in a considerable number of *raskol'niki* (schismatics) returning to settle on the Irgiz river near the new foreign Volga colonies;[56] though the relations of the schismatics with the official church remained problematic. In May 1763 a further Manifesto extended the advantages offered to Old Believers to all Russian subjects who would come back from abroad, including landlords' serfs; all were to be offered free choice of settlement and several years' tax freedom; landlords would receive compensation for their peasants.[57] This had the perverse effect of encouraging greater flight by serfs who hoped to return and benefit from the same terms, and further decrees had to be issued clarifying and restricting the terms of the offer. Government policy throughout the reign continued in this manner, both trying to interdict flight and also offering incentives to fugitives to return. But since the causes of flight remained largely unaddressed, the problem persisted.

Another question was the recording of population numbers. New forms of partial census introduced by Peter the Great for tax purposes (so-called 'revisions' [*revizii*]) had improved population counts, but these were still

---

53 *XVIII Vek*, ed. P. Bartenev, III (1869), pp. 192–3.
54 *PSZ*, no. 11618 (19 July 1762).
55 *PSZ*, no. 11725 (14 December 1762).
56 N. S. Sokolov, *Raskol v Saratovskom krae. Opyt issledovaniia po neizdannym istochnikam* (Saratov, 1888).
57 *PSZ*, no. 11815 (13 May 1763).

rough and ready; and their results were not always present in the minds of those governing Russia. A much-quoted anecdote tells how on Catherine II's accession she asked members of the Governing Senate the size of the Empire's population, and they could give no answer. The astonished Empress exclaimed, 'A great empire cannot live without registration of its population! [...] How am I, a weak woman, supposed to govern the Empire, if even the Senate doesn't know how many loyal subjects I have?' She called for a census, and was told it would be vastly expensive, because it was so oppressive that troops were needed to keep the population in place.[58] In fact a new census (third 'revision') had been started in 1761 and was still in progress. Now it was suspended until new procedures were introduced,[59] including the avoidance of military intervention and additional penalties for bribe-taking by officials, and finally completed – less oppressively – in 1765.

The next 'revision', in 1781, essentially followed the Austrian methodology of Sonnenfels.[60] This revision differed radically from previous ones in coverage, precision and speed. It was detailed, including both sexes and all social categories except nobles and government officials; it used printed forms, and flexible procedures for submission. It also covered the whole Empire, including peripheral provinces where the poll tax (Peter I's target) did not apply; however, this reflected not only statistical efficiency, but also government desire to extend the poll tax, which was introduced in these areas shortly afterwards. This format was followed for the fifth 'revision' (1794), still incomplete at Catherine's death.

Another existing form of population count were church registers (*metricheskie knigi*). Peter I had introduced them in 1702 in place of previous church records, but they scarcely functioned.[61] The German scholar and Academician August Ludwig Schlözer, working in Russia 1761–67, was inspired by Catherine's early populationist measures to propose better methods of acquiring raw data for Russian 'political arithmetic'. His proposals were presented to the Empress by the director of the Academy of Sciences, resulting in 1764 in an official requirement[62] for all St Petersburg parishes (only the capital in the first instance) to send in to the Holy Synod monthly returns of births, marriages and deaths, so that monthly summaries could be compiled. Schlözer produced model statistical forms, printed in several languages, to be distributed to clergy. He recorded early results in his work

58 See e.g. http://org-wikipediya.ru/wiki/Переписи_населения_в_России, accessed 10 Sept. 2015.

59 *PSZ*, no. 11632 (5 August 1762); no. 11755 (13 February 1763).

60 *PSZ*, no. 15278 (16 November 1781); Sonnenfels, *Grundsätze*, I, 3rd edn (Vienna, 1777), pp. 68ff.

61 Gregory Freeze, 'Bringing Order to the Russian Family: Marriage and Divorce in Imperial Russia, 1760–1860', *Journal of Modern History* 62 (1990), p. 716 (709–746).

62 *PSZ*, no. 12061 (29 February 1764).

On the Harmlessness of Smallpox in Russia and on Russia's Population in General (1768),[63] in which he also made other recommendations, including a state office of statistics on Swedish lines. (He also joined in the debate then simmering in Russia about the effectiveness of steam-baths in combating smallpox: his book republished an essay on the subject by the Portuguese Dr Antonio Ribeiro Sanches.)[64] Schlözer's statistical work was followed by Court Counsellor B. F. Hermann and Academician Wolfgang Ludwig Krafft, who published their results in the Academy's proceedings: their findings were used by Robert Malthus in editions of his *Essay*.[65] Throughout the reign efforts were made to enforce reporting of the poll tax-paying population by provincial governors.[66]

Having kept infants alive, and developed ways of counting them, Catherine also sought to ensure that after puberty they would marry and produce offspring. Encouragement of marriage and avoidance of marital disharmony and divorce were important topics among cameralists and in contemporary German legislation; Russia under Catherine followed suit. Marriage licences (*venechnye pamiati*, certifying absence of impediment to marriage) bore a tax. In 1765 Catherine issued a personal decree abolishing this charge,[67] whereupon the Holy Synod abolished the licences themselves: any matter of impediment was to be sorted out by the officiating priest using a different reporting system ('search registers'). At about the same time a set rate was prescribed for rural priests' marriage fees.[68] Those wishing to marry also had to pay a 'marriage tax' (*kunichnye den'gi*) for permission to do so from the head of their community, urban or rural. Peasants had to pay their community or landowner 'export payments' (*vyvodnye den'gi*) if their daughters married out of the village. These charges were progressively abolished during the reign.[69] Some confusion existed over the rather obscure Church rules governing days when marriage could take place, and degrees of kinship within which marriage was permitted: the Synod was ordered to publish clarifications.[70] Divorce and remarriage was made easier for women involuntarily

---

63 A. L. Schlözer, *Von der Unschädlichkeit der Pocken in Russland und von Russlands Bevölkerung überhaupt* (Göttingen-Gotha, 1768).
64 Bartlett, 'Russia in the 18th-Century European Adoption'; A. G. Cross, 'The Russian *banya* in the Descriptions of Foreign Travellers and the Depictions of Foreign and Russian Artists', *Oxford Slavonic Papers* 24 (1991), 34–59.
65 *Nova Acta Academiae scientiarum imperialis petropolitanae* IV (1786), 59–88, 174–210; T. R. Malthus, *An Essay on the Principle of Population; or, a View of its Past and Present Effects on Human Happiness [...] A New Edition, Very Much Enlarged*, 2nd edn (London, 1803): book II, chapter III.
66 *PSZ*, no. 12061 (29 February 1764); no. 14733 (19 April 1777).
67 *PSZ*, no. 12433 (14 June 1765).
68 *PSZ*, no. 12378 (18 April 1765).
69 *PSZ*, no. 14275, §17 (17 March 1775); no. 15468 (14 July 1782).
70 *PSZ*, no. 12408 (6 June 1765).

separated from their husbands – the wives of soldiers (conscripted for life) and of exiles – and wives of soldiers killed in action were to be informed of their husband's death, so that they could find another spouse.[71] On the other hand, over-easy separation or divorce was otherwise generally discouraged.[72]

Under-age marriage, previously tolerated, was increasingly frowned upon: marriages contracted by boys under 15 were to be annulled, and similar provisions were set out for girls.[73] A related problem arose from the peasant custom of arranging marriages between spouses of different ages: grown girls were married to young boys, whose families thus acquired a free worker. Such women could not expect a happy marriage, and were easy prey to abuse within the family – a special term, *snokhachestvo*, defined heads of households' practice of sleeping with such incomers. Decrees banning such marriage, which was in any case against church law, explained that it 'causes fathers-in-law to fall into sin with their daughters-in-law, and the latter kill their under-age husbands'.[74]

The Free Economic Society and the issue of serfdom

The problem of *snokhachestvo* caught the attention of the Free Economic Society, which proposed as one of its prize essays the topic 'Concerning the harm caused to population by marrying young lads to elderly spinsters'.[75] The St Petersburg Free Economic Society for the Promotion of Agriculture and Household Management was founded in 1765, with Catherine II's active benevolence, by 'a handful of courtiers, civil servants and academicians'.[76] It reflected the growing preoccupation with rational agriculture in Europe, and was Russia's principal contribution to the wave of 'economic' societies that swept the continent in the eighteenth century. As with the Academy of Sciences, members of the Society shared the common interest in population matters. It was unusual in its status in Russia, a body of private individuals under the direct protection of the Empress (hence 'Free'), and in

---

71 *PSZ*, no. 12289 (8 December 1764); no. 12934 (9 July 1767).

72 *PSZ*, no. 12860 (31 March 1767); no. 12935 (10 July 1767).

73 *PSZ*, no. 14899 (31 July 1779); no. 14229 (17 December 1774) confirmed by no. 15295 (10 December 1781); Freeze, 'Bringing Order', pp. 730–1.

74 *PSZ*, no. 14229 (17 December 1774); no. 14356 (5 August 1775); Shpilevskii, 'Politika narodonaseleniia', p. 39.

75 A. I. Khodnev, *Istoriia Imperatorskogo Vol'nogo Ekonomicheskogo Obshchestva s 1765 do 1865 goda* (St Petersburg, 1865), p. 369.

76 Leckey, *Patrons*, p. 1. See also Roger Bartlett, 'The Free Economic Society: The Foundation Years and the Prize Essay Competition of 1766 on Peasant Property', *Russland zur Zeit Katharinas II. Absolutismus-Aufklärung-Pragmatismus*, ed. E. Hübner, J. Kusber and P. Nitsche (Köln/Weimar/Wien, 1998), pp. 181–214.

its encouragement of membership from Russian educated society at large. It sought to spread useful practical information on farming, estate management and other economic matters, principally through publication of a series of *Proceedings (Trudy)*. It encouraged innovation by awarding gold and silver medals and by setting prize essay competitions; and it joined in the existing practice of gathering data about the national economy of Russia by circulating questionnaires – a sixty-five-question survey was attached to the first volume of the *Proceedings* (1765).[77] Essay competitions were a major activity of contemporary economic societies and academies; Justi first came to prominence with a controversial prize-winning essay on monadology for the Berlin Academy of Sciences.[78] The most famous of the St Petersburg Society's essay competitions was that of 1766 on the topic, 'What is more useful for society: that the peasant should possess property in land or only movable property, and how far should his rights to the one or the other extend?' This question, which involved agriculture, property rights and peasant status, and invited comment on the sensitive issue of Russian serfdom, aroused huge international interest.[79]

By the time of Catherine's accession in 1762 most cameralist writers expressed themselves against serfdom[80] – Justi wrote that 'it is difficult for serfdom to be compatible with the well-being of the state'.[81] Control and ownership of peasant land was a closely connected but separate issue. The laziness and fecklessness widely attributed to peasants was commonly explained by lack of any personal interest or stake in property, which would make them responsible and productive in caring for their children and family. Elagin in his memorandum already cited made the connection directly: rural husbandry was crucial to the economy, peasants neglected their farming or were even abandoning it for other occupations, so it was essential to give them property of their own, especially land.[82] This could be done with or without the abolition of servile status.

In Catherine Russia had for the first time a ruler who was troubled by serfdom. Not only did the serfs' status pose problems of population increase, economic progress and good social order: in the Empress' view serfdom was also un-Christian and immoral, as her 1761 notes and other early comments show. But Catherine was fully conscious of the political sensitivity of the question. Serfdom was built into Russian social and economic relations, and

77 Leckey, *Patrons*, pp. 45–57.
78 Reinert, 'Johann Heinrich Gottlob von Justi (1717–1771)', p. 5.
79 Khodnev, *Istoriia*, pp. 20–34; Bartlett, 'The Free Economic Society', pp. 192–214; Leckey, *Patrons*, pp. 61–75.
80 See the chapter by Marten Seppel in this volume.
81 Justi, *Gesammlete Politische und Finanzschriften*, I, pp. 518–19.
82 'Proekt D. S. S. i chlena Dvortsovoi Kantseliarii Ivana Elagina', §§6–27.

underlay military and financial systems.[83] Most nobles were strongly in favour of it, and at the Legislative Commission merchant deputies also aspired to own serfs. Catherine therefore avoided any direct action against the institution, and in fact some early decrees shored up the existing order; she hoped instead to encourage the serf-owning elite to take the lead in introducing change. 'Often', she wrote, 'it is better to inspire reforms than to order their enactment.'[84]

The first years of her reign are remarkable for a series of events that created space in which the status of the peasantry might be discussed without the absolute ruler laying down a policy – commissions, institutions, competitions, correspondence, publications. These encouraged educated members of the elite to think and talk relatively freely about peasants and how they should best be treated. At the same time the Empress as autocrat and fount of patronage could lead by example. Now Russia saw a series of projects and attempts at reform, by men who thought along similar lines to Catherine or hoped for her favour. Catherine's populationist immigration programme also introduced plans both for colonies of free foreign settlers, and for agricultural improvement. J. G. Eisen, a strong opponent of serfdom, was given a free hand in Grigorii Orlov's estate of Ropsha in 1764–66 to introduce hereditary peasant leasehold tenancies (*Erbzins*); this experiment, aborted for unknown reasons, was paralleled by reforms carried out in the late Peter III's patrimony of Holstein by Catherine's appointee Caspar von Saldern, and measures by Baron Schoultz von Ascheraden and Livonian Governor-General George Browne in Riga. The same period, 1762–74, saw other peasant reform projects: proposals by the aristocratic diplomat Prince Dmitrii Golitsyn; the plan of Governor-General of Tver and Novgorod Count Johann Jakob Sievers; Elagin's project already quoted; the work of Catherine's own estate manager Fedot Udolov; the plan of civil servant and Academician Timofei von Klingstedt. The issue was discussed in Catherine's *Nakaz*, and in the Legislative Commission. The 1766 Economic Society competition on peasant property resonated across Europe, attracting 162 replies – the essays crowned by the judges were all in favour of land for peasants and gradual abolition.[85]

---

83   David Moon, 'Reassessing Russian Serfdom', *European History Quarterly* 26 (1996), 483–526; Roger Bartlett, 'Serfdom and State Power in Imperial Russia', *European History Quarterly* 33 (2003), 29–64; Elise Kimerling Wirtschafter, *Russia's Age of Serfdom (1649–1861)* (Oxford, 2008), pp. xi–xii, 92–100, 135–43, 157–8.
84   *SIRIO* VII, 101.
85   V. I. Semevskii, *Krest'ianskii vopros v Rossii v XVIII i pervoi polovine XIX veka*, 2 vols (St Petersburg, 1888, reprint 1971); Erich Donnert, *Politische Ideologie der Russischen Gesellschaft zu Beginn der Regierungszeit Katharinas II* (Berlin, 1976); Madariaga, *Russia in the Age of Catherine the Great*; Roger Bartlett, 'J. J. Sievers and the Russian Peasantry under Catherine II', *Jahrbücher für Geschichte Osteuropas* 32 (1984), 16–33; Antje Erdmann-Degenhardt, *Im Dienste Holsteins. Katharina die Große und Caspar von Saldern*, 2nd edn

However, the final outcome of these events convinced Catherine that her dreams of doing something about serfdom or even facilitating peasants' secure tenure of land were premature: the issue roused furious passions, and not twenty people at Court, she wrote, thought about it as she did.[86] The 1768–74 Turkish war intervened, then the bloody and terrifying popular uprising of 1773–74 under the Cossack Emel'ian Pugachev, a vivid warning of the possible consequences of government loss of control, put an end to the matter. And in fact Catherine could and did successfully pursue her principal goals as ruler without needing to abolish serfdom. In the later years of her reign the Empress took some further cautious steps to ameliorate serfs' conditions,[87] but it was not until the reign of her grandson Alexander I (ruled 1801–25) that any real movement on the issue took place.

The impact and significance of populationism

Catherine's policies in the fields discussed, and her other populationist measures, were aimed at increasing population not only as an end in itself but also to achieve other state goals: economic productivity, national security and expansion, the development of civic society and territorial order and tranquillity. They must also be seen in the context of changing social attitudes in Russia over the course of the eighteenth century. In keeping with cameralist theory, which formulated social policy from the point of view of state interest, Russian officialdom tended to instrumentalise the population, approaching the mass of subjects as elements of production rather than as individual persons. The nineteenth-century liberal M. M. Shpilevskii observed, 'People were valued not for themselves, as human beings capable of living, suffering and dying, but as taxation and military units.'[88] This attitude, particularly pronounced in the case of the peasantry, underpinned the servile regime on which the Russian social order rested: the peasant was like a prize animal, to be protected, kept fed, healthy and fertile and made to work hard, but for others' advantage, not his own. In 1721 Peter I officially denounced the

(Rendsburg, 1987); A. I. Komissarenko, *Russkii absoliutizm i dukhovenstvo v XVIII veke* (Moscow, 1990), pp. 135–42; Bartlett, 'The Free Economic Society'; *Johann Georg Eisen, Ausgewählte Schriften*, esp. pp. 24–37; Medushevskii, *Proekty Agrarnykh Reform*, ch. 1; G. V. Ibneeva, *Imperskaia politika Ekateriny II v zerkale ventsenosnykh puteshestvii* (Moscow, 2009), ch. 3; Schippan, *Die Aufklärung*, pp. 297–335 (re note 1028: Korob'in was in fact ill, not dismissed); Leckey, *Patrons*, pp. 60–82.

86   *Zapiski imperatritsy Ekateriny II* (St Petersburg, 1907), p. 175.

87   Isabel de Madariaga, 'Catherine II and the Serfs: A Reconsideration of Some Problems', *Slavonic and East European Review* 52 (1974), 34–62.

88   Shpilevskii, 'Politika narodonaseleniia', p. 9. This is, of course, also true of classical economics.

sale of Russian peasants 'like cattle, which is not done anywhere else in the world', and 'all the more when a serf-owner sells a daughter or a son apart from their family, which causes much distress'. The decree had little effect, and such sales continued throughout the eighteenth century. On the other hand, over the same period social attitudes progressively softened – the 'discovery of childhood', the paternalism of 'Enlightened Absolutism' and 'popular enlightenment', the sentimentalist 'discovery of the common people' (expressed in the literary works of such writers as Aleksandr Radishchev and Nikolai Karamzin at the end of the eighteenth century), all brought the peasant increasingly into focus as a human being. The image offered by cameralism of the ruler as *Landesvater* merged with this development.[89] Attempts through the Foundling Houses to produce a 'new breed of people' reflected the utopian optimism of some Enlightenment thought, but were also both a recognition of individual human potential and a government attempt at social engineering for state purposes.

Catherine's activist population policy put in place a considerable body of legislation and institutions which effectively laid the groundwork for nineteenth-century Russian social policies. How far her work contributed to the increase of population is difficult to gauge. During her reign the Imperial population grew rapidly – by some 30% between 1765 and 1796, even excluding the substantial populations of annexed territories.[90] This was however part of an accelerating long-term demographic trend, essentially reflecting natural increase. In most areas the Imperial government's populationist efforts tended to facilitate growth. Better medical care, however thinly spread, and curtailment of epidemics, however incomplete; steps to influence marriage and fertility – such measures tended in some degree to favour the

---

89   Ransel, *Mothers of Misery*, pp. 22–3; H. M. Scott, ed., *Enlightened Absolutism. Reform and Reformers in Later Eighteenth-Century Europe* (Basingstoke/London, 1990); Roger Bartlett, 'German Popular Enlightenment in the Russian Empire: Peter Ernst Wilde and Catherine II', *Slavonic and East European Review* 84 (2006), 256–78; Wolfgang Gesemann, *Die Entdeckung der unteren Volksschichten durch die russische Literatur* (Wiesbaden, 1972); Leckey, *Patrons*, pp. 164–70. In 1768 the Free Economic Society sponsored a competition for a 'Peasant Mirror' explaining 'how to bring up children, so as to have healthy peasants', and providing a short instruction on husbandry; no entry or winner was recorded. In 1796 the competition was reprised, for a 'people's book' agreeable and accessible to peasants, with the German R. Z. Becker's folksy and popular *Not- und Hilfsbüchlein für Bauerleute, oder lehrreiche Freuden- und Trauergeschichte des Dorfes Mildheim* [A Little Book of Help for Peasant Folk in Need, or the Instructive Story of Joy and Sorrow in the Village of Mildhome] (Gotha, 1787–98) as a model. The resulting *Village Mirror* (*Derevenskoe Zerkalo*, 1798–99) was a Russian recasting of Becker. Khodnev, *Istoriia*, pp. 369, 390–1, 458–63; Leckey, *Patrons*, pp. 166–70. On Becker, see Ursula Tölle, *Rudolph Zacharias Becker. Versuch der Volksaufklärung im 18. Jahrhundert in Deutschland* (Münster/New York, 1994).

90   From 18.1 to 23.8 million within the boundaries of 1646: Boris N. Mironov, *Sotsial'naia istoriia Rossii perioda Imperii (XVIII–nach. XX vv.)* [...], 2 vols (St Petersburg, 1999), I, p. 20.

rise in population. On the other hand, the colonisation programme had only marginal effect on population numbers, and the maintenance of serfdom was evidently also to some extent a brake on growth: while it did not greatly hinder migration, in areas with a high proportion of peasant serfs natural increase appears to have been lower than elsewhere.

The predominance of cameralist theory and policies declined in Russia as elsewhere in Europe at the end of Catherine's reign. The ideas of Adam Smith (already partly introduced into Russia from the 1760s through Glasgow and Göttingen) became widely known and influential at the beginning of the new century. The Russo-German economist Heinrich Friedrich Storch was one of Smith's early European interpreters, and the *Wealth of Nations* was published in Russian in an official four-volume translation in 1802–06.[91] Nineteenth-century Russian political and economic theory moved into different fields.

91　A. H. Brown, 'Adam Smith's First Russian Followers', *Essays on Adam Smith*, ed. A. S. Skinner and T. Wilson (Oxford, 1975), pp. 247–73; Roderick E. McGrew, 'Dilemmas of Development: Baron Heinrich Friedrich Storch (1766–1835) on the Growth of Imperial Russia', *Jahrbücher für Geschichte Osteuropas* 24 (1976), 31–71; Susan P. McCaffray, 'What Should Russia Be? Patriotism and Political Economy in the Thought of N. S. Mordvinov', *Slavic Review* 59 (2000), 572–96 (579–81); Tatiana V. Artem'eva, 'Adam Smit v Rossii', *Filosofskii Vek* 19 (2002), 39–67; Tatiana V. Artem'eva, 'Adam Smith in Russian Translations', *A Critical Bibliography of Adam Smith*, ed. K. Tribe (London, 2002), pp. 153–67.

4

Cameralist Population Policy and the Problem of Serfdom, 1680–1720

MARTEN SEPPEL

Cameralist historiography has provided us with an overview of the ideas advanced by the leading cameralist writers of the seventeenth and eighteenth centuries. However, cameralist ideas, proposals and solutions are not only to be found in contemporary published literature; they are also contained in the administrative documents of the same period. This latter perspective on cameralist reasoning, although much more closely related to governmental actions, has hitherto been largely neglected in the historiography. The omission can be traced back to the positions originally taken by Albion Small and Kurt Zielenziger, who were of the opinion that the officials of the *Kammer* could be counted as cameralists only if they expressed their thoughts in writings which distinguished them from other officeholders.[1] Small called cameralist theorists 'cameralists of the books', and stressed that his 'investigation does not go into the evidence about the cameralists of the bureaus', i.e. the everyday administrative employees of governments who, according to Small, were 'men of affairs rather than of theory'.[2] Zielenziger labelled the latter 'fiscalists, the pure practitioners'.[3]

It can be questioned whether approaching cameralism in such a restricted sense remains justified, especially when studying the impact of cameralism on governmental policy and practice.[4] Early modern governments conducted

---

1   Albion W. Small, *The Cameralists: The Pioneers of German Social Polity* (Chicago/London, 1909), p. 6; Kurt Zielenziger, *Die alten deutschen Kameralisten. Ein Beitrag zur Geschichte der Nationalökonomie und zum Problem des Merkantilismus* (Jena, 1914), pp. 86–7, 104; Andre Wakefield, 'Books, Bureaus, and the Historiography of Cameralism', *European Journal of Law and Economics* 19 (2005), 314–15 (311–320).
2   Small, *The Cameralists*, pp. xv, 6, 18, 152–3, 479.
3   Zielenziger, *Die alten*, p. 395.
4   I have partly borrowed this argument from Andre Wakefield, who discusses this artificial separation between 'cameralists of the book' and 'cameralists of the bureau': Wakefield, 'Books,

different kinds of projects, and constantly received proposals from below (often outside the administration) that reflected the understandings of the economic ideas of the time. If an officeholder was affected by 'cameralist' ideas then he could design 'cameralist' solutions for the government, which might be quite independent of the theoretical literature of the time.

Population was a central issue that preoccupied early modern governments, and cameralism here had a strong influence on state policy and action.[5] From the second half of the seventeenth century cameralists devoted a great deal of attention to what was termed *Peuplierung* in German (borrowing from the French), and which we can translate as 'peopling'.[6] Cameralist *Peuplierungspolitik* presupposed that larger populations produced greater wealth (*'ubi populus, ibi obulus'*).[7] This idea was not, of course, original to cameralist teaching; we can find it in the Proverbs of Solomon, 'A large population is a king's glory, but without subjects a prince is ruined' (Proverbs 14:28).[8] Since the Middle Ages efforts had been directed to attracting new settlers and seeking to populate the land. After the Peace of Westphalia of 1648 tax exemptions and other privileges were seen as the main method for *Peuplierung*, or recruiting new settlers to German territories.[9] Early modern peopling policy was in fact not related to the influence of any one particular author, but arose from a relative consensus regarding policy aims.[10] There was a near-universal belief in early modern Europe that population growth would contribute to agricultural production, industry, trade, state taxes, and military manpower.[11]

Bureaus'; Andre Wakefield, *The Disordered Police State: German Cameralism as Science and Practice* (Chicago/London, 2009), pp. 3–4.

5   See the previous chapter by Roger Bartlett.

6   Matthias Asche, 'Peuplierung', *Enzyklopädie der Neuzeit*, vol. 9, ed. Fr. Jaeger (Stuttgart/ Weimar, 2009), cols 1042–5; Friedrich-Wilhelm Henning, *Handbuch der Wirtschafts- und Sozialgeschichte Deutschlands. Bd. 1: Deutsche Wirtschafts- und Sozialgeschichte im Mittelalter und in der frühen Neuzeit* (Paderborn, 1991), pp. 765, 775; Friedrich Lütge, *Deutsche Sozial- und Wirtschaftsgeschichte. Ein Überblick* (Berlin/Göttingen/Heidelberg, 1952), pp. 246–8.

7   The quote originates from 'Einrichtungswerk des Königreichs Hungarn' of 1689: János Kalmár and János J. Varga (eds), *Einrichtungswerk des Königreichs Hungarn (1688–1690)* (Stuttgart, 2010), p. 130.

8   For the reception of this passage from the Bible in the seventeenth century literature, see Johannes Overbeek, 'Mercantilism, Physiocracy and Population Theory', *The South African Journal of Economics* 41 (1973), 170 (167–174).

9   Justus Nipperdey, *Die Erfindung der Bevölkerungspolitik. Staat, politische Theorie und Population in der Frühen Neuzeit* (Göttingen, 2012), p. 285.

10   Martin Fuhrmann, *Volksvermehrung als Staatsaufgabe? Bevölkerungs- und Ehepolitik in der deutschen politischen und ökonomischen Theorie des 18. und 19. Jahrhunderts* (Paderborn, 2002), p. 26; Nipperdey, *Die Erfindung*, p. 22.

11   Frederick G. Whelan, 'Population and Ideology in the Enlightenment', *History of Political Thought* 12 (1991), 38–9 (35–72); Overbeek, 'Mercantilism', pp. 167–74; Johannes Overbeek, *History of Population Theories* (Rotterdam, 1974), pp. 28–34; Ted McCormick, 'Population:

As has been noted by Gustavo Corni, examining *Peuplierungspolitik* opens up some of the most important characteristics and tendencies of state economic policy.[12] Population policy has possibly been the most thoroughly studied issue connected to the theory and practice of cameralism. Justus Nipperdey has recently published an exhaustive survey of the theoretical foundations of population policy in Central Europe where he highlights the mutual relationship between population theory and political practice in the Electorate of Bavaria from the sixteenth century to the end of eighteenth.[13] Márta Fata has studied the practice of government by Joseph II in later the eighteenth century and the cameralist ideas that influenced the policy of *impopulation*, seeking to explain the relationship between theory and practice in the eighteenth-century Habsburgian 'cameralist state'.[14]

The present chapter discusses peopling policy in connection with the issue of serfdom, a question that has hitherto received only passing attention. It considers the plans to abolish serfdom that emerged in a number of East-Elbian territories during the last quarter of the seventeenth century and the first decades of the eighteenth century. Current historical understanding presumes that both serfdom and slavery were generally accepted until the second half of the eighteenth century, and only then were attacked by religious, physiocratic, liberal and enlightenment ideas that led to the reforms for the abolition of serfdom and slavery.[15] In this chapter I will argue that in fact serfdom became an economic problem for early modern state governments as early as the 1680s, precisely in relation to cameralist ideas that were already taking root. At that time governments of territories where serfdom dominated began for the first time to see serfdom, or components of it, as a problem hindering the growth of income, and an especial obstacle to peopling policy. Although the first plans to abolish serfdom received little support, it is still important to note that an economic and rational critique of serfdom had already emerged in the seventeenth century.

Modes of Seventeenth-Century Demographic Thought', *Mercantilism Reimagined. Political Economy in Early Modern Britain and Its Empire*, ed. P. J. Stern and C. Wennerlind (Oxford, 2014), p. 25.

12   Gustavo Corni, 'Absolutistische Agrarpolitik und Agrargesellschaft in Preussen', *Zeitschrift für Historische Forschung* 13 (1986), 296 (285–313).

13   Nipperdey, *Die Erfindung*.

14   Márta Fata, *Migration im kameralistischen Staat Josephs II. Theorie und Praxis der Ansiedlungspolitik in Ungarn, Siebenbürgen, Galizien, und der Bukowina von 1768 bis 1790* (Münster, 2014).

15   Michael L. Bush, 'Introduction', *Serfdom and Slavery: Studies in Legal Bondage*, ed. M. L. Bush (London/New York, 1996), p. 1; Peter Kolchin, 'In Defense of Servitude: American Proslavery and Russian Proserfdom Arguments, 1760–1860', *American Historical Review* 85 (1980), 819 (809–827); Werner Conze, *Quellen zur Geschichte der deutschen Bauernbefreiung* (Göttingen/Berlin/Frankfurt, 1957); Alessandro Stanziani, *Bondage: Labor and Rights in Eurasia from the Sixteenth to the Early Twentieth Centuries* (New York/Oxford, 2014), p. 23.

Serfdom as a hindrance to the goals of peopling policy

The population of the state became an increasingly important topic in the seventeenth century, and it was widely assumed that the state's power depended on its population size. Promoting population growth remained one of the main themes of cameralist teaching from the seventeenth century until its decline towards the end of the eighteenth.[16] According to Nipperdey, in German territories from the last third of the seventeenth century to around 1740 an 'economic population theory' (*ökonomische Bevölkerungstheorie*) developed that was directly connected with cameralist discourse. The foundations for this were laid by Johann Joachim Becher in his *Politischer Discurs* (1668), arguing that the development of the economy and the size of population were dependent on 'sustenance' (*Nahrung*). Population policy was now seen as an integral part of economic policy.[17]

The growing attention to peopling policy in the second half of seventeenth century faced, however, two fundamental questions: first, the state's confessional position, and its preparedness for religious tolerance.[18] In the East-Elbian region, the issue of serfdom became the second hurdle to the implementation of a successful peopling policy. Serfdom thus became a cameralist issue to which governments looked for options to increase their finances and population. From the 1680s at least it was understood that the strict enforcement of serfdom could severely damage attempts to people the land, since it could reduce the interest of migrants in settling. And this quickly led to the first plans and decrees to abolish 'serfdom' (at least for new settlers). The long-term socio-economic implications of this rather improvised solution were not discussed at any great length.

The first time a clear exemption from serfdom was promised to new settlers, in relation to peopling policy, can be found in a project for the repopulation of Brandenburg that was presented by the brothers Pierre and Hugues Lamy to Elector Frederick William (1640–88) in 1647.[19] Although the project was never carried out, the promise of freedom from serfdom became, however, one of

---

16 Fuhrmann, *Volksvermehrung*, p. 23; Nipperdey, *Die Erfindung*, p. 13; Fata, *Migration*, pp. 22, 41–2. See also e.g.: Johann Heinrich Ludwig Bergius, ed., *Policey- und Cameral-Magazin* […], vol. 1 (Frankfurt am Mayn, 1767), p. 293 (article 'Bevölkerung').

17 Nipperdey, *Die Erfindung*, pp. 299–300, 311–12, 320.

18 Niggemann, *Die Erfindung*, pp. 164, 268, 295–6, 350–1, 362; Gerhard Oestreich, *Geist und Gestalt des frümodernen Staates* (Berlin, 1969), p. 287; Ulrich Niggemann, '"Peuplierung" als merkantilistisches Instrument: Privilegierung von Einwanderern und staatlich gelenkte Ansiedlungen', *Handbuch Staat und Migration in Deutschland seit dem 17. Jahrhundert*, ed. J. Oltmer (Oldenbourg, 2016), pp. 182–97.

19 Matthias Asche, *Neusiedler im verheerten Land. Kriegsfolgenbewältigung, Migrationssteuerung und Konfessionspolitik im Zeichen des Landeswiederaufbaus. Die Mark Brandenburg nach den Kriegen des 17. Jahrhunderts* (Münster, 2006), pp. 411, 426–7; Ulrich Niggemann,

the typical privileges in edicts aimed at new settlers in many parts of Germany in the second half of the seventeenth century (e.g. in Mannheim in 1652).[20]

In Brandenburg-Prussia Elector Frederick William initiated an active peopling policy to restore agriculture, industry and population loss after the wars.[21] This culminated with the opening of the borders to religious refugees in the shape of French Huguenots with the Edict of Potsdam of 1685.[22] All the same, the Edict of Potsdam did not directly refer to the question of serfdom, and did not clearly promise its abolition. This was, however, the substance of the next order of 13 March 1699 directed to religious refugees, which assured to all refugee resettlers that 'they, their children and their descendants will remain free from serfdom in perpetuity (*von der Leib-Eigenschafft gäntzlich befreyet sein und bleiben*)'.[23]

While the privileges of 1685 and 1699 applied only to new settlers, the police ordinance of 16 December 1702 (*Flecken-, Dorf- und Acker-Ordnung*) introduced also the possibility of liberation from serfdom for local royal domain tenants, both in East Prussia and in the Margraviate of Brandenburg. In its final article (§61) it stated that it was His Majesty's wish to abolish serfdom (*die Leibeigenschaft aufheben*) for domain peasants in return for 'fair compensation' in money. This was open to all peasants who expressed such a wish, repaid all their debts (including support received for building their farmhouses, sowing, hardware and other movables) and bought themselves out.[24] It has

Immigrationspolitik zwischen Konflikt und Konsens. Die Hugenottenansiedlung in Deutschland und England (1681–1697) (Köln/Weimar/Wien, 2008), p. 403.

20 Niggemann, '"Peuplierung"', p. 180.

21 Asche, *Neusiedler*; Karl Heinrich Kaufhold, 'Preußische Staatswirtschaft – Konzept und Realität – 1640–1806. Zum Gedenken an Wilhelm Treue', *Jahrbuch für Wirtschaftsgeschichte* (1994), 49 (33–70); Markus Zbroschzyk, 'Die preußische Peuplierungspolitik in den rheinischen Territorien Kleve, Geldern und Moers im Spannungsfeld von Theorie und räumlicher Umsetzung im 17.–18. Jahrhundert' (Inaugural-Dissertation, Bonn, 2014), pp. 270–80.

22 Justus Nipperdey, 'Die Hugenottenaufnahme als Katalysator der Idee des Populationismus', *Francia: Forschungen zur westeuropäischen Geschichte* 40 (2013), 113–38; Meta Kohnke, 'Das Edikt von Potsdam. Zu seiner Entstehung, Verbreitung und Überlieferung', *Jahrbuch für Geschichte des Feudalismus* 9 (1985), 241–75; Asche, *Neusiedler*, pp. 409–16; the edict of Potsdam of 29 Oct. 1685 is published in: *Des Corporis Constitutionum Marchicarum* (= CCM), II Th., 1. Abt., pp. 183–8.

23 CCM, VI Th., 1. Abt., p. 660 (*Patent wegen der Freyheiten derer aus der Schweitz kommenden Frantzösischen Refugiers*, art. 8); Bertha v. Moeller, 'Luben von Wulffens Reformen, 1700–1710', *Altpreußische Monatsschrift* 55 (1918), 30 (1–49).

24 CCM, part 5–3 (Berlin, 1740), cols 245–6; Friedrich-Wilhelm Henning, *Herrschaft und Bauernuntertänigkeit. Beiträge zur Geschichte der Herrschaftsverhältnisse in den ländlichen Bereichen Ostpreussens und des Fürstentums Paderborn vor 1800* (Würzburg, 1964), p. 131; Lieselott Enders, 'Emanzipation der Agrargesellschaft im 18. Jahrhundert – Trends und Gegentrends in der Mark Brandenburg', *Konflikt und Kontrolle in Gutsherrschaftsgesellschaften. Über Resistenz- und Herrschaftsverhalten in ländlichen Sozialgebilden der Frühen Neuzeit*, ed. J. Peters (Göttingen, 1995), p. 404.

been argued that the main aim of the 1702 ordinance was to carry out a successful policy of repopulation.[25]

In 1708 King Frederick I ordered an investigation into whether or not the abolition of serfdom (*Leibeigenschaft*) could limit or prevent the flight of domain peasants to the neighbouring Kingdom of Poland, something that was a permanent problem for Prussia. The King demanded a report on what he would gain or lose by such an abolition of serfdom. According to a project drafted in response, the Prussian peasant would have been allocated a plot of land and farm equipment (*Hofwehr*) for a fixed payment. The peasant was then to hold his farm in hereditary tenure, also gaining personal freedom.[26] An ordinance to this effect was promulgated by the King on 21 February 1709, but in reality it had as little real effect as the ordinance of 1702.[27]

A similar idea was pursued by King Frederick William I (1713–40). Dubbed a real 'Cameralist King', though probably not competent in theory,[28] he declared his wish that the royal domain peasants should no longer remain serfs. In June 1718 he personally revealed to the provincial *Kammer* a plan according to which the domain peasants of East Prussia would be freed from serfdom and allocated their *Hofwehr*.[29] He justified this step by arguing that it would improve the cultivation of the land and also the situation of domain peasants: they would gain a sense of ownership with all its advantages, as well as understand the benefits of freedom. Further, peasants would have to pledge faith to the King and promise both to pay the taxes required of them, and maintain the farms in good order.[30] When the Chamber President of eastern Pomerania submitted counter-arguments to this plan, Frederick William I resolutely marked on the letter, '*Sollen aufheben!*' ('must be abolished').[31]

25 Enders, 'Emanzipation', pp. 404–7; Lieselott Enders, 'Bauern und Feudalherrschaft der Uckermark im absolutistischen Staat', *Jahrbuch für Geschichte des Feudalismus* 13 (1989), 251 (247–283); Lieselott Enders, *Die Uckermark. Geschichte einer kurmärkischen Landschaft vom 12. bis zum 18. Jahrhundert* (Weimar, 1992), pp. 437–8.
26 Henning, *Herrschaft*, p. 132.
27 Georg Friedrich Knapp, *Die Bauern-Befreiung und der Ursprung der Landarbeiter in den älteren Theilen Preußens* (Leipzig, 1887), vol. 1, pp. 81–4, vol. 2, p. 4. Cf. also the edict on populating Prussia by Frederick I on 22 November 1709: Günther Franz, ed., *Quellen zur Geschichte des deutschen Bauernstandes in der Neuzeit* (Darmstadt, 1963), pp. 189–91.
28 Hans Haussherr, *Verwaltungseinheit und Ressorttrennung vom Ende des 17. bis zum Beginn des 19. Jahrhunderts* (Berlin, 1953), p. 25; Kaufhold, 'Preußische Staatswirtschaft', pp. 48–9, 53.
29 Rudolph Stadelmann, *Preussens Könige in ihrer Thätigkeit für die Landeskultur*, part 4 (Leipzig, 1887), p. 195 (appendix no. 1); Wolfgang Neugebauer, 'Die Leibeigenschaft in der Mark Brandenburg. Eine Enquete in der Kurmark des Jahres 1718', *Brandenburgische Landesgeschichte und Archivwissenschaft. Festschrift für Lieselott Enders zum 70. Geburtstag*, ed. Fr. Beck and K. Neitmann (Weimar, 1997), p. 232.
30 Stadelmann, *Preussens*, part 4, pp. 195–7 (appendix no. 2).
31 Knapp, *Die Bauern-Befreiung*, vol. 2, p. 17; Oskar Eggert, *Die Massnahmen der Preussischen Regierung zur Bauernbefreiung in Pommern* (Köln/Graz, 1965), p. 34.

Preparations in 1718 resulted in the edicts of Frederick William I for the abolition of serfdom (*Leibeigenschaft*, i.e. personal bondage) in the royal domain estates of eastern Pomerania and Cammin on 22 March 1719, in East Prussia on 10 July 1719, and in the Lithuanian *Amt* estates on 20 April 1720. These edicts on the abolition of serfdom remained on the statute book throughout the eighteenth century.[32] An open edict of 10 July 1719 directly proclaimed that the abolition of serfdom would benefit domain lands, 'since our peasants, who have until today been serfs in the aforementioned *Amts*, can henceforth be treated as nothing other than free peasants (*Frey-Bauern*)'.[33] The edict made every effort to protect the proper management of farms and Crown incomes; this was apparently the main aim of the ordinance, and was in spirit very cameralist. It was thought that those who freed themselves would be better able to manage their farms and work with greater enthusiasm for themselves and their kin. Under the prevailing conditions peasants were more inclined to leave the land, thereby also diminishing the income of the estates.[34] And so the move to abolish serfdom in 1719 has been also seen as the expression of a wish on the part of Frederick William to promote the immigration of colonisers.[35]

Brandenburg-Prussia was not the only state to deal with the issue of serfdom as a cameralist problem from the 1680s onwards. Sharing an absolutist conception of power and following early cameralist principles of governance,[36] in April 1681 the King of Sweden, Charles XI, submitted a proposal to the Diet of Livonia demanding the abolition of 'wretched slavery

---

32 August Skalweit, *Die ostpreussische Domänenverwaltung unter Friedrich Wilhelm I. und das Retablissement Litauens* (Leipzig, 1906), p. 206; Knapp, *Die Bauern-Befreiung*, vol. 2, pp. 18–19; Eggert, *Die Massnahmen*, 35; Jan Ziekow, *Über Freizügigkeit und Aufenthalt. Paradigmatische überlegungen zum grundrechtlichen Freiheitsschutz in historischer und verfassungsrechtlicher Perspektive* (Tübingen, 1997), pp. 132–3; see also Sean A. Eddie, *Freedom's Price: Serfdom, Subjection, and Reform in Prussia, 1648–1848* (Oxford, 2013), pp. 108–9.

33 *Corpus constitutionum Prutenicarum, oder königliche Preußische Reichs-Ordnungen, edicta und mandata*, part 3 (Königsberg, 1721), pp. 352–3; Arthur Kern, 'Beiträge zur Agrargeschichte Ostpreußens', *Forschungen zur Brandenburgischen und Preußischen Geschichte* 14 (1901), 173–5 (151–258); Robert Stein, *Die Umwandlung der Agrarverfassung Ostpreußens durch die Reform des 19. Jahrhunderts*, vol. 1 (Jena 1918), p. 75; Henning, *Herrschaft*, p. 133; Ziekow, *Über Freizügigkeit*, p. 132.

34 Eggert, *Die Massnahmen*, p. 35.

35 Max Beheim-Schwarzbach, *Hohenzollernsche Colonisationen. Ein Beitrag zu der Geschichte des preußischen Staates und der Colonisation des östlichen Deutschlands* (Leipzig, 1874), p. 160.

36 Stellan Dahlgren, 'Karl XI:s envälde – kameralistik absolutism?', *Makt och vardag: Hur man styrde, levde och tänkte under svensk stormaktstid*, ed. S. Dahlgren, A. Florén and Å. Karlsson (Stockholm, 1993; 3rd edn, 1998), pp. 115–32; Stellan Dahlgren, 'Ekonomisk politik och teori under Karl XI:s regering', *Karolinska förbundets årsbok* (1998), 47–104 (here in particular pp. 50–1); Ralph Tuchtenhagen, *Zentralstaat und Provinz im frühneuzeitlichen Nordosteuropa* (Wiesbaden, 2008), pp. 316–18.

and serfdom' ('*dhet älendige Slafwerys och Lifegenhets afskaffande*') on the Crown estates of Livonia.[37] The Baltic provinces of Livland and Estland, together with western Pomerania and Rügen, were then regions of the conglomerate state of Sweden where serfdom still existed in the seventeenth century. During the final decades of the seventeenth century Sweden tried to stimulate population growth. One of the first Swedish cameralists, Johann Claesson, had already emphasised the need to increase the size of the population.[38] At the same time, the options of the state to influence population processes were rather limited in that period.

The reasons presented for the abolition of serfdom by Charles XI in 1681 were primarily cameralist, even if saturated with Christian rhetoric. He called serfdom, dominant in Livonia and Pomerania, a 'relic from the pagan era', since the landowners had arbitrarily seized much greater power over the peasants than that which was in accordance with 'Christian love'. This subordination of the peasant to the arbitrary rule of the landlord had to be halted on the Crown estates, since it robbed people of the trust and will necessary to for the 'general welfare of the country' (*till ett allgemehnt landets wälstånd*). This hindered population growth, for nobody would be willing to settle in a region governed in such a way. If the freeing of Crown peasants from the arbitrary rule of the lords could be realised it would open the way for the country to develop towards greater well-being.[39] In 1682 the head of the *Reduktion* Commission for Livland, Robert Lichton, also emphasised (and clearly in agreement with the King) that freeing the peasants in Livland would make them available for work in manufacturing (*gemehna folket giöras capablare till manufacturer*).[40]

In western Pomerania, which had fallen under Swedish rule in 1648 with the Peace of Westphalia, the issue of recruiting new settlers to towns and countryside despoiled by the ravages of the long war was even more acute. On 10 April 1669 the King of Sweden issued an ordinance that exempted all immigrants from all contributions, services, billeting and all other war duties. It was forbidden to use the constraints of serfdom (*das Recht der Leibeigenschaft*) against the new settlers or their children and grandchildren; instead they were granted freedom to leave, and the right for their children

---

37   RA, Riksregistraturet, vol. 460 (Charles XI's proposition, 27 Apr. 1681). Published in German: Carl Schirren, ed., *Die Recesse der livländischen Landtage aus den Jahren 1681 bis 1711. Theils im Wortlaute, theils im Auszuge* (Dorpat, 1865), p. 19; see also Anthony F. Upton, *Charles XI and Swedish Absolutism* (Cambridge, 1998), pp. 193–4; Aleksander Loit, 'Die baltischen Länder im schwedischen Ostseereich', *Die schwedischen Ostseeprovinzen Estland und Livland im 16.–18. Jahrhundert*, ed. A. Loit and H. Piirimäe (Stockholm, 1993), pp. 63–85.
38   Dahlgren, 'Karl XI:s envälde', p. 123.
39   RA, Riksregistraturet, vol. 460 (Charles XI's proposition, 27 Apr. 1681).
40   RA, Kammarkollegiet Kansliet, vol. A I a:48, p. 689 (Minute, 24 May 1682).

to take up apprenticeships in arts or crafts.[41] The government of Pomerania returned to this issue in the early 1680s.

In January of 1681 the Estates of western Pomerania – prelacy, towns and nobility – sent a joint letter to the King's commission in which they expressed support for the plans to revitalise trade and agriculture in a province that was 'totally in ruins', but one 'on which the soul of the wealth and livelihood of the country is based, as well as for the introduction of manufactures, that bring general prosperity'. However, the idea of abolishing serfdom was not included in the Estates' letter.[42] Resulting from this King's commission, a public edict for the restitution of prosperity in the duchy of Pomerania and Rügen was published in Stettin on 7 March 1681. It focused upon the specification of rights and freedoms for new settlers in towns on the one hand, and on aspects related to settlement in the villages on the other. Every landlord (*Grundherr*) should endeavour to bring his domains to the best condition possible. All new settlers interested in the cultivation and acquisition of empty *Hufen* were offered ten years' exemption from state taxes, together with exemption from all local dues and duties for an average of three years. Finally, immunity from serfdom (*das Recht der Leibeigenschaft*) was included, defined in the same way as in the ordinance of 1669 with the addition that it applied in perpetuity, except in the case of marriage to a local serf.[43] Incentives of this kind designed to attract settlers to depopulated parts of the country in principle remained in place for the rest of the eighteenth century, even if the safeguards against serfdom applied only on Crown lands.[44]

New settlers in the Duchy of Pfalz-Zweibrücken, belonging to Sweden between 1697 and 1719, were also offered a similar incentive. Charles XII ratified a so-called freedom ordinance (*Freiheitspatent*) for Pfalz-Zweibrücken on 6 November 1698, which guaranteed tax exemption for 15 years, together with freedom from serfdom and corvée for all immigrants and new rural settlers in the duchy.[45]

41 Johann Carl Dähnert (ed.), *Sammlung gemeiner und besonderer Pommerscher und Rügischer Landes-Urkunden Gesetze, Privilegien, Verträge, Constitutionen und Ordnungen*, vol. 3 (Stralsund, 1769), pp. 433–5 (Königl. Verordnung, wegen der Freyheiten derer, die sich in den Pommerschen Landen zu wohnen begeben wollen, 10 Apr. 1669); Jan Peters, 'Schwedische Bauernpolitik in Vorpommern vor 300 Jahren', *Wissenschaftliche Zeitschrift der Ernst-Moritz-Arndt-Universität Greifswald* 9 (1959/60, Gesellschafts- und sprachwissenschaftliche Reihe), no. 2/3, 151–7.

42 RA, Pommeranica, vol. 315, fols 9v–10, 45v–46 (The Estates of Pomerania to the commission of Pomerania, 15 Jan. and 25 Jan. 1681).

43 RA, Pommeranica, vol. 330 (Placard of the Royal Commission, 7 March 1681); Dähnert, ed., *Sammlung*, vol. 3, pp. 436–8.

44 Thomas Heinrich Gadebusch, *Schwedischpommersche Staatskunde*, vol. 1 (Greifswald, 1786), p. 299.

45 Lothar K. Kinzinger, 'Schweden und Pfalz-Zweibrücken: Probleme einer gegenseitigen Integration. Das Fürstentum Pfalz-Zweibrücken unter schwedischer Fremdherrschaft (1681–1719)' (unpublished diss., Saarbrücken, 1988), pp. 476–8.

The decisive steps towards improving the conditions of the peasants in Denmark can also be treated in part within the framework of peopling policy. In 1681 the Exchequer of Denmark took the view that peasants willing to settle in the Zealand area and who had arrived from other provinces or abroad should be promised freedom in perpetuity from *vorned* obligations (restricting peasants to one manorial estate). However, real steps in this direction were taken only on Crown estates. In the 1690s new ordinances followed that promised new settlers freedom from all *vorned* obligations.[46]

In Hungary too there was a project based on cameralist principles to protect new settlers from local serfdom, the details of which were quite similar to the ordinances for the new settlers in German lands. A reform project was ordered by Emperor Leopold I in 1688 and 1689, reconstructing *politica*, *cameralia* and *militaria* in the areas of Hungary that had been recaptured from the Turks. The principal author of the project ('*Einrichtungswerk des Königreichs Hungarn*') was the bishop and ex-president of the Hungarian Court Chamber, Leopold Kollonich.[47] It included substantial land rights for foreign settlers, who were also to retain the status of 'free subject' in contrast to Hungarian serfs, who could not change their place of residence without their landlord's permission.[48] In addition, the new settlers had to be guaranteed a certain number of years' exemption from duties and corvée (three years for Hungarians and five years for Germans). This was a reform project in support of Habsburgs' peopling policy that was in fact finally never implemented.[49]

The cameralist economic arguments against serfdom

Serfdom as a problem emerged in relation to the growing inclination on the part of early modern governments to attract new settlers to their territories by offering more advantageous conditions. This was not however the only reason for cameral administrations in the East Elbian territories to initiate the

---

46 Thomas Munck, *The Peasantry and the Early Absolute Monarchy in Denmark 1660–1708* (Copenhagen, 1979), p. 196–7.

47 Kalmár and Varga (eds), *Einrichtungswerk*, pp. 9, 24–6. For the background and the theoretical impulses of Kollonich, see: Nipperdey, *Die Erfindung*, pp. 357–8; Fata, *Migration*, pp. 42–7.

48 ... *das dise Untertanen und Bauern nicht adscriptitii glebae, wie tails der Mainung seind, noch weniger Leibeigne, sondern freie Untertanen ... bleiben sollen*: Kalmár and Varga (eds), *Einrichtungswerk*, p. 131.

49 Kalmár and Varga (eds), *Einrichtungswerk*, pp. 72–3, 131–3; I. Wellmann, 'Merkantilistische Vorstellungen im 17. Jahrhundert und Ungarn', *Nouvelles études historiques, I. Publiées à l'occasion du XIIe Congrès International des Sciences Historiques par la Commission Nationale des Historiens Hongrois* (Budapest, 1965), p. 345.

discussion of plans for the abolition of serfdom during the last quarter of the seventeenth century.

Lieselott Enders has established that in the mid-1680s the abolition of serfdom was in fact 'a general conversation piece' in the Uckermark of Brandenburg. In 1685 the *Amtskammer* of Brandenburg directly raised the question of whether serfdom (*Leibeigenschaft*) was detrimental to the income of the Uckermark domain. In the same year they concluded that serfdom (including unlimited corvée) had many harmful consequences. Serfdom could be seen as a burden for both the estates and for the peasantry. Where serfdom prevailed settling new tenants was a very significant manorial burden; the *Kammer* had to construct new farms, supply them with all equipment, and even provide the necessary seed corn. On the other hand, the peasants suffered the burdens of servitude, and their lack of property made them apathetic. Peasants were careless in the management of farms since they did not own them, with consequent losses to the estate. Hence the peasants would feel better served by fixed corvée obligations, and if serfdom were abolished altogether many people who were fearful of it would come and settle in the Uckermark. The *Kammer* pointed out that experience suggested that following the abolition of serfdom peasants quickly took over vacant farmsteads and cultivated them at their own expense.[50]

The most familiar of these projects is that linked to the Prussian clerk Christian Friedrich Luben, who sought to transform the domain estates of Brandenburg-Prussia into hereditary leasehold tenures (*Erbpacht*), and thereby abolish serfdom; this has long been controversial in Prussian historiography.[51] On 1 May 1700 Luben, who had already worked for fourteen years at the *Amtskammer* of Brandenburg and had recently obtained the title of *Kammerrat* of Magdeburg, submitted a project for the management of the domain lands to Elector Frederick III (the future King Frederick I).[52] Luben's project was not without precedent, and was a response to the inquiry initiated in 1697 by Frederick regarding the way in which domain estates could increase

50   Enders, *Die Uckermark*, pp. 387–8; Enders, 'Bauern', pp. 250–1.
51   E.g. Leopold von Ranke, *Neun Bücher Preußischer Geschichte*, vol. 1 (Berlin, 1847), pp. 128–36; Knapp, *Die Bauern-Befreiung*, vol. 1, pp. 81–4, vol. 2, pp. 3–5, 9–12; Curt Flakowski, 'Beiträge zur Geschichte der Erbpacht unter König Friedrich I', Inaugural-Dissertation (Königsberg, 1910); Moeller, 'Luben'; Siegfried Isaacsohn, *Das Preußische Beamtenthum des siebenzehnten Jahrhunderts* (Berlin, 1878), pp. 294–5; Hartmut Harnisch, 'Der preußische Absolutismus und die Bauern. Sozialkonservative Gesellschaftspolitik und Vorleistung zur Modernisierung', *Jahrbuch für Wirtschaftsgeschichte* (1994), pp. 14–18 (11–32); Asche, *Neusiedler*, pp. 126–7.
52   [Friedrich Ludwig Joseph Fischbach], *Historische politisch-geographisch-statistisch- und militärische Beyträge, die Königlich-Preußische und benachbarte Staaten betreffend*, part 2, vol. 1 (Berlin, 1782), pp. 94–105 (Beylage P); Flakowski, 'Beiträge', pp. 6–9.

their income.[53] Luben's project expressed a very cameralist concern for the 'prosperity and welfare' (*Wohlstand und Wohlfahrt*) of the provinces of Brandenburg. Luben argued that it would be in the interest of state finances to break up the domain estates (*Ämter* and *Amtsvorwerke*) into plots of land with hereditary leasehold tenure; their distribution among reliable burghers and peasants would not entail any risks. Luben's *Erbpacht* project clearly implied peopling. As he explained, 'the glory, force and wealth of a powerful potentate' rests in the number of his subjects. The aim was to retain current peasants, and to recruit foreign settlers (e.g. from western Pomerania).[54] He promised large sums and quick profits from the division of domain estates, while guaranteeing the loyalty of a satisfied peasantry. Luben criticised the current system of leasing the domain estates for fixed terms, a practice that had left the peasants in a 'wretched and miserable' condition that was also a result of heavy dues and burdensome corvée work that made demands on their farmhands and horses. Luben wanted to replace the burdens of corvée with a monetary rent, and so assumed a significant extension of the money economy. The replacement of domain estates by new farmsteads would enable the land to be populated, encouraging the heirs of the peasantry to dedicate themselves to agriculture and the cultivation of an inherited farm. Furthermore, the state would quickly make money from the sale of existing estate buildings, livestock and farm inventory.[55]

The King and his privy councillors were not against Luben's plans in principle, but nevertheless remained cautious; the privy councillors considered the project too radical and suggested starting with a smaller territory. In 1701 an order was given to test the new approach to domain management in the *Ämter* of Altmark. Even if King Frederick I was inclined to support Luben's project, his hesitations are reflected in the summoning of at least four commissions to review the viability of the project. Their reports varied according to the specific membership of the commission, as Luben also had opponents. In 1704 Frederick I ordered the application of *Erbpacht* on all his lands.[56]

In Prussian eastern Pomerania the King supported Luben's reform of

---

53 Moeller, 'Luben', pp. 4–6.

54 Jan Peters, 'Die Pommern als neue schwedische Untertanen. Über Ökonomie und patriotische Phraseologie in der 2. Hälfte des 17. Jahrhunderts', *Economy and Culture in the Baltic 1650–1700. Papers of the VIIIth Visby Symposium held at Gotlands Fornsal Gotland's Historical Museum, Visby August 18th–22th, 1986*, ed. S.-O. Lindquist (Visby, 1989), p. 125.

55 See also Rudolf Stadelmann, *Preussens Könige in ihrer Thätigkeit für die Landescultur*, part 1 (Leipzig, 1878), pp. 76, 216; Moeller, 'Luben', pp. 12–15; Corni, 'Absolutistische Agrarpolitik', p. 288; Enders, 'Emanzipation', p. 406; Lieselott Enders, 'Die Landgemeinde in Brandenburg. Grundzüge ihrer Funktion und Wirkungsweise vom 13. bis zum 18. Jahrhundert', *Blätter für deutsche Landesgeschichte* (1993), pp. 234, 240; Enders, 'Bauern', p. 249; Enders, *Die Uckermark*, p. 434.

56 Flakowski, 'Beiträge', pp. 19–44, 49–97.

domain lands, deciding to abolish serfdom in Pomerania. This was announced in Stargard on 12 July 1706, giving instructions for the abolition of serfdom (*Leibeigenschaft*) for all royal subjects.[57] This was seen as an unavoidable move, for conditions in Pomerania at the time deterred wealthier people from resettling, since they and their children were not willing to become serfs.[58]

By the end of 1708 the transition to *Erbpacht* had almost stalled, and was in crisis throughout the provinces of Prussia. In November 1710 the King ordered a new commission to examine domain management. Overall, the results of Luben's project in the provinces of eastern Pomerania, East Prussia and Neumark were very poor, being only slightly better in Magdeburg, Halberstadt and Kurmark.[59] At the end of 1710 it was decided to return to the previous *Zeitpacht* system (short-term lease), seen as more profitable than Luben's *Erbpacht* system. Luben (who had meanwhile been ennobled as von Wulffen) was released from all duties and his property pledged against debts. The whole *Erbpacht* experiment was abandoned by 1711.[60]

After being discharged from the services of the King of Prussia, Luben von Wulffen presented himself to the Duke of Mecklenburg Karl Leopold, who in January 1715 appointed him to the post of *Kammer-Director* for Mecklenburg, charged with leading the *Kammer* administration, improving state finances and increasing the income from domain land.[61] Luben von Wulffen immediately suggested his failed *Erbpacht* project to Karl Leopold and the Duke who, being very short of money, quickly agreed to its implementation in Mecklenburg. All that the Duke saw in Luben's project was the chance of a larger and more immediate income from his domain.[62] On 19 February 1715 Karl Leopold made an announcement in Rostock offering

57 Knapp, *Die Bauern-Befreiung*, vol. 2, p. 16; Otto Hintze, *Regierung und Verwaltung. Gesammelte Abhandlungen zur Staats-, Rechts- und Sozialgeschichte Preussens*, ed. G. Oestreich, 2nd edn (Göttingen, 1967), p. 408.

58 Flakowski, 'Beiträge', pp. 62–4.

59 For the realisation of the project in the different provinces of Prussia, see Flakowski, 'Beiträge', pp. 49–97; Enders, *Die Uckermark*, pp. 436–7; Lieselott Enders, *Die Prignitz. Geschichte einer kurmärkischen Landschaft vom 12. bis zum 18. Jahrhundert* (Potsdam, 2000), pp. 905–7; Lieselott Enders, *Die Altmark. Geschichte einer kurmärkischen Landschaft in der Frühneuzeit (Ende des 15. bis Anfang des 19. Jahrhunderts)* (Berlin, 2008), pp. 89–90.

60 Ranke, *Neun Bücher*, pp. 128–36; Corni, 'Absolutistische Agrarpolitik', pp. 288–9; Moeller, 'Luben', pp. 22–7; Flakowski, 'Beiträge', p. 109.

61 Georg Christian Friedrich Lisch, 'Der Kammerpräsident Luben von Wulffen und die Erbverpachtung, ein Beitrag zur Geschichte des Herzogs Carl Leopold von Mecklenburg', *Jahrbücher des Vereins für Mecklenburgische Geschichte und Altertumskunde* 13 (1848), 205–9 (197–234); Peter Wick, 'Versuche zur Erbverpachtung und Aufhebung der Leibeigenschaft in Mecklenburg zu Beginn des 18. Jahrhunderts', *Jahrbuch für Wirtschaftsgeschichte* (1961), p. 56 (45–60).

62 Peter Wick, *Versuche zur Errichtung des Absolutismus in Mecklenburg in der ersten Hälfte des 18. Jahrhunderts. Ein Beitrag zur Geschichte des deutschen Territorialabsolutismus* (Berlin, 1964), p. 51. For the fiscal situation of Duke Karl Leopold, see: Johannes Nichtweiss, *Das Bauernlegen in Mecklenburg. Eine Untersuchung zur Geschichte der Bauernschaft und der*

part of the domain estates to all takers in hereditary tenure, 'especially to the peasants'. Those accepting tenure had to buy out all the buildings belonging to the land as well as inventory at established rates, and also sign a lease contract. All peasants who rented such lands were freed from serfdom (*aus der beschwerlichen Leibeigenschafft*) to become free people (*Frey-Leute*), a status that was heritable.[63] However, by 1718 the whole project had totally failed in Mecklenburg as well.[64]

Why was Luben so unsuccessful with his projects? In Prussia the loss of royal domain lands became one of the strongest criticisms of the Luben project.[65] Some domain lands were sold for less than their real value. The new *Erbpacht* contracts did not fulfil expectations of increased revenues, the expansion of agricultural production and population growth. Luben presented the advantages of his project only from the cameralist viewpoint of the Prince; he did not take into account profitability and sustainability from the perspective of the new tenants. Here apparently the economic weakness of the peasantry played a role; there were insufficient numbers of well-off peasants capable of becoming prosperous *Erbpacht* tenants.[66] There were much lower numbers of settlers than had been expected (especially in the poorer areas). The high rent levels also played a role; the fixed rent had to be paid in cash by *Erbpacht* tenants, not in kind.[67] Georg Christian Lisch lists insufficient preparation, excessively harsh contract conditions and high prices demanded for farmstead, buildings, inventory and personal freedom as the factors behind the failure of the Luben project in Mecklenburg.[68] Peter Wick, however, considers the main reason to be the open hostility of the nobility to the Duke; nor did it help that an ongoing war led to the billeting military personnel in the countryside, further depressing conditions for innovation because of general instability. Furthermore, the Duke of Mecklenburg was impatient to obtain as much money as he could as quickly as possible, making it impossible for a serf peasant to purchase their contracts. However, there is surprisingly little in the sources that might give us some insight into what the peasantry thought about the matter.[69]

zweiten Leibeigenschaft in Mecklenburg bis zum Beginn des 19. Jahrhunderts (Berlin, 1954), pp. 89–102.

63   Lisch, 'Der Kammerpräsident', pp. 233–4 (supplement no. 2); Wick, 'Versuche zur Erbverpachtung', pp. 57–8.

64   See also Friedrich Lütge, *Geschichte der deutschen Agrarverfassung vom frühen Mittelalter bis zum 19. Jahrhundert* (Stuttgart, 1963), pp. 208–9.

65   Enders, *Die Uckermark*, p. 450.

66   See also Asche, *Neusiedler*, p. 128.

67   [Fischbach], *Historische*, pp. 50–1.

68   Lisch, 'Der Kammerpräsident', pp. 214–16. Later Nichtweiss corroborated Lisch: Nichtweiss, *Das Bauernlegen*, p. 94.

69   Wick, 'Versuche zur Erbverpachtung', p. 59; Wick, *Versuche zur Errichtung*, p. 52.

Finally, in 1719 the government of the Duchy of Holstein-Plön also proposed that serfs might buy their freedom. This plan was met however with the same negative reactions: it was described as an 'ungodly attempt' pursuing no other goal than 'earning quick money'.[70] In the end this plan was not carried out, but it still clearly belongs to the list of cameralist plans aimed at increasing the income of the state and attracting new settlers.

Critics of serfdom in the cameralist literature

Thus at the end of the seventeenth century and the beginning of the eighteenth century princes and *Kammer* administrations were developing projects to tackle the question of serfdom in a cameralist framework. We should note, however, that the contemporary programmatic texts of cameralism do not include any proposition to abolish serfdom. Before the mid-eighteenth century agrarian issues and the situation of the peasantry were not prominent topics in cameralist literature, even if in the seventeenth century some cameralists (for example, Johann Joachim Becher and Wilhelm von Schröder) had noted the importance of agriculture.[71] In the first half of the eighteenth century agricultural issues received even more attention in the writings of Simon Peter Gasser, Justus Christoph Dithmar and Georg Heinrich Zincke,[72] but there was no discussion of the idea that the unfree status of the peasantry was an obstacle to economic advancement. Serfdom is not discussed in these writings in the context of agriculture. At best, critical remarks are made on the 'enslavement' of the peasantry, as is briefly done by Veit Ludwig von Seckendorff in both of his central works, where he considers the 'enslavement' of subjects contrary to the laws of nature, Christianity and the state.[73] From the 1740s, Johann Michael von Loën spoke more generally of the cameralistic advantages of extending freedoms. Loën considered freedom (*Freiheit*) 'the true happiness of a state', and desired that peasant be prosperous and free.[74] Concrete references to serfdom are however absent from his texts.

70 Wolfgang Prange, *Die Anfänge der großen Agrarreformen in Schleswig-Holstein bis um 1771* (Neumünster, 1971), p. 69.
71 Ingrid Mittenzwei, 'Die Agrarfrage und der Kameralismus', *Deutsche Agrargeschichte des Spätfeudalismus*, ed. H. Harnisch and G. Heitz (Berlin, 1986), p. 146; Erhard Dittrich, *Die deutschen und österreichischen Kameralisten* (Darmstadt, 1974), p. 65.
72 Keith Tribe, *Strategies of Economic Order. German Economic Discourse, 1750–1950* (Cambridge, 1995), p. 9; Ulrich Adam, *The Political Economy of J. H. G. Justi* (Bern, 2006), p. 215.
73 Veit Ludwig von Seckendorff, *Teutscher Fürsten-Stat, [...]* (Franckfurth a. M, 1656), p. 26; Veit Ludwig von Seckendorff, *Christen-Stat, [...]* (Leipzig, 1685), pp. 271–2.
74 Johann Michael von Loën, *Entwurf einer Staats-Kunst, worinn die natürlichste Mittel entdecket werden, ein Land mächtig, reich, und glücklich zu machen,* 2nd edn (Frankfurt/Leipzig, 1750, originally 1747), pp. 5, 228–32.

There are no cameralist writings demanding the abolition of serfdom before 1750. The earliest cameralist treatises I have found with this direct proposal date from the beginning of the 1750s. The *Kammerrat* of Mecklenburg, Johann Georg Wachenhusen, argued against serfdom in his unpublished manuscript directed to the Duke, '*Gedanken über die Abstellung der Leibeigenschaft*' in 1750. According to his calculations, serfdom caused a yearly loss of 50 million Reichsthalers. He saw in serfdom an obstacle to all kind of progress, and therefore it had to be abolished.[75] Similarly, in a 150-page unpublished tract on the problem of serfdom that he probably finished in 1751, Johann Georg Eisen, a pastor, publicist and cameralist in Livland, wrote: 'Proof that that the condition of the peasantry whereby the peasant is subject to his lord as owner of his farm is the sole foundation upon which all possible happiness of a state can be based, whereas serfdom can be considered the principal cause of all imperfections therein.'[76] Eisen was the first to raise the question of the abolition of serfdom in the Russian Empire.[77] He referred to England, Scotland, Denmark (1702), and Prussia as examples of regions where serfdom had already been abolished, directly connecting this in the same paragraph with the need for the state to devote the greatest attention to increasing the size of the population. He was certain that 'liberty and property', i.e. the abolition of serfdom and guaranteed property rights for the peasants, would provide maximum 'happiness' and prosperity to the state.[78]

Only from the 1760s did the condemnation of serfdom become a more prominent topic in cameralist literature. Only from that time was serfdom seen as an obstacle to the further development of agriculture, and as having an adverse impact on the welfare of the state (*auf das Wohl des Staats*).[79] For example, Johann Peter Süßmilch in the second enlarged and rewritten edition

75   Carl Leopold Eggers, *Ueber die gegenwärtige Beschaffenheit und mögliche Aufhebung der Leibeigenschaft in den Cammergütern des Herzogthums Mecklenburg Schwerin* (Bützow/Schwerin/Wismar, 1784), pp. 260, 265; Hans Witte, *Kulturbilder aus Alt-Mecklenburg* (Leipzig, 1911), pp. 95–6.

76   Johann Georg Eisen, 'Beweis, daß diejenige Verfassung des Bauern, wenn selbiger seinem Herrn als ein Eigentümer von seinem Bauernhof untertan ist, der einzige Grund sei, worauf alle mögliche Glückseligkeit eines Staats gebauet werden kann; die Leibeigenschaft hingegen für die erste Ursache von aller Unvollkommenheit in derselben gehalten werden könne', *Johann Georg Eisen (1717–1779). Ausgewählte Schriften. Deutsche Volksaufklärung und Leibeigenschaft im Russischen Reich*, ed. R. Bartlett and E. Donnert (Marburg, 1998), p. 24.

77   Roger Bartlett, 'Russia's First Abolitionist: The Political Philosophy of J. G. Eisen', *Jahrbücher für Geschichte Osteuropas* 39 (1991), 161–76; Erich Donnert, *Johann Georg Eisen (1717–1779). Ein Vorkämpfer der Bauernbefreiung in Rußland* (Leipzig, 1978), p. 27. See also Bartlett's essay in this collection.

78   *Johann Georg Eisen, Ausgewählte Schriften*, p. 138. For a closer overview, see R. Bartlett, 'Russia's First', pp. 161–76.

79   Mittenzwei, 'Die Agrarfrage', pp. 163–8.

of his main work *Die göttliche Ordnung* ('The Divine Order'), published in 1761–62, considered the total abolition of serfdom (*die Leibeigenschaft ganz abgeschaffet werde*) to be indispensable, though this recommendation was missing from the first edition of the treatise in 1741.[80] In the published German-language cameralist literature demands to abolish serfdom are usually associated with the name of Johann Heinrich Gottlob Justi, who raised the problem of serfdom when arguing for agricultural improvement. On account of this he has been considered 'indisputably the most significant agrarian politician among the cameralists.'[81] However, according to Ingrid Mittenzwei, Justi in his *Staatswirtschaft* of 1758 wished only for the restriction (*die Einschränkung*) of serfdom, while in 1761 advocating the abolition ('*aufzuheben*') of serfdom.[82]

Justi did not so much seek to persuade the state of the necessity of agrarian reforms as the peasantry and landlords. He argued that serfdom (*Leibeigenschaft*) and the consequent lack of peasant land ownership were the main obstacles to agricultural advancement. He was a fierce opponent of corvée, especially when unregulated, as he believed it harmful both to the peasant and the estate; one cannot hope that the peasant would fully dedicate himself to his own work if in constant fear of being subjected to corvée.[83] Justi also suggested that large estates be broken up and divided into independent farmsteads. The division of royal domain lands would not have given the peasants ownership of the farms, but would have made them hereditary leasehold tenants (*Erbpächter*).[84]

It appears that, while the existence of serfdom was not discussed among cameralist authors until 1750, or subject to their criticism, in practice the question of serfdom had already emerged as the state authorities sought to implement cameralist objectives. Administrative practice preceded theoretical and historical attention to serfdom by half a century. Similarly, the issue of reforming the domain land became an issue in cameralist literature only in the 1750s (discussed e.g. by Johann Albrecht Philippi, Johann Christian von

80   Johann Peter Süßmilch, *Die göttliche Ordnung in den Veränderungen des menschlichen Geschlechts, aus der Geburt, dem Tode und der Fortpflanzung desselben*, 2nd edn (Berlin, 1762), p. 34; Johann Peter Süßmilch, *Die göttliche Ordnung in den Veränderungen Geschlechts, aus der Geburt, Tod, und Fortpflantzung desselben* (Berlin, 1741).

81   Prange, *Die Anfänge*, pp. 650–7; see also: Ernst Klein, 'Johann Heinrich Justi und die preußische Staatswirtschaft', *Vierteljahrschrift für Sozial- und Wirtschaftsgeschichte* 48 (1961), 170–8 (145–202).

82   Mittenzwei, 'Die Agrarfrage', p. 171.

83   Johann Heinrich Gottlob von Justi, *Abhandlungen von der Vollkommenheit der Landwirthschaft und der höchsten Cultur der Länder* (Ulm/Leipzig, 1761), p. 22; Adam, *The Political Economy*, p. 215.

84   Justi, *Abhandlungen*, pp. 19–21; Klein, 'Johann Heinrich Justi', pp. 175–6.

Zech and then by Justi),[85] while in practical and administrative terms this had already been proposed in Brandenburg by Bernd von Arnim in the 1530s; and the proposal repeated several times during the seventeenth century, before Luben's project.[86]

Conclusion

The size and growth path of the population became an important challenge to the politics of the early modern state of the seventeenth and eighteenth century.[87] Serfdom was also assessed in respect of its influence on population growth and the attraction of new settlers. The same argument held at least until the end of eighteenth century. And so, referring in 1796 to Schleswig-Holstein, Christian von Rantzau wrote that in the regions where serfdom prevailed 'the state can never hope for a surplus of people from the cities or the repopulation of emptied lands'.[88]

Thus we should not confine our attention only to cameralist literature in seeking to clarify the development of cameralist ideas, since different kinds of proposals and projects, political discussions and royal orders also provide evidence of the spread of cameralist principles. Most of the suggestions and orders to abolish 'serfdom' issued between 1680 and 1720 were the expressions of the will of kings or princes, and were justified by cameralist goals.

But was the aim in these orders and projects dating from the period 1689–1720 real, or only nominal?[89] The German term 'Leibeigenschaft' was certainly often used in a very loose and ambiguous way. However, with the rise of cameralism serfdom became an institution whose continuation was now assessed on the basis of rational economic arguments. Later

---

85   Adam, *The Political Economy*, pp. 220–1. In the 1760s and 1770s Johann Peter Süßmilch, Joseph von Sonnenfels, Joachim Georg Darjes and Johann Christoph Wöllner also criticised the corvée and serfdom and vehemently supported the idea of parcelling up of estates into smaller farmsteads on hereditary lease: Mittenzwei, 'Die Agrarfrage', pp. 167–8, 171, 173; Adam, *The Political Economy*, p. 221; Sigmund v. Frauendorfer, *Ideengeschichte der Agrarwirtschaft und Agrarpolitik im deutschen Sprachgebiet*, vol. 1 (Bonn/München/Wien, 1957), p. 138; Joseph von Sonnenfels, *Grundsätze der Polizey, Handlung und Finanzwissenschaft*, vol. 2, 2nd edn (Wien, 1771), pp. 71–5; Eva Ondrušová, 'Staatswirtschaftslehre des Kameralismus: Theorie und Praxis am Beispiel von den Kameralherrschaften im Mittelslowakischen Bergbaugebiet. Einführung in das Thema', *Economy and Society in Central and Eastern Europe: Territory, Population, Consumption, Papers of the International Conference Held in Alba Iulia, April 25th–27th 2013*, ed. D. Dumitran and V. Moga (Wien, 2013), p. 69.
86   Flakowski, 'Beiträge', pp. 3–4.
87   Nipperdey, *Die Erfindung*, p. 13.
88   Conze, *Quellen*, p. 65 (doc. no. 11).
89   Cf. Peter Blickle, *Von der Leibeigenschaft zu den Menschenrechten. Eine Geschichte der Freiheit in Deutschland* (München, 2003), pp. 162–3.

detailed calculations of the real economic losses of serfdom were made by Wachenhusen and also by Justi, who calculated the monetary loss of corvée for the peasants. Serfdom was clearly considered to be a hindrance to achieving the state's financial goals, and the abolition of serfdom was seen as one option for increasing state revenues and general welfare. Many arguments were similar to those used in the later eighteenth century and early nineteenth century for agrarian reforms.

On the other hand, while seventeenth- and eighteenth-century cameralist thinking treated the welfare of the population as its principal objective, in the period 1680–1720 the abolition of serfdom was not yet linked to the of the well-being of peasants; it was a purely a cameralist question of how best to fill the state's coffers. Serfdom was not criticised by cameralists on ethical or humanistic grounds, but in terms of financial and political needs and cameralist principles. Characteristic of all these plans to abolish serfdom was that they were solely confined to domain lands (with the exception of Denmark). And so there was intention to mount a direct attack on the nobility. The main impulse to abolish serfdom came not from a wish to exert political pressure on the nobility, but from a desire to find a solution to revise and stabilise the situation on the domain lands. Nor did this mean that foundations were being laid for more extensive social reform, or that the emancipation of peasants was an objective; they started instead from declarations announcing the abolition of 'serfdom'. What was meant by 'serfdom' in different edicts and projects is a separate question.

Andre Wakefield lays emphasis on the fact that cameralists never had any practical success, and that their simple practical solutions were idealised or utopian.[90] One can agree with Wakefield that the official cameralist suggestions and solutions of the seventeenth and eighteenth centuries were indeed idealised, normative and often doomed to failure. Cameralists often sought ground-breaking reforms rather than piecemeal changes and revision of low-level police ordinances. The proposals made during the period 1680–1720 to abolish 'serfdom' were ultimately not achieved. Serfdom was abolished only in the last quarter of the eighteenth century and during the early nineteenth century by order of the state, this time in close co-operation with the nobility who for several reasons (cultural, political and economic) were then ready to accept it.[91] In the seventeenth century and in the first half of the eighteenth century cameralist argument only articulated the benefit to the state, and so the plans lacked both understanding and support among the nobility. This has indeed been considered to be the main weakness of cameralism – it paid attention only to state governance and state finances, involving top-down

90   Wakefield, The Disordered.
91   Michael L. Bush, 'Serfdom in Medieval and Modern Europe: A Comparison', Serfdom and Slavery: Studies in Legal Bondage, ed. M. L. Bush (London/New York, 1996), p. 220.

orders and decisions that might not have been socially motivated.[92] For this reason plans to abolish 'serfdom' failed in reality before 1780.

However, we can see already in 1680–1720 that suggestions and demands to abolish 'serfdom' arose before visions of a free peasantry were developed by Physiocrats and Enlightenment thinkers. It is also surprising how quickly governments agreed to abolish serfdom on domain lands. Projects, suggestions or draft bills were often introduced without further reflection. Cameralist thinking was deceptively convincing in suggesting easy solutions.

92 Cf. Dan Ch. Christensen, 'Physiocracy – the Missing Link?', *Modernisation and Tradition: European Local and Manorial societies 1500–1900*, ed. K. Sundberg, T. Germundsson and K. Hansen (Lund, 2004), p. 81 (78–106).

5

Cameralist Writing in the Mirror of Practice: The Long Development of Forestry in Germany

PAUL WARDE

Over the past three decades, historians of cameralism have moved away from treating it as a largely intellectual exercise, a specific school of political and economic thought, to drawing attention to the way it was (or was not) embedded as a discourse in particular practices: university education, alchemical endeavour, experimental agriculture, or just looking for a job.[1] In 2005 Andre Wakefield went back to Albion Small's distinction between 'book cameralists' and 'practical cameralists', calling for more attention to be given to the interaction of literary production with administrative practice.[2] In truth, even this distinction describes, in most cases, rather than different biographies, different moments in an individual's career trajectory, moving between managerial responsibility in a private or state capacity and periods of accelerated writing, publication or involvement in education. Some managed each with rather more distinction than others, and perhaps the most prolific writers, precisely because they had time to write and build their reputation through writing, were the least representative of either the usual run of cameralist administrators, or of the everyday expectations of those who did the drudge work of running states. In cases where historians have tied the stages of this trajectory into a more coherent analysis, this has generally been done in a biographical mode, explaining the context of particular writings, or indeed examining whether individuals practised what they preached. Studies that broadly contextualise cameralist thought within

---

1 Keith Tribe, 'Cameralism and the Science of Government', *Journal of Modern History* 56 (1984), 263–84.

2 Andre Wakefield, 'Books, Bureaus and the Historiography of Cameralism', *European Journal of Law and Economics* 19 (2005), 311–20; Albion W. Small, *The Cameralists. The Pioneers of German Social Policy* (New York, 1909), pp. 142–3; Eli F. Heckscher, *Mercantilism*, vol. II (2nd edn, London, 1955).

long-term trends in administration and governance in the germanophone
territories remain scarce.

One theme that consistently emerges in cameralist works is forestry.
Forestry was a major aspect of state activity in central Europe, employed
large numbers of people (as foresters, woodwards, or as part of the provision
of princely hunting), and both could supply significant revenues to the fisc,
or underpin the activities of strategically important industries such as metal-
smelting or saltworks. Some states managed woodlands directly, or leased
concessions to supply significant timber export industries. Territorial rulers
both exercised extensive direct ownership of woodlands, which could be used
to generate income; enjoyed rights both of *regal* claimed over unutilised space
and in regard to hunting over their entire territory; and also asserted rights
to govern the provision of basic resources to ensure basic welfare (*Notdurft*).
Forests and forestry appeared in cameralist literature in a range of aspects:
as a theme in legal practice pertaining to sovereign's rights to govern certain
activities and spaces; as regulatory practice concerned with good order
(*Polizei*), and as an economic concern contributing to wealth, revenue and
happiness. Parallel to cameralist writing was a burgeoning literature directly
focused upon the practice of forestry itself, but often involving considerable
overlap with cameralists' concerns. Yet one can also observe that much of
the rich seam of recent research on forest history has not explicitly investi-
gated the relationship between these literatures. Indeed, it is only compara-
tively recently that the study of forest history has turned to consider more
directly the influence of *Forstwissenschaft* as a historical genre on the well-
documented reforms and conflicts around the wood resources of many
states.[3] We could call the early authors of such works 'book foresters', for
foresters did write books, and rare indeed was the man who wrote about
forestry without some direct experience. But this symbiosis between learning
and practice in forest writing has usually been treated as an ornament, a kind
of hinterland of commentary on wood shortage in studies that are more
interested in social conflict and the contested authority of central authorities
vis-à-vis peasant and forest communities.

This chapter seeks to provide an overview of the relationship between
writings of various kinds on forests that also addressed government and
economic issues, and the actual administrations and systems of governance
in place in a range of German territories. The literatures involved include the
Hausväterliteratur that, from the latter decades of the sixteenth century, drew
on classical antecedents to provide advice manuals on the running of country
estates, but also strongly influenced early cameralist writing; cameralists'
textbooks and compilations; and writings squarely directed at foresters. They

3   Exemplary in this regard is Richard Hölzl, *Umkämpfte Wälder. Die Geschichte einer ökologischen Reform in Deutschland 1760–1860* (Frankfurt, 2010).

will be examined over a long timespan stretching back to the middle of the sixteenth century, for two reasons. Firstly, as will be seen, works from the later eighteenth century still cited forest legislation and *Polizeiordnungen* that were promulgated two hundred years previously, and remained a significant point of reference. Secondly, and relatedly, much of what was presented as desirable in regard to forest management had already been quite normal, although not universal, practice in the sixteenth century. The literature was therefore *descriptive* rather than *prescriptive*. Henry Lowood noted this property of cameralist literature in an influential essay published in 1990, but gave no clear sense of precisely how long-established the practices were.[4]

The survey will be far from exhaustive, but indicative of the kinds of relationships that can be found between the content of the texts, legislation, and practice. A first section will provide a short account of the widespread emergence of legislation for forests in the sixteenth century, the administrative divisions set up at that time to implement regulation, and the earliest writing to take up forestry as a theme (largely juridical). The second section will survey the period from the appearance of Veit Ludwig von Seckendorff's *Teutscher Fürsten-Staat* in 1656 to the publication of Hans Carl Carlowitz's *Silvicultura oeconomica* of 1713, considered the first major work of a recognisably modern forestry that focused largely on practice.[5] This was also the period that saw the publications of major works in the *Hausvater* tradition, by Wolf Helmhard von Hohberg, Johann Joachim Becher, and under the pen-name of Florinus, among others.[6] Such was the publishing environment in which the first teaching chairs in cameralism were founded. The final section deals with the period after 1750 that saw the florescence of both cameralist and forestry writing, and will utilise texts from Dithmar, Justi, Zincke and Pfeiffer in the case of cameralists, and Moser and Beckmann among foresters. These works will be assessed against the practice of forest regulation and management, to evaluate both the sources they drew upon, the 'realism' of their recommendations, and the distinctiveness of particular genres of writing. I will argue that

---

4   Henry E. Lowood, 'The Calculating Forester: Quantification, Cameral Science, and the Emergence of Scientific Forestry Management in Germany', *The Quantifying Spirit in the 18th Century*, ed. T. Frängsmyr, T. L. Heilbron and R. E. Rider (Oxford, 1990), p. 336.

5   Veit Ludwig von Seckendorff, *Teutscher Fürsten-Staat* (Jena, [1656] 1737 edn) with additions by Hn. Andres Simon von Biechling (Geheimen-Rat in Sachsen-Meiningen); Hans Carl von Carlowitz, *Sylvicultura oeconomica oder haußwirtschaftliche Nachricht und naturmäßige Anweisung zur Wilden Baum-Zucht nebst gründlicher Darstellung wie zu förderst durch göttliches Benedeyen dem attenthalben und insgemein einreissenden grossen Holz-Mangel …* (Leipzig, 1713).

6   Johann Joachim Becher, *Kluge Haus-Vater. Verständige Haus-Mutter* (Leipzig, [1685] 1747); Wolf Helmhard von Hohberg, *Georgica curiosa aucta* (Nürnberg, [1682] 1701); Francis Philipp Florinus, *Oeconomus Prudens et Legalis oder allgemeiner kluger und Rechts-verständinger Haus-Vatter* (Nürnberg, [1701] 1750).

there was no essential disconnection between 'book cameralism' and forestry practice, but that the core challenge for forestry administrations remained exactly what it had been in the sixteenth century: achieving a *uniform* quality of personnel and enforcement across regions where ordinances had always been *partially* implemented.

Foundations in the sixteenth century

Stipulations regarding rights to woodland, and the need to conserve it as a resource, can already be found in *Landesordnungen* (general territorial law ordinances) of the fifteenth century, and networks of princely foresters certainly already existed in some states at this time, primarily occupied with duties relating to the chase. During the general period of reform following the religious upheavals that began in 1517 territories also began to promulgate distinct *Forstordnungen* concerned with the wider governance of forests, including both those directly under princely control, or owned by cities, village communes, monasteries and private individuals.[7] Some measures, particularly relating to stipulations on land use and the marketing of wood, were included among *Polizeiordnungen*, the 'police ordinances' that covered very wide-ranging aspects of life and were intended to create good order in the polity.[8] Over time these ordinances tended to become much more extensive

---

7 Many lordships, communes and cities had provided earlier regulations and by-laws of various kinds, recorded in 'manifests' (*Weistümer*) and ordinances. Many are provided in the collection of Jakob Grimm, *Weisthümer gesammelt von Jakob Grimm* (Göttingen, 1840–78); also examples in August Bernhardt, *Geschichte des Waldeigenthums, der Waldwirtschaft und Forstwissenschaft in Deutschland* (Berlin, 1872–5); Helmut Brandl, *Der Stadtwald von Freiburg* (Freiburg, 1970); Albert Hauser, *Wald und Feld in der alten Schweiz* (Zürich, 1972), pp. 110–12; Ernst Schubert, 'Der Wald: wirtschaftliche Grundlage derspätmittelalterlichen Stadt', *Mensch und Umwelt im Mittelalter*, ed. B. Herrmann (Stuttgart, 1987), pp. 257–69; Siegfried Epperlein, *Waldnutzung, Waldstreitigkeiten und Waldschutz in Deutschland im hohen Mittelalter. 2. Hälfte 11. Jahrhundert bis ausgehendes 14. Jahrhundert* (Stuttgart, 1993); Uwe E. Schmidt, *Der Wald in Deutschland im 18. Und 19. Jahrhundert* (Saarbrücken, 2002), p. 6; Hans Heinrich Vangerow, *Vom Stadtrecht zur Forstordnung. München und der Isarwinkel bis zum Jahr 1569* (München, 1976); Paul Warde, 'Imposition, Emulation and Adaptation: Regulatory Regimes in the Commons of Early Modern Germany', *Environment and History* 19 (2013), 313–37.
8 On the 'police ordinances' and the historiographical debate about the degree to which they were implemented, see Karl Härter, *Polizey und Strafjustiz in Kurmainz. Gesetzgebung, Normdurchsetzung und Sozialkontolle im frühneuzeitlichen Territorialstaat* (Frankfurt a.M., 2005); Thomas Simon, *'Gute Polizey'. Ordnungsleitbilder und Zielvorstellungen politischen Handelns in der frühen Neuzeit* (Frankfurt a.M., 2004); Michael Stolleis, 'Was Bedeutet "Normdurchsetzung" bei Policeyordnungen der frühen Neuzeit?', *Grundlagen des Rechts*, ed. R. H. Helmholz (Paderborn, 2000), pp. 740–57; Jürgen Schlumbohm, 'Gesetze, die nicht durchgesetzt waren – ein Strukturmerkmal des frühneuzeitlichen Staates', *Geschichte und Gesellschaft* 23 (1997), 647–63; K. Härter (ed.), *Policey und frühneuzeitliche Gesellschaft*

and prescriptive, in particular providing significantly more detail as to how woodlands should be managed, consumption restrained and certain kinds of wood reserved for particular purposes. In some cases such ordinances very clearly reflected local preoccupations and might apply only to some districts of a state, related for example to the supply of salt mines and saltpans at Reichenhall in the Tyrol; in other cases such laws covered the entirety of a polity, as was the case in the Duchy of Württemberg.[9] First examples, generally episodically revised and extended, were promulgated in (among others) Hesse in 1532, Württemberg in 1540, Wolfenbüttel in 1547, Siegerland in 1553, Saxony in 1560, Upper Palatinate in 1565, Zweibrücken 1568, Bavaria in 1568, the Palatinate in 1572, Ducal Prussia in 1582, Westphalia in 1590, Homburg in 1569, Nassau-Dillenburg in 1562, Trier in 1584, and Cleves-Mark in 1649.[10] This impression considerably understates activity because many other kinds of ordinances also contained regulations relating to the forests.

To enforce such rules a network of forestry officials was also created, usually with assigned districts or wards to police.[11] The expectation was usually (although not solely) that stands of timber trees or coppice woods (deciduous trees cut back after a period of years to 'stools' that sprouted

(Frankfurt a.M., 2000); André Holenstein, 'Gute Policey' und lokale Gesellschaft im Staat des Ancien Régime. Das Fallbeispiel der Markgrafschaft Baden(-Durlach) (Epfendorf/Neckar, 2003); Achim Landwehr, Policey im Alltag: Die Implementation frühneuzeitlicher Policeyordnungen in Leonberg (Frankfurt a.M., 2000); Achim Landwehr, 'Die Rhetorik der "Guten Policey"', Zeitschrift für historische Forschung 30 (2003), 251–87; Marc Raeff, The Well-ordered Police State. Social and Institutional Change through Law in the Germanies and Russia, 1600–1800 (New Haven, CT, 1983); Andre Wakefield, The Disordered Police State. German Cameralism as Science and Practice (Chicago, 2009).

9 Dorothea Hauff, Zur Geschichte der Forstgesetzgebung und Forstorganisation des Herzogtums Württemberg im 16. Jahrhundert (Stuttgart, 1977); P. Piasecki, Das deutsche Salinwesen 1550–1650 (Idstein, 1987).

10 Kersten Krüger, Finanzstaat Hessen 1500–1567. Staatsbildung im Übergang vom Domänstaat zum Steuerstaat (Marburg, 1980), p. 153; Joachim Allmann, Der Wald in der frühen Neuzeit (Berlin, 1989), pp. 35, 44; Burkhard Dietz, 'Wirtschaftliches Wachstum und Holzmangel im bergisch-märkischen Gewerberaum vor der Industrialisierung', http://www.lrz-muenchen-de/MW/Hardenstein/Dietz.htm, pp. 5–6, accessed 27 Apr. 2006; Christoph Ernst, Den Wald entwickeln. Ein Politik- und Konfliktfeld in Hunsrück und Eifel im 18. Jahrhundert (München, 2000), p. 52; Christa Graefe, Forstlete. Von den Anfängen einer Behörde und ihren Beamten Braunschweig-Wolfenbüttel 1530–1607 (Wisebaden, 1989), p. 74; Friedrich Mager, Der Wald in Altpreussen als Wirtschaftsraum (Köln, 1960), pp. 36, 54; Kurt Mantel, Forstgeschichte des 16. Jahrhunderts unter dem Einfluß der Forstordnungen und Noe Meurers (Hamburg, 1980), pp. 158, 273; Joachim Radkau, Holz – wie ein Nahrstoff Geschichte schreibt (München, 2007), p. 127; Ingrid Schäfer, 'Ein Gespenst geht um.' Politik mit der Holznot in Lippe 1750–1850. Eine Regionalstudie zur Wlad und Technikgeschichte (Detmold, 1992), p. 17; Rolf-Peter Sieferle, The Subterranean Forest. Energy Systems and the Industrial Revolution (Cambridge, 2001), p. 72; see also Peter-Michael Steinsiek, Nachhaltigkeit auf Zeit. Waldschutz in Westharz vor 1800 (Münster, 1999), pp. 92–5.

11 Allmann, Der Wald, p. 72.

again) would naturally rejuvenate, although more systematic planting had been carried out in a few spots such as the *Reichswald* of Nürnberg since the late fourteenth century.[12] Rules were often in place for the protection of 'staddles' that would grow into timber, or just as importantly, provide mast for pigs and game. Such habits and oversight were by no means unique to princely forest legislation; many cities or lordships had such officers as well. As was typically the case with early modern officialdom and laws, the *Forstordnungen* enjoyed rather episodic and variable fortunes; it is clear in Württemberg, for example, that the further one went from the residence of a forester, the less likely it was that the rules were adhered to, and the woods directly owned by the duke were much more likely to see them observed than other property types.[13]

At this time the printed literature addressing woodlands was very limited both in volume and indeed in its substantive content regarding the management of the woods. Until the dawn of *Forstwissenschaft* texts (still *avant le mot*) in the eighteenth century, the contents of forest ordinances were far richer in detail on the practice of forestry than anything to be found in the literature, although we do have evidence that some foresters took an interest in botany and agronomic works. There was, then, a widespread and recognisable practice of state forestry that existed long before it became an academic discipline; this is equally true of *Polizei*, which existed as an extensive and refined system of codes for generating order long before anyone spoke of *Polizeiwissenschaft*, or indeed *Kameralwissenschaft*. In the context of a broader academic education, the much later texts that dealt with such things were, to quite a large degree, providing pedagogically orientated intro-ductions to the basic administrative norms that had existed for a very long time.[14]

Those men that did write on such topics in the sixteenth century were also precisely the kind of experienced and active officials that cameralists wished their readers to become. Noé Meurer, a trained jurist who published two volumes on princely hunting and forest rights in 1560 and 1576, had been active in forest matters as counsellor and judge in Württemberg and the Palatinate, was familiar with discussions of conifer planting long practised

12 Lore Sporhan and Wolfgang von Stromer, 'Die Nadelholzsaat in den Nürnberger Reichswäldern zwischen 1369 und 1600', *Zeitschrift für Agrargeschichte und Agrarsoziologie* 17 (1969), 79–99.
13 Paul Warde, *Ecology, Economy and State Formation in Early Modern Germany* (Cambridge, 2006), pp. 226–42.
14 Keith Tribe has commented that within cameralist works, 'Cameralism assembles the objects that *Polizei* then orders for the good of the state and its subjects', but in truth the assembly of objects subject to *Polizei* had occurred much earlier and, as Tribe also points out, had developed its own reflective dynamics. Keith Tribe, *Strategies of Economic Order. German Economic Discourse 1750–1950* (Cambridge, 1995), pp. 20–2.

around Nürnberg, and contributed to the drafting of *Forstordnungen*. His work was intended as a compilation of existing forest law to avoid future confusion, establishing a tradition that would have much more extensive successors.[15] These were the two first really substantial works dedicated to the theme, although in 1557 a work on 'the art of saving wood' had been presented as a book to the Imperial court.[16] Conrad von Heresbach, author in 1570 of the *Quatres libri rustici*, was venerable enough a counsellor in the Duchy of Cleve that he had been involved in marital negotiations with the court of Henry VIII three decades previously; his English contacts meant the work was soon translated in 1577 and went on to be one of the best-known books of husbandry in England during the Elizabethan and Jacobean reigns.[17] Johann Colerus played a similar role in Brunswick before writing and compiling his *Oeconomica ruralis et domestica* in the 1590s.[18]

Heresbach and Colerus are now seen as the founders of the *Hausväter* tradition, providing handbooks for the running of large country estates that were consciously modelled on writers of classical Rome: Cato, Varro, Columella, Palladius, and drawing extensively on them. Advice focused on the raising of individual species of tree, and arboreal matters were placed in a section towards the end of an imagined tour of the estate, together with gardens and orchards.[19] This arboriculture was not the much more widespread practice of woodland management that at the time provided fuelwood and timber to millions in the villages, cities and industrial centres of central Europe. Nevertheless, neither in matters of farming nor arboriculture did these authors slavishly follow the ancients, and comments about the necessity of experience and learning-by-doing were seriously meant.[20] Colerus went on to recommend and quote from the ordinance requiring the planting of trees on Lüneburg Heath under pressure from the demands of the famous salt industry, with more detailed consideration of the best times for planting (also typically preoccupied with planting according to the moon, a practice

15   Noé Meurer, *Vom Forstlicher Oberherrligkeit und Gerechtigkeit* (Pforzheim, 1560), pp. 2–4; Noé Meurer, *Jag und Forstrecht* (Frankfurt a.M., 1576); see also Allmann, *Der Wald*, p. 44; Karl Hasel and Ekkehard Schwartz, *Forstgeschichte. Ein Grundriss für Studium und Praxis*, 3rd edn (Kassel, 2006), p. 314; Mantel, *Forstgeschichte*, passim; for a later, much more extensive example that however was less orientated towards advice on the practice of woodland management, see Ahasver Fritsch, *Corpus Iuris Venatorio Forestalis* (Jena, 1676).

16   Fritsch, *Corpus*, p. 47.

17   Conrad Heresbach, *Foure bookes of husbandry, collected by M. Conradus Heresbachius, counseller to the hygh and mighty prince, the Duke of Cleue: conteyning the whole arte and trade of husbandry, vvith the antiquitie, and commendation thereof. Newely Englished, and increased, by Barnabe Googe, Esquire* (London, 1577).

18   Johannis Colerus, *Oeconomiae oder Hausbuch*, 2 vols (Wittenberg, 1598).

19   Heresbach, *Foure bookes*, pp. 100–10; Colerus, Bd. II.

20   Colerus, *Oeconomica*, pp. 209, 272; see also Bernhardt, *Geschichte des Waldeigenthums*, p. 247.

particularly recommended by Palladius), and maintain coupes protected from grazing animals.[21] Certainly in some regions industrial demand provided the stimulus to the relatively precocious development of forestry administration.[22] He also provided a detailed price list of wood products from districts in Saxony and Meissen.[23] It was, therefore, official publications that provided some of the real detail in his work.

The emergence of new genres, c.1650–1750

In 1656, a young court librarian and administrator of Saxony-Gotha in central Germany called Veit von Seckendorff published the *Teutscher Fürsten-Staat*, a work in many ways unlike any that had previously appeared. Eventually this and further editions of the acclaimed book would lead to a professorial post, but Seckendorff first wrote as someone who had been charged with helping rebuild the state after its withdrawal from the Thirty Years' War. With rather donnish care he documented juridical and administrative tasks *in extenso*. This was no fantastical wish-list; or at least, if it did not entirely correspond to practice in Gotha, much of what he recommended was nonetheless precisely the kinds of things active administrators had been doing in the decades running up to the war and during it, as anyone familiar with the administrative archives of that time would recognise. Soon Seckendorff was himself in charge of the treasury (*Kammer*), where, like any administrator, he struggled to turn such ideas into effective practice – which is not the same as saying that they had no effect.[24] His interest in the forests was, however, for the most part limited to establishing the nature of a sovereign's rights.[25] In this he was again perhaps typical. Whilst princely counsellors were certainly interested in good management of the forests, arbitrating disputes as efficiently as possible, and raising revenues from traditional fees and sales, in Württemberg they generally left the business of guarding and harvesting the trees to the men on the ground. Although almost complete surveys of forests were made in 1556,

---

21 Colerus, *Oeconomica*, passim.

22 Bernhardt, *Geschichte des Waldeigenthums*, p. 223; Elisabeth Johann, *Geschichte der Waldnutzung in Kärnten unter dem Einfluss der Berg- und Hütten- und Hammerwerke* (Klagenfurt, 1968); Schäfer, *Ein Gespenst geht um*, p. 16.

23 Colerus, *Oeconomica*, pp. 218–20.

24 The gap between promise and practice in von Seckendorff's work has been argued by Andre Wakefield to be cynical and self-serving rhetoric, although it is not clear that Seckendorff intended the book to be a statement of what was done. Doubtless there would be a significant gap between the private discussions of treasury officials and the public pronouncements of ministers today, just as presidents and prime ministers turn out not to be as virtuous as their public image suggests. Wakefield, *The Disordered Police State*, pp. 18–20, 133–7.

25 Seckendorff, *Teutsche Fürsten-staat*, pp. 460–74.

1583 and 1682 in that state, these surveys were not employed to co-ordinate the exploitation of the resource, but rather as reference tools in legal cases and to help define boundaries.[26] Seckendorff himself did not cite others in regard to the forest (his own state had just received a new forestry ordinance in 1644). He hardly needed to do so, since he just wrote about what was already generally known. Andre Wakefield has argued that 'we cannot read these texts in isolation', and we must always remember that these were 'idealized texts, originally crafted to please powerful people by sketching well-ordered possible worlds'.[27] Yet they were plausible precisely because what was being suggested had frequently already been put into practice somewhere (although very far from everywhere). If we remove them from the isolation of individual authors, we find their context in many little worlds where state officials were generating their own order, here falteringly, there more effectively, although it would be a century before such men ventured into print in any numbers.

In the subsequent post-war decades, a range of authors returned to the *Hausväter* traditions with major works: Becher (who was active as a counsellor and projector for several states, and also wrote for the Imperial government the stimulation of commerce and industry),[28] Hohberg, and the author who used the pen-name 'Florinus'.[29] None of these added much to the canon of understanding about woods, which found their place, if at all, nestled after viticulture, gardens and orchards in the now traditional fashion in the *Hausväterliteratur*.[30] Of more interest were the annotations to Florinus provided by the jurist, Christoph Donauer, which provide much more extensive commentary on woodland management, and cite very many of the forest and territorial ordinances of the sixteenth century. These show how the ordinances provided the reference point for good practice, and indeed also provided a textual corpus upon which to draw. Of course, by no means were the ordinances universally observed and enforced. But they were nearly all observed and enforced somewhere. Donauer's work represents, perhaps, a particular juridical tradition in his use of legal authority and citation, but in doing so he actually provided an account that related to real *praxis* rather more than any that evoked a canon running back to antiquity.

At the time that Donauer edited the text of Florinus, Hans Carl von Carlowitz, scion of a minor dynasty of forest and mining officials in Electoral Saxony, was coming to the end of a long career. His *Silvicultura oeconomica*

26 Warde, *Ecology*, pp. 105–11; on a variety of surveys taken in the Palatinate, see Allmann, *Der Wald*, pp. 162–76.
27 Wakefield, *The Disordered Police State*, pp. 20–1.
28 Johann Joachim Becher, *Politischer Discurs von den eigentlichen Ursachen deß Auf- und Abnehmens der Städt, Länder und Republicken* (Frankfurt, 1668).
29 Heinz Haushofer, 'Franz Philipp', *Neue Deutsche Biographie* 5 (1961), p. 255.
30 Florinus, *Oeconomus Prudens et Legalis*, Book IV.

of 1713 was a work that, in its inception, might be said to be *sui generis* and quite unlike anything previously written. Carlowitz was certainly aware of the compilation of knowledge regarding trees written (or perhaps more accurately stated, edited) by John Evelyn in 1664 at the behest of the Royal Society following concern expressed by naval administrators about the supply of timber in England: *Sylva, or a discourse of forest trees*.[31] Yet while there are some overlaps in style and content, *Sylva* was not a practical work for someone in charge of swathes of forest. In 1710 Réaumur was also compiling his observations on French forestry practice on the instruction of Louis XIV for much the same reasons as Evelyn, but this was not published until 1721.[32] Carlowitz did not obviously lift anything important from the *Hausväterliteratur*, but he was clearly widely read in classical literature, travelogues, and aspects of current science.

Carlowitz's interest was, as he put it, in the 'raising (*Zucht*) of wild trees', by which he meant raising large stands of those trees that normally constituted woodlands, as opposed to the growing and grafting of garden and orchard trees in the nursery. It was *silviculture* properly conceived, in that it aimed to augment or replace the processes of natural rejuvenation to create a more productive forest. This was the true conceptual novelty of his writing, rather than the oft-quoted use of '*nach haltend*' as a direct precursor to modern concepts of sustainability (*Nachhaltigkeit*) – which was not, in truth, a new sentiment at all when applied to the need to ensure trees for future generations.[33] Nine of the seventeen chapters in the first part of the book were devoted to detailed discussion of the collection and planting of seed, preparation of the ground, transplanting trees and their maintenance, comparisons with natural processes, and the possible introduction of foreign species. The first eight sections constituted a somewhat arbitrarily ordered justification and contextualisation of the importance of Carlowitz's work, and his emphasis, new in a literary mode, upon the necessity of active intervention in shaping the forest in order to keep in step with the demand for fuel from the smelting industry, the main preoccupation of his career. He discussed

31   John Evelyn, *Sylva, or, A discourse of forest-trees, and the propagation of timber in His Majesties dominions* (London, 1664); Beryl Hartley, 'Exploring and Communicating Knowledge of Trees in the Early Royal Society', *Notes and Records of the Royal Society of London* 64 (2010), 229–31.

32   See Kieko Matthieson, *Forests in Revolutionary France. Conservation, Community and Conflict, 1669–1848* (Cambridge, 2015), p. 58.

33   Carlowitz, *Silvicultura oeconmica*, p. 69; for a slightly hagiographical take on Carlowitz, see Ulrich Grober, *Die Entdeckung der Nachhaltigkeit. Kulturgeschichte eines Begriffs* (München, 2010); Sächsische Carlowitz-Gesellschaft (ed.), *Die Erfindung der Nachhaltigkeit. Leben, Werk und Wirkung des Hans Carl von Carlowitz* (München, 2013). Much of the management of woodlands in medieval times essentially enshrined the principle of the 'eternal wood', but for seventeenth-century examples, see Radkau, *Holz*, p. 97.

the previously vast extent of Germanic woods (Tacitus always appeared in this connection), the high regard in which they were treated, the current lamentable 'wood shortage' (*Holzmangel*) and its causes; alongside sections on the physiology of trees and their pests, and historical and foreign efforts to conserve woodland (Carlowitz uses the word *Conservation* frequently).[34] It is notable that he made so much of what might appear to be more 'glamorous' invocations of famous historical figures who valued trees, a rather typical trope in early modern literature, as well as citing states such as Venice (as did Evelyn); he clearly felt the need to elevate his banal subject, although this was a common conceit in learned writing about the land.[35] Germany was already replete with forest ordinances, and Carlowitz refers to no fewer than 18 (a small sample, to be sure). Seckendorff is cited too.[36] However, it seems that these familiar laws carried neither the weight of authority nor expressed the desired degree of novelty adequate to Carlowitz's desire to disseminate his project; although the law and practice to which he referred was no recent innovation, but established forestry practice of in some regions.[37] His project of extending awareness of such techniques required something beyond an appeal to laws that were, perhaps, much observed in the breach.

The second edition of Carlowitz, with appended and extended sections by Christian von Rohr, appeared in 1732. At this time the cameralist Christoph Dithmar was active as a counsellor in Prussia and Professor of Police, Cameralism and Economy (*Oeconomie*) at Frankfurt an der Oder, after Gasser had taken up the first chair in the 'cameral sciences' (*Kammer-Sachen*) at Halle in 1727.[38] Dithmar turned his lectures into compendious works published in 1731, and which posthumously went through expanded editions until the mid-1750s. He represents, of course, a cameralist discourse, but the breadth of work that he combined is notable for the purposes of our considerations here. He was widely read in the classics, von Carlowitz, and foreign authors such as Richard Bradley (the first professor of botany at Cambridge, but perhaps best understood as a kind of hack gentleman scientist rather than an education-alist). Dithmar's works were structured very like the *Hausväterliteratur*, but extended their managerial purview from the bounds of the great estate to the polity as a whole. Trained as a jurist, he was also studious in his referencing: a

34 Carlowitz, *Silvicultura oeconmica*, pp. 3–4, passim.
35 Carlowitz, *Silvicultura oeconmica*, pp. 52–8, 74–82.
36 Carlowitz, *Silvicultura oeconmica*, pp. 58–9.
37 In Lippe, to take but one example, conifers were planted in the 1680s and again in the 1740s, although such measures did not stop the gradual attrition of larger trees. Schäfer, *"Ein Gespenst geht um"*, pp. 43, 63; also Winifried Schenk, *Waldnutzung, Waldzustand und regionale Entwicklung in vorindustrieller Zeit im mittleren Deutschland* (Stuttgart, 1996), p. 95.
38 Heinrich Grimm, 'Dithmar, Justus Christoph', *Neue Deutsche Biographie* 3 (1957), p. 746, http://www.deutsche-biographie.de/pnd128453230.html, accessed 16 May 2015; Tribe, 'Cameralism', pp. 263–4.

new generation of forest ordinances were dutifully evoked, such as those from Prussia in 1688 and 1719; Venetian law; and publications advocating fuel-saving devices and stoves.[39] His direct discussion of woodland management rests however on reference to a range of pre-existing legislation.[40] This was in reality a kind of reportage on established good practice, because any reader would know that to invoke forest ordinances was to invoke the administrative paraphernalia and personnel that went with their enforcement. No act of imagination was required; it was already there. In this regard he might be seen as writing in the tradition of von Seckendorff with whom we began this section, but profiting from the extended library and literary habits to be found a century after his predecessor's work.

Practice and publication at the high point of cameralism

After 1750 the rate of publication on forestry matters and cameralism accelerated, assisted by the self-plagiarism of some of the more prolific writers, but also paralleling the emergence of a journal literature, such as the *Forst-magazin* of Zanthier, which enjoyed a short-lived life from 1763. It also reflected a general upsurge in publications on agriculture at this time in much of Western Europe.[41] The burgeoning cameralist texts (also in the sense that many became enormously long multi-volume works) integrated more substantive details on forestry practice, but the literature of *Forstwissenschaft*, which really became established with von Moser's *Grundsäze der Forst-Oeconomie* of 1757, also positioned itself more clearly as a genre of pedagogy situated *within* the cameralist traditions, as one of the essential sciences of the state.[42] There was less of the appeal, still very present in von Carlowitz, to the litany of virtuous figures from sacred and secular history that would justify a learned man's interest in mere trees. Equally, a requirement for technical mastery that had previously appeared in more isolated forms (such as Penther's work on mensuration, aimed at surveyors)[43]

---

39   Christoph Dithmar, *Einleitung in die Öconomischen, Policey- und Cameral-Wissenschaften* (5th edn, Frankfurt an der Oder, [1731] 1755), pp. 40–1, passim.

40   Dithmar, *Einleitung*, pp. 188–92.

41   Isabelle Knap, 'Die Anfänge "wissenschaftlicher" Forstlehre am Beispiel des *Allgemeinen oeconomischen Forst-Magazins* (1763–1769)', *Landschaften agrarisch-ökonomischen Wissens. Strategien innovativer Ressourcennutzung im Zeitschriften und Sozietäten des 18. Jahrhunderts*, ed. M. Popplow (Münster, 2010), pp. 61–78; Peter Jones, *Agricultural Enlightenment. Knowledge, Technology, and Nature, 1750–1840* (Oxford, 2016); André J. Bourde, *The Influence of England on the French Agronomes 1750–1789* (Cambridge, 1953).

42   Wilhelm Gottfrid Moser, *Grundsäze der Forst-Oeconomie* (Frankfurt/Leipzig, 1757).

43   Friedrich Penther, *Praxis geometriae worinnen nicht nur alle bey dem Feld-Messen vorkommende Fälle, mit Stäben, dem Astrolabio, der Boussole, und der Mensul, in Ausmessung*

was blended into a more comprehensive range of skills that it was thought the progressive forester should command, much in the way that cameralist writers provided exhaustive and doubtless exhausting compendia of what the 'clever statesman' should know.

In this light we nevertheless should remember that cameralist comment on the forests comprised only a small part of their output, although some authors, like Pfeiffer, entertained a particular interest in fuel economy.[44] Like many of the men discussed in this chapter, most cameralist writers spent time in public office, although unsurprisingly the time of their greatest *literary* output tended to be when they were out of a job and had time to advertise their skills, whether in search of academic posts, or of further patronage as administrators and innovators. This can make vast and apparently programmatic works appear more fantastical than they would have seemed to contemporaries, who would have recognised their role both as collected lectures and a conspectus of skills as in a *curriculum vitae*.

However they chose to couch their political philosophy in regard to the origins of the state and human nature, or the end purposes of government (generally the 'happiness' of the subjects), cameralist writers of the mid-eighteenth century argued that security and welfare had to be built upon a flourishing and large population, economic prosperity and a capacity to extract revenue for the prince.[45] When Georg Heinrich Zincke writes about the forests, for example, he begins with a legalistic outline of the various rights lending possibilities for extracting income, where the juridical issues regarding the forest are not simply a prelude to a discussion of *Polizei*. For this he was able to use the collection of examples gathered in Stisser's history of the German forests published in 1737, an example of how the expansion of literature in the Enlightenment could gradually supplant the old law codes as a source of information. And yet the list of what Zincke thought achievable, and how woodlands might be managed to realise these goals, could already be found virtually entire in forest codes going back to Württemberg's ordinance

eintzeler Linien, Flächen und gantzer Revier, welche, wenn deren etliche angräntzende zusammen genommen, eine Land-Carte ausmachen, auf ebenen Boden und Gebürgen, wie auch die Abnehmung derer Höhen und Wasser-Fälle, nebst beygefügten practischen Hand-Griffen, deutlich erörtert, sondern auch eine gute Ausarbeitung der kleinesten Risse bis zum grösten, mit ihren Neben-Zierathen, treulich communiciret werden (Augsburg, 1761).

44 Anton Felix Napp-Zinn, *Johann Friedrich von Pfeiffer und die Kameralwissenschaften an der Universität Mainz* (Wiesbaden, 1955), p. 21.

45 Johann Friedrich von Pfeiffer, *Grundsätze der Universal-Cameral-Wissenschaft* (Frankfurt, 1783), pp. 1–4; Johann Friedrich von Pfeiffer, *Lehrbegrif sämmtlicher oeconomischer und Cameralwissenschaften* (1st edn, 1764–65; 2nd edn, Mannheim, 1773–78); see also Paul Warde, 'Sustainability, Resources and the Destiny of State in German Cameralist Thought', *Nature, Action and the Future: Political Thought and the Environment*, ed. K. Forrester and S. Smith (Cambridge, 2018) (forthcoming).

of 1552. The prescriptions of that ordinance could also be widely encountered as actual management practice for the Duchy's forests, as could for example procedures for keeping proper accounts.[46] Perhaps the one genuine novelty we find in Zincke, who after work as a Prussian bureaucrat lectured in Halle, Weimar, Leipzig and then Brunswick, is the suggestion that the *Holztag*, the long-established day that consumers came and presented foresters with bids for what trees they wished to purchase that year, should somehow be co-ordinated at the level of the polity and involve the all sources of demand, including the ordinary populace, state officials and industry.[47] Such a level of co-ordination was, however, never achieved.

    Johann Heinrich Gottlob von Justi published a flurry of works in the years around 1760, among them *Die Grundfeste zu der Macht und Glückseeligkeit der Staaten; oder ausführliche Vorstellung der gesamten Policey-Wissenschaft*.[48] In this he worked from first principles of the social and economic order in addressing the need for and needs of a population, the appropriate supply of wood, and the economics of supply and demand; this was something of a departure from authors who preferred to deal with legal entitlements first. As such, and as so often, Justi presents in this work a peculiar mix of the strikingly insightful and blindingly obvious. He had quickly absorbed literature on political economy appearing at the time, discussing for example Mirabeau's observations on the rising fuel demand of Paris (including the idea that spoiled modern maidservants who enjoy not only their own chambers, but heat and light in them, are part of the problem of the pressure on fuel supplies, a variety of the discourse on 'luxury'). Yet he also noted recent experiments with the growing of cedars in Wernigerode, whose innovative forest ordinance of 1747 was an oft-cited and talismanic implementation of modern forestry for the proselytisers of *Forstwissenschaft*.[49] Justi also introduced the essential insight of political economy: if the price is

46   Georg Heinrich Zincke, *Anfangsgründe der Cameralwissenschaft worinne dessen Grundriß weiter ausgeführet und verbessert wird*. Part II (Leipzig, 1755); A. E. Reyscher, *Vollständige, historisch und kritisch bearbeitete Sammlung der württembergischen Gesetze* (1828–), esp. vol. 16.

47   For examples of requirements to hold a *Holztag*, which clearly was widely implemented in several states, see Allmann, *Der Wald*, p. 100.

48   Johann Heinrich Gottlob von Justi, *Die Grundfeste zu der Macht und Glückseeligkeit der Staaten* (Königsberg, 1760); *Gutachten von dem Vernünftigen Zusammenhange und practischen Vortrage aller Oeconomischen und Cameralwissenschaften wobey zugleich zur Probe die Grundsätze der Policeywissenschaft* (Leipzig, 1754); *Die Natur und das Wesen der Staaten als die Grundwissenschaft der Staatskunst, der Policey, und aller Regierungswissenschaften, desgleichen als die Quelle aller Gesetze* (Berlin, 1760); *Oeconomische Schriften über die wichtigen Gegenstände der Stadt- und Landwirtschaft* (Berlin, 1760); *Gesammlete Politische und Finanzschriften über wichtige Gegenstände der Staatskunst, der Kriegswissenschaften und des Cameral- und Finanzwesens*, 3 vols (Copenhagen/Leipzig, 1761–64).

49   Justi, *Die Grundfeste*, I, pp. 82–4.

not right for the interested parties, any amount of instruction is futile. This lesson was perhaps not learned by his suzerain, Frederick the Great, whose instructions sought to impose a more regular pattern of management on domain forests, avoiding 'selection' cutting (logging out prized trees rather than systematically felling whole stands), creating a monopoly supply for Berlin, and by 1769 seeking to abolish commons, all of which measures had a limited effect.[50] Nevertheless, while some argued that the effect of high prices would be to encourage planting and conservation, the short-run prospect of returns and the pressures of supplying industry clearly also encouraged logging reserves out. Different interests articulated ideals of the 'good forest' in disputes over jurisdiction and appropriate practice, as indeed happened to Justi himself in his management of ironworks at Vietz in Prussia's Neumark.[51] The desire to increase fiscal returns, especially in economically peripheral states, offered the same temptation to cash in. Further down the fiscal chain, communities sold off wood to meet tax demands; while price competition put pressures on traditional industries like salt-making or metal-smelting, making them sensitive to the secular rise in prices and increasing demands for protection against 'shortage', as argued by Ingrid Schäfer.[52]

Around two decades later, Johann Friedrich von Pfeiffer was the leading cameralist writer in both eminence and output; he too engaged very widely with contemporary writing on political economy, producing extended commentaries, but also setting out considerations on management of the land that stood squarely within the traditional ordering of the *Hausväterliteratur*.[53] He also produced rather eclectic collections of essays on topics of interest that were typical of the journal literature at the time, to be found in periodicals such as the *Leipziger Sammlungen*.[54] As with Justi, we find that his stipulations regarding forestry, whilst certainly ambitious as a project for complete implementation across the entirety of a state, were not at all out of line with the ambitions of foresters already at work, and indeed in some regions established for over two centuries. All woodlands were to be assigned to particular administrative districts (*Forstrevier*), with their boundaries

---

50   Radkau, *Holz*, p. 143.

51   As there was by no means a consensus over what constituted good forest management, it could be that (self-interested) individuals could well defend quite opposing views over what was best practice perfectly legitimately in the eyes of themselves or contemporaries (as is frequently found today). On the dispute, see Wakefield, *Disordered Police State*, pp. 93–102.

52   Schäfer, *"Ein Gespenst geht um"*, pp. 47, 52–3, 167–8, 180; Schmidt, *Der Wald*, p. 114.

53   Napp-Zinn, *Johann Friedrich von Pfeiffer*; for recent essays on von Pfeiffer's output, including a complete bibliography, see Jürgen Georg Backhaus, *Physiocracy, Antiphysiocracy and Pfeiffer* (Berlin, 2011).

54   For example, Johann Friedrich von Pfeiffer, *Vermischte Verbeßerungsvorschläge und freie Gedanken über verschiedene, den Nahrungszustand, die Bevölkerung und Staatswirtschaft der Deutschen betreffende Gegenstände* (Frankfurt a.M., 1777).

properly measured, and a record made of kinds of trees and their qualities, the character of the ground and extent of waste, and bare patches ripe for plantation. Aside from the last stipulations, these would fall comfortably within the ambitions of activist renaissance foresters. Like Justi, with the elevated perspective of a man writing for the polity as a whole, Pfeiffer also wrote of the need for a single co-ordinating authority to match all sources of supply and demand. Implausible as it might seem, this was in fact precisely the kind of consideration being worked into documents on forest policy by his contemporary Peter Kling for the demand and supply of wood in the Palatinate, with quantification of different kinds of use and a calculation of the annual shortfall, roughly sketched out in Nassau-Saarbrücken as early as 1750. Indeed, such calculations had been made in relation to particular mines and smelting works for much longer.[55]

This brings us to the numerous writers of *Forstwissenschaft*. As exemplars I will take Wilhelm Moser and Johann Beckmann, both pioneers in the genre whose works were widely received before the 'classics' of forestry were first published by Heinrich Cotta and Georg Hartig towards the end of the century.[56] Before writing his *Grundsätze* Moser had worked both in the mining and smelting centre of the Harz in north-central Germany and as a forester in Württemberg, which was more orientated towards the supply of domestic households and timber for export. He argued that *Forst-Oeconomie* was to be considered a branch of *Cameralwissenschaft*, being critical of foresters who did not consider their profession in this context, but he also clearly broke with the *Haus-Vater* tradition in arguing that forestry must be treated distinctly from farming and horticulture (which included arboriculture and orchards).[57] He was familiar with the works of Zincke and Justi published before 1757, as well as Stisser and Réaumur's 1721 discussion of French forestry.[58] In this he brought a mix of authorities that was typical: praising the forest ordinances that directed the woods towards a providing a 'continual use' (*beständiger Nutzen*), and drawing on Justi to justify and historically legitimate state oversight of forests, while also commending the practitioner, the man who trod the woods, as 'Whoever wants to learn economy (*Wirtschaft*) must seek out people, who practice it (*wirtschaften*) themselves.'[59]

As with his cameralist contemporaries and indeed Carlowitz, wood shortage was conceived by Moser as a threat to the state, and he set out cause

---

55   Pfeiffer, *Grundsätze*, pp. 155–62; Allmann, *Der Wald*, pp. 55–6; Grewe, *Der versperrte Wald*, p. 229; Lowood, 'The Calculating Forester', p. 324; Schmidt, *Der Wald*, pp. 49, 149; Steinsiek, *Nachhaltigkeit*, pp. 114,119, 125.
56   On the reception of these two authors in Bavaria, and an excellent discussion of the southern German literature of the time, see Hölzl, *Umkämpfte Wälder*, pp. 42–90.
57   Moser, *Grundsäze*, pp. 5–6.
58   Moser, *Grundsäze*, pp. 137–8.
59   Moser, *Grundsäze*, pp. 9, 12, 25–6.

and effect before detailed prescriptions for forestry practice. Again, while the point might seem laboured, preambles of this kind were very typical in much earlier forest ordinances. In turn, rather as *Cameralwissenschaft* had become provided with a core purpose to provide for 'happiness' and welfare, so forestry, just like a programme of 'rational economy' (*vernünftigen Wirtschaft*) in general, had a 'primary purpose ... of drawing such advantage from the available woodlands, which is possible and advisable to achieve according to their nature'. Indeed, this was a duty of the ruler if he was to fulfil that obligation to promote the 'happiness' and 'welfare of the state'. Such an aim relied on, in turn:

(1) the sustainable use and economical division of the available forests and woods, (2) the managing of wood with all kinds of means and arts of thrift, (3) the continual cultivation of individual trees and bushes suited to woods, (4) the encouragement of the natural growth of wood in the woodlands, (5) but also on the new plantation of woods on barren patches and other suitable areas and places.[60]

So far, so cameralist. Moser went on however to provide considerable detail on how the optimal times for cycles of felling and regrowth should be assessed, as well as including an earlier section discussing the properties of individual species that harked back to Evelyn and Carlowitz.[61] In setting out forestry practice, Moser was highly reliant on forest ordinances, including especially those of the County of Stolberg-Wernigerode (1745), Württemberg (1733), Nassau-Saarbrücken (1750), Hesse-Cassel (1740), Hessen-Hanau-Münzenberg (1736), Sachsen-Gotha (1667), Brandenburg-Onolzbach (1736), Mainz (1692) and the somewhat older ordinance of Brandenburg in 1613. In short, he was very well acquainted with the forestry legislation of the age, which itself was quite prescriptive of forestry practice, being the prime means by which such practice was communicated in print until the second half of the eighteenth century. Indeed, he was sufficiently aware to be able to comment on regional differences.[62]

By no means, however, were Moser's sources limited to laws. He also drew upon recently published journal articles to be found in the *Leipziger Sammlungen* and *Hanoverischen Gelehrten Anzeigen*, as well as refer-encing more specialist text: the Comte de Buffon on felling and de-barking, Böse's industrially orientated work on mining, saltworks and forestry of 1753, and especially Langen, the influential forester and cartographer who had seen official service in both Denmark and German territories including

60 Moser, *Grundsäze*, pp. 82–3.
61 Moser, *Grundsäze*, pp. 32–60.
62 Moser, *Grundsäze*, pp. 101, 123, 128, 133–4, 154, passim.

Stolberg-Wernigerode where von Moser served under him in the early 1750s.
Carlowitz and Hohberg feature too.[63] Whilst the attention to the detail
of practical forestry (and its wider social justification) is reminiscent of
Carlowitz, Moser then moved on to give much more attention to the distribution of wood and the regulation of the market, a typical theme for cameralists (among which Moser would include himself, of course); but above all, he
took account of forestry ordinances for which market regulation had been a
major theme from the very beginning, in common with territorial ordinances
of the sixteenth century.

Johann Gottlieb Beckmann had served as a forest inspector in several
minor states in Saxony, and was a dutiful member of the local ökonomische
Gesellschaft. He coined the term Forstwissenschaft in a work of 1759.[64]
Himself the same age as the century, his first work was not penned until
1755, and by its reissue in 1777 he was able to enter into a relatively new
phenomenon associated with the rise of printed works on forestry: the literary
spat. Beckmann took aim at several of his critics but especially Döbel, who
had published a critical article in the Leipziger Ökonomischen Nachrichten,
and among other things had objected to Beckmann's didactic, question-and-
answer approach to writing. Beckmann retorted however that, 'I did not write
this work for the learned, but for huntsmen, foresters, estate managers and
the like, people not accustomed to deep reflection'; this style was, he thought,
'more easy to grasp for their instruction'.[65] Nevertheless Beckmann certainly
did not eschew learning himself, citing Moser, Geutebrück, Büchting,
Carlowitz (that 'oft-mentioned book'), Duhamel du Monceau and others.[66]
Nonetheless Beckmann, more like Carlowitz and in distinction to Moser, did
not attempt to place his work so unambiguously as a branch of cameralism.
He maintained a narrower focus on the practice of preparing seed and sowing
trees, and he is also famed for developing practical ways for calculating the
growth rates of trees and the quantity of standing timber in a given area
(although by no means the first to tackle such topics).[67] Beckmann evoked
the Saxon forest ordinance of 1560 as an example that such sowing had long
been practised, rather than as a source of technique or prescription, and
often preferred to highlight his personal experience.[68] As much as he berated
the ignorance of his peers who ventured into print, he was also lambasted

63   Moser, Grundsäze, pp. 128, 155, 182–3, 413; see Hasel and Schwartz, Forstgeschichte,
pp. 319, 325.
64   Hasel and Schwartz, Forstgeschichte, p. 317.
65   Johann Gottlieb Beckmann, Gegründete Versuche und Erfahrungen der zu unsern Zeiten
höchst nöthigan Holzsaat, zum allgemeinen Besten (4th edn, Chemnitz, 1777), pp. 10–13.
66   Beckmann, Gegründete Versuche, pp. 13, 36, 103, 175.
67   Beckmann, Gegründete Versuche; Johann Gottlieb Beckmann, Anweisung zu einer pfleglichen Forstwirthschaft (Chemnitz, 1759); see also Lowood, 'The Calculating Forester'.
68   Beckmann, Gegründete Versuche, p. 4.

by critics who claimed that in the whole Ore Mountains of central Germany there were hardly ten peasants who understood the techniques of sowing he proposed. Beckmann, with his long experience, was at least able to point to the success of specific plantings he had made in the 1720s, and additionally to the evidence of well-kept forestry accounts if anyone desired a paper trail, confidently asserting the likely success of clear instruction from forester to the peasantry.[69]

The salutary lesson for the modern reader, however, is the limits of what we can gather from disputatious sources when rather violently phrased contestation was typical. We need to refer to other sources to find out what was actually happening, and what made a difference. And in connection with this, much was at stake in the decision to adopt or reject new techniques that entailed considerable capital investment; it is not surprising that arguments could become heated when livelihoods and reputation were at stake. The sowing of conifers had been practised in Germany since the 1360s, and was certainly widely familiar among foresters (as was the sowing of acorns), yet the actual extent of plantations was small, regionally focused, and clearly many were ignorant of the entire approach.[70] The printed literature had a tendency, at times, to present a picture of simple steps to a well-oiled machinery of optimal resource management; or alternatively, of a dismal wasteland of ignorance and sloth observed from afar by bewigged improvers with little grasp of what was possible. The reality was, as ever, more varied and complex.

Conclusions

Cameralist writing, from its inception in the seventeenth century, drew broadly on genres already established in legal writing, in the *Hausväterliteratur* on agriculture, and perhaps most significantly, in administrative practices already long embodied in German territories from before the Thirty Years' War. Indeed, what seems retrospectively to be a rather eclectic and unsystematic mix of topics was actually well-established among the police and territorial ordinances of the sixteenth century as the means to secure sovereignty and order. This juridical framing of policy, and the legal training of many authors, serves to explain the significance of those earlier ordinances and style of referencing to be found in many cameralist works, and in particular those sections that we have examined here concerned with forestry. They were largely descriptive of long-established norms and practices, even if there is also, it must be noted, a considerable historiographical debate on the degree to which

---

69 Beckmann, *Gegründete Versuche*, pp. 28–9, 49–50.
70 On the sowing of spruce in the Harz, see Steinsiek, *Nachhaltigkeit*, p. 153.

Polizeiordnungen were actually enforced.[71] This is not to say that cameralism brought no novelty to the table. While the literature of forestry developed to some degree in parallel with it, forestry itself was powerfully shaped in some regions of central Europe by the needs of fiscally remunerative industries, and thus some foresters and officials engaged in mining and smelting works were quite familiar with the kind of integrated administration that cameralists espoused.[72] Equally, such demand stoked an interest in developing more productive forestry, while foresters could argue that they could save the state from incipient wood shortages. Of course, one cannot take claims about wood shortage at face value, as undoubtedly regulation benefited certain vested interests (from industry to princely hunting or timber exporters). While there is evidence that closer management of the forests improved yields over time in some places from early in the eighteenth century, some of the treasury officials who had final oversight in forestry matters were more interested in a stable *monetary* return than guaranteeing the sustainability of wood yields.[73] Christoph Ernst has noted how closer management of a woodland divided into more regular coupes and subject to systematic felling regimes from around 1760 in the Archbishopric of Trier did not prevent a declining stock of timber by the end of the century.[74] But when levels of consumption are high, this was the inevitable effect of the new forestry regime, because even if regeneration matches consumption, the available stock will initially decline as stands of old growth are logged, and there is then a long wait until new stands reach the desired age. Equally, as production switched more towards conifers and longer cutting cycles for timber, the available annual supply of 'lop and top' or small-diameter wood for fuel may also decline.[75] These short- to medium-term trends may well cause difficulties for consumers, but are not indicators of unsustainability in a purely quantitative sense. Equally, measures were not always without effect.[76]

If Carlowitz represents a threshold for a new era of more activist and transformatory forestry, he did report on a lifetime of practice, and he

71   See above note 7.

72   In some areas this pattern was very long established; see Johann, *Geschichte der Waldnutzung*; see also Hasel and Schwartz, *Forstgeschichte*, p. 317.

73   Ernst, *Den Wald entwickeln*, pp. 116–17, 123–4.

74   Ernst, *Den Wald entwickeln*, pp. 124, 337–8; also Christoph Ernst, 'Neue Zugänge zur historischen Waldentwicklung. Die Auswertung von Forst- und Landrentmeisterrechnungen (Kurtrier, 1759–1792)', *Langer Reihen zur Erforschung von Waldzuständen und Waldentwicklungen*, ed. W. Schenk (Tübingen, 1999), pp. 215–18.

75   This did not go unnoticed by the 'classics' of forestry. See Bernd Stefan Grewe, *Der versperrte Wald. Ressourcenmangel in der bayerischen Pfalz (1814–1870)* (Köln, 2004), pp. 248–9.

76   Dietz, 'Wirtschaftliches Wachstum', pp. 8–9. Ernst notes how yields increased soon after woodlands were more widely divided into coupes in Hunsrück. Ernst, *Den Wald entwickeln*, p. 95; Schenk, *Waldnutzung*, pp. 104–5, 131.

justified his activities in traditional ways. By the time of Moser, forestry was becoming a *Wissenschaft* imagined alongside cameralism, and would in subsequent decades follow it into the university, although more importantly into the school of forestry. The career of the first ever university lecturer in *Forstwissenschaft* followed a progression not unlike the history of literature on forests, like an embryo recapitulating phases of evolution in its development. Johann Jakob Trunk initially studied and practised law, before becoming a senior forestry official and then lecturing at Freiburg in 1787 after the new Outer Austrian forest ordinance required professional qualifications for foresters. Five years later he became professor of *Cameralwissenschaft* at Bonn.[77] At the same moment there was a proliferating output of the printed word on woodlands and the use of wood itself, and it must be remembered that if the blandishments of a Justi at times seem troublingly distant from practical considerations, they were writing in the context of numerous other works that did provide such details within the framework they proposed.

---

77   See Hasel and Schwartz, *Forstgeschichte*, pp. 326–7.

6

Cameralist Theoretical Writings on Manufacturing and Administrative Practice in the German Principalities: Conflict and Coherence[1]

GUILLAUME GARNER

Introduction

During the eighteenth century the rise of manufactures and manufacturing became one of the central concerns for economic policymakers in the territorial states of the Holy Roman Empire. This theme also occupied a prominent place in the treatises on cameralism that proliferated during the second half of the century. This essay explores this relationship through an examination of the institutional framework of 'industrial policy' (*Gewerbepolicey*) as discussed in cameralist works and applied to policy.

Consideration of the economic and social context of the Holy Roman Empire explains why the focus on manufacturing and manufactories is typical for cameralism in the second half of the eighteenth century. This sector offered possibilities for the employment of a growing population and so resolve the increasingly acute problem of poverty, in particular after the grain shortage of 1771–72. For these reasons the states governments in the Holy Roman Empire were under pressure,[2] and were also prompted to introduce measures of *Gewerbepolicey* advocated by the flourishing economic discourse of the second half of the eighteenth century, including the cameral sciences. Furthermore, this sector had to be developed to offset a perception of economic backwardness in comparison to France, England, and the Dutch Republic, and to confront economic competition among the states of Holy

1   The author is grateful to Marten Seppel and Keith Tribe for editorial support.
2   John Komlos, 'Institutional Change under Pressure: Enlightened Government Policy in the Eighteenth-Century Habsburg Monarchy', *Journal of European Economic History* 15 (1986), 435 (427–482).

Roman Empire. Given the impossibility of most German states increasing their power through territorial and colonial conquest, development of their industry was a primary objective.[3] According to recent studies, this is a criterion that distinguishes German cameralism – centred on agricultural and industrial production – from trade-oriented English mercantilist discourse, which gave priority to a positive balance of trade.[4]

A few preliminary observations will be useful. First, an analysis of the relationship between cameralist proposals and their application in German states (in other words, the relationship between theory and practice) points to a number of unresolved issues.[5] Showing that theoretical proposals and particular policies have similarities is one thing; demonstrating that the former influenced the latter is quite another.[6] One can also ask to what extent cameralists took any account of policies already in place, thereby reversing the terms of the question. Second, distinguishing an interventionist mercantilism or cameralism from a liberalism hostile to state intervention is not a helpful approach to the writings of the cameral sciences. Recent studies have abandoned this interpretive framework.[7] Third, while the historiography subsequent to Eli Heckscher and Jacob van Klaveren has been rather negative about the achievements of mercantilist economic policies and theories,[8] it has been emphasised that they were quite adequate to the economic context and to the concrete problems faced by governments during the eighteenth century.[9] Beyond these – positive or negative – assessments, the present study examines how economic policy was implemented, so that we might gain a

---

3   Sophus A. Reinert, *Translating Empire: Emulation and the Origins of Political Economy* (Cambridge, MA, 2011), pp. 242ff.
4   Thomas Simon, 'Merkantilismus und Kameralismus. Zur Tragfähigkeit des Merkantilis-musbegriffs und seiner Abgrenzung zum deutschen "Kameralismus"', *Merkantilismus. Wiederaufnahme einer Debatte*, ed. M. Isenmann (Stuttgart, 2014), pp. 65–82; Lars Magnusson, 'Was Cameralism Really the German Version of Mercantilism?', *Economic Growth and the Origins of Modern Political Economy: Economic Reasons of State, 1500–2000*, ed. Ph. R. Rössner (London, 2016), pp. 57–71.
5   Karl Heinrich Kaufhold, '"Wirtschaftswissenschaften" und Wirtschaftspolitik in Preußen von um 1650 bis um 1800', *Wirtschaft, Wissenschaft und Bildung in Preussen: Zur Wirtschafts-und Sozialgeschichte Preussens vom 18. bis zum 20. Jahrhundert*, ed. K. H. Kaufhold and B. Sösemann (Stuttgart, 1998), pp. 51–72; Hans Joachim Braun, 'Economic Theory and Policy in Germany, 1750–1800', *Journal of European Economic History* 4 (1975), 301–22.
6   Kaufhold, '"Wirtschaftswissenschaften" und Wirtschaftspolitik', p. 53.
7   Keith Tribe, *Governing Economy. The Reformation of German Economic Discourse 1750–1840* (Cambridge, 1988), pp. 66, 74–5. See also Marcus Sandl, *Ökonomie des Raumes. Der kameralwissenschaftliche Entwurf der Staatswirtschaft im 18. Jahrhundert* (Cologne/Vienna/Weimar, 1999), pp. 38, 422ff.
8   Eli F. Heckscher, *Mercantilism* (London, 1994), 2 vols; Jacob van Klaveren, 'Die Manufakturen des Ancien Régime', *Vierteljahrschrift für Sozial- und Wirtschaftsgeschichte* 51 (1964), 145–91.
9   Komlos, 'Institutional Change'.

basic understanding of the intended objectives and the methods employed to achieve them.

Manufactories and manufacturing in the cameral sciences

Cameralist works published after the creation of the first chairs in the cameral sciences in 1727 at Halle and Frankfurt (Oder) had an essentially professional orientation. Their purpose was to train the territorial states' future officials in the fundamentals of cameralism: economy (agricultural, artisanal and industrial production), finance, and above all 'police science'. This professional orientation explains the central place of *'Policeywissenschaft'*, or the systematic study of measures that would ensure the 'common good' and promote the economic prosperity of the German states. During the second half of the eighteenth century cameralist tracts multiplied, as did university chairs in the cameral sciences across the Empire.[10] However, this close link between cameralist writings and professional training has to be treated with some care. It is clear that during the second half of the eighteenth century cameralist authors sought to reach a broader readership. In particular, they addressed an emergent public opinion progressively more interested in economic issues. Increasingly, their works adopted a critical view of the *status quo*. This constituted part of the politicisation of the Enlightenment (which included several noteworthy cameralist figures).[11]

The fluctuation of the cameral sciences between the education of loyal and competent officials and political criticism can be explained in part by the writers' social status. Some were academics whose careers were devoted to serving the university and the state,[12] such as Joseph von Sonnenfels, who taught cameral sciences in Vienna from 1763 until his death, and who was

---

10   Tribe, *Governing Economy*, pp. 91–118; David Lindenfeld, *The Practical Imagination. The German Sciences of State in the Nineteenth Century* (Chicago/London, 1997), pp. 22ff. See also the collection of case studies in two important publications: Wilhelm Stieda, *Die Nationalökonomie als Universitätswissenschaft* (1st edn, 1906; 2nd edn, Vaduz, 1978); Norbert Waszek, ed., *Die Institutionalisierung der Nationalökonomie an deutschen Universitäten. Zur Erinnerung an Klaus Hinrich Hennings (1937–1986)* (Sankt-Katharinen, 1988).

11   On Justi, see Horst Dreitzel, 'Justis Beitrag zur Politisierung der Aufklärung', in *Aufklärung als Politisierung – Politisierung der Aufklärung*, ed. H. E. Bödeker and U. Herrmann (Hamburg, 1987), pp. 158–77; on Pfeiffer, see Horst Dreitzel, 'Universal-Kameral-Wissenschaft als politische Theorie: Johann Friedrich von Pfeiffer (1718–1787)', *Aufklärung als praktische Philosophie. Werner Schneiders zum 65. Geburtstag*, ed. F. Grunert and Fr. Vollhardt (Tübingen, 1998), pp. 149–71.

12   The implication of cameralists in the administrations of German states has been underestimated according to Andre Wakefield, 'Books, Bureaus, and the Historiography of Cameralism', *European Journal of Law and Economics* 19 (2005), 311–20.

also associated with the government of the Habsburg Monarchy. By contrast, Johann Heinrich Gottlob von Justi and Johann Heinrich Jung-Stilling moved among different states within the Empire, at times taking up temporary university positions and administrative responsibilities, at others living off the sale of their works. Similarly, Johann Friedrich von Pfeiffer took on a number of roles in various states before being named professor of cameral sciences at the University of Mainz in 1782. In other words, cameralist discourse and proposals have to be located in at least three fields:[13] the field of administrative and governmental practice, the academic field (which was centred on the universities and the chairs of cameral sciences), and the learned field of the emerging public sphere (*Öffentlichkeit*). To understand the relationship between the discourse and practice of *Gewerbepolicey* we need to keep in mind that cameralists had to define their position with respect to these three fields. Justi sought to legitimise the cameral sciences within academic and learned fields by organising them around the unifying principle of 'general happiness' (*allgemeine Glückseligkeit*). This notion was closely associated with the economic prosperity of the state.[14] Importance was placed, therefore, on expanding production and the circulation of wealth, defined as the totality of goods that could satisfy human needs.[15] Given this perspective, manufacturing and manufactories occupied a central place in cameralist discourse for several reasons.

First, manufactories and manufacturing contributed to the production of wealth. According to many cameralists, human needs had increased and diversified in such a way that the agricultural sector alone could not satisfy them. Manufacturing and manufactories made it possible to fulfil not only primary needs (such as clothing), but also those associated with convenience and luxury.[16] However, manufactories and manufacturing could only expand if they made use of inexpensive and abundant raw materials, which in turn implied a prior increase in the output of agriculture and mining. Justi noted in 1758 that an increase of this kind reduced the cost of 'industrial' production – especially since low food costs kept workers' wages down and thus promoted

13   Pierre Bourdieu, 'Quelques propriétés des champs', in: Pierre Bourdieu, *Questions de sociologie* (Paris, 1984), pp. 113–20.
14   Ulrich Engelhardt, 'Zum Begriff der Glückseligkeit in der kameralistischen Staatslehre des 18. Jahrhunderts (J. H. G. v. Justi)', *Zeitschrift für Historische Forschung* 8 (1981), 45, 52–3 (37–79).
15   Johann Heinrich Gottlob von Justi, *Staatswirthschaft, oder systematische Abhandlung aller oeconomischen und Cameral- Wissenschaften, die zur Regierung eines Landes erfordert werden* (1st edn, 1755; 2nd edn, Leipzig, 1758), vol. 1, p. 152. Hence cameralists do not consider that wealth consists in money: Tribe, *Governing Economy*, pp. 69–70, 74–5.
16   See for example Joseph von Sonnenfels, *Grundsätze der Polizey, Handlung und Finanz* (1st edn, 1765–71; 5th edn, Vienna, 1787), vol. 2, pp. 5–16.

the sale of manufactured goods.[17] A state's prosperity rested, therefore, not only on the production of raw agricultural and mineral materials, but above all on the transformation of these materials into marketable merchandise.[18] Here the cameralists took up a widespread theme in seventeenth- and eighteenth-century European economic thought, the importance of 'industry' (*Fleiss*) in the creation of wealth.[19] In the 1770s, they used this dualist theory of value to criticise the Physiocratic idea that agricultural production was the source of wealth.[20]

Second, since 'industrial' output added value, it made the development of new foreign markets possible. In seventeenth- and eighteenth-century European economic thought it was common to emphasise the benefits of a positive trade balance, ensured through the export of manufactured goods. While some authors considered exports the sole method for enriching the state, many cameralists argued that a surplus trade balance was not only the precondition but also the consequence of a state's economic prosperity.[21] Therefore, the goal was to create a virtuous circle linking a positive trade balance and economic growth, a process that ultimately depended on successful manufactories. According to this logic, the prosperity of a state (such as the Dutch Republic) with a positive balance of trade but no industry was illusory.[22]

The balance of trade was also a central theme in cameralist discourse, since this literature underlined the economic backwardness of the German states compared to the Dutch Republic, France and England. In the late seventeenth century, mercantilist thinkers and German territorial states took up this theme at the Imperial Diet, which from the 1670s to the 1720s attempted to create

17   Johann Heinrich Gottlob von Justi, *Vollständige Abhandlung von den Manufakturen und Fabriken* (1st edn, 1758; 2d edn, Berlin, 1780), vol. 1, pp. 41–2.

18   Tribe, *Governing Economy*, p. 76 (on Justi). This assertion was repeated during the second half of the eighteenth century.

19   Hans Frambach, 'Cameralism and Labour in von Justi's Economic Thinking', *The Beginnings of Political Economy. Johann Heinrich Gottlob von Justi*, ed. J. G. Backhaus (New York, 2009), pp. 133–45.

20   Johann Friedrich von Pfeiffer, *Der Antiphysiocrat oder umständliche Untersuchung des sogenannten Physiocratischen Systems vermöge welchem eine allgemeine Freiheit, und einzige Auflage, auf den reinen Ertrag der Grundstücke, die Glückseligkeit aller Staaten ausmachen soll. Von dem Verfasser des Lehrbegrifs sämtlicher Oekonomischer- und Cameralwissenschaften* (Frankfurt a.M., 1780), pp. 21ff. On German physiocracy and the debate with cameralism, see Tribe, *Governing Economy*, pp. 119–31.

21   Justi, *Abhandlung*, vol. 1, p. 22; Johann Friedrich von Pfeiffer, *Grundriß der Staatswirthschaft zur Belehrung und Warnung angehender Staatswirte* (Frankfurt a.M., 1782), p. 55.

22   See for example the comment of Johann Beckmann in Johann Heinrich Gottlob von Justi, *Grundsätze der Policeywissenschaft in einem vernünftigen, auf den Endzweck der Policey gegründeten, Zusammenhange und zum Gebrauch academischer Vorlesungen abgefasset* (1st edn, 1756; 3rd edn, Göttingen, 1782), pp. 180–1.

an Imperial mercantilism (*Reichsmerkantilismus*) to protect manufactures from French competition.[23] Lagging development remained a central concern during the second half of the eighteenth century, especially as the aftermath of the Seven Years' War underscored the urgency of stimulating economic progress through manufacturing.[24] This context provides some explanation for the close links that began to form between the academic cameral sciences and technology from the 1730s onwards, and particularly after the 1770s,[25] when Johann Beckmann (one of the champions of technological development in Germany) republished two of Justi's treatises on manufacturing and police science,[26] and several cameralists also published manuals on technology and 'manufacturing science' (*Fabrikwissenschaft*).[27] As the population continued to grow in the final decades of the eighteenth century the problem of economic activity became particularly acute. Manufactories and manufacturing were seen as a means to make use of increasing manpower, and to promote the virtues necessary for wealth creation.[28]

Objectives and preferential sectors

When making concrete proposals cameralists used three criteria to determine which sectors took priority.[29] The first was tied to a country's trade balance; manufacturing and manufactories had to be developed in sectors with the largest cash flow, and those with potential export markets. The second

23   Ingomar Bog, *Der Reichsmerkantilismus. Studien zur Wirtschaftspolitik des Heiligen Römischen Reiches im 17. und 18. Jahrhundert* (Stuttgart, 1959).

24   This was for example the case in the Prussian states: Ingrid Mittenzwei, *Preußen nach dem Siebenjährigen Krieg: Auseinandersetzungen zwischen Bürgertum und Staat um die Wirtschaftspolitik* (Berlin, 1979), pp. 129–35.

25   Ulrich Troitzsch, *Ansätze technologischen Denkens bei den Kameralisten des 17. und 18. Jahrhunderts* (Berlin, 1966), pp. 87–103; Ulrich Troitzsch, 'Manufakturen in Deutschland und ihre theoretische Behandlung in der kameralistischen Literatur. Ansätze zu einem Vergleich', *Wirtschaftskräfte und Wirtschaftswege. Festschrift für Hermann Kellenbenz*, ed. J. Schneider (Stuttgart, 1978), vol. 4, p. 615 (611–624).

26   Birger P. Priddat, 'Die unbekanntere Seite: Joh. Beckmann als Herausgeber und Kommentator der Von Justi'schen "Policeywissenschaft"', *Johann Beckmann-Journal. Mitteilungen der Johann Beckmann-Gesellschaft e.V.* 4 (1990), no. 2, pp. 23–44.

27   Johann Heinrich Jung-Stilling, *Versuch eines Lehrbuchs der Fabrikwissenschaft zum Gebrauch Akademischer Vorlesungen* (Nürnberg, 1785); Torsten Meyer, *Natur, Technik und Wirtschaftswachstum im 18. Jahrhundert. Risikoperzeptionen und Sicherheitsversprechen* (Münster/New York, 1999), especially pp. 161–4.

28   Pfeiffer, *Staatswirthschaft*, p. 51.

29   Johann Friedrich von Pfeiffer, *Die Manufacturen und Fabricken Deutschlands nach ihrer heutigen Lage betrachtet und mit allgemeinen Vorschlägen zu ihren vorzüglichsten Verbesserungs Mitteln begleitet* (Frankfurt a.M., 1780), vol. 2, Einleitung.

criterion was economic activity: for example Sonnenfels stressed the necessity of encouraging industries that employed the greatest number of workers.[30] The presence within the territory of raw materials (agricultural and mineral) that could be processed was the third consideration. The combination of these three factors explains why the textile sector (woollens, linens, cottons, silks) took priority. Justi devoted the entire first volume of his *Abhandlung* to this sector and, in 1780, Pfeiffer detailed the leading textile products in his treatise about German manufacturing.[31] Enterprises that exploited mineral resources made up another primary sector. Pfeiffer therefore repeatedly lamented the underdevelopment of the processing of metallic ores in Germany.[32]

In most of the territorial states of the Holy Roman Empire 'industrial policy' was not a coherent practice, but instead resulted from the accumulation of different kinds of measures: laws, police ordinances, fiscal measures, customs regulations and privileges. These were enacted in a piecemeal fashion, especially in small states or in those with scattered territory,[33] while larger states (the Habsburg Monarchy, Brandenburg-Prussia, Bavaria) created policies that seemed more coherent; the most famous case of this is the *Rétablissement* carried out in Saxony after 1763.[34] Beyond these differences, governments pursued similar objectives overall: stimulating widespread engagement in economic activity and exploiting domestic natural resources, especially mineral reserves. In general, these measures were undertaken to catch up with French and English economic (industrial) development, avoid cash expenditures, and possibly attain a positive trade balance.[35] This approach can be observed in the Habsburg Monarchy after the War of the Austrian Succession and the Seven Years' War, as Maria Theresa sought to offset the loss of Silesia, an important manufacturing region.[36] In Saxony too the *Rétablissement* programme aimed

---

30   Sonnenfels, *Grundsätze*, vol. 2, pp. 154ff.

31   Justi, *Abhandlung*, vol. 1; Pfeiffer, *Manufacturen*, vol. 1, pp. 1–415.

32   See for example Johann Friedrich von Pfeiffer, *Grundsätze der Universal-Cameral-Wissenschaft oder deren wichtigsten Säulen nämlich der Staats-Regierungs-Kunst, der Policey-Wissenschaft, der allgemeinen Staats-Oekonomie, und der Finanz-Wissenschaft zu akademischen Vorlesungen und zum Unterricht angehender Staatsbedienten* (Frankfurt a.M., 1783), vol. 2, p. 851.

33   Rudolf Schäfer, *Die Förderung von Handel und Wandel in Kurmainz im 18. Jahrhundert* (Frankfurt a.M., 1968); Rudolf Endres, 'Wirtschaftspolitik in Ansbach-Bayreuth im Zeitalter des Absolutismus', *Jahrbuch für Wirtschaftsgeschichte* (1994), no. 2, 97–117.

34   Katrin Keller, 'Saxony: *Rétablissement* and Enlightened Absolutism', *German History* 20 (2002), 309–31.

35   Günther Chaloupek thus mentions a 'policy of import substitution' in the Habsburg Monarchy: Günther Chaloupek, 'J. H. G. Justi in Austria: His Writings in the Context of Economic and Industrial Policies of the Habsburg Empire in the 18th Century', *The Beginnings of Political Economy*, ed. J. G. Backhaus (New York, 2009), p. 149 (147–156).

36   Gustav Otruba and Harald Steindl, 'Einleitung', *Österreichische Fabriksprivilegien vom 16. bis zum 18. Jahrhundert und ausgewählte Quellen zur Frühgeschichte der Industrialisierung*, ed. G. Otruba (Graz/Cologne/Vienna, 1981), pp. 58–9 (11–120).

at strengthening the mutual growth of agricultural production and manufacturing; only then would a positive trade balance be possible.[37]

In the second half of the eighteenth century, a number of states attempted to revitalise and streamline prospecting for and the exploitation of mineral resources. Institutions devoted to teaching mining sciences and the training of competent administrators were created; the most famous among them was the Freiberg Mining Academy, founded in Saxony in 1765.[38] Andre Wakefield has underscored the importance of the mining sector within cameralism;[39] indeed, here governmental initiatives and cameralist propositions were intertwined.[40] Not only was mining science integrated into cameral science curricula, some cameralists were directly involved in the exploitation of mineral resources.[41] Moreover, and particularly after the 1740s, the authorities of many states considered metallurgy to be another sector to be fostered, not only in the larger but also in the smaller and more scattered territorial states.[42]

As in the cameralist treatises, another primary production sector was the textile industry. In Brandenburg-Prussia Frederick William I fostered cloth manufacturing to support his army;[43] and Frederick II similarly backed the nascent silk industry, mainly located in the central provinces of his realm.[44] Through varied measures many governments in the imperial states assisted the textile industry. In the Habsburg Monarchy and in Bavaria privileges were granted to the textile sector after 1740, and this policy was also followed in smaller states, such as the County of Hanau, where from the 1730s onwards the government attempted to halt the decline of industry and cloth manufacturing.[45]

---

37   Horst Schlechte, ed., *Die Staatsreform in Kursachsen, 1762–1763: Quellen zum kursächsischen Rétablissement nach dem siebenjährigen Kriege* (Berlin, 1958), p. 103.

38   Andre Wakefield, *The Disordered Police State. German Cameralism as Science and Practice* (Chicago, 2009), pp. 34–41; Jakob Vogel, 'Felder des Bergbaus. Entstehung und Grenzen einer wissenschaftlichen Expertise im späten 18. und 19. Jahrhundert', *Figurationen des Experten: Ambivalenzen der wissenschaftlichen Expertise im ausgehenden 18. und frühen 19. Jahrhundert*, ed. E. J. Engstrom, V. Hess and U. Thoms (Berlin, 2005), pp. 82–6 (79–100).

39   Wakefield, *The Disordered Police State*, p. 20.

40   Justi, *Staatswirthschaft*, vol. 1, pp. 243–58; Johann Heinrich Jung-Stilling, *Lehrbuch der Staats-Polizey-Wissenschaft* (Leipzig, 1788), pp. 498–500.

41   Wakefield, *The Disordered Police State*, p. 28. On Justi's commitment in the mining sector, see ibid., pp. 93–9, 108–10; Pfeiffer was also involved in the mining sector in the Electorate of Mainz: see Schäfer, *Förderung*, pp. 16–19, 27.

42   Otruba and Steindl, 'Einleitung', p. 38; Stefan Gorißen, *Vom Handelshaus zum Unternehmen. Sozialgeschichte der Firma Harkort im Zeitalter der Protoindustrie (1720–1820)* (Göttingen, 2002), pp. 88–90; Endres, 'Wirtschaftspolitik', pp. 109–10.

43   Klaus-Peter Tieck, *Staatsräson und Eigennutz. Drei Studien zur Geschichte des 18. Jahrhunderts* (Berlin, 1998), pp. 89ff.

44   Jutta Hosfeld-Guber, *Der Merkantilismusbegriff und die Rolle des absolutistischen Staates im vorindustriellen Preussen* (Munich, 1985), p. 207; Tieck, *Staatsräson*, p. 101.

45   Otruba and Steindl, 'Einleitung', pp. 35–8; Gerhard Slawinger, *Die Manufaktur in Kurbayern: die Anfänge der großgewerblichen Entwicklung in der Übergangsepoche vom*

The wish to limit imports of merchandise included luxury goods. Beginning in the 1750s, a number of German states – including the principalities of Bavaria and Mainz, with their Nymphenburg and Höchst manufactories near Frankfurt (Main) – sought to emulate the successes of the Meissen manufactory, which exported Saxon porcelain throughout the Empire and Europe.[46] Governments and cameralists alike appreciated the value of economic sectors where consumer demand was increasing. Tobacco was a case in point; Pfeiffer asserted that, despite its noxious effect, the creation of tobacco manufactories should be encouraged. Not only would this end the importation of the popular consumer product, but also the raw materials could be produced and processed domestically.[47] Governments that backed tobacco manufactories – in Saxony and Bavaria, for example – were driven by similar motivations.[48]

The allocation of resources

In response to numerous complaints about the insufficient quantity and low quality of raw materials many states sought to ensure that manufactures and manufactories were well supplied with adequate vegetable, animal and mineral resources. In some cases, governments prohibited the export of raw materials. Frederick William I's decision to prohibit wool exports in 1718 is a well-known example;[49] identical measures were introduced in Saxony from the sixteenth to the mid-eighteenth century, and in the Habsburg Monarchy following the War of the Spanish Succession.[50] However, the efficacy of such measures was debated. They were difficult to enforce and, because they limited the market, they discouraged the production of these raw materials. Additionally, they risked provoking reprisals, a particularly

Merkantilismus zum Liberalismus 1740–1833 (Stuttgart, 1966), pp. 75ff; Harm-Hinrich Brandt, *Wirtschaft und Wirtschaftspolitik im Raum Hanau 1597–1962. Die Geschichte der Industrie- und Handelskammer Hanau-Gelnhausen-Schlüchtern und ihrer Vorläufer* (Hanau, 1963), pp. 37–41; Marcus Ventzke, *Das Herzogtum Sachsen-Weimar-Eisenach 1775–1783. Ein Modellfall aufgeklärter Herrschaft?* (Cologne/Weimar/Vienna, 2004), pp. 193–203.

46   Mario Monti, *Der Preis des "weißen Goldes". Preispolitik und -strategie im Merkantilsystem am Beispiel der Porzellanmanufaktur Meißen 1710–1830* (Munich, 2011); Slawinger, *Manufaktur in Kurbayern*, pp. 196–208; Ventzke, *Herzogtum*, pp. 213–18.

47   Pfeiffer, *Manufacturen*, vol. 1, pp. 594–601.

48   Christian Hochmuth, *Globale Güter–lokale Aneignung. Kaffee, Tee, Schokolade und Tabak im frühneuzeitlichen Dresden* (Konstanz, 2008), pp. 186–7, 189–94; Slawinger, *Manufaktur in Kurbayern*, pp. 273–300.

49   Tieck, *Staatsräson*, p. 91.

50   Rudolf Forberger, *Die Manufaktur in Sachsen vom Ende des 16. bis zum Anfang des 19. Jahrhunderts* (Berlin, 1958), pp. 97–105.

acute fear in the period following the Seven Years' War. And so instead of banning them outright, authorities were more likely to regulate exports through customs duties.[51] The cameralists advanced similar ideas. While they often recommended banning exports of raw materials,[52] their approach was tempered by the considerations mentioned above. By the end of the eighteenth century, they tended to advocate duties on exported raw materials to give domestic manufactories a competitive advantage over foreign enterprises.[53]

Furthermore, premiums and subsidies stimulated the production of raw materials, especially to supply textile manufactories with a variety of plant and animal products, and plant-based dyes (such as woad and madder). While these policies were not new, they were used more frequently during the second half of the eighteenth century. They were most commonly employed in Saxony for example after 1763, within the political framework of the *Rétablissement*.[54] The measures instituted in Saxony during the last third of the eighteenth century were consistent with arguments proposed by the cameralists. They saw this type of policy as a means to not only supply manufacturing, but also to support the countryside's integration into the monetary economy through the commercialisation of its products.[55]

Theoretical proposals and actual policies also converged in support of manufacturing through the payment of premiums and subsidies. Enterprises were thought to lack sufficient capital to start up and develop. Some writers suggested using capital advances to develop particular sectors (the cloth industry, for example).[56] These advances could be in the form of cash, tools, or raw materials. However, some writers, like Justi, were reluctant to encourage cash investments for the creation of new manufactories, since subsidies often exhausted the state's resources. Justi, along with Pfeiffer, proposed alternatives, such as the allocation of premiums based on production output or the number of looms in operation. Here they referred to the example of Colbert and of Frederick William I.[57] German states did apply these measures, but in an uneven manner. One example was launched on a grand scale in Saxony after

51   See the reports of the 'Landes-Oeconomie, Manufactur- und Commercien-Deputation' in the last third of the eighteenth century: Forberger, *Manufaktur in Sachsen*, pp. 105–7.

52   Johann Albrecht Philippi, *Die wahren Mittel zur Vergrößerung eines Staats* (Berlin, 1753), pp. 70–1; Justi, *Abhandlung*, vol. 1, p. 144–5, who lauds the decision of Frederick William I.

53   Johann Friedrich von Pfeiffer, *Natürliche aus dem Endzweck der Gesellschaft allgemeine Policeiwissenschaft* (Frankfurt a.M., 1779), vol. 1, pp. 215–17.

54   Forberger, *Manufaktur in Sachsen*, pp. 81–93.

55   On Sonnenfels, see Karl-Heinz Osterloh, *Joseph von Sonnenfels und die österreichische Reformbewegung im Zeitalter des aufgeklärten Absolutismus. Eine Studie zum Zusammenhang von Kameralwissenschaft und Verwaltungspraxis* (Hamburg/Lübeck, 1970), pp. 83–4.

56   Johann Friedrich von Pfeiffer, *Lehrbegrif sämmtlicher oeconomischer und Cameralwissenschaften* (1st edn, 1764–65; 2nd edn, Mannheim, 1773–78), vol. IV-2, p. 15.

57   Justi, *Staatswirthschaft*, vol. 1, p. 30; Pfeiffer, *Manufacturen*, vol. 1, p. 179.

1764 by the 'Prämien-Casse', while in Prussia this type of assistance, which was aimed at the silk industry in particular, amounted to a quite modest outlay.[58]

Following Johann Joachim Becher and Paul Jacob Marperger, Justi suggested creating a 'manufacture house' (*Manufakturhaus*) that could encourage production by training workers and loaning entrepreneurs the tools and materials they needed.[59] It could in addition, serve as a warehouse for finished goods, assisting the sale of manufactured products. Sonnenfels advanced a similar proposition by recommending the creation of state-financed local warehouses (*Zwischenniederlagen*), but he stressed that this type of support should be provisional, to lapse once new manufactories were established.[60] Projects of this kind had already been partly developed in Saxony and in Prussia during the late seventeenth and eighteenth centuries. Storehouses were here used strategically, to compensate for fluctuations in the price of raw materials (particularly of wool).[61] However, this example shows the particular difficulties in analysing the relationship between theory and practice in industrial policy. The Saxon cameralist Carl Gottlob Rössig also mentioned the utility of such a *Manufakturhaus*, but made no reference to these experiments and referred only to the writings of Justi. When the Prussian cameralist Georg Friedrich Lamprecht mentioned this measure in 1784 he specified no concrete undertaking, but instead weighed the pros and cons of Justi's theoretical proposal.[62]

The institutional framework of industrial policy

Some cameralist writers considered the institutions that would have to be established to foster manufacturing.[63]

Since the later seventeenth century, cameralist writers agreed that the beauty, quality, durability, and affordability of manufactured goods promoted

---

58 Forberger, *Manufaktur in Sachsen*, pp. 244ff; Hosfeld-Guber, *Merkantilismusbegriff*, pp. 206–7.

59 Johann Heinrich Gottlob von Justi, *Die Grundfeste zu der Macht und Glückseeligkeit der Staaten; oder ausführliche Darstellung der gesamten Policey-Wissenschaft*, 2 vols (Königsberg/Leipzig, 1760–61), 1, pp. 450–8; Justi, *Abhandlung*, vol. 1, pp. 107–19.

60 Sonnenfels, *Grundsätze*, vol. 2, pp. 297–9.

61 Forberger, *Manufaktur in Sachsen*, pp. 82, 106, n. 1; see also Hugo Rachel, 'Der Merkantilismus in Brandenburg-Preußen' (1st edn, 1881), *Preußische Geschichte 1648–1947. Eine Anthologie*, ed. O. Büsch and W. Neugebauer (Berlin/New York, 1981), vol. 2, p. 980 (951–993).

62 Carl Gottlob Rössig, *Lehrbuch der Polizeywissenschaft* (Jena, 1786), pp. 409–10; Georg Friedrich Lamprecht, *Versuch eines vollständigen Systems der Staatslehre mit Inbegriff ihrer beiden wichtigsten Haupttheile der Polizei- und Kameral- oder Finanzwissenschaft. Zum Gebrauch academischer Vorlesungen* (Berlin, 1784), vol. 1, pp. 521–2.

63 Guillaume Garner, *État, économie, territoire en Allemagne. L'espace dans le caméralisme et l'économie politique 1740–1820* (Paris, 2005), pp. 195ff.

their circulation, especially abroad. These observations led to two proposals. First was a recommendation that regulations be adopted defining precise specifications for production processes and standards of quality. Justi laid emphasis upon this idea, both in his treatise on manufactories and manufacturing and in a complementary work on the regulation of production.[64] In these texts he confined his discussion to the regulation of the textile sector and related enterprises (such as the manufacturing of dyes), and included extracts from existing regulations, mainly those adopted in Prussia, but also Saxon regulations concerning blue dye. He also referred to French regulations, which he considered exemplary. Both Justi and other cameralist writers thought highly of Colbert and credited him with originating this style of regulation.[65] The second proposal was the institution of stamping offices (*Beschauanstalten*) that could verify and certify product quality. Here again, this recommendation reflected established practices in not only Prussia, the Habsburg Monarchy and Westphalia,[66] but also in France and England, whose procedures were held up as models. Here we have a clear example where cameralist writers made proposals for the improvement of manufactures that referred back to existing and established practice.

Of interest are the justifications behind this array of regulations. First, it was necessary not only to verify, but above all to certify, product quality. As cameralist writers repeatedly claimed, such endorsements bolstered consumer confidence; a positive reputation boosted a product's success in the marketplace.[67] Another argument was made in response to manufacturers' protests against these measures: manufacturers did not understand their own interests, consequently, it was up to the state to guide them.[68] The historiography has traditionally argued that manufacturers were hostile to regulations and controls that limited their freedom. Often cited is the failure to regulate Prussian silk production in 1766, especially since this failure caused tensions between Krefeld silk manufacturers and the Prussian authorities.[69]

64 Johann Heinrich Gottlob von Justi, *Abhandlung von denen Manufactur- und Fabriken-Reglements zu Ergänzung seines Werkes von denen Manufacturen und Fabriken* (Berlin/Leipzig, 1762).
65 Pfeiffer, *Policeiwissenschaft*, vol. 1, pp. 225–6.
66 Horst Krüger, *Zur Geschichte der Manufakturen und der Manufakturarbeiter in Preussen: die mittleren Provinzen in der zweiten Hälfte des 18. Jahrhunderts* (Berlin, 1958), pp. 88–90; Karl Pribram, *Geschichte der österreichischen Gewerbepolitik von 1740 bis 1860. Auf Grund der Akten*, vol. 1: *1740 bis 1798* (Leipzig, 1907), pp. 76–7; Clemens Wischermann, *Preußischer Staat und westfälische Unternehmer zwischen Spätmerkantilismus und Liberalismus* (Cologne/Weimar/Vienna, 1992), pp. 82ff.
67 Sonnenfels, *Grundsätze*, vol. 2, pp. 253–7.
68 Justi, *Abhandlung von denen Manufactur- und Fabriken-Reglements*, p. 13.
69 Krüger, *Zur Geschichte der Manufakturen*, p. 89; Tieck, *Staatsräson*, p. 112; Peter Kriedte, *Taufgesinnte und großes Kapital. Die niederrheinisch-bergischen Mennoniten und der Aufstieg des Krefelder Seidengewerbes* (Göttingen, 2007), pp. 275–6.

More recently attention has turned to the way that manufacturers worked with local authorities in matters of quality and quantity. In Westphalia canvas manufacturers co-operated with officials charged with stamping offices whose work eased the export of their goods, manufacturers' demands being taken into account by local administrators.[70] Indeed, these regulations and the checking of weights and measures made it possible to reduce the uncertainty typical of the early modern economy, avoiding asymmetries of information between producers and merchants, or between producers and consumers. It is for this reason that such regulations were just as widespread in France and England, examples that the cameralists considered worth following.[71] Cameralist writers defended these institutions not principally in response to the needs of entrepreneurs, but rather to advance the interests of the 'state economy' (*Staatswirtschaft*), which benefited from increased exports.

Nonetheless, we should note that cameralist writers did criticise some of the measures taken by the governments of the German states, notably with regard to monopolies and state-run enterprises. Their stance rested on the principle that freedom and competition in industrial production provided overall benefits. Present in Justi's *Staatswirthschaft*, this theme was developed by Sonnenfels in a 1777 treatise, 'Vom Zusammenflusse'.[72] From Justi onwards, the cameralists were critical of manufactories run by or exploited by the state.[73] First, they harmed a country's inhabitants by exposing them to unfair competition and discouraged investment in their economic sector.[74] Second, such enterprises tended to be badly managed and resulted in wasted public resources (here, critics targeted officials who oversaw manufactories on the state's behalf). Finally, they produced inexpensive, low-quality goods that were difficult to export, although – due to their monopolies – these enterprises were content merely to satisfy domestic demand.

In the later seventeenth and early eighteenth centuries a wave of state-run manufactories were founded and they were, despite these criticisms, widespread by the late eighteenth century, especially in sectors such as porcelain, textiles and glass. In addition to questions of prestige

---

70 In Westphalia, this was still the case in the first half of the nineteenth century: Wischermann, *Preußischer Staat*, pp. 97ff.

71 Philippe Minard, 'L'inspection des draps du West Riding of Yorkshire, ou le jeu des normes au XVIIIe siècle', *Fraude, contrefaçon et contrebande de l'Antiquité à nos jours*, ed. G. Béaur, H. Bonin and C. Lemercier (Geneva, 2006), pp. 621–38; Philippe Minard, 'Facing Uncertainty: Markets, Norms and Conventions in the Eighteenth Century', *Regulating the British Economy 1660–1850*, ed. P. Gauci (Aldershot, 2011), pp. 177–94.

72 Joseph von Sonnenfels, 'Vom Zusammenflusse', id., *Politische Abhandlungen* (Vienna, 1777), pp. 271–342.

73 Justi, *Abhandlung*, vol. 1, pp. 85–7; Osterloh, *Sonnenfels*, pp. 90–1.

74 Jung-Stilling, *Staats-Polizey-Wissenschaft*, pp. 495–6.

and profitability,[75] their proliferation can be explained by the difficulty of mobilising private capital to invest in expanding sectors. The state's willingness to capitalise on rising consumer demand for certain goods was in fact welcomed; Justi recommended the creation of state-run mirror manufactories in response to increased demand, noting the prosperity of such manufactories in the Electorate of Mainz and in Saxony.[76] Furthermore, there are examples of states taking over private enterprises that were in trouble, for instance in Mainz, and in the Habsburg Monarchy.[77] Initially the granting of monopolies should have strengthened enterprises by securing internal markets. In many cases, however, internal demand was insufficient and manufacturers were dependent on exports.[78] If officials frequently misappropriated funds, governments sometimes contracted entrepreneurs to run firms for fixed periods. It was for instance the case when it came to the exploitation of certain mineral resources and in the supplying of armies. For Justi, such a solution was preferable to a direct takeover by the state, but opinions remained divided on this issue.[79]

Cameralist analyses of monopolies were driven by the same concern about competition. They asserted that monopolies should only be temporary expedients, intended to support a new and difficult-to-establish industrial sector, requiring significant initial outlays.[80] However, monopolies were problematic for the same reasons that cameralist writers objected to state-run enterprises.[81] Furthermore, they were also hostile to import prohibitions for similar reasons.[82]

Very many studies have claimed that monopolies and privileges were a basic tool of the Imperial states' industrial policy to the late eighteenth century.[83] This explains the currency of privileges, even in supposedly non-mercantilist

---

75 Monti, *Der Preis*, pp. 62–3; Slawinger, *Manufaktur in Kurbayern*, pp. 19–20.
76 Justi, *Abhandlung*, vol. 2, pp. 424, 465. On the mirror manufactory of Lohr (in the principality of Mainz), see Schäfer, *Förderung*, pp. 66ff.
77 Gerhard Pfeisinger, *Arbeitsdisziplinierung und frühe Industrialisierung 1750–1820* (Cologne/Weimar/Vienna, 2006), pp. 46–7. On the porcelain manufacture of Höchst (principality of Mainz), which was founded in 1746 and came into state's property in 1778, see Rudolf Schäfer, *Die kurmainzische Porzellanmanufaktur zu Höchst a.M. und ihre Mitarbeiter im wirtschaftlichen und sozialen Umbruch ihrer Zeit (1746–1806)* (Frankfurt a.M., 1964), pp. 17–18.
78 Monti, *Der Preis*, pp. 314ff; Slawinger, *Manufaktur in Kurbayern*, pp. 51–2.
79 Justi, *Abhandlung*, vol. 1, p. 89.
80 See for example Pfeiffer, *Staatswirthschaft*, pp. 60–2; Rössig, *Lehrbuch der Polizeywissenschaft*, p. 408; Lamprecht, *Versuch*, pp. 522–3, 677–9.
81 Justi, *Staatswirthschaft*, vol. 1, p. 209; Justi, *Abhandlung*, vol. 1, p. 149.
82 Garner, *État, économie*, p. 192.
83 Heinz Mohnhaupt, 'Fabriksprivileg', *Enzyklopädie der Neuzeit*, ed. Fr. Jaeger, vol. 3 (Stuttgart/Weimar, 2006), cols 753–6.

states like the Duchy of Berg.[84] They also allowed states to attract and retain entrepreneurs from abroad, together with a skilled workforce, for example in the silk and porcelain sectors.[85] For this reason some writers, including Justi, recommended granting various 'liberties', such as fiscal exemptions, financial advances, and freedom of religion.[86] Furthermore, privilege was a means of stimulating competition by weakening the monopoly of a single corporation over an economic sector and giving manufacturers a free hand to conduct their business.[87] Besides, governments did not only grant exclusive privileges but also non-exclusive privileges;[88] in the second half of the eighteenth century, in states like Prussia, privileges had begun to resemble licences (i.e. authorisations to operate businesses).[89] In other words, some governments shared the cameralist goal of promoting and regulating competition between actors within the state, and did not think conferring non-exclusive privileges and licences to be incompatible with this objective.

Cameralism and 'industrial policy': actors, interests and institutions

What has this overview of the relationship between the theory and practice of industrial policy revealed? Let us begin with the divergence between cameralist writers and governments regarding monopolies and state-run manufactories. This split can be explained in two ways. The first concerns the spatial frame of reference; privileges allowed authorities in a territorial state to compete with other states by attracting entrepreneurs and workers, made possible by existing political divisions within the Holy Roman Empire. However, some writers approached the problem from a different perspective, dealing not only

---

84   Stefan Gorißen, 'Interessen und ökonomische Funktionen merkantilistischer Privilegien-politik. Das Herzogtum Berg und seine Textilgewerbe zwischen 16. und 18. Jahrhundert', *Die Ökonomie des Privilegs, Westeuropa 16.–19. Jahrhundert. L'économie du privilège, Europe occidentale XVIe–XIXe siècles*, ed. G. Garner (Frankfurt a.M., 2016), pp. 279–329.

85   Forberger, *Manufaktur in Sachsen*, pp. 39–44; Brandt, *Wirtschaft und Wirtschaftspolitik*, p. 24.

86   Justi, *Grundfeste*, vol. 1, p. 449.

87   Robert Walz, 'Privilegien zum württembergischen Gewerberecht im 18. Jahrhundert', *Das Privileg im europäischen Vergleich*, ed. B. Dölemeyer and H. Mohnhaupt, vol. 1 (Frankfurt a.M., 1997), pp. 435, 445–6 (419–462); Forberger, *Manufaktur in Sachsen*, pp. 236–7; Pribram, *Geschichte der österreichischen Gewerbepolitik*, pp. 13–14; Ventzke, *Herzogtum*, pp. 275–8.

88   Pribram, *Geschichte der österreichischen Gewerbepolitik*, pp. 15, 72–5.

89   Dietmar Willoweit, 'Gewerbeprivileg und "natürliche" Gewerbefreiheit. Strukturen des preußischen Gewerberechts im 18. Jahrhundert', *Vom Gewerbe zum Unternehmen. Studien zum Recht der gewerblichen Wirtschaft im 18. und 19. Jahrhundert*, ed. K. O. Scherner and D. Willoweit (Darmstadt, 1982), pp. 98–9 (60–111); Walz, 'Privilegien', pp. 447–52; Otruba and Steindl, 'Einleitung', pp. 76–9.

with the different territorial states of the Holy Roman Empire, but with the Empire as a whole. They condemned the negative economic consequences of competition among manufactories in the territorial states,[90] just as they criticised the multiple internal customs barriers that paralysed commerce in 'Germany'.

The second reason is more sociological. Cameralist writers referred to a 'common good', to 'general happiness', sometimes addressing future administrators and sometimes an informed public opinion. In Pierre Bourdieu's terminology, they elaborated a discourse of the 'universal' that prioritised the general interest over particular interests, a discourse typical for the specific state's point of view.[91] However, as we have seen, most of these thinkers were academics whose viewpoint was in part different from that of concrete administrative practice, and it was precisely this viewpoint – the primacy of the general interest of the state – that led them to criticise some aspects of industrial policy (for instance monopolies or state-run manufactories). Because of their academic position, they were remote from negotiations between authorities and economic actors, though such negotiations played an important role in the practice of industrial policy.[92] This interaction often led to compromises between particular and general interests, and sometimes to instances of corruption or the embezzlement of funds by privileged entrepreneurs or by those put in charge of the state's manufactories. Yet, at the same time, many cameralist writers understood the state's need to collaborate with economic actors. For instance, Justi suggested establishing a *Manufaktur-Collegium* ('manufactory council') responsible for the direction of this sector, and recommended that it include entrepreneurs who could bring their experience to the table.[93] Indeed, many German states did create institutions like this, inviting economic actors to participate in them because they possessed knowledge that state officials lacked.[94] However, these institutions also often welcomed merchants, which Justi considered ill-advised, since they promoted their own interests over the general interest.[95] The conflict between

90   Johann Friedrich von Pfeiffer, *Grundriß der wahren und falschen Staatskunst*, 2 vols (Berlin, 1778–79), vol. 2, p. 178.

91   Pierre Bourdieu, *Sur l'État. Cours au Collège de France 1989–1992* (Paris, 2012), pp. 55–6, 64–5.

92   See for example Rolf Straubel, *Kaufleute und Manufakturunternehmer: eine empirische Untersuchung über die sozialen Träger von Handel und Großgewerbe in den mittleren preußischen Provinzen (1763 bis 1815)* (Stuttgart, 1995), pp. 397–411.

93   Justi, *Abhandlung*, vol. 1, pp. 119–20; Justi, *Grundfeste*, vol. 1, pp. 458–9.

94   For an overview, see Friedrich Facius, *Wirtschaft und Staat. Die Entwicklung der staatlichen Wirtschaftsverwaltung in Deutschland vom 17. Jahrhundert bis 1945* (Boppard am Rhein, 1959), pp. 11–38.

95   Justi, *Grundsätze der Policeywissenschaft*, pp. 187–8. However, in his remark, Beckmann approves the presence of merchants in such institutions, provided that those merchants have

producers' and states' interests on the one hand and merchants' interests on the other was a common problem, since merchants tended to be hostile to protectionist customs' policies, and to monopolies granted to manufactories and manufacturing. Justi, and later other writers,[96] did not seek a compromise between these conflicting interests, but instead argued for the subordination of merchant interests to the general interest of the state: to the development of manufacturing and manufactories.

Important here is that cameralist writers adopted a perspective partly out of step with the way that economic policy was conceived and implemented. This discrepancy is demonstrated by the fact that some cameralist writers, having transferred into state administration, advanced policies contrary to their previous theories.[97] This change of attitude could be explained in part by dishonesty or opportunism; but also by the move from one field (that of academic and critical discourse) to another (that of administrative practice and of the prince's service), making compromise necessary.

A final question concerns the influence that cameralist discourse on manufactories and manufacturing may have had on the concrete measures authorities put into practice. The historiography offers a range of interpretations, as this influence is sometimes thought to have been quite strong, and otherwise quite weak (in Prussia for example).[98] Justi's writings have also been interpreted in divergent ways, depending on whether the discussion centres on Prussia or on the Habsburg Monarchy.[99] Here, I will confine myself to a few points.

The first concerns the training of officials and officers. Not all were trained in cameral sciences, but studies reveal that a non-negligible percentage of the German states' administrative personnel had attended university lectures in the cameral sciences. In eighteenth-century Prussia, one third of officials studied cameral sciences; although it is also true that law remained the dominant preparatory discipline for administrative posts.[100] Furthermore, the dissemination of works in the cameral sciences was not confined to the university, but passed through other channels as well. Especially important

been educated to the right principles of the commercial science (*Handlungswissenschaft*): ibid., p. 188.

96   For example Pfeiffer, *Staatswirthschaft*, p. 199.

97   This was the case for Justi in Prussia: Wakefield, *The Disordered Police State*, pp. 86–8.

98   Frederick II applied the principles of cameralism, according to Karl Heinrich Kaufhold, '"Wirtschaftswissenschaften" und Wirtschaftspolitik', pp. 66–8. The opposite thesis is formulated by Hosfeld-Guber, *Merkantilismusbegriff*, pp. 221–31, 266–71.

99   See respectively Ernst Klein, 'Johann Heinrich Gottlob von Justi und die preußische Staatswirtschaft', *Vierteljahrschrift für Sozial- und Wirtschaftsgeschichte* 48 (1961), 145–202, and Chaloupek, 'J. H. G. Justi in Austria'.

100   Kaufhold, '"Wirtschaftswissenschaften" und Wirtschaftspolitik', p. 70.

were the patriotic societies that flourished after the Seven Years' War.[101] These institutions, which were central to the German Enlightenment, made cameralist ideas accessible, and we know that some cameralist professors were active in learned societies. Noteworthy here was the Leipziger Ökonomische Sozietät, in which Daniel Gottfried Schreber, who taught cameralism from 1764 at the University of Leipzig, was an active member. The Lautern Society (founded in 1769) was another example of a learned institution where administrators, local officials, and priests mingled. The teaching of cameralism was one of its initiatives and Jung-Stilling was one of its professors of cameral sciences.[102] He offered courses and gave lectures, including some on manufactories and manufacturing, at the Palatinate's 'Economics Society'.[103]

Second, we need to use conceptions of 'government' and 'authorities' carefully, since these were not unitary and homogeneous bodies, especially with regard to manufactories and manufacturing. In the Prussian states, the monopolies held by the state's manufactories were the subject of intense debates between the General Directory and the administration of the province of Kurmark ('kurmärkische Kammer'). The latter criticised the state's 'Lagerhaus' monopoly, while the General Directory bitterly defended it.[104] The years following the Seven Years' War were marked by intense controversies and, after the death of Frederick II in 1786, argument extended to a number of subjects, including freedom of trade, the reform of craft guilds, and monopolies on production.[105] However, it is difficult to ascertain whether members of provincial administrations based their critique of monopolies on cameralist writings. If these works played a role, they were probably not the only factor, because administrators maintained close relationships with merchants and entrepreneurs who also denounced these monopolies.[106]

A third point of debate is the importance given to state or princely revenues, particularly when these revenues were derived from monopolies. Authorities and the princes themselves did not always make 'general happiness' a guiding principle in decision-making and administration. They sought above all to

101   Rudolf Vierhaus, ed., *Deutsche patriotische und gemeinnützige Gesellschaften* (Munich, 1980).

102   Tribe, *Governing Economy*, pp. 99–111.

103   See for example Johann Heinrich Jung-Stilling, 'Bemerkungen über den natürlichen Standpunkt der Fabriken' (1784), *Sachgerechtes Wirtschaften. Sechs Vorlesungen*, ed. G. Merk (Berlin, 1988), pp. 63–90; Johann Heinrich Jung-Stilling, 'Bemerkungen über die wichtigsten Theile der Gewerbepolizei' (1787), *Sachgerechtes Wirtschaften. Sechs Vorlesungen*, ed. G. Merk (Berlin, 1988), pp. 17–41.

104   Krüger, *Zur Geschichte der Manufakturen*, pp. 82–4.

105   Mittenzwei, *Preußen*, pp. 71–100, 135–47; Straubel, *Kaufleute*, pp. 411ff.

106   Rolf Straubel, 'Preußische Kaufleute und Beamte um 1800. Ausgewählte Aspekte ihrer sozialen, wirtschaftlichen und gesellschaftlichen Lage', *Wirtschaft, Wissenschaft und Bildung in Preussen: Zur Wirtschafts- und Sozialgeschichte Preussens vom 18. bis zum 20. Jahrhundert*, ed. K. H. Kaufhold and B. Sösemann (Stuttgart, 1998), pp. 179–90.

increase state revenues from taxes and customs, so that a positive trade balance and the growth of industrial production were sometimes merely secondary goals.[107] Cameralist writers routinely denounced this emphasis on the extraction of fiscal revenues and customs taxes, and these criticisms were sometimes adopted by members of state administrations. In this regard, one can cite the case of the jurist Johann Jakob Moser who served on a number of committees in the Duchy of Württemberg, including the Council of Commerce, founded in 1755. Moser defended a governmental practice that closely tied 'Policey' to the cameral sciences, leading him to reject monopolies on production. Twenty years later, Jakob Friedrich Autenrieth took a similar stance. He entered the duchy's financial administration in 1765 and taught cameral sciences at Karlsruhe from 1777 while retaining his administrative duties. But, as with the case of Moser, when his proposals were applied, they only faintly echoed his theories. In 1787 Autenrieth was relieved of his duties.[108]

Finally, the case of Autenrieth is also interesting because James Steuart's *Inquiry into the Principles of Political Œconomy* (1767) was one of his major theoretical sources. This should remind us that, in spite of cameralism's 'German' particularities, their discourse did not arise in a vacuum, but borrowed from French, English, and Italian theories.[109] For instance, when cameralists claimed that commerce, as well as manufactories and manufacturing, needed 'liberty and protection', they regularly cited the French economist Jean-François Melon and his *Essai sur le Commerce*, published in 1734.[110] Sonnenfels integrated theories elaborated by Forbonnais[111] and the six volumes of the *Berichtigungen berühmter Staats-, Finanz-, Policei-, Cameral-, Commerz- und ökonomischer Schriften dieses Jahrhunderts* published by Pfeiffer between 1781 and 1784 demonstrate his extensive knowledge of eighteenth-century French, English, Spanish, and Italian political economy.[112] This same eclecticism is found in administrators' theoretical references, as an examination of the sources used by the principal actors of the Saxon *Rétablissement* demonstrates.[113] A similar conclusion has been drawn regarding

---

107   Hans Medick, *Weben und Überleben in Laichingen 1650–1900. Lokalgeschichte als Allgemeine Geschichte* (1st edn, 1996; 2nd edn, Göttingen, 1997), pp. 39–44.

108   Medick, *Weben und Überleben*, pp. 53–8.

109   This point has been stressed by Tribe, *Governing Economy*, pp. 134ff.

110   On Melon and this treatise (which was translated in German in 1740), see Simone Meyssonnier, *La balance et l'horloge. La genèse de la pensée libérale en France au XVIIIe siècle* (Montreuil, 1989), pp. 61–72.

111   Tribe, *Governing Economy*, pp. 79, 82; Sandl, *Ökonomie*, pp. 419–22.

112   Sandl, *Ökonomie*, pp. 417–19, 423–6.

113   Christine Lebeau, 'Beispiel eines Kulturtransfers zwischen Frankreich und Sachsen: die neue Regierungskunst in Sachsen zur Zeit des Rétablissements (1762–1768)', *Von der Elbe bis an die Seine. Kulturtransfer zwischen Sachsen und Frankreich um 18. und 19. Jahrhundert*, ed. M. Espagne and M. Middell (Leipzig, 1999), pp. 121–35.

the theoretical culture of the higher officials of the Habsburg Monarchy in the second half of the eighteenth century.[114] To understand the work of German states' administrators, then, it is important to ask whether cameralism was not just one theoretical source among others, including many borrowed from countries perceived to be more economically and industrially developed.[115]

Concluding remarks

1. The grid that opposes state intervention and 'liberalism' is quite inappropriate to the comprehension of cameralist discourse, since cameralist writers elaborated a mix of protection and of promotion of internal competition from the mid-eighteenth century. One of their major concerns was the stimulation and regulation of competition in order to foster the development of manufacturing and manufactories. Consequently the dichotomy of state intervention v. *laissez-faire* does not correspond to the way in which cameralist writers conceived the *Gewerbepolicey*. It is not accidental that their propositions have some theoretical roots in the French 'libéralisme égalitaire', which attempted to render individual freedom and economic competition compatible with state regulation.

2. To what extent does the above illustrate convergences or divergences between cameralism and mercantilism? It is difficult to give a clear answer, since the mercantilism is an indistinct notion.[116] While cameralism differs from English trade-oriented mercantilism of the seventeenth century, it has common features with mercantilist discourse in which the promotion of the industrial production was a central theme.[117] Cameralists promoted the optimum exploitation of the economic resources of the German states, based on intensive relations between the agricultural and the industrial sector. In these theoretical writings as well as in the practice of *Gewerbepolicey* in the German states, one important goal was to keep the money within the state. It does not mean that cameralist writers and administrators had a bullionist conception of wealth: instead, they considered that a sufficient quantity of

---

114   Christine Lebeau, *Aristocrates et grands commis à la Cour de Vienne (1748–1791). Le modèle français* (Paris, 1996), pp. 91–100, 141–52, 193–210.
115   Sonnenfels laments the backwardness of German theoretical economic knowledge in comparison to other European countries (especially France and England): Joseph von Sonnenfels, *Antrittsrede von der Unzulänglichkeit der alleinigen Erfahrung in den Geschäften der Staatswirthschaft* (Vienna, 1764), pp. 12–15.
116   Isenmann, ed., *Merkantilismus*.
117   Reinert, *Translating Empire*, pp. 242ff.

money was needed both in order to allow the extraction of fiscal resources and to finance the investment in industrial production.[118]

From this perspective, the agents involved in industrial production were not primarily the state and its officials – as the rejection of state-run manufactories shows – but individual actors. According to cameralist writers, they could be economically free so long as they were driven by an adequate set of measures and institutions. Hence the tasks and the scope of *Gewerbepolicey* were redefined from the middle of the eighteenth century with the writings of Justi and Sonnenfels: the government had principally to guide the economic activity of subjects in order to guarantee that they conformed to the general interest (or 'general happiness'). Consequently, cameralistic textbooks sought to provide state officials with the necessary knowledge to fulfil this task. Related to manufactories and manufacturing, this knowledge encompassed production processes (the 'technology'), the leading principles of industrial policy, and the concrete measures to be put into practice (such as the regulations regarding quality and quantity).

3. This chapter has highlighted the strong similarities between cameralistic discourse and the concrete measures of *Gewerbepolicey* in the states of the Holy Roman Empire. However, these similarities are not sufficient to demonstrate an immediate influence of the latter on the former, for at least two reasons. First, in many cases cameralist writers elaborated their propositions in reference to measures that had already been put into effect in other states. Second, both cameralist writers and administrators borrowed from various theoretical sources, which were not confined to the German-speaking area. This makes a clear-cut delimitation of strictly cameralist influences rather difficult, because in both cases there was an intensive reception and assimilation of European economic discourses. If we try to analyse the relationship between cameralist discourse and the concrete industrial policy implemented in the German states, we need to use the notion of 'influence' with caution, because it tends to blur the way foreign discourses were received, appropriated, and adapted to the specific context of the German states in the eighteenth century, as well as to the discursive structure of the cameral sciences.

4. Moreover, some cameralist proposals were neglected or rejected, and agreement between cameralist writers and policymakers ceased as soon as the general interest (as promoted by cameralist writers) no longer conformed to the immediate interest of the *Kammer*, or of the ruler. This is an explanation

118 Lars Magnusson, 'Was Cameralism Really the German Version of Mercantilism?', *Economic Growth and the Origins of Modern Political Economy: Economic Reasons of State, 1500–2000*, ed. Ph. R. Rössner (London, 2016), p. 65 (57–71).

for the persistence of such measures and institutions as monopolies or state-run manufactories.[119] One could object that the difference between 'cameralists of the books' and 'cameralists of the bureaus' (Wakefield) should not be overestimated, insofar as some academic cameralists were simultaneously involved in the administration of the German principalities and in the application of *Gewerbepolicey*. Nevertheless, academic discourse and policy-making were anchored in two different fields, with some strong peculiarities. The field of a concrete *Gewerbepolicey* was thus distinguished by negotiations with economic actors and by the differences and rivalries between the various administrations and institutions involved. These formed notable obstacles to a direct application of cameralist theories into practice, which might partly explain the misadventures and the reversals of some cameralists with administrative responsibilities.

119   As only alluded in this essay, customs policy is another case of such as divergence between 'general happiness' and the immediate interest of the *Kammer*.

7

Administrative Centralisation, Police Regulations and Mining Sciences as Channels for the Dissemination of Cameralist Ideas in the Iberian World

ALEXANDRE MENDES CUNHA

Introduction

In the opening pages of the *Elementos da Policia Geral de hum Estado*, translated from French to Portuguese by João Rosado de Villalobos e Vasconcellos and published in Lisbon in 1786, the translator made a dedication to the Lieutenant General of Police of the Portuguese kingdom, Diogo Inácio de Pina Manique, requesting his patronage for the book. The translator tells us in these opening pages that the work does not offer more than the theory behind the rules and principles already put in practice for many years by Pina Manique.[1]

This very interesting book – which introduces itself as fully aligned with the spirit of the actions and establishments created in the field of 'police matters' in Portugal since the mid-eighteenth century – was originally published in French in 1781 by the famous publishing house of Fortuné-Barthélemy De Felice at Yverdon (Switzerland). Because of that, the *Elémens de la police générale d'un Etat* (1781), which does not contain any indication of authorship, would be traditionally assigned to De Felice.

---

1   In the original, in Portuguese: 'Nesta traducção não offereço a V. S. mais do que a theorica daquellas mesmas regras, que V. S. ha tantos annos tem posto em pratica: mais do que a especulação, e as provas daquelles mesmos estabelecimentos, que vemos ha tanto tempo fundados em Portugal com gloria da Nação e authoridade do Ministerio de V. S.' [Eli Bertrand], *Elementos da Policia Geral de hum Estado / traduzidos do Francez, que ao senhor Diogo Ignacio de Pina Manique, offereceo Joao Rosado de Villalobos e Vasconcellos (...)* (Lisbon, 1786 [1781]).

However, as indicated by Marc Weidmann,[2] the author of the book is in fact another important name associated with the Swiss Enlightenment: the pastor and naturalist Eli Bertrand. What went unnoticed however by those who have dedicated themselves to this subject, and this book in particular, is that the *Elémens de la police générale d'un Etat* is actually not an original work of Bertrand, but an abridged and annotated version of a fundamental cameralist work written by Johann Heinrich Gottlob von Justi: *Die Grundfeste zu der Macht und Glückseeligkeit der Staaten; oder ausführliche Vorstellung der gesamten Policey-Wissenschaft* (1760/61) created for Bertrand's teaching purposes.[3] Hence, even if inadvertently, the Portuguese translator, who also added his own notes linking the content of the book to Portuguese reality, assigned an important compendium of cameralist police science (*Policeywissenschaft*) as the foundation for actions and institutions in Portugal during the second half of the eighteenth century.

I will return to the topic of police matters and its regulations in more detail, but this example serves to highlight some of the issues that are central to discussion of the influence of cameralist ideas in Portugal. The first is that we should locate this influence in the field of practice, i.e. the concrete actions carried out in the political, economic and administrative institutions of the contemporary Portuguese state, rather than in the theoretical speculations of academic authors.

A second and more epistemological issue in discussing the international diffusion of cameralist ideas in the eighteenth century (and more broadly, the question of the contemporary diffusion of economic ideas) is that it does not necessarily imply a transmission of a specific and well-defined set of ideas or doctrines as a whole. For receptors in this process, the assimilation or emulation of certain ideas, concepts or practices was more important than learning a system of ideas. Particular ideas were selected because they connected to very specific topics or concrete problems, such as for example the instruments to improve financial administration. What could in a certain context be a specific doctrinal apparatus, like the science of cameralism itself (*Cameralwissenschaft*), could in other contexts end up being assimilated in just some of its dimensions and in response to specific concerns – such as, for example, general concerns with the strengthening of monarchical power, or with the increase of state wealth.[4] The basic condition for understanding

---

2   Marc Weidmann, 'Un pasteur-naturaliste du XVIIIe siècle: Elie Bertrand (1713–1797)', *Revue historique vaudoise* 94 (1986), 102.

3   For detailed analysis of this case, see: Alexandre Mendes Cunha, 'A Previously Unnoticed "Swiss Connection" in the Dissemination of Cameralist Ideas during the Second Half of the 18th Century', *History of Political Economy* 49/3 (2017).

4   We should recall here that these topics of strengthening monarchical power and increasing state wealth were not exclusive to one or another European monarchy between the sixteenth

the diffusion of cameralism in distant places, such as the Iberian world of the eighteenth century, is to pay attention first to the dissemination of "certain cameralist ideas", however presented, and not to a comprehensive system of ideas. Moreover, the spread of cameralism may have taken place through the adoption of a number of these ideas or practices (for example in the different issues covered by police ordinances), without actually being recognised by its receivers as an importation. In certain cases, the ideas assimilated may have been assumed to belong to the same framework held by its receptors, given that the ends were the same, when in fact it these ideas were elements from very different and specific doctrinal frameworks.

Some of these ideas were thus spread in both direct and indirect ways; they might have had an original cameralist connection, or even have been merged with singular ideas produced in other contexts, such as that of France, for example.[5] So we can here talk of dual processes, and not only of a transmission mechanism with well-defined poles of emission and reception.

A third and final point here is the extent to which it makes sense to discuss the influence of cameralism beyond the Germanic world, and in particular in such distant places such as the Iberian world, where as a rule knowledge of German language and literature was virtually non-existent, to note just one of the impediments. There is point in such discussion, however, because it helps clarify important aspects that inform economy, politics and state administration of the Iberian world throughout the period, while also clarifying issues related to cameralism itself. Considering the diffusion of cameralism beyond the Germanic world can help render cameralism itself less defined and unified than traditional literature has presumed. Cameralism is a relatively amorphous set of practices with multiple paths of theorisation, taking shape from the seventeenth century onwards, but only being systematised in the mid-eighteenth century. In the process this matrix would be subject to overlays and diverse influences from other parts of continental Europe (French ones especially). Because of influence or because of the importance of natural law as a common starting point, cameralism as finally systematised in the mid-eighteenth century in the work of authors such as Justi was less 'exclusively' German than often supposed.

In this chapter I first deal with the particular context of Portuguese administration in the years following the Lisbon earthquake of 1755, highlighting the process of political centralisation and reform in the administration

and eighteenth centuries, but rather a broad framework for the European states marked by what came to be generically called 'mercantilism' in the older literature.
5   The French context would provide several ideas that were assimilated by cameralism, either in the way that French police provided elements that would be worked into the German science of police; or in the specific influence of writers such as Montesquieu or Forbonnais on the work of cameralist authors such as Justi and Sonnenfels.

of finance. Then I turn to the importance that police matters assumed in mid-eighteenth century Portugal where the king was taking more direct legislative action. Finally I present a reflection on how mining academies, such as the *Bergakademie* of Freiberg, were important for the spread of cameralist ideas in the Iberian world, providing sources of inspiration for reforms of mining activities in the Portuguese state. In conclusion the importance of enlightened reformism is highlighted as a platform of ideas, including cameralist ideas, when connected to arguments over the practical, eclectic and indirect diffusion of cameralism in the Iberian world.

The centralisation of financial administration in the period following the Lisbon earthquake

In a series of papers published since the later 1980s Ernest Lluch has raised for the first time the issue of the diffusion cameralist ideas in the Iberian context.[6] Lluch analysed in particular the case of the territories linked to the Crown of Aragon (the parts of Spain defeated in the War of Spanish Succession, 1702–14), which, being marked by a distinct economic organisation within the Spanish context, were more particularly open to the assimilation of cameralist ideas in the second half of the eighteenth century. His argument is undoubtedly a highly original one, and has extended understanding of changes in the Spanish economic thought throughout the eighteenth century. Nonetheless it might be noted that Lluch's argumentation has some problematic peculiarities, such as in the definition of cameralist authors, with little distinction being made between very different authors such as Justi, Bielfeld or even Frederick II weakening to some extent his general case.

While there is not space here for a detailed exploration of Lluch's arguments and a review of the Spanish historiography on these issues, it must be said that the primary point of departure for Spanish discussion of the influence of cameralist ideas, sharply contrasting with the Portuguese case,

---

6   Some elements of this discussion were already presented in Lluch's Ph.D. dissertation at the University of Barcelona: 'El pensamiento económico en Cataluña entre el Renacimiento económico y la Revolución Industrial: La irrupción de la escuela clásica y la respuesta proteccionista' (1970). One of the first papers to explicitly address the theme of cameralism in Spain is: Ernest Lluch, 'El déficit de la hacienda pública española y las propuestas del cameralismo', *II Seminario de Historia de la Real Sociedad Bascongada* (Donostia, 1988). An interesting selection of papers were collected in *Treballs sobre cameralisme a Catalunya i a Espanya*, ed. J. M. Gay i Escoda (Barcelona, 1992). But the most important ones for this discussion are: Ernest Lluch, 'El cameralismo más allá del mundo germánico', *Revista de economía aplicada* 4 (1996), 163–75 and Ernest Lluch, *Las Españas vencidas del siglo XVIII: claroscuros de la Ilustración* (Barcelona, 1999); and the only one written in English: Ernest Lluch, 'Cameralism Beyond the Germanic World: A Note on Tribe', *History of Economic Ideas* 5 (1997), 85–99.

is concrete evidence for the translation into Spanish of works by cameralist authors (Justi in particular), as well as the influence of these books on various Spanish authors of the period, particularly in areas linked to the Crown of Aragon and the Basque Country.

This contrast is very important to an understanding of the Portuguese case, since there is no comparable route of translations providing direct evidence of the influence of cameralist ideas in Portugal. There is all the same a strong and concrete similarity with regard to initiatives, actions and institutions created in Portugal in the mid-eighteenth century with other contexts directly informed by the cameralist ideas. As I have argued elsewhere,[7] cameralist influence in Portugal occurred more in indirect than direct ways, and was undoubtedly more informed by practice than by theory.[8]

The administrative reforms orchestrated in the post-Lisbon earthquake under the baton of Sebastião José de Carvalho e Melo, future Count of Oeiras and Marquis of Pombal,[9] offer some of the best measures of this influence. The aftermath of the Lisbon earthquake of 1755 can be associated directly with profound change in political and administrative structures, corresponding largely to a centralisation of monarchical power. It is likewise a moment of retreat from power of the upper courts and councils of the kingdom, and the effective consolidation of the power of state secretariats (created in the 1730s, but until then disputing pre-eminence with the courts and councils). It is also, essentially, the moment of ascension of the State Secretariat of the Kingdom's Affairs, headed by Pombal, which would progressively amass very considerable decision-making powers. Together with this, there is likewise the creation of new specialised administrative (and non-legal) agencies connected to the Secretariat of the Kingdom's Affairs, working as a support for this centralisation process.

As pointed out by José Subtil, it was the earthquake that effectively created the conditions for new political dynamics in Portugal, which would otherwise not have developed as abruptly and comprehensively. Two aspects were

7   Alexandre Mendes Cunha, 'Polizei and the System of Public Finance: Tracing the Impact of Cameralism in Eighteenth-Century Portugal', *The Dissemination of Economic Ideas*, ed. H. D. Kurz, T. Nishizawa and K. Tribe (Cheltenham/Northampton, MA, 2011); Alexandre Mendes Cunha, 'Police Science and Cameralism in Portuguese Enlightened Reformism: Economic Ideas and the Administration of the State during the Second Half of the 18th Century', *European Journal of the History of Economic Thought* 8 (2010), 36–47.
8   This perspective is to some extent connected with (and influenced by) Andre Wakefield, 'Books, Bureaus, and the Historiography of Cameralism', *European Journal of Law and Economics* 19 (2005), 311–20. Wakefield notes the importance of administrative practice for cameralist texts, and how in the eighteenth century cameralists were seen more as practitioners than as theorists.
9   Sebastião José de Carvalho e Melo would be made Marquis of Pombal only in 1769, but this is how he is commonly referred in the historiography.

important here: firstly, the effective destruction of the courtiers' public space and the violent and unexpected interruption of the baroque political practices of the symbolic representation of power; and secondly, the need to create autonomous political control to address the immediate problems created by the catastrophe, achieved with the creation of a crisis cabinet headed by Pombal, enabling him to progressively concentrate power and strengthen administrative centralisation.[10]

The political and administrative innovations introduced in this context tended to enforce governance and establish political control over the old-style juridical and synodal administrative apparatus, until then deeply associated with the corporatist nature of the Portuguese monarchy. This shifted powers from the courts and councils to the state secretariats, in particular to that headed by Pombal. This also produced an opportunity to create different agencies related to the secretariats. The emblematic cases are the Royal Treasury (*Erário Régio*), created in 1761, superseding the functions of the Council of Finance, which would be redefined exclusively as a financial and administrative court of litigation; and the Lieutenancy General of Police, created in 1760, which removed functions from the superior courts and the Senate Chamber of Lisbon. The creation of these institutions reinforced the intendancy system in the political administration of the contemporary Portuguese government.[11]

In the post-earthquake context, a symbol of these shifts of power is the competition for influence between Pombal, whom would finally emerge victorious, and D. Pedro de Bragança Sousa Tavares da Silva Mascarenhas, Duke of Lafões, cousin of the monarch and president of the *Casa de Suplicação*, the High Court of Appeals of the kingdom. This dispute between Pombal and Lafões is itself a clash between the traditional political system of courts and councils and the new administrative scheme that separated political from economic governance and centralised matters in the Secretariat of the Kingdom's Affairs.

In the financial administration, there was a major reorganisation of all practices and procedures with the creation of the Royal Treasury in December 1761. Envisaged as a means for the unification of the revenues and expenditures of the kingdom and its domains, the foundation of the Royal Treasury was a key element in the political centralisation effected by Pombal. Measures were then introduced to improve the collection of royal rights and revenues, until then controlled by the old court of finance of the kingdom, the *Casa dos Contos*. This old court of finance, dating back to the thirteenth century,[12]

---

10   José Subtil, *O terramoto político (1755–1759): memória e poder* (Lisbon, 2007), pp. 11–12.
11   Subtil, *O terramoto*, pp. 93–4.
12   The institution was probably inspired by the *Chambre des Comptes* of Paris, created a few decades earlier.

was responsible for organising and inspecting the revenues and expenditures of the Portuguese state, being characterised by its dispersion over many government offices, by all sorts of abuses on the part of tax collectors, and by delay in the deposit of revenues.

The creation of the Council of Finance (*Conselho da Fazenda*) in the later sixteenth century, to which the *Casa dos Contos* was subordinated (like other institutions, such as the *Casa da India*, warehouses and customs), was the first step in forming an instance of effective financial administration, although still subordinated to the traditional political logic of the councils and law courts. At the time financial accounts were dispersed among various institutions and subordinated to various legal authorities.

The foundation of the Royal Treasury can be seen as an attempt to address these challenges. If the *Casa dos Contos* did little more than compare revenues received against expenditures made by tax collectors, the Royal Treasury was responsible for a substantial innovation. The treasury itself now paid and received everything, dramatically increasing control over accounts and also auditing the use of funds. The institution was internally structured in a very hierarchical fashion, and at its head was Pombal himself. In other words, the principal minister of the King was also the General Inspector of the Treasury.[13] But, more than this, the creation of the Royal Treasury not only replaced the *Casa dos Contos* but also, in parallel, restricted the Council of Finance functions to those connected exclusively to litigation issues, suppressing its deliberative position within finance administration.

Centralised financial administration, with a solid accounting framework, producing an unified financial overview of the Kingdom and its Empire, converging exclusively on the Secretary of State (and General Inspector of the Treasury), together with the suppression of the deliberative functions of the Council of Finance – all this added up to a comprehensive centralisation of Portuguese financial administration.

There is a striking resemblance between these Portuguese reforms and those introduced in the Austrian empire from the 1740s, directly influenced by cameralist ideas. Administrative centralisation in the Austrian lands is closely connected with the name of Count Friedrich Wilhelm von Haugwitz. The final decision on the adoption of the Haugwitz system was taken by the Privy Conference (*Geheime Konferenz*) in January 1748, and began immediately with the establishment of a body for political and financial administration, the *Directorium in publicis et cameralibus*, which had as its function the virtual centralisation of all existing administrative structures in Austria

13   Alzira Teixeira Leite Moreira, *Inventário do Fundo Geral do Erário Régio, Arquivo do Tribunal de Contas* (Lisbon, 1977), pp. x–xii.

and Bohemia, as well as the creation of new agencies subordinated to it, such as the Commission of Police (*Policeyhofkommission*), formed in 1749.[14]

The rise of Haugwitz to a central position in Viennese circles was due in particular to his success with political reform and financial administration for Silesia, securing the attention of Empress Maria Theresa, mediated by her husband, Francis I, and her closest adviser, the Portuguese Manuel Teles, Earl and then Duke of Silva-Tarouca.[15]

Haugwitz was deeply interested (even practically) in cameralist doctrines.[16] He was directly influenced by authors such as Wilhelm von Schröder, to whom he made frequent reference in regard to the importance of well-structured financial administration based on a trained and loyal bureaucracy overseen by centralised direction. In his famous text proposing reforms in Silesia, the *Notata*, he had already insisted for example that a 'well-arranged financial administration is the soul of the state'.[17] One of the central points of the reforms in Silesia, which would later be incorporated by the central government in Vienna, involved the separation of political and economic from judicial structures, aiming at the strengthening of the administration of finances and improving arrangements for the collection of revenue, but at the same time representing a direct confrontation with the complex inter-penetration between administrative and judicial powers (one of the pillars of feudal corporate particularism) prevalent under the Ancien Régime.[18]

Although there is a substantive historiographical discussion on the extent to which the reform process in the Austrian Empire at the time of Maria Theresa (1740–80) was capable of effecting political, administrative and financial centralisation in the empire, and even the idea that in some respects *de facto* centralisation would only be achieved during the reign of Joseph II (1780–90), it is intentionality and ideas that are more important here than the results themselves. In these terms, it is not difficult to realise that already in the 1740s Haugwitz's plans represented a specific Austrian plan to promote the centralisation of political power, based on a process of reform, institution building, and bureaucratisation inspired by cameralist ideas.

It is possible to select key features of the Austrian reforms of the 1740 and 1750s for comparison with the Portuguese experience. First, there is the separation of political and economic administration from the administration

14 Franz Szabo, *Kaunitz and Enlightened Absolutism 1753–1780* (Cambridge, 1994), pp. 77–9, and Ulrich Adam, *The Political Economy of J. H. G. Justi* (Bern, 2006), pp. 28–31.
15 Anton Victor Felgel, 'Haugwitz, Friedrich Wilhelm', *Allgemeine Deutsche Biographie* 11 (1880), pp. 66–9, http://www.deutsche-biographie.de/pnd118773437.html?anchor=adb, accessed 5 Feb. 2016; Szabo, *Kaunitz*, pp. 74–5.
16 He was, for example, the responsible for Justi coming to Vienna for a position at the *Theresianum* (see Adam, *The Political Economy*, pp. 26–7).
17 Szabo, *Kaunitz*, p. 75.
18 Szabo, *Kaunitz*, pp. 75–6.

of justice as a central axis in the centralisation process. In Austria, this was progressively achieved by the strengthening of the *Directorium* orchestrated by Haugwitz; in the Portuguese case this occurred through the centralisation orchestrated by Pombal around the Secretariat of the Kingdom's Affairs following the earthquake, having suppressed the opposition of the Duke of Lafões.[19]

A second aspect for comparison is related to the centralisation of the administration of finance in Austria, which went beyond centralisation of economic governance under the *Directorium*, subordinating the functions of the Treasury (*Hofkammer*) itself.[20] There are many possible associations with the Portuguese case in these aspects, with the complete reform of the financial administration of the kingdom after the creation of the Royal Treasury, obliterating the functions of the Council of Finance and promoting a direct subordination of the Treasury to Pombal's Secretariat of the Kingdom's Affairs, as explained above.

A third aspect is the attention to training specialised staff and the orientation of the educational system to state interests. In the Austrian context this already began to take shape with the creation of the *Theresianum* in 1746, and its connection with the idea of preparing the children of the monarchy's elite for future positions within the state (to which would be added later other institutions such as the Theresian Military Academy, founded in 1751, and the Oriental Academy, founded in 1754). This process related to the effort on the part of the monarchy to wrest control of the educational system from the Jesuits, one of its first battlefronts opening with the progressive resumption of control over the censorship process on the new commission (*Zensurkommission*). In 1751 this would have as its president Gerard van Swieten, the personal physician to the Empress, accompanied by Justi and Karl von Martini, although at first still having two Jesuits in the group.[21] The most important reform, however, was related to the changes introduced by Swieten at the University of Vienna, which gradually removed the influence of Jesuits over secular colleges and promoted a comprehensive curricular reform, based on the specific interests of the state. This directly corresponds with the Portuguese case, which under the baton of Pombal promoted the expulsion

---

19   Not in terms of cross-influences, but simply of presenting the similarities in their positions as *de facto* Prime Ministers, see the analysis done by H. M. Scott comparing Kaunitz to Pombal: Hamish M. Scott, 'The Rise of the First Minister in Eighteenth-century Europe', *History and Biography: Essays in Honour of Derek Beales*, ed. T. C. W. Blanning and D. Cannadine (Cambridge, 1996).

20   Haugwitz even suggests that the Treasury could be completely incorporated into the *Directorium*, which only did not happen because of the Treasury's duties relating to Hungary, which was kept outside the scope of the reforms then implemented (Szabo, *Kaunitz*, p. 78).

21   Charles Ingrao, *The Habsburg Monarchy, 1618–1815*, 2nd edn (Cambridge, 2000), p. 166–7.

of the Jesuits from Portugal and its empire in 1759 (raising myriad issues, but having a direct impact on state control of the educational system). Laicisation and the direct influence of state decision-making in these matters took shape in the 1760s, and an important part of this process is the publication of *Cartas sobre a educação da Mocidade* (1760), written by Antonio Ribeiro Sanches (a close friend of Swieten) and praising the virtues of the experimental method in science education and the contribution of mathematics to logical thinking. This had a direct impact on the creation of the Royal School for Noblemen (*Real Colégio dos Nobres*) by Pombal in 1761, and also some time later in the substantive educational reform process conducted at the University of Coimbra in 1772.

Pombal had the opportunity of being closely acquainted with the reforms initiated in Austria in the late 1740s during the period that he spent in Vienna as a Portuguese diplomatic envoy – although formally linked to a very specific mission: obtaining the support of Austria in a dispute with the Vatican. This period allowed him to establish many connections and receive influences that certainly can be related to his political actions a few years later in Portugal, beginning a comprehensive reform of the political and administrative apparatus of the kingdom following the 1755 earthquake.

Although the influences probably guiding Pombal's reforms are often associated by Portuguese historiography with seventeenth-century sources,[22] it is important to recognise that, based on examples gathered and ideas shared with his closest partners in the period, the Austrian influence (and by extension, some cameralist perspectives) can also be included in this framework of influences guiding his political and economic actions.

Pombal was in Vienna between 1745 and 1749, in 1745 marrying Eleanore Ernestine, Countess of Daun, a young woman from an important noble imperial family, daughter of Heinrich Reichard Lorenz, Count Daun and Violante Maria Josepha von Boymont, Countess of Payrsberg. This ensured him privileged entry to the Viennese court, and some proximity to the Empress Maria Theresa, which was of vital importance for his diplomatic mission.

Among the witnesses to the marriage were names close to the political core of the empire and the Empress's inner circle, such as (on the groom's side) the Count of Silva-Tarouca, the Empress' main intimate adviser of the period and chairman of the Flemish Council (*Niederländischen Rates*), or (on the bride's side) the Count Rudolf Colloredo, Imperial Vice-Chancellor (*Substitutes des Reichsvizekanzlers*).[23]

---

22   Pombal's influences are usually credited to French authors such as the Duke of Sully or Jean-Baptiste Colbert as well as to some English sources, such as the political arithmetic of William Petty.
23   Maria Alcina Ribeiro Correia, *Sebastião José de Carvalho e Mello na corte de Viena de Áustria: elementos para o estudo da sua vida pública, 1744–1749* (Lisbon, 1965), p. 76.

Pombal received daily visits from important Viennese personalities. Although there is no record of the matters discussed at each meeting, we can form an idea of the circles in which Pombal moved from the list of the persons who visited him throughout the period, and which were preserved in his personal documents.[24] Among these names we can for example find the aforementioned personal physician of the Empress, who was also Pombal's physician, the Dutch-Austrian physician Gerard van Swieten (a friend of António Nunes Ribeiro Sanches and a future collaborator of Pombal in educational reforms for the kingdom, both of them Herman Boerhaave's disciples). There are also individuals to whom he was close because of family ties, like his wife's cousin, Count Leopold Joseph von Daun, already at that time one of the most important military commanders of the empire and one of those directly responsible for subsequent reforms to the Austrian army, having been appointed by the Empress as the first head of the Theresian Military Academy (*Theresianische Militärakademie*), created in 1751.

Pombal's guest books from that period list many other frequent visitors who may have provided him with first-hand information about the political transformation of the Austrian empire. A good example here is Karl Maximilian, Prince of Dietrichstein, *Imperial Kämmerer, Oberst-Erblandmundschenk* and, between 1745 and 1754, *Oberst-Hofmarschall* of Emperor Francis I, Maria Theresa's husband; or the "Count" of Khevenhüller, probably a reference to Prince Johann Joseph Khevenhüller-Metsch, who in 1742 was appointed Court Marshal (*Obersthofmarschall*), rising to Chamberlain (*Oberstkämmerer*) to the imperial couple in 1745 and head of the Court Household (*Obersthofmeister*) in 1760. Johann Joseph's son, Johann Sigismund Friedrich, 2nd prince of Khevenhüller-Metsch, was very close to Pombal in Lisbon years later, while serving between 1756 and 1760 as a diplomatic envoy in Portugal. Less frequent meetings also took place with leading decision-makers for the empire, such as Count Philipp Ludwig Sinzendorf, Count Alois Raymund Harrach, Count Philipp Joseph Kinsky or Wenzel Anton, Prince of Kaunitz-Rietberg and who would be central in the reform in Austria after the Seven Years' War.

During the four years that Pombal lived in Vienna, in the period immediately prior to his ascension to the central administration of the Portuguese state, he met almost on a daily basis either in connection with their public duties or with his personal life many who were directly involved in the substantive political, administrative and economic reform of the Austrian empire. Although there is at this time no direct evidence of conversations, or ideas that may have been exchanged at these meetings, the existence of this network is suggestive of a strong connection between his Viennese experience

---

24 Biblioteca Nacional de Lisboa (Portuguese National Library) – BNP, *Col. Pombalina*, cod. 718; Correia, *Sebastião José*, pp. 81–5.

and his understanding, more practical than theoretical, of Austrian cameralist ideas that would, together with other sources of influences, guide the reforms he conducted in the Portuguese government a few years later.

Police regulations and the legislative action of the king

Another institutional example of great interest is the Lieutenancy General of Police, created by Pombal in 1760. The law establishing this agency states that experience had demonstrated the impossibility of maintaining the link between the judiciary and the exercise of police in the kingdom, and placed the new body under the immediate and exclusive supervision of the Secretariat of the Kingdom's Affairs. Its main inspiration was French, as with many other similar institutions created in Europe: it was primarily focused on crime and the maintenance of mores and public order.[25]

Nevertheless, this new institution rapidly came to include a wide range of functions, such as being the disciplinary and supervisory instance for other bodies of state administration, the conduct of population censuses, surveys on sanitation, movement of people and also supporting related activity in the Secretariat of the Kingdom's Affairs, including surveys of geography, production, commerce and trade.[26]

One of the main results in this regard was the Portuguese population censuses in 1776 and 1798, conducted by the Lieutenancy General of Police under the direction of Pina Manique, who as Secretariat of Overseas Affairs was also involved in the first comprehensive population count in the Brazilian colony. There is an interesting similarity between the survey formats and data processing followed in Portugal with the census carried out in Spain under the command of Pedro Pablo Abarca de Bolea, the Count of Aranda in 1768–9. This is particularly interesting because this Spanish census was an important source of information for Aranda's reforms during his period as president of the Council of Castile, which is seen as one of the key elements of cameralist influence in Spain, as analysed by Lluch.[27]

However, in addition to practices associated with institutions such as the Lieutenancy General of Police, it is important to understand the specific

---

25 'Alvará, com força de Lei, em que se determina a Polícia da Corte, para conseguir a pública paz da mesma Corte e Reino', 25 June 1760, in António Delgado da Silva, *Collecção da Legislação Portugueza desde a ultima compilação das Ordenações* (Lisbon 1830), pp. 731–7.
26 Subtil, *O terramoto*, pp. 99–100.
27 Lluch, *Las Españas vencidas*, pp. 129–62; Dauril Alden, 'The Population of Brazil in the Late Eighteenth Century: A Preliminary Study', *Hispanic American Historical Review*, 43 (1963) and Joaquim Veríssimo Serrão, *A população de Portugal em 1798. O censo de Pina Manique* (Paris, 1970).

content of policies, and in particular the nature of the legal apparatus throughout Pombal's period. In this regard it is obvious that there was in Portugal from the 1750s onwards an increasing attention to police matters relating to police regulations and other legal instruments, including a variety of topics such as urban planning, food supply, public safety and the suppression of vagrancy, road construction, river works, public health, mining and forestry, separation of educational institutions from the clergy, issues relating to the discipline and increase of the workforce, population growth, and measures related to the indigenous populations in Brazil.[28] The emphasis on the interdependence between population size and the progress of economic activities, or the country's prosperity and its importance at the international level, gave particular significance to issues relating to population, in particular in relation to colonial territories, a typical and prominent theme for police matters.

This helps us understand how police matters came to constitute a central focus of legislative action on the part of the direct will of the sovereign, i.e. legal documents emanating directly from the king-legislator, mediated by the Secretariat of the Kingdom's Affairs. This is related to the separation of political and administrative power from the functions of the courts and councils of the kingdom. A key moment in this process of separation and centralisation of powers was when Pombal, having become State Secretary, decreed that all courts should submit any query or legal proposition to the king to the Secretariat of the Kingdom's Affairs.[29]

There is an interesting example reflecting a broadly cameralist agenda in a legal document from this period, which establishes a major reorientation of policies regarding the indigenous populations of Brazil. The primary purpose of the new strategy was the incorporation of native populations into 'white society', ending slavery and servile bondage and turning them into active workers, ensuring territorial settlement, territorial defence and a stimulus to the economy and the growth of state revenue.

Royal decrees (*alvarás*) from 1755 freed the indigenous populations of Brazil, encouraging marriages and promoting settlements. The culmination of this process was the legal enforcement by the king of a large collection of rules and regulations from 1757 called the 'Directory to be observed in the Indian settlements of Pará and Maranhão',[30] which had been carefully

---

28   For an analysis of the importance of police matters in the Portuguese legislation of the period, see: Airton L. Cerqueira-Leite Seelaender, *Polizei, Ökonomie und Gesetzgebungslehre: ein Beitrag zur Analyse der portugiesischen Rechtswissenschaft am Ende des 18. Jahrhunderts* (Frankfurt a.M., 2003).

29   Subtil, *O terramoto*, p. 99.

30   'Diretório que se deve observar nas Povoações dos Índios do Pará, e Maranhão, enquanto Sua Majestade não mandar o contrário', 3 May 1757, in: Silva, *Collecção*, pp. 507–30.

drafted by Pombal and his brother, Francisco Xavier Mendonça Furtado,[31] governor of the territories of Pará and Maranhão, and which listed a series of measures and set out a specific rationale that deserves mention here.

What is noticeable here is the similarity with cameralist arguments, such as those articulated by Johann Joachim Becher. Pombal may possibly have had contact with Becher's ideas in Vienna – the idea that economic development and population size are directly connected with the level of food supplies and subsistence. This is one of the points stressed by Joseph Schumpeter in his analysis of Becher's ideas, that popular consumption is the soul of economic life.[32]

The 'Directory to be observed in Indian settlements' presents a logic that goes beyond the simple positive association of a large population with the wealth of a kingdom. There are here some elements that can be associated with different ideas, such as late mercantilism, political arithmetic or cameralism – all of which share the centrality of state in the direction of economic action, part of the eclectic panorama of ideas that directly or indirectly inspired the policies implemented by the Portuguese colonial administration during the second half of the eighteenth century.[33]

With regard to the 'populationist argument', it is also important to note that this broadly corresponds to the change of perspective regarding the problem of population from roughly the seventeenth century onwards: from a dissociation of the threat of overpopulation (as in Plato or Aristotle) to a progressive association with the practical economic problems of countries 'poor in goods but rich in possibilities', the population problem becoming one of underpopulation. This was particularly true for some Germanic states, or for Spain, both of which had experienced the concrete problem of depopulation.

---

31   The instructions received by Mendonça Furtado to guide his government included explicit orders of stimulating the creation of settlements and the enlargement of the population, with the final and direct objective of increasing royal incomes. See: Marcos Carneiro de Mendonça, *A amazônia na era pombalina: correspondência do governador e capitão-general do estado do Grão-Pará e Maranhão Francisco Xavier de Mendonça Furtado: 1751–1759*, 2nd edn (Brasília, 2005), vol. I, p. 170.

32   Joseph Schumpeter, *History of Economic Analysis (with a New Introduction)* (Oxford, 1996 [1954]), pp. 283–4. A key term for this discussion is *Nahrung*, and more specifically *Nahrungsstand*, as frequently used by Justi in his considerations of *Policeywissenschaft*. Literally, *Nahrungsstand* refers to the level or state of nourishment, or livelihood – a 'state of subsistence', primarily in reference to the question of supplies, but also, as used by Justi, designating different dimensions, associated for example with the labouring classes, subsistence and commerce in general. More than this, in line with the ideas of authors such as Ulrich Adam on Justi, or Schumpeter on Becher, the concept of *Nahrung* is also important for the understanding of the place of cameralist ideas within the history of economics, because it conveys a conception of the 'demand side'.

33   José Luís Cardoso and Alexandre Mendes Cunha, 'Discurso Econômico e Política Colonial no Império Luso-Brasileiro (1750–1808)', *Tempo* 17 (2011), 69.

The English populationists of the seventeenth and early eighteenth centuries, such as William Petty, tended to consider the rapid increase of population as a motor, or a condition and symptom, of economic development, and not as a risk of overpopulation.[34] From his time as ambassador in London Pombal was familiar with the writings of Petty and with his political arithmetic;[35] Pombal himself considered these ideas, along with the idea of 'state economy', to be central elements of his political thought.[36]

Nevertheless, the general argument of the *Directory* goes beyond the exclusive terms of Petty's reflection, and shows specific concern for the link between population and access to means of production and economic activity, something that is similar to cameralist ideas.[37] For example, the document presents a discussion of the links between the greatest happiness of a country and the plentifulness of supplies,[38] the first building block for population increase and state wealth. There is also emphasis that the rationale of this process is that 'in order to conduct any Republic to a complete happiness, any means would be more effective than the introduction of commerce because it enriches peoples, civilises nations, and consequently makes powerful the monarchies'.[39] The cultivation of the land is thus understood as the foundation of commerce, but at the same time connected, via the stimulus to

34 Schumpeter, *History*, pp. 250–8.
35 Pombal had copies of William Petty and other various English and French mercantilist authors in his extensive London library (see: Sebastião José de Carvalho e Melo, *Escritos económicos de Londres (1741–1742)*, ed. J. Barreto (Lisbon, 1986), pp. 167–77). Among Pombal's remaining personal papers was also preserved an interesting working manuscript with the title: 'Differents Essais sur l'Arithmetique politique, dont les titres sont aux pages suivantes, Par le Chevalier Guillaume Petty' (Londres, 1699), composed of partial translations into French of five treatises of Petty (version of: Petty, *Five Essays in Political Arithmetick*, London, 1687), BNP, Col. Pombalina, cod. 168.
36 Antonio Cesar de Almeida Santos, 'Luzes em Portugal: do Terremoto à Inauguração da Estátua Equestre do Reformador', *Topoi* (Rio de Janeiro) 12 (2011), 79.
37 See note 32 above on the concept of *Nahrungsstand*. It is also worth noting that there are similarities not only with the cameralist tradition, but also, for example, with Forbonnais' *Elemens du commerce* of 1754, translated into Portuguese in 1766 by a person close to Pombal in the period (on the Portuguese translation, see Monica Lupetti and Marco Guidi, 'Translation as Import Substitution: The Portuguese Version of Veron de Forbonnais's *Elemens du commerce*', *History of European Ideas* 40 (2014), 1151–88). This similarity with Forbonnais, moreover, is suggestive of a certain degree of contact between French ideas and elements of cameralist doctrine. Joseph von Sonnenfels used Forbonnais in his *Grundsätze der Polizei, Handlung und Finanzwissenschaft* of 1765–67 (on this, see: Keith Tribe, *Governing Economy: the Reformation of German Economic Discourse, 1750–1840* (Cambridge, 1988), pp. 87–90). This leads us again to the question of how these sources and others may have been eclectically combined according to the reformist intentions of the Portuguese government during the second half of the eighteenth century.
38 'Diretório', §20.
39 'Diretório', §36.

the production of genres such as cotton, to the necessary basis for the future introduction of manufactories in the colonies.[40]

The *Directory* continues, stating that all this should however converge naturally, so that indigenous peoples must also be freed from the 'diabolical abuse of not paying tithes' (i.e. 'the tenth part of all fruits that grow and of all goods purchased, without exception') owed to the Portuguese monarch.[41] And it adds, again in relation to the state, that 'freedom is the soul of trade', but that Indians, given their 'rusticity and ignorance, needed the state's protection. This, however, does not constitute an infringement of freedom, since such protection is addressed to 'the common good of the state and the particular usefulness of these traders'.[42]

The increase of farming and its links with commerce and manufacturing is also clearly expressed in the *Directory*, being a direct result of the latter and even a mechanism for the attraction of farmers, traders and workers, and the encouragement of the marriage of Indians with white people,[43] ensuring advantage and dignity to their offspring. The general rationale of the document is emphasised at the end, proceeding from the growth of faith, the civilisation of the Indian and the promotion of the common good of vassals through increased farming and agriculture and the introduction of commerce, finally achieving 'the establishment of the opulence and total happiness of the State'.[44]

Attention to police matters beyond the logic of French police, approaching elements that can be associated with the reasoning of the Germanic science of police, would recur in the second half of eighteenth-century Portugal. The translator of the *Elémens de la police générale d'un Etat* makes a direct association with the actions of Portuguese police authorities noted above, without suspecting that what seemed to be a French book was actually an abridged translation of a cameralist compendium of *Policeywissenschaft* written by Justi (*Die Grundfeste*). The same can be said of the popularity that the French translation of Justi's previous book on this theme – *Die Grundsätze der Polizeywissenschaft*, in 1756 – had enjoyed in Portugal. The influence of the French translation of Justi's *Grundsätze* – *Eléments généraux de police*, in 1769 – can be traced through its presence in many private libraries of important statesmen of the period; or, for example, in the importance that the book would have in the chair of Homeland Law (*Direito Pátrio*) created after the reform of the University of Coimbra, and in the lectures by its professor, Pascoal José de Melo Freire. In Freire's teaching and reflections

40   'Diretório', §24.
41   'Diretório', §27.
42   'Diretório', §37.
43   'Diretório', §80.
44   'Diretório', §95.

economic issues were clearly marked by natural law; it is easy to find frequent references to writers such as Justi and his 'elements of police'. This would certainly had an effect on some of the students that studied at the Faculty of Law of the University of Coimbra at that time, remembering that this faculty was the traditional common point of access to all the superior positions in state administration for the Portuguese kingdom.

Mining sciences and the *Bergakademie*

The mining sciences played an important role in cameralism, and it can be said that the way they were developed, taught and used in the Germanic world of the eighteenth century made them an integral part of cameralist knowledge. All the same, this does not lend mining issues any kind of prominence in the more theoretical realms of cameralist knowledge. The importance of mining sciences to cameralism was more practical than theoretical, being closely related to the linkage of this technical knowledge to taxation, particularly in those contexts where the revenues and fiscal possibilities of territorial states were linked to mining activity.

Major improvements and advances of the sciences were oriented towards practical applications for mining activities and the increase of state revenues, centred upon the traditional mining areas of the Holy Roman Empire. Important for such developments were the establishment of mining schools, which were not only technical institutions but also significant centres for the production and dissemination of cameralist ideas, especially throughout Saxony, Prussia, Hungary and Bohemia.

This links readily to the Iberian world, and in particular the Portuguese case. Mining activity had a significant impact upon Portuguese state revenues, emphasising the relationship between economic knowledge and practical knowledge. The wealth of the kingdom depended after all on the extraction of gold and diamonds in Brazil. This factor plays a very important part in the influence of cameralism on Portuguese–Brazilian economic thought.

There was a close connection between cameralism and the idea that the natural sciences were sources of useful knowledge, especially chemistry and mineralogy. This was not a matter of what we would now call fundamental (or pure) science, but predominantly of applied scientific knowledge. Cameralism created a junction between the sciences of mining and metallurgy and the practical and applied contents of chemistry and mineralogy (among others); it also created a connection between knowledge related to the operation and administration of the mines on the one hand, and taxation and state regulation on the other. The establishment of institutions such as the *Bergakademie* of Freiberg directly reflected the accumulation of such knowledge, where advances in the natural sciences were connected to fiscal concepts, and specific ideas about administration and the improvement of state economy.

As pointed out by Andre Wakefield,[45] the establishment of the *Bergakademie* of Freiberg was one part of a wider movement in which the production of academic knowledge was treated as one component of a fiscal logic and as a strategy to generate state revenue; this also included the revenues generated by attracting wealthy foreign students to the cities in which these institutions were located. Preparation of the local elite for functions in state financial administration was a deliberate objective in the creation of the academy, and determined the nature of the knowledge that would be produced and disseminated within the institution, explicitly linking the fields of chemistry, mineralogy and 'montanistic' studies to cameralist principles. The original purpose of the mining academy was this combination of subjects, more than any formal education of 'mining engineers'.[46]

We can here identify a path of transmission of cameralist ideas to the Iberian world through the careers of particular men of science who, for some reason, had direct ties to the German academic environment, and who in the course of their scientific careers also became closely involved in state administration. During the second half of the eighteenth century a significant number of students from Spain and Portugal attended the *Bergakademie*, including two individuals who were actually born in Brazil but who were enrolled at Freiberg as Portuguese natives.[47]

After studying at the *Bergakademie* many of them pursued careers in mining and mineralogy, sometimes becoming recognised as important men of science, and in some cases acquiring administrative or political functions. There has in the past been a tendency to interpret these careers as examples of men of science being diverted into political life, abandoning science for politics; a conception that has been particularly influential in the case of these Portuguese/Brazilian students. We need however to understand that this shift from the world of science to that of politics and administration was quite normal in the eighteenth century. Indeed, a career that followed this path represented an ideal of someone well trained in mining sciences and cameralist knowledge, for which knowledge of the natural world, the administration of state revenues and the practice of state functions were perfectly compatible.

45 Andre Wakefield, 'The Fiscal Logic of the Enlightened German Science', *Making Knowledge in Early Modern Europe: Practices, Objects, and Texts, 1400–1800*, ed. P. H. Smith and B. Schmidt (Chicago, 2007), and Andre Wakefield, *The Disordered Police State: German Cameralism as Science and Practice* (Chicago, 2009).

46 Wakefield, 'The Fiscal Logic', p. 279.

47 For a list of students enrolled at the *Bergakademie* from 1766 to 1865, see: Bergakademie, *Festschrift zum hundertjährigen Jubiläum der Königl. sächs. Bergakademie zu Freiberg, am 30. Juli 1866* (Dresden, 1877).

Useful knowledge of the natural world, application of this knowledge to the increase in state revenues, and concrete and holistic concerns with administration and government of the state economy represented, in this sense, the typical ideal of a good cameralist (even if in practice the execution of all this was imperfect).[48] It is exactly these ideas that we see transplanted to the Iberian world and its American colonies through the careers of some of these men.

Among the prominent Spanish *Bergakademie* alumni are the brothers Juan José and Fausto Delhuyar, the first of whom was the discoverer of tungsten, and the second the founder of the Royal Mining Seminary (*Real Seminario de Minería*) of Mexico. They enrolled in the *Bergakademie* in 1778, but not alone. Throughout the second half of the eighteenth century various other Spanish natives also studied there. The Delhuyar brothers benefited from initiatives of the Royal Basque Society of Friends of the Country (*Real Sociedad Bascongada de Amigos del País*), like the Seminary of Vergara, founded in 1776.[49] This society was an important centre for the reception of police science in Spain as studied by Lluch,[50] being created in 1765 by the Count of Peñaflorida, which was actually the first Spanish student enrolled at the *Bergakademie*.[51] It would be interesting to explore any cameralist connections between the *Bergakademie* and the Seminary of Vergara, but to do so would take us beyond the scope of this essay.

Nonetheless, the Delhuyar brothers draw attention to the most striking example of a direct application of the *Bergakademie* as a model cameralist mining academy: the foundation of the Royal Mining Seminary of Mexico in 1792. The influence of cameralist doctrines on its founder Fausto Delhuyar would still be apparent even in his writings of the early nineteenth century, dealing with mining and its influence on agriculture, industry, population and civilisation, or with issues such as the minting of coin.[52]

Regarding the Portuguese *Bergakademie* alumni, one of the important names is the Brazilian-born José Bonifácio de Andrada who, years later, would be one of the founding fathers of the Brazilian nation. Like many of his colleagues, after his experience at the *Bergakademie* he pursued important

---

48   See Wakefield's discussion of this involving 'bad cameralists and disordered police states': Wakefield, *The Disordered Police State*, pp. 1–25.

49   On the importance of the Royal Basque Society of Friends of the Country, and the Seminar of Vergara, for the Spanish history of economic thought, see: Jesús Astigarraga, *Los ilustrados vascos: ideas, instituciones y reformas económicas en España* (Barcelona, 2003).

50   Lluch, *Las Españas vencidas*, p. 160.

51   Bergakademie, *Festschrift*, p. 226.

52   See Fausto Delhuyar, *Memoria sobre el influjo de la minería en la agricultura, industria, problacion y civilizacion de la Nueva-España en sus diferentes épocas …* (Madrid, 1825); Fausto Delhuyar, *Indagaciones sobre la amonedacion en Nueva España sistema observado desde su establecimiento, su actual estado y productos …* (Madrid, 1818).

academic and administrative functions related to mineralogy and mining, becoming, for example, professor of Metallurgy at the University of Coimbra and Superintendent of Mines and Metals of the Portuguese Kingdom. However, the clearest connection between mining sciences and the cameralist knowledge can be found in the career of another Brazilian-born student of the *Bergakademie*: Manuel Ferreira da Câmara.

Câmara was born in Minas Gerais, Brazil, around 1764. He preliminary studies were completed in his homeland, and in 1783 he enrolled as a Law student at the University of Coimbra. In the following year he also began to study Philosophy, from which he became familiar with the natural sciences. Coimbra's Faculty of Philosophy was a direct product of the educational reforms carried out by Pombal from 1772, functioning as a centre for disseminating scientific knowledge focused on the development and practical implementation of economic activities. Câmara was at this time mainly influenced by a prominent scientist, the Italian naturalist and chemist Domenico Vandelli.[53]

Câmara's knowledge of cameralist authors was yet to come. In 1790 the Portuguese government sent him and two fellow students, José Bonifácio de Andrada and Joaquim Pedro Fragoso, on a lengthy tour of the European continent. First they spent some time in France, attending courses at the *École Royale des Mines*. Then, after a brief period in the Netherlands, they arrived at their main destination, the *Bergakademie* in Freiberg, where it was intended that they should enrol, as is stated in the instructions they received from the Portuguese government. There they took the course of geognosy (historical geology) and oryctognosy (descriptive mineralogy) taught by Professor Abraham Gottlob Werner, whose teachings strongly influenced their careers. Câmara actually published two articles in the prestigious *Bergmanniches Journal* on experiments with obsidian, in which he shows its affinity to Werner's neptunistic theory.[54] The Portuguese envoys not only had in this way

---

53 Marcos Carneiro de Mendonça, *O Intendente Câmara: Manoel Ferreira da Câmara Bethencourt, e Sá – Intendente Geral das Minas e dos Diamantes (1764–1835)* (Rio de Janeiro, 1933); Alex Gonçalves Varela, 'A trajetória do ilustrado Manuel Ferreira da Câmara em sua "fase européia" (1783–1800)', *Tempo* 23 (2007), 150–75; Alex Gonçalves Varela, 'Atividades Científicas no Império Português: um Estudo da Obra do Metalurgista de Profissão Manuel Ferreira da Câmara (1783–1820)', *História, Ciências, Saúde-Manguinhos* 15 (2008), 1201–8; Alex Gonçalves Varela, 'Ciência e Patronagem: análise da trajetória do naturalista e intendente das minas Manuel Ferreira da Câmara (1808–1822)', *Revista do Instituto Histórico e Geographico Brazileiro* 446 (2010), 67–92.
54 Varela, 'A trajetória'; Manuel Ferreira da Câmara, 'Über das Verhalten des Obsidians vor dem Löthrohre, von Hr. Da Camera – Aus dem französischen übersetzt', *Bergmanniches Journal* 6 (1794), 280–5; Manuel Ferreira da Câmara, 'Schreiben von Herrn da Camera de Bethencourt an Herrn Hawkins einige Versuche mit dem Obsidiane betreffend', *Bergmanniches Journal* 6 (1794), 239–49.

direct contact with advanced studies in mineralogy and mining, but also an overview of the cameralist doctrine.

After their time in Freiberg the three would take resume their travels, but separately. In 1796 Camera travelled to the mining areas of Transylvania and Banat, and before his return to Portugal he visited mining districts in Sweden, Norway, Denmark and England. He returned to Portugal in 1798 and immediately joined the inner circle of the then most powerful minister of the king, the Secretary of the Overseas Affairs, Rodrigo de Sousa Coutinho, being given significant functions in the central mining administration in Portugal and Brazil.

Several reports, memoirs, letters and other documents of the period attest to the close connection between the scientific understanding of mining practice acquired by Camera and his colleagues, and a keen awareness of fiscal and administrative demands.[55] A direct example of this can be read in a key document for the administrative reform of mining activity at the heart of gold production in the Portuguese Empire: Minas Gerais, Brazil. The document is a Royal Decree containing new directives for mining activities in Minas Gerais from 1803.[56] Câmara, appointed Superintendent of Mines and Diamonds in Minas Gerais, would return to his homeland after being away for several years and put into practice reforms to activities and fiscal regulations. The document deals with numerous technical and economic issues, for example: rules for preventing the circulation of gold dust and the establishment of a local Mint, the introduction of technical improvements to gold mining, encouragement to exploit other metals, and the establishment of mineralogical and metallurgical schools in the area. The proposals and goals of the document were certainly very ambitious, and would ultimately be only partially implemented given the unwillingness of a ruler with financial problems to invest a large amount of money in the restoration of mining activities in Minas Gerais, even with the incentive provided by the promise of future earnings.

This Royal Decree of 1803 is directly connected to another text produced by Câmara a few years before: the 'Note on mining extraction in the Principality

---

55 See Mendonça, O Intendente Câmara and Andrée Mansuy-Diniz Silva, Portrait d'un homme d'État: D. Rodrigo de Sousa Coutinho, Comte de Linhares – 1755–1812, vol. II: L'homme d'État, 1796–1812 (Paris, 2006).

56 The legal document was officially presented to the Sovereign (who signed the Decree) by his minister Sousa Coutinho, but the original text, which suffered some minor modifications in the final drafting, was in fact written by Câmara, as has been amply demonstrated and documented by Marcos Carneiro de Mendonça (see O Intendente Câmara, ch. 8). Nevertheless, it should be noted here that in one of the few references to this question published in English, by Brazilian historian Júnia Ferreira Furtado, 'Enlightenment Science and Iconoclasm: The Brazilian Naturalist José Vieira Couto', Osiris 25 (2010), 207–8, Furtado is mistaken in seeking to demonstrate that the author of the document was José Vieira Couto.

of Transylvania', written in 1796. The legal document of 1803 in several parts closely follows the text of the 'Note on mining', and does actually seek to convey the general logic of Transylvanian cameralist administration and gold exploitation to the reality of Minas Gerais and other mining areas in Brazil. A problem that recurred during the the second half of the eighteenth century was the need to prevent gold dust circulating as currency in Minas Gerais. The local colonial government and the central government proposed, without success, to tackle this by replacing gold dust with an official currency through the activities of exchange houses (*casas de permuta*).[57] Here Câmara found in the example of the gold mines of the Principality of Transylvania a model that could be copied, as he explained in the document.[58]

The paper on Transylvania also provides many details of the influence of cameralist logic upon the fiscal administration of gold mining in that region. Câmara notes, for example, the importance of the administration of the mining districts being in the hands of a Board headed by the Sovereign, including a general director, councillors, lawyers familiar with the art of mining, one director of mining activity work and another for ironworks, together with subordinate officials.[59] Years later the principal board for mining administration in Minas Gerais still conformed to the model that he described in the document of 1796.[60] This superior board, or *Kammer* in Câmara's description of the administration of the mines in Transylvania, is very similar to the proposed organisation presented in the decree of 1803. Its essential function was also the same: to promote the administrative centralisation of mining revenues in the context of the kingdom's financial administration. This work of centralisation was also consistent with efforts made to centralise financial administration when Pombal created the Royal Treasury in 1761. Câmara explains, for example, in the document that in the mines of the Austrian and German states mine institutions are independent of all political or civil jurisdiction apart from the Treasury (*Hofkammer*) which is in charge of the inspection of mines, noting that this inspection is done by

57 Alexandre Mendes Cunha, 'A Junta da Real Fazenda em Minas Gerais e os projetos de abolição da circulação de outro em pó (1770–1808): limites às reformas econômicas na colônia dentro da administração fazendária portuguesa', *História Econômica & História de Empresas* 15 (2012), 9–46.
58 Manuel Ferreira da Câmara, 'Nota sobre a extração das minas do Principado da Transilvânia escrita em Zalathna aos 5 de março de 1796', Arquivo Nacional da Torre do Tombo (Lisboa), Núcleo do Ministério dos Negócios Estrangeiros, box 526, in Alex Gonçalves Varela, 'Um manuscrito inédito do naturalista Manuel Ferreira da Câmara: nota sobre a extração das minas do Principado da Transilvânia (1796)', *História, Ciências, Saúde-Manguinhos* 17 (2010), 195.
59 Câmara, 'Nota sobre a extração', p. 190.
60 Ferreira, ed., *Repertorio juridico*, p. 49.

councillors who 'not only had learned the art mines and mining economy, but had worked as chiefs in the mining districts'.[61]

Among several other observations regarding the way that this Transylvania model marked the treatment of mine administration and the fiscal structure of the Portuguese in the decree of 1803 can be cited: the establishment of a clear relationship between the mining administrations understanding of the importance of forestry, woods and waters to fiscal benefits for the state;[62] or in the importance of providing specific and comprehensive education in this field, leading some years later to the establishment in Minas Gerais of 'mineralogical and metallurgical schools, similar to the ones of Freiberg and Schemnitz'.[63]

Final considerations

The examples included here stretch over half a century, and converge with many different political contexts in Portugal: from the transition of corporatist power, the imposition of a centralised model by Pombal, and the decisive influence of enlightened reformism that played such a strong role in Portugal during the 1790s. These are diverse contexts, but all of them can be associated with the utility of cameralist ideas for the ever-present concern with the strengthening of state power. Further, the points made above could be extended to consider how some aspects of cameralist doctrines, in the post-earthquake context of 1755 and the 'opportunities' it provided for political change, would over the subsequent decades combine with several other ideas, shaping the eclectic platform of enlightened reformism that guided political actions at the end of the century in Portugal.[64]

Returning to some of the ideas advanced at the beginning of this essay, it is important to emphasise here that cameralism (or perhaps it would be more appropriate to say *quasi-cameralism*)[65] was never a pure influence in Portugal, i.e. it was not adopted as an organic and complete system of ideas. In most cases it can be detected more in relation to the practical action of state administration, rather than in theoretical or analytical reflection. This is true for Portugal and also for the Iberian world to some extent, although we can see

61   Câmara, 'Nota sobre a extração', p. 191.
62   Ferreira, ed., *Repertorio juridico*, p. 63.
63   Ferreira, ed., *Repertorio juridico*, p. 49.
64   On enlightened reformism in Portugal and its relation with cameralism, see: Cardoso, Cunha, 'Discurso econômico'.
65   The idea of 'quasi-cameralism' is explained in José Luís Cardoso and Alexandre Mendes Cunha, 'Enlightened Reforms and Economic Discourse in the Portuguese-Brazilian Empire (1750–1808)', *History of Political Economy* 44/4 (2012), 622.

in the Spanish case some direct influence of cameralist ideas in the writings of certain authors. This influence was nonetheless always one of individual ideas, and not a full theoretical system. In spite of that, these ideas diffused throughout the second half of the eighteenth century and even crossed to the Western Atlantic, being remembered, disseminated and linked to ideas of state economy; or to elements of police science as in the work of Fausto Delhuyar in Mexico; or in a very interesting partial translation published in Brazil in 1823 of Bielfeld's *Institutions Politiques*, adopted by the government of Brazil after its independence, and dedicated to the country's youth.[66]

---

66   Anon. [Gervásio Pires Ferreira], *Resumo das instituições políticas do Barão de Bielfeld, parafraseadas e acomodadas à forma actual do governo do Império do Brasil* ... (Rio de Janeiro, 1823). For a discussion of this book, see: Cardoso and Cunha, 'Enlightened Reforms', pp. 631–8.

8

Balancing the Divine with the Private: The Practices of *Hushållning* in Eighteenth-Century Sweden

GÖRAN RYDÉN

A cupboard of coins at Leufsta *bruk*

In 1739 the 19-year-old Charles De Geer travelled from Stockholm to Leufsta *bruk* to claim his inheritance. Nine years earlier he had inherited from a childless uncle the largest iron-making estate in Sweden, with Leufsta as its centrepiece. For nine years the estate had been run by a group of guardians, including his father Jean Jacques and his older brother Louis. In charge of the day-to-day business was the *Directeur* at Leufsta, Eric Touscher, and it became his task to prepare Charles De Geer, his master and the future *brukspatron* at Leufsta, for the life that lay ahead of him, an assignment Touscher took seriously.[1]

De Geer's arrival was the beginning of a new era at Leufsta, a new *brukspatron* taking possession of his estate, and a poem was written for the occasion: 'Rejoice, those who make all his work, those who make his iron ... your master will arrive. Welcome our Master, our father ... to your estate, inheritance and table, we long to obey your commands.'[2] De Geer was also presented with two hand-written manuscripts, nicely leather-bound as books, by Touscher, and a newly drawn-up plan of the *bruk*. The first manuscript was a directory of a collection of coins, medallions, books, scientific instruments, etc., assembled for the new master. Touscher noted that he had always

---

1 Chris Evans and Göran Rydén, *Baltic Iron in the Atlantic World in the Eighteenth Century* (Leiden, 2007); Göran Rydén 'Provincial Cosmopolitanism – An Introduction', *Sweden in the Eighteenth-Century World: Provincial Cosmopolitans*, ed. G. Rydén (Farnham, 2013).

2 Magnus Waller, *Enfaldig och wördsam Lyckönskan til den Högädle och Wälborne Herren /Herr Carl De Geer/* 1739. Quoted from Thomas Anfält, 'Herrgård och bruk. Om livet på Leufsta på 1700-talet', *Vallonerna*, ed. T. Anfält (Skärplinge, 1996), pp. 66f.

had an inclination to collect 'Historical' things, but his lack of wealth had prevented him to do so. However, in a deferential mood he had ignored these constraints and established a small collection for his master; the manuscript and the items were a sign of this ambition. It was a foundation on which De Geer, with his exquisite taste and knowledge, could create a collection worthy someone as 'well-born' as the new owner of Leufsta.[3]

Some features of this catalogue should be emphasised. One is Touscher's deferential tone. He made sacrifices in order to present his master with a collection and expected some kind of recognition; he acted in accordance with the poem, of obeying, but also as the highest official in the estate's hierarchy. Another feature is the emphasis upon utility; books and scientific instruments should 'serve ... as an edifying pleasure, in one or the other science'. Touscher used the Swedish word *brukas*, indicating a consumption of an endless, or renewable, resource, as science was useful. There was a spatial dimension to this utility, as books and instruments were allocated to different rooms where 'the walls are with essential books clothed [...] for them to be close at hand and useful'. This was also highlighted in the manuscript, with a drawing of a designed cupboard for storing coins, in separate drawers; the collection was catalogued and stored in an ordered and systematic way.[4]

The second manuscript dealt with the management of a large iron-making estate, a *bruk*. Touscher's introduction explained how he had acquired the knowledge to run such an estate. The former manager, Georg Swebilius, had been his mentor, but he had also spent time in 'discourse, talk and reasoning with all kinds of people' to improve his understanding of what was required. The deferential tone was there. He stressed that this would be easier for 'my master', but the *Handbok*, as the manuscript was called, might be a useful foundation for De Geer's future life as a *brukspatron*. Touscher's first task was to familiarise the new owner with his 'subordinates', at the *bruk* itself, the estates and mines, and the treatment began with pages filled with names, titles, tasks and wages for bookkeepers and clerks in many offices scattered around the gigantic estate. At the top of the structure he placed himself in charge of the *bruks-contoir* at Leufsta. Below the clerks were the working people, but they were 'too numerous to describe [and] could be found out from tax ledgers'. In 'Leufsta Bruk alone 300 people shall have nourishment and clothing, lodging, and allotments.'[5]

The next task was to give a thorough description of all parts belonging to

3   Touscher, Katalog öfver Carl De Geers samlingar på Leufsta, 1739. ATA: A** Topografiska Arkivet. Vitterhetsakademins handskriftssamling. 'Top. O. Hist. Samlingar' Typotius, vol. 29. Riksantikvarieämbetets arkiv och bibliotek.

4   Touscher, Katalog öfver Carl De Geers samlingar.

5   Leufstaarkivet, vol. 152, RA. En liten handbok angående Leufsta Bruk &c. Wälborne Herren Herr Carl de Geer, wid ankomsten i Orten af En Des Tienare, öfwerlemnat 1739.

iron making, from pig-iron making, in the blast furnaces, to bar-iron making in the forges. Touscher took care to tell his new master what was expected from his workers, as well as their 'daily chores'. The manuscript ends with the *Directeur* merging the working people with the 'material side' of the estate; people with technology and natural resources. These were the internal conditions of a *bruk*, and the word Touscher used to describe this was *hushållning*. The overarching aim of a good *brukspatron* should always be to keep a sound *hushållning*, and to balance the estate's resources of people and natural endowments to a desired output of bar iron.[6]

There is a similarity between these two manuscripts, quite apart from being bound in matching books. The first volume was a list of items in a collection of useful 'things', while the second was a manual on how to manage an iron-work estate, but from a broader perspective they dealt with economic matters, or better still, in *hushållning*. This is obvious in the second case, on iron-making, but it was also an integrated feature in the first manuscript; collections were sources for scientific enquiries. Borrowing from the French philosopher Michel de Certeau, and his dictum 'manipulation by users', it is clear that Touscher prepared De Geer for a life as *brukspatron* by stressing that he had to use (in Swedish 'bruka') both the collections and the estate's properties of people and natural resources. The two spheres were also connected, since it was the profits from the iron trade that made collecting a possibility.[7]

Both Touscher and de Certeau stress the *practice* of using, with the concept of *hushållning* seen as a practice; the Leufsta *Directeur* wanted his master to 'manipulate' himself into a *brukspatron*, and the way to do so was to enforce a *hushållning* that balanced people with natural resources in a systematic way. This systematic practice of *hushållning* envisioned by Touscher had three salient features. The first was utility; iron was useful but so was everything that Touscher had collected for his master. A second feature was hierarchy, and even if Touscher saw himself as superior to his clerks and forgemen he was still a servant to De Geer. The poem stated that 'our Master, our father' was welcomed with the promise that 'we long to obey your commands'. Touscher's *hushållning* was also spatial, with coins in different drawers, but there was a larger spatiality as well with a plan of the *bruk*, placing people in houses and workplaces; the cupboard of coins mimicking the ordering of the larger mercantile universe of Leufsta. The two manuscripts set the boundaries for the *hushållning* of which Charles De Geer was placed in charge.

Hushållning was a concept frequently used by a variety of Swedish eighteenth-century writers, whether natural historians or those who discussed economic matters. Travellers used it; one could talk about a specific region's

---

6 'En liten handbok'.
7 Michel de Certeau, *The Practice of Everyday Life* (Berkeley, 1988).

hushållning, while the metallurgist Sven Rinman dealt with the *hushållning* of iron-making. Carl Linnaeus used the concept when attempting to bridge the spheres of natural history and economic thinking. Anders Berch, the professor of economics, devoted a book to the theme, with a world divided into three related layers, each with its specific *hushållning*: a divine, a public and a private *hushållning*.[8]

This essay takes these manuscripts as a starting-point for an analysis of economic matters in Sweden around the mid-eighteenth century, by using the concept of *hushållning* as a tool.[9] The Swedish concept, along with the German *Haushalten*, can be translated into the English 'householding', although this is seldom used. There is a link to Aristotelian thinking with concepts elaborated from ideas around *oikonomia*, linking *oikos*, or dwelling place, to *nomos*, or regulations and laws, and Swedish writers sometimes replaced *hushållning* with *oeconomia*. I have decided against translating the Swedish concept, but will sometimes use the Latin form used by Swedish writers.[10]

The manuscripts in Touscher's hand might be placed in the sphere of what Anders Berch thought of as private *hushållning*, and there are links to public *hushållning*; but an analysis of the two manuscripts must be inserted into a wider, and more diverse, setting of different usages of *hushållning* in mid-eighteenth-century Sweden. I will start with a treatment of Berch's publications, mainly his *Inledning til almänna hushålningen*, followed by an examination of texts devoted to the *oeconomia* of iron-making, before returning to the concrete practice of *hushållning* as the one found in the manuscripts given to Charles De Geer at Leufsta *bruk* in 1739.

An ordered society and regulated households

In a book published some three decades ago Susan Dwyer Amussen stated: 'The family was not only the fundamental economic unit of society; it also provided the basis for political and social order [and] the family served as a metaphor for the state ...'. In a micro study she has analysed the 'inextricable' relationship between 'the family and state' in early modern Britain,

8   Anders Berch, *Inledning til almänna hushålningen, innefattande grunden til politie, oeconomie och cameral wetenskaperne* (Stockholm, 1747).
9   Recently Karin Hassan Jansson has discussed the concept of a 'Haushaltskultur' for a society in which a dominant form of social relationships was based on the household. See Karin Hassan Jansson, 'Haus und Haushalt im frühneuzeitlichen Schweden', *Das Haus in der Geschichte Europas*, ed. J. Eibach and I. Schmidt-Voges (Oldenbourg, 2015).
10   Keith Tribe, *The Economy of the Word: Language, History, and Economics* (New York, 2015), ch. 2. Tribe is one of few writers who actually uses the English word 'householding'.

with questions about class and gender. English society was made up of small households, with a husband, father or a master at their helm; this was a 'private Commonwealth', or a 'Castle', as 'every man's house' was perceived. Together with other households and houses, the English people acted as servants to God and were subjects to the King, in accordance with an organic view of society where both smaller parts and the larger universe had a similar structure. It was the obligation of the subjects to follow rules and regulations enhanced through household manuals and political treatises. Amussen studies how English households lived up to these rules.[11]

Amussen's book had been preceded by other studies also linking society's larger structures to its smaller parts. Keith Tribe had published a book in 1978 also dealing with England. He began by stating that we are dealing with a tradition from at least Plato when making the analogy between the state and the household, and this became an essential part of the political literature of Hobbes, Locke and others, and their discussion of power and property. To Tribe it is clear that the 'organisation of the economy' must be 'conceived as a branch of the organisation of the polity', but he also relates this to the even grander structure of God's creation of the world; 'God makes man, and man makes objects, the process of *making* being that which creates the right to the object.' His analysis moves from philosophical treatises to manuals on husbandry, but contrary to Amussen this work remains within the bounds of a textual analysis, and he does not deal with the social implications of the 'family [as] the basis of social order'.[12]

In later studies Tribe poses similar questions to the tradition of cameralism in central Europe, and once again he shows a correspondence between the 'administration of the state' and 'the running of the household'; to 'deduce the existence of the state from the natural order of men in society, i.e., in families'. Again Tribe takes up the classical Greek tradition, with its trinity of politics, ethics and oeconomy, but in cameralism gave precedence to former; it was *policey* that was the key to the structure, and 'there is no motion that is not the outcome of proper government'. Tribe makes a case for linking the concepts of politics and oeconomy to that of 'household', 'householding' and even 'management' (from the French 'ménage'), and by doing so he adds the aspect of ordering to the central European tradition. His defines cameralism

---

11   Susan Dwyer Amussen, *An Ordered Society. Gender and Class in Early Modern England* (Oxford, 1988), pp. 1, 2 and 37. Julia Adams has more recently attempted to 'bring gender studies closer to the discussion about political authority', but on a different analytical level. See Julia Adams, *The Familial State. Ruling Families and Merchant Capitalism in Early Modern Europe* (Ithaca, NY, 2005), p. 3.

12   Keith Tribe, *Land, Labour and Economic Discourse* (London, 1978), pp. 37, 45, 47.

as the practice of governing the economy for the material well-being of citizens and subjects.[13]

The main feature in both Amussen and Tribe is the close connection between the state and the family/household, something that is strengthened by the merging of more general treatises on economic matters, whether we call these mercantilism or cameralism, and the more practical manuals of husbandry or housekeeping. In the German-speaking world the latter was called *Hausväterliteratur*, and according to Torsten Meyer the 'cognizance of their normative character' makes it easy to link them to other layers in society. We are thus dealing with principles that permeated society on all levels.[14]

Thomas Buchner would concur regarding the 'permeating principles', but he has also added a more 'practical aspect' to this. On a general level it is hard to maintain the view that we are dealing with doctrines as such, and instead he stressed that these texts were actively written with a specific political purpose; mercantilist writers aimed at advancing the interests of merchants, while cameralism was created by royal servants in the interest of an absolute ruler. Cameralists strove to fill the prince's chambers with tax revenues, and in doing so they viewed both people and 'things' as 'resources' to be mobilised to create wealth. This was *hushållning* at a general level, with the realm seen as a 'castle' and with the princes as the *Hausväter* viewed as political authorities, with the family as a model.[15]

Even if Andre Wakefield has not dealt with the *Hausväterliteratur* he has, to a certain extent, developed what Meyer and Tribe thought of as the 'normative character' of the early modern German economic literature, and he has also elaborated on what might be seen as the social implications of cameralism, and thus moved beyond strictly textual analysis; cameralism was not only a doctrine being taught, but also something being 'done, a practice'. These two

13   Keith Tribe, 'Cameralism and the Science of Government', *The Journal of Modern History* 56 (1984), pp. 265–6, 268, 275 and 277. See also Keith Tribe, *Strategies of Economic Order: German Economic Discourse, 1750–1950* (Cambridge, 1995). For two brief introductions to cameralism, see Keith Tribe, 'Cameralism and the Science of the State', *Cambridge History of Eighteenth-Century Political Thought*, ed. M. Goldie and R. Wokler (Cambridge, 2006), and Andre Wakefield, 'Cameralism. A German Alternative to Mercantilism', *Mercantilism Reimagined: Political Economy in Early Modern Britain and its Empire*, ed. P. J. Stern and C. Wennerlind (Oxford, 2013).

14   Torsten Meyer, 'Cultivating the Landscape: The Perception and Description of Work in Sixteenth- to Eighteenth-Century German Household Literature (*Hausväterliteratur*)', *The Idea of Work in Europe from Antiquity to Modern Times*, ed. J. Ehmer and C. Lis (Farnham, 2009), p. 221.

15   Thomas Buchner, 'Perceptions of Work in Early Modern Economic Thought: Dutch Mercantilism and Central European Cameralism in Comparative Perspective', *The Idea of Work in Europe from Antiquity to Modern Times*, ed. J. Ehmer and C. Lis (Farnham, 2009). See also Marion W. Gray, *Productive Men, Reproductive Women. The Agrarian Household and the Emergence of Separate Spheres during the German Enlightenment* (Oxford, 2000).

sides were intimately tied together, but scholars have for the most part concentrated their analysis on the former, and it is time to rectify this. Wakefield begins by claiming that cameralists 'were simply artisans', at least in their own voices, and 'servants of the Kammer'. Cameralism was an art of linking the ruler's house, or his 'castle', to the smaller households of the realm. Wakefield, however, only ties cameralism to that of the households of the cameralists themselves; his beginning is with the 'Bad Cameralist', and how their 'art', aimed at promoting their own personal interests at the expense of enhancing the wealth of their rulers. In doing so he expands the study of cameralism from pure textual analysis to that of social history, but his concentration on the bad cameralist hides the fact that many 'good' cameralists also affected the lives of many more subjects by governing their lives in the interests of the princes.[16]

With a recent book by Karen Harvey we are back to the approach used by Amussen: what could be seen as the social implications of a society with the household as the template for most social relations, but with a more advanced practice-oriented approach; her sources are everything from 'general household manuals' to 'political treatises'. She prefers the concept of 'oeconomy' instead of analysing the family, households or 'householding', but she sees that as a 'social practice' combining 'day-to-day management [...] and the macro- or global management of people and resources [...] Oeconomy was, first, a specific way of organizing the household. But, second, oeconomy was also a discourse that comprised values, structures, and practices.' Her analytical beginning is the discourse, but, as 'oeconomy was lived in material ways, rather than existing only in words on a page', her analysis proceeded to a study of the practice of everyday life. A central feature is the practice of accounting, as it 'expressed authority that men wielded over other members of the household'.[17]

It is interesting to note that this practical approach, visible in recent studies about hushållning, is also prevalent in recent family history; there is a clear trend away from the structural approach advocated by scholars like Peter Laslett, with his many 'family forms', and Otto Brunner, and his concept of 'das ganze Haus'.[18] People like Naomi Tadmor and David Sabean have made important contributions to an opening-up of these rigid structures, treating households instead as flexible and open units, as well as conferring power to individual decision-making; 'the household [was] a place where various

---

16   Andre Wakefield, The Disordered Police State. German Cameralism as Science and Practice (Chicago, 2009). Quotations from pp. 3, 5 and 9.

17   Karen Harvey, The Little Republic. Masculinity and Domestic Authority in Eighteenth-Century Britain (Oxford, 2012), pp. 14, 15, 17, 23 and 72. For a discussion of the role of accounting during the early modern period, see Mary Poovey, A History of the Modern Fact. Problems of Knowledge in the Sciences of Wealth and Society (Chicago, 1998).

18   Peter Laslett, Household and Family in Past Times (Cambridge, 1972). Otto Brunner, 'Das "ganze Haus" und die alteuropäische "Ökonomik"', Neue Wege der Verfassungs- und Sozialgeschichte, 2nd edn (Göttingen, 1968).

exchanges took place [and] the house was a locus of exchange'.[19] Joachim
Eibach has developed this further and disputed the very concept of 'das ganze
Haus'. Instead he prefers the idea of 'das offene Haus'; the house was spatially
loose, as he gave it a materiality that was not present in earlier approaches.
The house existed in the midst of 'kommunikativen Praktiken' and human
performances, pointing towards the practice of *hushållning*.[20]

Bruk, 'bruka' and using Michel de Certeau

When Charles De Geer came to Leufsta in 1739 to claim his inheritance he
was not entirely unfamiliar with its work. Even though he had been brought
up in Holland, he had been to Leufsta before, and most likely seen iron being
made. More importantly, however, he belonged to a family very much involved
in Swedish iron-making for more than a century. His great-great grandfather,
Louis De Geer, came to Sweden from Amsterdam in the early seventeenth
century and acquired Leufsta in the 1620s.[21] Charles De Geer's arrival in Leufsta
in 1739 was about a young heir's transition to the helm of a family estate, but
it also signalled an important event in Sweden at large: a *brukspatron* was
adapting to a new phase in his life, and a *bruk* being reinstated to its role of
generating national wealth. Touscher's manuscripts are a testament written by
someone involved in the Swedish public *oeconomia*, but this was also about
generating wealth from Leufsta *bruk*. The latter was all about balancing the
estate's resources, and as such it became the *private hushållning* of the De Geer
family, as well as that of the forgemen, peasants and other workers.

The Swedish word *bruk* is related to the verb *bruka*, meaning to use
renewable resources in making something new, and so it is connected to a
spatial entity with close affinity to the practice of *hushållning*. A *bruk* was
a combination of an industrial enterprise, a landed estate and mines; raw
material, such as charcoal and iron ore, was supplied to the *bruk*, where
bar iron was made. Much of the labour needed was undertaken by tenants,
paying rent in the form of charcoal. The *bruk* itself was arranged around the
manor house and the workers' cottages. The master had his own park, and the
workers had their plots. These places were not, however, closed communities,

19 Naomi Tadmor, *Family and Friends in Eighteenth-century England: Household, Kinship, and Patronage* (Cambridge, 2001). David Warren Sabean, *Property, Production, and Family in Neckarhausen, 1700–1870* (Cambridge, 1990): quotation from pp. 122f.
20 Joachim Eibach, 'Das offene Haus. Kommunikative Praxis im sozialen Nahraum der europäischen Frühen Neuzeit', *Zeitschrift für Historische Forschung* 38 (2011). Quotation from p. 639.
21 See for instance Erik Wilhelm Dahlgren, *Louis De Geer 1587–1652. Hans lif och verk* (Stockholm, 1923).

as the iron was traded globally. A *bruk* was an organic entity 'utilising' what the divine creator had installed in nature, and the De Geer *hushållning* is linked to the divine sphere, as a place where metal was 'brought to its purity and proper condition', making respectful use of God's bounty.[22]

One way to approach the layered structure of *hushållning* noted above is to apply de Certeau's idea of 'manipulation by users'. Touscher and others, like Anders Berch, envisioned *hushållning* as a systematic practice, stressing utility and consumption in the making of 'things'. To Touscher, collections as well as people and natural endowments were resources that could be utilised in both the making of iron and in the 'manipulation' of De Geer into a *brukspatron*. These ideas correspond with the dual approach proposed by Amussen and others, of linking the family to that of political authority, emphasising especially a historiographical movement towards a practice-oriented approach, circulating less around abstract principles and directing attention to the practices of the people involved. This might be the moment to study the practice of *hushållning*, linking cameralism to that of 'das offene Haus' in a study of the Swedish eighteenth-century society.

Mercantilism, cameralism and the all-present divinity

In 1741 Anders Berch was appointed to the first Swedish professorship of economics at Uppsala University, formally to a chair in *Jurisprudentiæ, Oeconomiæ & Commerciorum profession*. The new chair was only the fourth such foundation in Europe. His inauguration had been preceded by some complicated machinations that involved scientific, political and economic spheres, and had been made possible through some complex manoeuvring within the university. That Berch was a suitable candidate is beyond doubt: Sven-Eric Liedman has called him 'a man of the future'. Berch had enrolled at Uppsala in 1726, studying mathematics. In 1731 he defended a thesis on economic matters, written in Latin. He then joined the Board of Commerce in a junior position, and had a brief bureaucratic career. During the years in Uppsala and at the Board in Stockholm he made valuable contacts with powerful people as well as important economic thinkers. In 1741 he was well prepared for the chair that was created for him.[23]

22   Sven Rinman, *Bergwerkslexicon* (Stockholm 1788–89), p. 314. See also the entry 'Bruka' in the *Svenska Akademiens Ordbok*, http://g3.spraakdata.gu.se/saob/, accessed 3 March 2016.
23   Anders Berch, http://sok.riksarkivet.se/sbl/artikel/18514, Svenskt biografiskt lexikon (art. av K. Petander.), accessed 18 Feb. 20168; Sven-Eric Liedman, *Den osynliga handen. Anders Berch och ekonomiämnena vid 1700-talets svenska universitet* (Värnamo, 1986), pp. 47–53 and 62–9.

Berch is a key figure in the Swedish discussion on economic matters. Karl Petander stated in 1912 that Berch was in many aspects 'a precursor and innovator [as well as] a founder of the science of economics in Sweden'. Eli Heckscher was not that impressed, but maintained that Berch has a special place in the Swedish development: it was vital to acknowledge his dominant position in the decades around 1750, but his lack of 'originality' might also provide an issue for more thorough analysis. Later scholars, like Liedman and Lars Magnusson, have confirmed his importance. The former dedicated a book-length study to Berch, describing him as 'a typical state intellectual', while the latter noted that he 'is perhaps the best known of the "mercantilists" from the Age of Liberty'. Karin Johannisson has added that Berch was a key figure in the introduction of 'political arithmetic' to Sweden, and as such crucial in the development of *Tabellverket* from 1749, the state-fostered initiative to statistically investigate 'the conditions of the country'.[24]

Even if Magnusson puts quotation marks around Berch as a 'mercantilist', as if to question whether he really should be seen as one, few scholars have distanced themselves from such a characterisation. Lisbet Koerner, an exception, stated that the chair created in Uppsala 1741 was in cameralism, and Berch was 'its first holder'.[25] However, no-one has doubted the importance of influences from German cameralism, and some have tried to pinpoint the exact nature of this influence. To Petander this might in fact be what made him so 'innovative', but to Heckscher it pointed instead to the reverse; in his search for the origins of the modern liberal economy Heckscher made it clear that cameralism 'stood on a much lower level', and that Berch was stuck there as well. To Liedman, the connection to cameralism is obvious, with Berch tied to the development of the early modern state, with its regulated and systematic economic development as a crucial feature.[26]

It is not enough, however, to view Berch in the light of the cameralist tradition, or, for that matter, with respect to his links to English mercantilists. He must be analysed in a wider context. Magnusson, in his quest for

24 Karl Petander, *De nationalekonomiska åskådningarna i Sverige sådana de framträda i litteraturen. Del I: 1718–1765* (Stockholm, 1912), p. 53; Eli F. Heckscher, *Sveriges ekonomiska historia från Gustaf Vasa. Andra delen. Det moderna Sveriges grundläggning* (Stockholm, 1949), p. 827; Liedman, *Den osynliga handen*, p. 8.

25 Lars Magnusson, *Äran Korruptionen och den Borgerliga Ordningen. Essäer från svensk ekonomihistoria* (Stockholm, 2001), p. 37; Lisbet Koerner, 'Daedalus Hyperboreus: Baltic Natural History and Mineralogy in the Enlightenment', *The Sciences in Enlightened Europe*, ed. W. Clark, J. Golinski and S. Schaffer (Chicago, 1999), p. 398. Recently Hjalmar Fors, although without detailing Anders Berch, has stated that Sweden was a cameralist country: see Hjalmar Fors, *The Limits of Matter. Chemistry, Mining and Enlightenment* (Chicago, 2015), pp. 101ff.

26 Petander, *De nationalekonomiska åskådningarna i Sverige*; Heckscher, *Sveriges ekonomiska historia*, p. 827; Liedman, *Den osynliga handen*; Magnusson, *Äran Korruptionen*, p. 37; Karin Johannisson, *Det mätbara samhället. Statistik och samhällsdröm i 1700-talets Europa* (Stockholm, 1988), p. 157.

'a more historically inspired reading' of eighteenth-century economic texts, has advocated a closer integration of economic writings with the tradition of Natural Law. According to him Berch, and other Swedish "mercantilists", were deeply influenced by Christian Wolff, and 'the Wolffian philosophical system' with its emphasis upon 'order' and the 'perfection' of everything; Swedish eighteenth-century economic thinking was always dominated by 'principles of order'.[27]

Leif Runefelt has developed these ideas by deepening the views of an overarching system of 'orders', adding a discussion of physico-theology and natural history. To Runefelt, the key issues in Swedish economic writings during the early modern period were virtue and utility: everything on earth had two purposes, to honour God and render mankind blissful. It was a virtue for all humans to make use of the generous endowments granted by a benevolent God. Natural history was the way to investigate these endowments and to discover the greatness of the Divinity. Virtue and utility were entangled as were nature, humans and God. Runefelt adds that Berch was aware that people sometimes acted contrary to a virtuous life, and that they needed guidelines and regulations. It was the state that had been given the onerous task of supplying this; to Berch this was what he called *Politien*, or *Politie-Wetenskapen* (the science of policing).[28]

It is clear that the study of Anders Berch, and other Swedish economic writers in the eighteenth century, has changed since the early twentieth century. Petander and Heckscher were foremost interested in tracking the roots to a modern, and liberal, economic thinking, while later scholars, such as Liedman and Magnusson, have stressed the need to understand 'economic' texts in their contemporary context. This has also meant a development away from an interest in features such as 'the balance of trade', 'import substitution', etc., to a more inward-looking approach dealing with links between economic writings and natural history, divinity, etc. Runefelt has been most radical in that sense, and stated that 'trade' was totally 'subordinated' to the aim of 'independence', and that in political as well as economic and cultural ways. With such a reading it is hard to maintain Berch as a mercantilist, and Runefelt has recently stated, at a seminar, that 'there was no such thing as

27 Magnusson, *Äran Korruptionen*, p. 42. Here Magnusson builds heavily on Tore Frängsmyr, 'Den gudomliga ekonomin. Religion och hushållning i 1700-talets Sverige', *Lychnos. Lärdomshistoriska samfundets årsbok* (1971–1972); Tore Frängsmyr, *Wolffianismens genombrott i Sverige* (Uppsala, 1972). Frängsmyr has added that these 'orders' were to be formulated in mathematical terms. See Tore Frängsmyr, 'Christian Wolff's Mathematical Method and its Impact on the Eighteenth Century', *Journal of the History of Ideas* 36 (1975), 653–68.
28 Leif Runefelt, *Dygden som välståndets grund. Dygd, nytta och egennytta i frihetstidens ekonomiska tänkande* (Stockholm, 2005), pp. 33ff.

a Swedish mercantilism'. Instead he prefers to talk about an 'Aristotelian *hushållning* ideology', but with a closer affinity to cameralism.[29]

Even if scholarly attention to Swedish early modern economic writings has changed in recent decades, it has not quite reached the position envisioned by people like Amussen and Tribe, in fully merging political authority, economic writings and family history, or in analysing the day-to-day business of *hushållning*; Swedish scholars have yet to link ideas of mercantilism and cameralism to texts such as the *Hausväter* literature. Runefelt's writings, including his rejection of a Swedish mercantilism, are a welcome move away from texts that focus upon finding the roots to modern economic thinking, but his attention to 'virtue' and 'utility' still remains within the sphere of ideology, or what can be viewed as a discourse. The aim of the following is to take one further step, and attach this discourse to the sphere that most intimately connected the 'economy' to Swedish everyday life, by asking what people should do if they are to be virtuous and useful. One way of doing this is to replace the discussion of mercantilism or cameralism by the concept of *hushållning*, which was a common term in the period. This makes it possible to integrate Swedish society, with all its spheres, connecting everyday life with that of state and church. I will begin with Anders Berch and his discussion of *oeconomia* as a three-layered structure: of a divine, a public and a private *hushållning*.

***

The influences of 'the Wolffian philosophical system' on Swedish economic thinking were pronounced; it was all about order and structures. No-one was better equipped to live up to these rules than the systematic Anders Berch, and it is obvious that he strived for 'perfection', to use Magnusson's word,[30] in his main publication of 1747, *Inledning til almänna hushålningen*. The book begins with a preface in a deferential tone that resembles that used by Eric Touscher when he welcomed De Geer to Leufsta. Berch addressed the new-born prince, the future Gustav III, by stating that 'every Swedish Man' would 'kneel' in front of the future King, 'the Heavenly gift'. 'All the Children of Swea' would strive to make the future Monarch happy and glorious. Berch noted that his book might not have anything to offer to a future king, for he would learn everything from the 'Honourable Company of his parents', but it might be of service to the Swedish 'Youth' by teaching them how to be 'industrious and rich subjects'.

29   Runefelt, *Dygden som välståndets grund*, p. 78. See also Leif Runefelt, *Att hasta mot under-gången. Anspråk, flyktighet, föreställning i debatten om konsumtion i Sverige 1730–1830* (Lund, 2015). The seminar took place at Drottningholm Castle, 22 August 2014, and was part of the conference *Practices and Performances Between Materiality and Morality in Pre-Modernity*.
30   Magnusson, *Äran Korruptionen*, p. 42.

Berch placed himself in the middle of a hierarchy – with the heaven-sent prince at the top – as a teacher to Swedish subjects.[31]

Berch's agenda was directed to the middle part of the trinity, to public *hushållning*, but in doing that he first had to establish links to the other layers. The preface set the frame for what was to come, beginning with the glorification of God, and he proceeded to talk about 'the Laws of God and Nature'. Considering a kind of divine *hushållning*, Berch imagined a beginning before time, with the 'benefits' of the Universe, created by God, 'flowing' from a generously furnished nature. Religion was to Berch an 'auxiliary tool' for his nascent economic thinking. God had not only created 'nature' but mankind as well, and it was their duty to take nature into possession. The way to do this, to be 'virtuous' in Runefelt's words, was by 'diligent labour'.[32]

The globe had been designed by a benevolent Creator, and it was in this benign nature, replete with generous endowments, that *hushållning* took place. The great Carl Linnaeus concurred, and talked about an *oeconomia naturæ* at the highest level of existence; 'the Oeconomia of the great God is one and the same all over the world', even if the *hushållning* of the 'Sami', 'the European peasant' or the 'Brazilian savage' differed. Linnaeus even talked about 'the strange *hushållning* of the skuas' and 'the extraordinary *hushållning* of the bees', as parts of this large entity.[33] Carl Gustaf Löwenhielm stated: 'The mighty world-building' was the result of God's 'wisdom' and endeavour. In his creation humans had been allotted an 'understanding and gifts of genius, to discover and to set in motion all inventions for common as well as individual well-being'. People were to act in accordance with the great plan of the Creator. Lars Salvius agreed, and all *hushållning* began with the 'all-wise Creator ... who furnished the Earth with the benefits of Nature'. This was the beginning of everything, and people should glorify God by acting in accordance with his plan.[34]

Berch was more thorough when setting the boundary between public and private *hushållning*, an important issue especially since Sweden 'had got a taste' for both. These two layers had a common foundation and shared

31   Berch, *Inledning*, without pagination.
32   Berch, *Inledning*, pp. 2, 6, 7, 17f and 272.
33   Carl von Linné, *Oeconomia naturæ eller Skaparens allvisa inrättning på vår jord, i agttagen vid de skapade tingens betraktande i de tre naturens riken, till deras fortplantning, vidmagthållande och undergång* (Uppsala, 1750), pp. 69, 82 and 87. For a full treatment of Linnaeus and his approach to economic thinking and the divinity, see Lisbet Koerner, *Linnaeus: Nature and Nation* (Cambridge, MA, 1999), especially pp. 82–94.
34   Carl Gustaf Löwenhielm, *Tal om landt-skötsel, hållit för Kongl. Svenska Vetenskaps academien* (Stockholm, 1751), pp. 5–11; Lars Salvius, *Beskrifning öfver Sveriget, Första Tomen om Upland* (Stockholm, 1741). See also Tore Frängsmyr, *Svensk idéhistoria. Bildning och vetenskap under tusen år*, 1: 1000–1809 (Stockholm, 2000), pp. 192–4, and Tore Frängsmyr, 'Den gudomliga ekonomin'.

important features; *hushållning*, as a general idea, was 'a science [and] an art of acquiring, managing and maintaining property', and it should be practised, according to a contemporary, with 'principles and systems'.[35] Berch stated that 'the science of *hushållning* was ... a twofold topic ... namely People and Things'. The split between the public and private spheres had a historical explanation. Since creation 'People lived in their Natural state', and originally only private *hushållning* existed. It was only when people left their 'freedom', and together with other people founded a 'bourgeois coexistence', that a public *hushållning* developed. The smaller sphere should strive for 'profits and utility [from] property', but always with the well-being of the larger entity in mind. The crucial link was that wealth-creation took place among individual people, also aiming to benefit the whole society; people should live according to 'common rules regarding a proper life' and 'arrange their way of life and *hushållning* in such a way that other members of society would benefit'.[36]

A striking feature in this way of reasoning is the simultaneously organic and ranked structure. The three-layered practice of *hushållning* was seen as an indissoluble entity with an almost self-evident hierarchy. Private *hushållning* was subordinated to the sphere of the public, while the latter was outranked by that of the divine order. A second aspect of inequality also existed within each layer, as *hushållning* always was subordinated to a ruling *Hausvater*; the Creator, the king and the master of the household. There was a clear gender aspect of this structure, as Berch saw *hushållning* as a male domain; 'the female sex can appropriate a fair share [of it]', but it was the task of men to undertake its 'administration'. The structure was often expressed in bodily terms; Germano Maifreda has reminded us that there was often an overlap between early modern practitioners of medicine and of economics.[37] Isaac Johan Uhr, to whom we will return, elaborates on this:

> A living body cannot lose any of its limbs, and do without the service of either, as all, the smallest and the largest, are from the Creator's wise ordination [and] contributing to the ability and skills owned by the body, to remain in its order and execute the effects to which it has been designed. [...] In a natural body ... a limb serves ... according to the purpose it has been given by the all wise Creator's Systematic cohesion ... it cannot be dislocated [but must remain] in perfect balance.[38]

---

35 'Om Hushållning', Anders Nordencrantz, Börstorpsamlingen, A. Nordencrants arkiv, Koncept E3011.
36 Berch, *Inledning*, pp. 8ff.
37 Berch, *Inledning*, p. 56. Germano Maifreda, *From Oikonomia to Political Economy. Constructing Economic Knowledge from the Renaissance to the Scientific Revolution* (Farnham, 2012).
38 Isaac Johan Uhr, *En Brukspatrons Egenskaper* (Uppsala, 1750), pp. 1f.

It was the middle section of this systematic structure, the *oeconomia publica*, that was crucial to Berch, a layer that was divided into three integrated parts; *Polity*, *Oeconomie* and taxation. In Swedish the latter was called *Cammar* science, a clear indication of Berch's affinity to what we today see as cameralism; taxation was essential to the state.[39] None of these parts was given priority but policing, or the 'administration of orders', would give 'force and effect' to the others as well as 'paving the way' for a 'civil felicity'. The *Polity* strived for three goals: to enhance the wealth of the mind, the body and 'the happiness'. Divine service was one of the tools for achieving that, according to Berch, thus creating a link between the divinity and the public sphere.[40]

The 'economic' sphere was also divided in Berch's version, and he talked about four different parts, with agriculture as well as mining and metal-making consigned to the countryside, while crafts and trades had their home in the towns. The motives for such a structure were quite apparent, since rural sectors were rooted in the actual soil; but the reasons for locating craft and trade in towns were different. To Berch it was clear that concentrating these activities to a small number of places would not only make taxation easier, but also raw materials cheaper. However, the most obvious reason for Berch was that he saw the economy as a rational structure; what he was describing was not any actual economy, but the most rational spatial division of labour.[41]

Scholars have previously emphasised that the division of labour was important in Berch's thinking, and that he was greatly influenced by the political arithmetic that was developed in Britain by people like William Petty and Gregory King.[42] He had published a book on that theme a year ahead of his *Inledning*, and the crucial aspect is that he always thought of the division of labour as something imposed from 'above'. Johannisson has dubbed this the 'dehumanised' aspect of these ideas: 'Population was a crowd or materia to be divided and structured in profitable combinations.' It was the task of the *Polity* to enforce a suitable 'combination' within the *Oeconomie*. Between its four parts 'there is a quite strong connection', but it was the duty of people like Berch to regulate the internal links. Political arithmetic, with all its newly developed statistical tools, aimed at balancing human resources with natural endowments.[43]

39   See Tribe, 'Cameralism and the Science of the State' for a similar structure used by many German cameralists.

40   Berch, *Inledning*, pp. 23f.

41   Berch, *Inledning*, pp. 10ff.

42   For an introduction, see Julian Hoppit, 'Political Arithmetic in Eighteenth-century England', *Economic History Review* 49 (1996), 516–40. See also Per-Arne Karlsson, 'Housekeeping Ideology and Equilibrium Policy in Eighteenth-century Sweden', *Scandinavian Economic History Review & Economy and History* 37 (1989), 51–77.

43   Anders Berch, *Sätt, at igenom politisk arithmetica utröna länders och rikens hushåldning* (Stockholm, 1746); Berch, *Inledning*, p. 10. Johannisson, *Det mätbara samhället*, pp. 99f.

It is interesting to note that Berch presented his public *hushållning* as consisting of three parts placed side-by-side, and with *Polity* only given priority as something setting the structure in motion. It is very much a vertical structure being explained in horizontal terms. However, his 'verticality' becomes obvious since this 'mid-layer' in his trinity is always connected to other layers as well, and that the hierarchies in his model – and those of the Swedish society – are always present; it was the task of the *Hausvater* to delegate duties to other members, whether we are dealing with God, the king or the masters of individual households. Within the framework of the *oeconomia publica* people like Berch had the task of assisting the ruler. They were the true cameralists, and Berch was aware of his position, as subordinate to both God and King. In the deferential preface to his *Inledning* he made that perfectly clear: He would 'kneel' in front of the future King and be content to be of service to Swedish 'Youth'.

In Berch's book the dividing line between *oeconomia publica* and *oeconomia privata* was clear. In chronological terms a line was drawn by the establishment of a 'bourgeois coexistence', and from a 'systemic' angle the division was between what we now call the individual household and the state, the same distinctions dealt with by Amussen, Tribe and others. However, Swedish cameralism, if such a label can be used, was more diverse and complicated. Some writers, including a few of Berch's students, presented a more complex picture. One 'diversion' is a spatial division of the public sphere, with 'economic' descriptions of regions or towns.[44] Lars Salvius dealt with the county of Uppland, systematically dividing the county into different spatial entities, ending with a meticulously detailed narrative of the *hushållning* of all the parishes. On page 348 he reached his concluding chapter, *Hushållning in General*, where he noted that the people of Uppland could support themselves from the fields, but also from what could be had from the sea and employment in iron-making. This was a study of the division of labour in spatial as well as social terms, where everybody had their specific place and pre-set tasks and duties.[45]

Salvius's approach was spatial, a public *hushållning* on a smaller scale, but it also opened another 'diversion' to the three-layer structure. It anticipated a *hushållning* of specific trades. Uppland was an iron-making region, the location of Leufsta *bruk*, and aspects of mining and metal making were analysed. This theme was elaborated by others, such as Sven Rinman. He also stressed that the essential aim of iron-making was to make ends meet, and that through an improved knowledge about the 'generous nature' in which

44 Mattias Legnér, *Fäderneslandets rätta beskrivning. Mötet mellan antikvarisk forskning och ekonomisk nyttokult i 1700-talets Sverige* (Helsingfors, 2004). See also Magnus Örnberg, *Oeconomisk Beskrifning öfwer Stapel Staden Gefle* (Stockholm, 1755).
45 Lars Salvius, *Beskrifning öfver Sveriget, Första Tomen om Upland* (Stockholm, 1741).

hushållning took place. Rinman also touched upon the boundary to the private *hushållning* of skilled artisans; it would be good if the 'best workers' were given 'some support for their *hushållning*' in the form of allotments. This would make 'their love for the place greater' as well as decrease their wages.[46]

Isaac Johan Uhr, introduced above, is a perfect bridge from the public *hushållning* to an analysis of the layers placed below. Uhr defended a short thesis, *The Properties of a Brukspatron*, with Berch as supervisor. It is a text highlighting aspects of order and hierarchy. Its first paragraph reiterated the general outlook of Swedish economic thinking, as well as stressing the importance of iron-making. Nature provided a foundation for humans to 'toil and work', something that should be done with 'mature senses and skills', as well as 'order'. The latter was enforced by people with special 'abilities', and they had been entrusted to their roles by the Creator. A *brukspatron* was, of course, such a person, and his task was to 'make his estate useful, for both himself and his country, and [make] himself a useful limb of Society'. To create 'order' and run an estate, 'the chores entrusted to him', a *brukspatron* had to be educated in a number of different fields. He had to be conversant with 'the Sciences' which he should have 'acquired through … keeping company with bookish and free arts'; it was important to know chemistry, physics, mathematics and geometry, and to adopt these to the work undertaken in the estate's different workshops. Uhr stressed that a *brukspatron* had to 'keep thorough accounts of credits and debits, and to adopt the former after the latter'. His 'Objectum' was to keep an *Arithmetisk hushållning*, meaning to 'supervise and press the actual labour'.[47]

Berch's writings fit well with the agenda set by Amussen, but with the addition of an outer 'shell' in the guise of a plentiful nature created by a benevolent God; his world was the three-layered trinity of a divine, a public and a private *hushållning*. It was a world that was ordered, systematic and hierarchical. The divine sphere represented the upper part of the hierarchy, with the public and private layers subordinated, although a generous nature was also the foundation on which private and public *hushållning* were practised. Berch's *hushållning* was about 'people and things', with work and toil bringing them together, but labour also created a unity within the trinity. With a phrase worthy of de Certeau, Berch stated that: 'The means whereby all created things are used [*nyttjas och brukas*] is diligent labour.' This was *hushållning* in the view of a cameralist writer – from above![48]

---

46   Sven Rinman, *Anledning Til Kunskap Om Den gröfre Jern- och Stål-Förädlingen Och des Förbättrande* (Stockholm, 1772), p. 74.

47   Uhr, *En Brukspatrons Egenskaper*, quotations from pp. 4–5, 7–8 and 30. See Jacob Orrje, *Mechanicus. Performing an Early Modern Persona* (Uppsala, 2015), pp. 106f, for a slightly different discussion about Uhr.

48   Berch, *Inledning*, p. 6.

Eric Touscher's *brukshushållning*

On 24 September 1780 the owner of Gimo *bruk*, Jean Lefebure, had
summoned a meeting with *bruksfolket*, the 'people of the *bruk*', probably
in the church after they had attended the sermon. The meeting was a
recurring event each autumn, and Lefebure wanted to establish his authority.
Hushållning, along the lines of an ordered and hierarchical structure, had a
central place in what the *brukspatron* conveyed to 'his people'. Gimo was an
estate close to Leufsta, and previously owned by the De Geer family. In 1764 it
had been purchased by Lefebure.[49]

The first point on the agenda was that the *bruksfolket* should live a life filled
with 'godliness' and be 'faithful, sober, industrious and united', but it was not
a horizontal unity that Lefebure strove for. He stood apart as their 'master
and *Hausvater*', and it was their duty to pay him respect. His second point
was directly related to *hushållning*: 'I have stated that all and sundry must
arrange their *hushållning* so that their debit does not exceed their credit,' and
especially regulate remuneration in such a way that people not end up in debt.
If that happened Lefebure would 'take unpleasant' steps. The ironworkers had
a monetary wage, but seldom received any cash since all necessities had to be
purchased in a warehouse at the *bruk*; Lefebure thus controlled both their
debits and credits. Then followed precise instructions: it was forbidden to fish
in the pond, pigs had to be kept behind fences, and everyone had to accept the
restrictions on haymaking. The workers were reminded that the latter took
place on *his* fields, and that each household could only collect enough hay in
relation to their stipulated number of animals. If they kept more cattle, that
was their problem and not one of their *brukspatron*.

Lefebure's instructions bear clear similarities to themes discussed by writers
on the public *hushållning*. He did not deal with iron-making, the main task
for a *bruk*, but other instructions were issued for that; letters were regularly
sent from his office in Stockholm to *bruks-contoiret* at Gimo specifying the
amount and dimension of the bars they should make. Instead Lefebure dealt
with pigs, hay and debts, but still these instructions touch upon features from
the previous analysis. One thing to note is that 'nature' was the foundation
for Lefebure's argument since 'his people' had to make a living from what
nature gave. A second argument follows from this, because it was *his* nature
they used; God might have furnished the land with resources, but their use
was in the gift of the *brukspatron*.

Eric Touscher's *Handbok* from 1739 also dealt with *brukshushållning*, its
two factors 'people and things' being joined by 'diligent labour'. Touscher's
point of departure was similar to Lefebure's, with the Leufsta people that

---

49   Gimo bruksarkiv, Lövstaarkivet, fack 43: Gimo Bruk. Handlingar från 1700-talet, No 29.

had 'nourishment, clothing, lodging and allotments'; but he proceeded to a detailed description of labour, and there were four different types. First there was the tedious work done by the skilled artisans in the furnaces and forges, working around the clock from Sunday evening until dusk the following Saturday. Their work set the pace for other activities at the estate. A second group was the day-labourers and craftsmen undertaking auxiliary tasks and supplying the population with shoes, clothes and other necessities. The clerks did non-manual tasks, such as keeping the accounts and controlling the other groups. At the top sat Touscher himself, the *Directeur*, in charge 'of all the estate [and] the workers, peasants and crofters ... for the benefit of the Lordship'. Lastly there were the lease-holding peasants.[50]

To Berch, *hushållning* was 'a science [and] an art of acquiring, managing and maintaining property', and Touscher agreed. He was busy trying to expand iron production, but without disturbing the balance between output and resources. He was active on the iron market, trying to complete lucrative contracts with English merchants, but also busy in the land market to increase the supply of charcoal. He was also trimming the organisation of labour. Memoranda were written with calculations about production costs, supply of charcoal and man-power, and when the organisation was too large he tried to down-size; he wanted to make redundant some of the artisans at the 'carpenter workshop ... as soon as it can be done'.[51]

Fine-tuning was one way of securing a good *brukshushållning*, but Touscher had at least two other tools to enhance the efficiency of 'managing and maintaining [the] property' at Leufsta. One measure was to assure that the workers actually practised 'diligent labour'. The forges were the 'heart-beat' of the *bruk*, and the forgemen worked according to the rhythm set by the work of refining iron, but for the rest of the workers other means were used to make sure that everybody was 'diligent', and that an efficient *oeconomia* prevailed. Work began at five o'clock, when a bell signalled the beginning of the working day, but the *Directeur* also had a clerk walking around the place to make sure that 'work was done with fidelity'; to Uhr the 'objectum' was to 'press the actual labour'. The same bell also announced the breaks for food and the end of the working day.[52]

Leufsta was a gigantic estate, with many people attached to it, and direct supervision was practically impossible. It might have worked at the *bruk* itself, but was not feasible for the estate at large. There were, however, other means of control, and none as powerful as elaborate bookkeeping techniques. Much of the *Handbok* dealt with this. Mary Poovey has stated that double-entry

50   'En liten handbok'.
51   Georg Swebilius to J. J. De Geer, 5 April 1731, Volym 106, Leufsta Arkivet, Riksarkivet, Stockholm.
52   'En liten handbok'.

bookkeeping, a 'rule-governed system' of accounting, was essential in the making of modernity, and in the creation of what she calls 'the modern fact'. The crucial feature was the systematic approach of gradually transforming, and abstracting, real business transactions into figures and numbers that fitted into the balanced scheme of credits and debits. According to Poovey, this gave accounts a transparent character that mirrored 'God's order'. Balancing books became a virtue, and a way of establishing what constituted the truth. Merchants used different account books, the *Inventory*, a list of all belongings, the *Memorial*, containing the day-to-day business and the *Journal*, a summary of the memorial. The final book was the *Ledger*, which transformed the journal's entries into thematically arranged double-entry accounts.[53]

If systematic accounting was a sign of modernity Swedish iron-making was a part of this process. Conforming to Poovey's argument, archives are filled with meticulously kept accounts from the beginning of the seventeenth century, including inventories, journals, memorials and ledgers. In Sweden three books were used. There was the day-to-day *Journal*, sometimes divided between different areas of the *bruk*. These were compiled into the *Avräkningsboken*, kept as double-entry accounts of all the people related to the *bruk*. These accounts were transferred into *Capitalboken*, the main ledger. The same process of abstracting day-to-day transactions into figures that could be transformed into the double-entry system was thus at work.[54]

There were differences as compared to Poovey's narrative: *Avräkningsboken* at Leufsta contained individual accounts with everybody attached to Leufsta, and business transactions with merchants, but these ledgers also included accounts with the workers and peasants. The credit side gives information about jobs, tasks or services the workers had performed, calculated as wages, while the debit side shows how this was paid for, mainly in kind. *Capitalboken* begins with a summary in the form of a 'balancing account' of all the individual accounts, and an inventory, valuing all 'material wealth' at the *bruk*. The largest part of the ledger is however devoted to capturing what can be called 'internal' commodity chains. There is a concentration on different types of iron, but ample information is also given on charcoal and other necessary materials used in iron-making; these ledgers are clearly divided into accounts dealing with 'people and things'.[55]

After the 1750s new volumes were being added to the accounts,

53 Poovey, *History of the Modern Fact*.
54 For a brief introduction to bookkeeping at Swedish *bruk*, see Karl-Gustaf Hildebrand, *Swedish Iron in the Seventeenth and Eighteenth Centuries. Export Industry before the Industrialization* (Stockholm, 1992), pp. 71–6.
55 See the account book from several different *bruk*, including those from Leufsta and Gimo, Lövstaarkivet.

strengthening the emphasis upon the material side, particularly on iron and charcoal, but the aspect of controlling labour was also taken to a new level. A volume with weekly reports from the forges, with output figures and the uses of pig iron and charcoal, was created. A second volume, aptly called *Diarium*, takes this information to yet another level, with minute details about what the working people did on a daily basis. In large spreadsheets, one for each month, we can follow what type of work was undertaken by each of the *bruk*'s subordinates.[56]

Touscher's version of *brukshushållning*, along with Lefebure's instructions and the new bookkeeping practices, are good examples of inserting 'layers' of *hushållning* between the public sphere and the private domain in the trinity elaborated by Berch, while keeping to the same internal structure; *brukshus-hållning* was all about systematic order along hierarchical principles. It began with a benign nature, but framed by the boundaries set by the *brukspatron*, and it was about balancing between 'people and things' using 'diligent labour', or 'supervise and press the actual labour' as Uhr formulated it. Elaborate bookkeeping principles were a way of ensuring that this 'act of balancing' was undertaken in an ordered and systematic way, as well as remaining in control; it was about abstracting concrete relationship and transactions into abstracted numbers in double-entry accounts of credits and debits. From the beginning there was an emphasis upon people and things, but towards the end of the century monitoring labour gradually became more important. Throughout the period, however, these principles demanded of the clerks that they spent hours on end trying to write down what workers had done.

To an extent one might be tempted by Touscher's writings to see the whole *bruk* as one large household in itself, with Charles De Geer as a grand *Hausvater*; the poem from 1739 used household metaphors such as 'obeying and working for our father', with the estate seen as a 'table'. However, that is not the whole story, as Touscher was aware of a layer below the *bruks-hushållning*. This was the private *hushållning* of the many workers, artisans and peasants, with their own much smaller households, trying to balance their credits and debits. It is not clear how the lines between this larger entity and the many smaller subordinated households were drawn, or if they made such a demarcation at all. Lefebure's remark about the ability of 'his people' to actually balance between debit and credit is a sign that they did, but if they did not it is clear that they were interested in the viability of the private

---

56   These accounts are gender-blind. Most accounts are in men's names, but they deal with the whole household. For an elaboration, see Göran Rydén and Chris Evans, 'Connecting Labour. Organising Swedish Ironmaking in an Atlantic Context', *Labour, Unions and Politics under the Northern Star. The Nordic Countries, 1700–2000*, ed. M. Hilson, S. Neunsinger and I. Vyff (New York/Oxford, 2017), pp. 71–87.

hushållning of their subordinates; no *brukshushållning* would have existed without a well-functioning private domain.

Swedish *hushållning*: concluding remarks

This essay opened with an event that was seen as a generational shift at Leufsta *bruk*; in 1739 the young heir Charles De Geer arrived to claim his inheritance. On arrival he was presented with two hand-written manuscripts, a poem and a new map of the place. These four gifts, and especially the *Handbok* by Eric Touscher, gave an initial first insight into the issue that has been dealt with in this essay, that of *hushållning*. The practice of *hushållning* was a systematic and ordered 'art of acquiring, managing and maintaining property' and people; it was all about 'people and things' and how these were combined in 'diligent labour', as well as 'used' [*nyttjas och brukas*] in the making of iron. *Hushållning* had a spatial character, and to the new *brukspatron* it was the boundaries of his estate that set the limits to his iron-making; but spatiality also meant more in Swedish eighteenth-century economic discourse. Touscher's texts must be inserted into the wider framework of Swedish cameralism, and into the triad of divine, public and private *hushållning*, all with their distinct spatial settings.

A central feature of the *hushållning* Touscher wanted De Geer to follow, but also in the writings on the public *oeconomia*, is a hierarchical structure; both Touscher and Berch had clearly adopted a deferential tone in what they wrote. There was an overarching structure to their texts, in which a divine *hushållning*, headed by the Almighty Creator, was seen as superior to the public and private spheres, with the *brukshushållning* placed in between the latter two. The hierarchical principle also works within each of these levels, with a well-defined *Hausvater* at its helm. It was their duty to oversee the practice of their subordinated people. In line with this it was the assignment of Touscher to monitor that the people of De Geer's estate did what they were supposed to do, namely practise 'diligent labour'; his task was to 'press the actual labour'.

A central feature of this hierarchical structure was the work of ordering and controlling. To Berch it was clear that the *Polity* was given the role of supervising the *oeconomia*, and De Geer was assured that his workers 'long to obey [his] commands'. Within the public *hushållning*, political arithmetic was seen to be a crucial tool in the quest for a rational structure that enhanced both the power of the sovereign and the happiness of the people. In *brukshushållning* an elaborated accounting technique, with double-entry bookkeeping, performed a similar role. Both Berch and Touscher were clear about these structures, but they also allotted themselves a very specific position within these hierarchies. They were subordinated to their masters, but also indispensable; Berch was the self-appointed teacher to Swedish youth, and Touscher the man who elaborated the bookkeeping at the Leufsta estate. Their practice was to spend hours at their writing desks, trying to find new ways of transforming everyday tasks and duties of common people into abstract figures and numbers. In many ways they can both be seen as Swedish cameralists, working on different levels of Swedish society.

The 'lowest' of the levels discussed here, the private *hushållning*, has only been touched on in passing, because most writers of the time ignored it, or only made occasional reference to it. We have been told that this had a hierarchical structure similar to that of the other layers, with a master at its helm, but we have not been told anything about the actual practice of private *hushållning*. In partial compensation for this, the last words will be those of Anders Berch. In a letter written to Pehr Wargentin, one of the men behind *Tabellverket*, he compared the public and the private layers:

> The *hushållning* of States and Kingdoms are kept in the same fashion as is those of private persons. If I have a farm in the country, then I must adopt one branch of *hushållning* after the other, if it shall work well: I cannot keep all my farmhands in the stable with all my expensive horses, but some must be out on the fields and meadows: if I want so much food preparation in the kitchen, or cleaning in the chambers, so that the maids have no more time, then the cattle in the shed will perish. [...] If I am ignorant about how much a man can ditch, fence, plough, thresh, on one day, then I cannot control his sloth: I then do not know how many hands I need for my chores; with one word am I in confusion and will turn into a beggar. It is the same with the Kingdom's *hushållning*: there must be a proportion between Land and people, people and trade, trade and trade, and these things come from a thorough investigation of the country's area, fertility, climate, number of inhabitants, orders, trade, store of money, etc. [...] then the *hushållning* would be in order [...].[57]

57   Anders Berch to Pehr Wargentin, 4 September 1759, quoted in Johannisson, *Det mätbara samhället*, p. 136.

9

Johan Ludvig Reventlow's
Master Plan at the Brahetrolleborg Estate:
Cameralism in Denmark in the 1780s and 1790s

INGRID MARKUSSEN

Introduction

The brothers Johan Ludvig and Christian Ditlev Reventlow can be seen as later eighteenth-century representatives of cameralist thinking in Denmark. The reforms to agriculture, education and poor relief that Johan Ludvig Reventlow (1751–1801) introduced on his Brahetrolleborg estate, Funen island, were largely cameralist in inspiration. His brother Christian Ditlev Reventlow (1748–1827) was leader of the *Rentekammer* and one of the highest cameral officials in Denmark; he reformed his Christianssæde estate on Lolland island in like manner. However, in the following I will primarily concentrate on the work of Johan Ludvig Reventlow.

During the second half of the eighteenth century there were plans for reform in every social sector of the Danish-Norwegian dual monarchy. New ideas generally came from the South, passing through the two duchies of Schleswig and Holstein that were part of the Danish monarchy. These two duchies were windows open not only to the ideas of the Continental Enlightenment, but were also influenced by ideas originating in England.

Despite the closed collegial system of the Danish–Norwegian absolute monarchy, its central administration was relatively receptive to new ideas. At mid-century one of the best-known officials in the country was the theologian Erik Pontoppidan, a man who combined pietist faith with enlightened economic ideas. In 1759 his *Eutropii Philadelphi Oeconomiske Balance* argued for greater emphasis upon Danish raw materials and Danish labour, highlighting awareness of Enlightenment economic ideas in Denmark. At about the same time he published *Collegium Pastorale Practicum*, a manual in which he counselled newly educated clergymen who would take over local parishes. This connection between religion and economy would be a characteristic feature of Danish cameralist policy in the 1780s and 1790s.

In 1755 the Danish–Norwegian government invited proposals for economic improvements, and many contributions were later published in the first Danish economic periodical, *Danmarks og Norges økonomiske Magasin*. Erik Pontoppidan was the motive force here, having had encouragement from the King's closest adviser, Adam Gottlob Moltke, an estate owner and high official, the *overhofmarskal*. On his Bregentved estate Moltke practised so-called *holstensk kobbelbrug* (a system of crop rotation); he also sought to extend the arable cultivated area of his property by draining and clearing, and encouraged his tenant farmers to adopt improved agricultural techniques and better seed. He turned to Johann Heinrich Gottlob von Justi for advice on cultivating Danish heathlands, seeking to accelerate the economic development of the country with the help of 'the German expert'. Justi had of course published a very great deal on the ways in which the economy of a state could be improved, and he became a notable voice in the Danish social debate.

Unlike their Norwegian counterparts, Danish peasants did not own their farms. They rented land and farm buildings from the estate, so that farms remained the property of the estate owner. There was lifetime security of tenure, but not the right to sell or extend their holding. Tenant farmers were liable for annual dues, and had to carry out corvée work for the estate.[1] They were protected by law; only when a tenant farmer was no longer capable of maintaining his farm could his tenure be terminated. Even though most tenant farms were passed on to the children of a sitting tenant, this was a practice that lacked legal foundation and could not be presumed; the estate owner retained the right to take control of a farm after a peasant's death and pass it to another household head. Land was still distributed in an open field system, laid out in narrow strips around villages. Each tenant farmer had a mixture of all types of land, good and bad. Working the dispersed strips called for a great deal of collaboration, and the estate owner had many opportunities to interfere with the working lives of his tenants.[2]

Danish peasants had since 1733 been bound to their estate (*stavnsbåndet*, i.e. adscription). Between the ages of 4 and 40 male peasants were not allowed to leave the estate without the permission of the manor. The estate owner was also required to provide soldiers for the monarch, and so this was an

---

1   Carsten Porskrog Rasmussen, 'Modern Manors?', *Modernisation and Tradition. European Local and Manorial Societies 1500–1900*, ed. K. Sundberg, T. Germundsson and K. Hansen (Malmö, 2004), p. 50.
2   Fridlev Skrubbeltrang, *Det danske Landbosamfund 1500–1800* (Copenhagen, 1978); Harald Holm, *Kampen om Landboreformerne i Danmark i Slutningen af det 18. Aarhundrede* (Copenhagen, 1888).

added burden for the peasantry. It is generally agreed that the peasants' lack of property rights, the system of *stavnsbånd* and corvée labour all fostered a condition of stagnation in eighteenth-century Danish agriculture.

Many eighteenth-century estate owners and publicists were of the opinion that the peasants were just lazy, stupid, reluctant, sly and suspicious of everything new, especially when innovations were made by estate owners and government officials.[3] The impact of Physiocracy and cameralism during the 1760s and 1770s altered this perception. Cameralism especially played an increasingly important part in the later eighteenth century, influencing not only government economic initiatives and private ventures supported by the government, but also developments related to education and the church.

Cameralist arguments and policy was oriented to the state, seeing an increasing population as a important factor in national prosperity. Agriculture was considered to be the most important economic sector, and there was also an emphasis on the ethical and economic value of work. A cameralistic watchword was that every well-regulated state should give work to every man, that every man naturally loved working. Moral education and popular enlightenment were important for cameralists who saw an enlightened and educated people as an essential foundation for improved agriculture and a well-regulated state.[4]

Education in cameralist sciences at the Academy of Sorø

After 1750 the cameralist sciences could be studied at a new educational institution in Denmark, the Academy of Sorø. This was a modern alternative to the University of Copenhagen, which was generally thought to serve only theological ends. The Academy was founded by Ludvig Holberg, a famous writer and professor at Natural Law at the University of Copenhagen. Holberg was also an estate owner, and he funded the new institution from his Tersløsegaard estate on Zealand. He had in mind a modern higher educational institution with modern languages, philosophy, geography, history, moral sciences and, above all, public law and cameral sciences: natural law, economic and financial management, and *Polizeiwissenschaft*.

Professor Andreas Schytte (1726–77) lectured on cameral sciences at the Academy in the 1760s. Johan Ludvig and Christian Ditlev Reventlow were his students at the Academy from 1763 to 1766, and they later remained in

---

3 Peter Henningsen, *I sansernes vold. Bondekultur og kultursammenstød i enevældens Danmark*, 1–2 (Copenhagen, 2006).
4 Ingrid Markussen, *Til Skaberens Ære, Statens Tjeneste og vor egen Nytte. Pietistiske og kameralistiske ideer bag fremvæksten af en obligatorisk skole i landdistrikterne i Danmark* (Odense, 1995).

close contact with him. During the 1780s and 1790s the brothers introduced many of the ideas to which Andreas Schytte had introduced them at Sorø. In the introduction to volume 4 of *The Government of the State* (*Staternes indvortes Regiering 1773–75*), entitled *Politievæsenet* (*Polizei*), Schytte cited Aristotle as the great teacher of the Greeks in arguing for the importance of Polizei:

> *Polizei* is the life of the state, it reflects on everything, educates the whole, gives humans what they need, protects the people from the evil things as they are afraid of, ... the Romans called *Polizei* the mother of sciences, the nurse of arts, the school of wisdom and the source of all order.[5]

Schytte considered *Polizei* to be the spirit that imbued the state system, a guide for cameral policy. *Polizeiwissenschaft* was a body of knowledge whose influence ranged from the most domestic level to systematic schooling and qualification, also identifying the penal code as a powerful regulator of human behaviour. 'Polizei' was the morality of 'state and church', Schytte concludes, but with a significant difference: the measures enforced by the church were gentle, those used by secular powers were harsh,[6] and so to be a good cameralist one needed to pay attention to *Polizei*.[7]

In this publication Schytte describes the cameral sciences as a part of *Staatswissenschaft*, the science that shows what is right and of use to society. What is right is law, and what is useable is *Polizei*. The first volume deals with natural law, public law, private law, international law, the concept of state, different forms of governmental systems – despotism, aristocracy, monarchy, democracy, republicanism, limited governments – and finally, the ideological foundations of a government. Volume 2 and a part of volume 3 cover state revenues, and volume 3 covers state expenditure. In the introduction to volume 2 Schytte describes the state as an artificial body which, like a human body, needs sustenance. Cameralism is closely connected to *Polizei* and the household arts. Schytte argues that there are two types of households in the state: the public household and the domestic household. The domestic household relates to the private economy of subjects, which is crucial for

5   Andreas Schytte, *Staternes indvortes Regiering*, 4 vols (Copenhagen, 1773–75), vol. 4, pp. 1–2: 'Politiet er Statens Liv, den giør i Staten den samme Virkning, som Sielen i Legemet: Den tænker på alt, danner det Heele, forskaffer Borgerne det fornødne, afvender fra Selskabet det Onde der har at befrygte. Romerne, der havde deres Love, deres Statskunst, og næsten alt af de vittigere Grækere, kaldte Politiet Videnskabernes Moder, Kunsternes Amme, Viisdommens Skole og Kilden til al Orden.'
6   Schytte, *Staternes indvortes Regiering*, vol. 4, p. 46: 'Politiet er Moralisten i Staten, saavel som Gejstligheden, men med Forskiel. Den geistlige Magt bruger Glat-Høvlen og Polere-ernet, den verdslige Raspen og Skrub-Høvlen.' See Markussen, *Til Skaberens ære*, pp. 71–2.
7   Schytte, *Staternes indvortes Regiering*, vol. 4, p. 2.

the economic health of the state. *Polizeiwissenschaft* contains the laws, rules and arrangements of the state appropriate for the management of all income sources for both public and private good.

In the fourth volume Schytte also writes about religion, education and the sciences, because the education of the citizenry in these areas (of *Polizei*) was necessary for the successful development of the state.[8] Schytte considered that a good cameralist could not limit his work to the public household, but should have effective oversight over all the many sources of state income, at the same time understanding the laws, rules and arrangements that apply to both the public and private realms for the good of all. The task of the cameralist was to maximise public and private economic benefits for the common good. *Polizei* was the instrument at the disposal of the cameralist, conducting education and religion as a 'state moralist'.

Two cameralist educators

Leader of the *Rentekammer* from 1784, Christian Ditlev Reventlow characterised himself in a letter to his sister Louise Stolberg as 'ein Cammer Mensch',[9] and in a letter to his *hofmester* Carl Wendt he called himself a Cameralist.[10] During the 1770s Johan Ludvig Reventlow was also employed in the government administration at the Økonomi- og Kommercekollegiet, but in 1787 he returned to his estate to pursue local reforms. During their educational studies during the later 1760s the two brothers had had excellent teachers and authors at Halle, Göttingen and Leipzig University. Among them was Christian Garve, who became a close friend. Garve talked and later wrote about the need to free German serfs, and he naturally influenced the young Danish brothers.

On his estate Johan Ludvig Reventlow wanted to be free from the intervention of the state. He was closer to the Physiocrats than the cameralists in this regard.[11] However he was in constant contact with the government and was a member of advisory commissions to reform Danish agriculture, education and poor relief. In the same way as his brother, he here acted like a

---

8   Schytte, *Staternes indvortes Regiering*, vol. 1, pp. v–vi.
9   Louis Bobé, *Efterladte Papirer fra den Reventlowske Familiekreds i Tidsrummet 1770–1827*, 10 vols (Copenhagen, 1895–1931), vol. 1, p. 93.
10   Bobé, *Efterladte Papirer*, vol. 1, pp. 30–2.
11   Christian Ditlev Reventlow warned his brother that freedom could not be given to estate owners and peasants until the government was sure that they were capable of effective administration, so that freedom would not bring ruin to owners, peasants and the state. Until this time all reforms had to be made within existing legislation. Bobé, *Efterladte Papirer*, vol. 1, p. 40.

governmental official: as Schytte would have said, as a *genuine* cameralist and educator.

Following a *coup d'état* in 1784 that removed the conservative Guldberg regime of 1772–84,[12] the Danish government was favourable to reform. Johan Ludvig Reventlow had been active in the *coup*, and the government appointed a commission to reform agriculture on the royal domains of north Zealand island. He was himself an active member of the commission engaged with small farms, the *Lille Landbokommission*. The commission's recommendations were accepted and enacted: all royal open fields were enclosed, many tenant farms were moved out of villages, the corvée was limited and peasants were given hereditary tenure (*arvefæste*). There were however conditions attached, since the government wanted to control land development and be sure that peasants were capable of dealing with their new responsibilities. Reforms were similar to those that Johan Ludvig Reventlow hd introduced on his Brahetrolleborg Estate, revising both the legal status of his peasants and agricultural practice at the same time.

Johan Ludvig Reventlow as estate owner and cameralist

Johan Ludvig Reventlow and his brother belonged to one of the leading noble families in the country whose lands were scattered and not consolidated into one single estate. Like other leading noble families in the German circle of aristocrats, the Reventlow family had migrated to Denmark from northern Germany in the seventeenth century and quickly established itself in the Danish absolute system. Louise Stolberg, sister to the two brothers, once wrote in a letter that these German noble families were like a tree whose roots went back to the rivers Elbe and Weser.[13] These German roots connected the Reventlow family to the two duchies of Schleswig-Holstein and to the north of Germany. During 1783–1800 Hamburg was seen to be an area of Danish interest, and Altona was part of Holstein, where a branch of the Reventlow family lived. Johan Ludvig Reventlow and his brother and sister generally wrote to each other in the German language.

Johan Ludvig inherited the Brahetrolleborg Estate on Funen island in 1775. The manor had been established in the Middle Ages as a Cistercian monastery, 'Insula Dei'. In the sixteenth century the monastery extended in total over 964 *tønder hartkorn*,[14] divided into 125 farms. This was broadly

---

12   Ove Hoegh Guldberg (1731–1808) followed the Struensee regime. Johann Friedrich Struensee (1737–72) died by beheading in 1772.

13   Bobé, *Efterladte Papirer*, vol. 1, p. viii.

14   An average tenant farm of 15–20 hectares of arable land was estimated to be 5–6 *tønder hartkorn*.

how the property was arranged in 1775.[15] In 1803 there were 105 farms, and by 1818 again 125 farms on the estate. Most of the tenant farms were of about 5 or 6 *tønder hartkorn*. The name Brahetrolleborg derived from earlier noble families that had owned the estate, the families Brahe and Trolle.

Agricultural reforms at Brahetrolleborg

Soon after taking over the estate in 1775 Johan Ludvig initiated long-term reforms that had far-reaching consequences both for tenants and estate owner. Reforms were continued until 1801 when Johan Ludvig Reventlow died at the age of 51.

On inheriting the land in 1775 Reventlow began a survey of manorial lands, and in 1782 continued with peasant lands. The survey covered fields, pastures and forests, following which a valuation was made. During 1786–88 the open fields were consolidated into more compact units; meadow and woodland was also distributed among the peasants according to the assessed value of the land. The objective was that all tenant farms should have an equal share of land by value. Following from these arrangements, 40 tenant farms (one third of all the tenant farms) were moved out of the villages and established as detached farmsteads.

Reventlow did not only direct his attention to tenant farmers. He also parcelled out land to 90 smallholdings, each of 3 *tønder land* (1 *tønde land* was equal to 0.55 hectares). Some of the smallholdings – like the tenant farms (*arvefæstegårde*) – were conveyed to smallholders on terms of a hereditary tenancy (*arvefæste*).[16] According to the census survey of 1787, the tenant farm households had between 3 and 5 unmarried farmhands (land workers), but by the 1801 census survey numbers had fallen by nearly half. This was in part a result of the Reventlow smallholding reforms. In 1801 a large percentage of agricultural work on the estate was done by married smallholders, a group that contributed to a growing population.[17]

Moving out of the villages was very painful for tenants. Reventlow cushioned the process by building new modern farms with stables and outbuildings at a price of 600–800 rigsdaler per farm, equipping them with new tools and implements. A building boom broke out on the estate. During 1786–88 40 new farms and 90 smallholdings were built, and at the same time

15 René Schrøder Christensen, 'Udskiftningen på Brahetrolleborg. Et eksempel på godsejerens store indflydelse på kulturlandskabet', *Fynske Årbøger* (2005), p. 41.

16 Schrøder Christensen, *Udskiftningen på Brahetrolleborg*, p. 45.

17 The census surveys for 1787 and 1801 show that the population at Brahetrolleborg was 1,181 persons in 1787; 14 years later, in 1801, the population had grown to 1,522 persons.

many other permanent brick buildings constructed for other purposes.[18] Tenants who remained in the villages had to provide for those moving out to their new farms, transporting building materials or assisting with the enclosure of land. Reventlow facilitated loans to tenants from the Royal Kreditkasse (established in 1786), guaranteeing their repayment. He also extended credit to his tenants at an interest rate of 4%. These loans were used for extensive land improvement (clearing land, removing stones, planting hedges and and building stone walls, for example). Reventlow had a positive view of his tenants and believed that they could work harder and be more productive if freed from *stavnsbånd* (adscription) and corvée, holding their farms on hereditary tenure.

Reventlow established a 'farmer parliament' of eight elected tenants at the beginning of his reforms, four appointed by Reventlow and four elected by the tenants. These acted as mediators between the manor and the peasants during the time of the estate's transformation. Reventlow also appointed his special advisers, attendants and valuers from among these eight farmers. The eight farmers often met at the estate around an eight-sided table that Reventlow had had made, and this is now displayed in the estate's library.

Arvefæstereformen: tenure reform

The high point of agricultural reform was in 1788, when Reventlow was authorised by the government, *Danske Kancelli and Rentekammer* to introduce a system of hereditary tenure. Hereditary tenure (*arvefæste*) is a half-way house between renting and possession. The farmers gained the right to sell parcels of land to a lodger, for instance. Tenants knew that the farm would be inherited by their children. But similarly to the farms at the royal domains in the north of Zealand, some conditions were imposed. Tenants had to pay rent to the estate, farms had to be enclosed by hedges, and the young men of the household had to be engaged in running the farm. If these conditions were not fulfilled, and if the family had no children, Reventlow could reassume control of the farm and give it to another household head. Both the state (in the north of Zealand island) and Reventlow at Brahetrolleborg retained their rights of land ownership.

At the beginning of September 1788 Reventlow gathered together all his tenants to fully inform them about the *arvefæstereform* and seek their approval. He was aware that not all tenants were enthusiastic about his plan.

---

18   Agricultural buildings and a large dairy at the manor, plus two schools. The two school-buildings still exist as private housing and a local archive. See N. Rasmussen Søkilde, *Gamle og nye Minder om Brahetrolleborg og Omegn* (Brahetrolleborgs Folkemindesamling og Øster Hæsinge lokalhistoriske arkiv, 2001).

Farmers could look forward to increased rights over the land they farmed and being freed from *stavnsbånd* and a greater part of corvée, but they had to pay a great deal for these gains, paying off the large loans they had taken out and in addition annual rents to the estate owner.

Reventlow gathered all the tenant farmers together on his wife's birthday, 14 September 1788, and gave them their documents. In his address he made it clear that he had for many years pursued a master plan for his reform project, and that he now wanted to complete this. His master plan had three steps: first to reform children's schooling, secondly to reform poor relief, and thirdly to reform agriculture. He argued that together, these three steps would produce new farmers for the estate, and new subjects for the state. He extolled freedom, independence and responsibility within a governmental framework.

Reventlow began his talk to his tenants as follows:

> Children! My wish is to quickly give you a final and most long-term proof of my true love for you and my dear friendship, placing all of you in such condition that can preserve you from arbitrary treatment in future; making you free, rational, good and active, useful, industrious and godly subjects of the state. My wish is that you be as happy as I want you to be; that is what has encouraged me all these years, and today I see myself in a position to realise this in the most solemn way.[19]

For Reventlow, of the many advantages that would come about with *arvefæste* freedom was the most essential factor, and with this freedom many of the other advantages would come about of themselves.

Promoting industry and new initiatives at Brahetrolleborg

Reventlow hoped that after 1788 tenants would be keen to test new techniques and agricultural products and so produce greater profits. He established factories to process their products. During the years of the building boom Reventlow established six brickworks not only to build the 40 new farms and 90 new smallholdings, but also to build new dwelling-houses for landless agricultural workers. New workers' houses had accommodation for eight families, with individual plots of land for each family to grow vegetables. By

---

19 Bobé, *Efterladte Papirer*, vol. 2, pp. 193–216: 'Børn! Mit Ønske, i en kort Tid, at kunne give Eder det sidste, det varigste Beviis paa min oprigtige Kiærlighed, paa mit ømme Venskab for Eder, ved at sætte Eder alle, Børn, i saadan en Forfatning, som kunde sikre Eder mod al vilkaarlig Behandling ved at giøre Eder til frie, fornuftige, gode og virksomme, nyttige, stræbsomme og gudfrygtige Statens Borgere, at I derved kunne blive saa lykkelige, som jeg attraaer, dette Ønske, som har oplivet alle mine Foretagender, seer jeg mig nu i Stand til i Dag paa det høitideligste at opfylde' (p. 193).

1788 there were two water mills on the estate. Reventlow also had a canal dug from a nearly lake to bring water to one of the mills, and he renovated it so that it could mill tenants' cereal products. The mill was a great success.

On the advice of his brother Christian Ditlev, Reventlow established a forge in 1784, assisted by the local smith. Christian Ditlev, living at Christianssæde on Lolland island, was there called 'the big smith' because of the great interest he took in the blacksmith's craft on his estate.[20] Reventlow's new project had assistance from the government (and it could be that Christian Ditlev also had a hand in that). The local smith had learned his trade during travels to Hamburg and Holstein. The forge produced farm equipment, such as parts for ploughs and scythes; knives and axes were also made. The scythes made by 'Søren the smiths' became well-known locally and brought in a good income, the forge continuing in use until 1858.

Another important initiative was the growing of flax on the estate. This was directed by Henning Schroll who had in the course of eleven years travelled through Westfalia, the Netherlands, Flanders and Scotland. When he returned to Brahetrolleborg in 1790 he became 'arvefæster' and started experimentally producing flax, a *høravlingsinstitut*, an institute for producing flax. The production was such a success that by 1801 flax was being farmed on 76 *tønder* land at the estate. The rent for the land was 552 rigsdaler but his income was over 6,000, so that after all the expenses were paid there was a profit of 2,000 rigsdaler. He also received economic aid from the government, and was able to attract young men from all over the country to learn not only flax growing, but also modern agricultural methods. The trainees were given free food, lodging and money, but had to commit themselves to working on the farm growing flax for nine years, later reduced to five. The trainees were also freed from military conscription if they were growing flax on at least 1 *tønde* of land per year, and were given 100 rigsdaler from the government to buy tools and linseed. This institute for flax growing continued until 1863. Reventlow established a flax manufactory on the estate, which employed 20 people, among them seven weavers, the first linen master having been educated in England. In 1801 the flax factory closed, but it reopened some years later.

There is no doubt that Reventlow had the intention of pursuing cameralist objectives with these manufacturing initiatives, establishing opportunities for work on the estate. He wanted young women of the region to be able to learn spinning and weaving, increasing household and manufacturing good quality cloth for clothing and household use. He therefore founded a spinning school linked to the linen manufactory. Later he established further schools for spinning and other training centres on the estate, so that schoolchildren might be able to learn handicraft skills.

20   In letters to his sister he sometimes calls himself 'Christian der Schmidt'. Bobé, *Efterladte Papirer*, vol. 1, p. 88.

At the beginning of his reform project Reventlow had established a dairy on the estate, on the recommendation of a German estate administrator, Schmeltz. This venture failed initially, for Schmeltz proved quite incompetent. It was at his suggestion that Reventlow put grass for the stall-fed cows into salted cellars,[21] which ruined the fodder and the Reventlow family then had to buy their milk from other farms.[22] Once Schmeltz had been dismissed milk production increased, and by 1801 there were seven milkmaids and a dairyman on the estate. Schmeltz had come from Saxony; he was replaced by an English estate administrator, Somerwell, who was more successful. He imported light ploughs from England, and also improved the cultivation of potatoes and turnips.

Reventlow was the first estate owner on Funen island to use his fallow land to grow peas, vetches, buckwheat and flax. He also grew red onions and clover, and was the first to cultivate rape. He planted in his garden fruit trees bought from Holstein and Hamburg. Together with the trees came German gardeners. They helped tenants to plant fruit trees and grow vegetables in the new gardens of the outlying farms. At the teacher training college founded at Brahetrolleborg in 1794 each student had his own small garden where he could grow vegetables and plant fruit trees.

Reventlow also introduced new cattle breeds. One came from Scotland, a cow suitable for the production of both meat and milk. From Holstein and southern Schleswig he imported another breed that was raised in tenants' cattle sheds after cattle epidemics in the 1770s. 'Funen red cattle' was a mix of the two breeds, and later became a famous Danish cattle breed. Reventlow also introduced a new breed of horse, the Trolleborg, equally suitable for riding and transport. Sheep farming was established with a mix of Spanish and English breeds, with 260 sheep and 15 Spanish rams; later the flock grew to number more than 500. Their wool was used in the spinning schools.

Brahetrolleborg was, and is still today, quite heavily wooded. During the eighteenth century the forests were not fenced, and tenants were accustomed to gathering wood and other materials from them for household use. Reventlow ended this custom by fencing off the forests. When Johan Ludvig took over the estate in 1775 the woodland was not systematically exploited. Here again, he took advice from his brother, and had his forests valued by experienced foresters who drew up plan for felling and reseeding. During the later 1790s revenue from Brahetrolleborg woodland saved the estate at a time when many of Schmeltz's projects had failed at great expense. Reventlow, together with his brother-in-law, the minister of finance Ernst Schimmelmann, concluded an agreement between 1793 and 1796 that secured Reventlow a major loan

21   Carsten Porskrog Rasmussen, *Det sønderjyske landbrugs historie 1544–1830* (Åbenrå, 2013), pp. 421–2. Stallfeeding was in fashion in the 1760s.
22   Bobé, *Efterladte Papirer*, vol. 2, p. xxiv.

from Schimmelmann, paid off through the sale of logged timber, a clerk being deputised by Schimmelmann to oversee the work, The greater part of the oak timber was sold to the Danish Navy.[23]

Schooling and poor relief in Reventlow's master plan

Reventlow talked of three steps in his master plan, beginning with the schooling of children:

> Education and the teaching of children is without doubt most essential, lending hope of more enlightened peasants and promoting their true future happiness. Their way of thought, their intellectual formation depends on their education in their early years, and without education they will not be able to acquire properly useful knowledge.[24]

Reventlow saw schooling as a way to defeat the ignorance of peasants. This would alter their mentality, give them a sense of independence and under-standing of what freedom required them; and this had to begin in their very early years. In 1783 new school instructions were implemented and three new schools were established, two of them were in new modern buildings. According to the school rules, all boys and girls between the ages of 6 and 15 had to attend school for 2–4 hours every day. The school was divided into two classes. Younger children went to school in the afternoon, the older in the morning. In the pre-1783 school system all children attended all day to learn how to read and also learn Luther's small catechism by heart. After 1783 young children did not have to learn anything by heart. They had to form concepts by talking to the teacher about well-known affairs and by reading a textbook. It was essential for Reventlow that children would learn how to think and reflect. Children had to study reading, writing, arithmetic, religion, geography, history and the natural sciences, together with practical disciplines such as gymnastics, spinning and weaving. The new teachers were trained at the Kiel Seminar, where they had been exposed to ideas about enlightened education. The new school system was modelled on that of Friedrich Eberhard von Rochow's at his Brandenburg estate, Reckahn.

Rochow's reading book, *Der Kinderfreund*, was translated into Danish in

---

23 Bobé, *Staternes indvortes Regiering*, vol. 2, pp. xxv–xxvi; Elers Koch, *Brahetrolleborg Skovdistrikt 1786–1886* (Copenhagen, 1893), pp. 36–8.

24 Bobé, *Staternes indvortes Regiering*, vol. 2, p. 195: 'Børnenes Opdragelse og Underviisning er ustridig det meest vigtige, som skal give et grundet Haab om en mere oplyst Almue og fremme deres egen sande Lyksalighed i Fremtiden siden. Deres Tænkemaade, Forstandens dannelse beroer paa de Indtryk og den Anviisning de faaer i de første Aar, og uden hvilken de ikke ville være i Stand til at opnaae de dem fornødne og nyttige Kundskaber.'

1784 at the initiative of Reventlow and was used as the principal textbook in his schools. In religion Reventlow introduced Johan Andreas Cramer's rationalist catechism *Kurzer Unterricht im Christenthum*, translated into Danish. Cramer was the principal of the seminar in Kiel, and also a close friend of Johan Ludvig Reventlow.[25]

In 1794 Reventlow founded a teacher-training seminar at Brahetrolleborg where local peasants' sons, among others, could be educated, and a few years later he established a boarding school (philantropinum) in the same building. Teachers at the seminar and the philantropinum taught in both institutions, and the students in both institutions lived together, since the seminar also boarded its students. The philantropinum closed in 1808, and the seminar in 1828.

The second step of the master plan concerned poor relief. In 1788 reform was here already in progress. Reventlow argued that the new form of poor relief had the most beneficial prospects: 'if we are to continue supporting each other, for all depends on that'.[26] Support did not imply the direct distribution of alms. The poor must have help, but not through receiving alms or begging; help should be tailored to their actual needs. Reventlow observed that there were many beggars in the parish asking for help. A tenant farmer could have as many as twenty beggars a day at the door. The faith and support of the tenant was not shown by giving alms to all these poor beggars, but instead helping them by finding them work. Beggars had to be educated to work.

Poor relief was reformed in 1787.[27] The estate was divided into a number of smaller districts, in each of which a bailiff for the poor was elected. In addition, eight overseers were elected from past and present members of Reventlow's farmer parliament, each for a limited period. Altogether with the administrative staff of the estate, the priest, the three schoolteachers and Reventlow, the poor commission numbered some 15 to 20 persons, and the group met regularly to discuss poor relief matters. A poor box was set up. All persons who could work had to contribute to the poor box, Reventlow giving the large amount of 500 reichsthalers annually. The poor box had to meet the expenses for feeding and housing orphans, the disabled and the elderly poor. A hospital for the old and the sick was established near the estate house.

The third step of the master plan involved the reform of agriculture, as outlined above, seeking to create independent and industrious peasants who

25   Johann Andreas Cramer, *Kurzer Unterricht im Christenthum zum richtigen Verstande des kleinen Catechismus Lutheri, zum allgemeinen Gebrauche in Schleswig und Holstein* (Pinneburg/Ranzau, 1781).

26   Bobé, *Efterladte Papirer*, vol. 2, p. 196: 'naar vi, som vi have begyndt, vedblive at være hinanden troe, thi derpaa beroer alting'.

27   Rigsarkivet Odense. Brahetrolleborgs kommune. Fattigkommissionens forhandlingsprotokol 1787–1853.

could benefit from the first and second steps. These three steps involved much more than was usually expected of the owner of a private estate. Reventlow thought and acted in his own domain as a cameralist did in the context of the state. He envisaged his estate as a miniature monarchy, a demonstration for the leading politicians of the country. If the government ensured that girls and boys had a good rational education, that poor relief was reformed across the country so that the able-bodied poor could learn to work, then government would have secured a happy people producing economic benefit for the state.

Opposition from the tenants

However, many tenant farmers were opposed to the *arvefæste* and they complained of it to the government. To Reventlow's astonishment, in 1791 the government agreed with the complainants, although it had endorsed the reforms in 1788. Reventlow was compelled to revise his project. He was well connected with the government, which included his brother (Christian Ditlev Reventlow in *Rentekammeret*) and his brother-in-law (Ernst Schimmelmann (1747–1831) in *Finanskollegiet*); provision had been made for security of tenure, which Reventlow considered should have given the tenants freedom and security from arbitrary interference. Reventlow found it paradoxical that the government considered that it knew what was good for his peasants better than he did, and he was furious. Perhaps he had forgotten something that Schytte wrote in his book, about the way that people behaved like a flock of sheep.[28] It is likely that the government was worried that tenants would not be able to pay their taxes to the state because Reventlow would take too large a share for himself – in which case the reforms at Brahetrolleborg, would neither be of benefit to the state, nor the peasants.

A patriarchal perspective from the standpoint of Lutheran ideas

One could ask why Reventlow began his address to his tenants with what appears to be a sermon. But there is a clear logic here, and it can also be seen in Schytte's definition of *Polizei*. By emphasising the connection between his actions as an estate owner and Luther's teaching Reventlow lent religious legitimation to his project. He was aware that many tenant farmers were opposed to the changes involved in his reforms. He wished therefore to remind them about the nature of a Christian relationship between estate owner and

---

28   Schytte, *Staternes indvortes Regiering*, vol. 2, p. 33: 'Folket, lad være det er et Faar, der skal klippes, saa er det dog ikke et Faar, der skal slagtes.'

his peasants in a Christian state. Christian education was an essential part of the project.

Reventlow also preached Lutheran ideas regarding the dominant role of the father in every rank of society. Lutheran doctrine included a conception of the three estates, including all persons in society divided into subordinates and superiors within three estates: the household (the head of the household and his family and servants); the clergy (the priest and his congregation); and the government, with its civil servants and subjects.[29]

According to Luther, in each estate those who were superior should be like fathers to their subordinates, reflecting a paternal order. Superiors were to be given love and respect in the same way as a father was loved and respected by his wife, children and servants. Luther argued that God had called humans to live in special estates and positions (*stænder*). Every person therefore had to be satisfied with the position in which he or she was placed and perform the duties appropriate to that estate and calling.[30] If one was in a subordinate position then one had to obey, and act as a faithful servant; if one was in a superior position, then one had to take care of subordinates in an honourable manner, as if one was their father.[31] If one was rich one had to be grateful, but there was no reason to be excessively proud. Gratitude had to be shown by helping the less fortunate and acting in such a way that the common good was promoted. If one was poor one should not be envious, because it was God's will that one had this special challenge; patience was needed, and gratitude had to be shown to those who proffered assistance.[32] Actions of both rich and poor would be valued once earthly life had ended.[33]

The common good

Agriculture reform was intended to give peasants freedom and security from arbitrary rule and long-term benefit from their work. But Reventlow did not only talk about the benefit accruing to peasants, he also stressed the common good that would result from reform:

29 Markussen, *Til Skaberens Ære*; Michael Bregnsbo, *Samfundsordning og statsmagt set fra prædikestolen* (Odense, 1997).
30 Ingrid Markussen, 'Hustavlen og Aristoteles – en disciplinerende affære', *ARR. Idehistorisk tidsskrift* 4 (2013). Ingrid Markussen, *Sagens sande Beskaffenhed. Skolereformen på Brahetrolleborg 1783 set i lyset af en forældreklage* (forthcoming).
31 This is the content of the 'Haustafel'. Markussen, 'Hustavlen og Aristoteles'.
32 Writing test. 'Akter i Retssagen mod skoleholder Johannes Hansen Pade'. Exam, 29 July 1796. *Brahetrolleborg Archive*.
33 Reventlow shared the view of Cramer. Cf. J. A. Cramer's sermons in Bregnsbo, *Samfundsorden og statsmagt*.

You who are so fortunate that the plough has fallen into your hands ... when you are tilling your acres, and take from those acres all the riches with which providence will reward your tireless diligence, so you will increase the amount of sustenance nor only for yourselves, but also for the state; that is the common good. When everyone does his duty in his *stand og kald* estate, each person contributes to the common good and all society will be happy.'[34]

Reventlow's address could have been made by Andreas Schytte. Reventlow argued that the reform would teach the *arvefæster* industry, and the tenants would learn to use their time for useful pursuits so that they might be capable of performing the duties required by estate and calling. They would not only work for their own good, but also for the common good. Reventlow did however point out that the common good could sometimes require more than working for one's own good. It was when the common good came into conflict with one's own good that a man could show best how to perform his duties. There is no doubt that Reventlow saw himself in that position. He would have been wealthier if he had not sought to reform the working of his estate. But he knew of a better way for agricultural work, the tenant farmers and their families. He was certain, however, that one day in the future his heirs would reap the economic benefits of his reforms.

Brahetrolleborg as a fief of the crown, and Johan Ludvig Reventlow's loyalty to the Danish king

Reventlow's engagement for the common good was not only influenced by cameralism. He had in fact close connections with the Danish state, the Reventlow family belonging to an especially privileged section of the landowning class. In 1671 King Christian V had introduced the ranks of count and baron in Denmark. The Reventlow family belonged to this new elite nobility, as did other German noble families. The act establishing this new elite stipulated that counts and barons had to serve and promote the Danish crown.[35] As *lensbesiddere* noblemen were automatically linked to the King, and acted as officials (*amtmænd*) for the peasants on the estate. The estate was located in an

34   Bobé, *Efterladte Papirer*, vol. 2, p. 204: 'I som have den Lykke, at se Ploven er falden Eder til Deel, ... naar I dyrker Eders Marker og udaf Jorden drager alle de Riigdomme, som Forsynet vil tildeele Eders utrættelige Fliid, saa forøger I Fødevarernes Mængde, forøger Eders egen men og tillige Statens, det er: den almindelige Velstand. Naar enhver saaledes er og giør det, hvad han i sin Stand og i sit Kald skulde være, kan og bør giøre, saa vil enhver bidrage sit til det almindelige Bedste, og hele Samfundet ustriidig blive lykkeligt.'
35   Erik Gøbel, *De styrede rigerne. Embedsmændene i den danske civile centraladministration 1660–1814* (Odense, 2000).

independent court district (*birketing*). Reventlow had the right to appoint the judge, *birkedommer*, although the King's authorisation was needed. His court had the status of *landsting*, directly accountable to the King and the central administration, but outside the authority of regional civil servants.

Reventlow – as a local *Polizeiherr* – had to fulfil many administrative functions, involving a great number of reports to be sent to the central administration – reports on criminals, probate, public trustees, civil servants' duties, reconciliations, vaccinations, the harvest, forestry, factories and manufactures. In addition, reports were sent to the prefect (*stiftamtmand*) on people's health, road conditions, and the like. All Danish manors were included in the government's local system of administration, and the nobility were deeply involved in it.[36] As a count and estate owner Reventlow was also responsible (alongside the *birketing* and the church) for the proper behaviour of his peasants, in legal, moral and religious matters.

Reventlow was a private estate owner, with a manor; but also, as a count, an official with special responsibility to the state. As a private estate owner he implemented the three steps of his master plan, while as a count he was responsible for the local court and was himself a counsellor. Often the two functions overlapped, and he probably gained by not making a clear distinction between them. The fact that he worked for the king gave him an advantage when dealing with his tenants.[37] The state to which Johan Ludvig Reventlow was faithful was not one that could directly intervene in the management of his estate, as did happen when the tenant farmers appealed against his *arvefæste* reform in 1789. From Reventlow's point of view, the state and the king were patriarchal figures – a king who, backed by the heavenly father, required that each person, in his own estate and calling, did his duty by using capabilities given to him by God's providence. This duty had to be performed even when any benefit to oneself (the estate owner) was less than the benefit for the state. If an estate owner knew how to make his peasants happier than by employing his knowledge to introduce reforms that would cause him great expense for many years, it was nonetheless still his duty to implement these reforms, because it was for the common good.

Conclusion

Johan Ludvig Reventlow is therefore an interesting example of cameralist thinking in the Danish state in the late eighteenth century. He would probably

---

36   Lotte Dombernovsky, *Lensbesidderen som amtmand. Studier i administrationen af fynske grevskaber og baronier 1671–1849* (Copenhagen, 1983). 'Der Lehnsbesitzer als Amtmann'. Diss.
37   Cf. Dombernovsky, *Lensbesidderen som amtmand.*

not have called himself a cameralist, as his brother did. He was proud of being an estate owner who could manage his estate as he thought best according to genuine cameralist ideas. In this he followed his teacher Andreas Schytte. In the third volume of his *Staternes indvortes Regiering* Schytte compares a genuine cameralist with a landowner who has much work to do to raise the flow of income.[38] He has to take into account nature, soil fertility, seed quality and related matters. So in this respect he was a genuine cameralist, whose task was to take into account the quality of citizens, teaching them how to work productively for the state. Because of that, Schytte argues that all education in the state, whether related to science, art or work, has the same relevance to the citizen as the soil has to the landowner. Education will provide citizens with capital that will be of benefit to themselves and to the state.

Johan Ludvig Reventlow followed this path on his estate, where he educated the children and taught adults about new agricultural technology and manufacturing, reforming agriculture and giving the peasants property and freedom from corvée work. The were able to work for their own benefit, for the benefit of the estate and, by paying taxes, for the benefit of the state. Reventlow was also a member of advisory commissions for the government, so acting both outside and inside the governmental system. His master plan was a state-plan, much more than a reform plan simply for his own estate.

38   Schytte, *Staternes indvortes Regiering*, vol. 3, p. 12.

10

Maasreguln wider die Unglücksfaelle: Cameralism and its Influence on the Establishment of Insurance Schemes

FRANK OBERHOLZNER

There was a great service in the Cathedral. The bodies of the victims were approximately collected and approximately separated from one another, and there was a great searching of hearts in the beautiful city of Lima. ... Yet it was rather strange that this event should have so impressed the Limeans, for in that country those catastrophes which lawyers shockingly call the 'acts of God' were more than usually frequent. Tidal waves were continually washing away cities; earthquakes arrived every week ... [and diseases] ... were forever flitting in and out of the provinces.[1]

These sentences from the first page of Thornton Wilder's famous novel *The Bridge of San Luis Rey* describe the feelings of many people in early modern times towards epidemics or natural catastrophes. It does not matter for us that the novel takes place in South America in 1714, because misfortunes and perils like diseases, city fires, and last but not least natural hazards were quite common for the majority of people in Europe too. Until the eighteenth century these phenomena were often interpreted as divine retribution for earthly sin.[2]

---

1   Thornton Wilder, *The Bridge of San Luis Rey* (London, 2000), p. 8.
2   Marie Luisa Allemeyer, '"Dass es wohl recht ein Feuer vom Herrn zu nennen gewesen ...". Zur Wahrnehmung, Deutung und Verarbeitung von Stadtbränden in norddeutschen Schriften des 17. Jahrhunderts', *Um Himmels Willen. Religion in Katastrophenzeiten*, ed. M. Jakubowski-Tiessen and H. Lehmann (Göttingen, 2003), pp. 201–34; Christian Rohr, *Extreme Naturereignisse im Ostalpenraum. Naturerfahrung im Spätmittelalter und am Beginn der Neuzeit* (Köln, 2007); Christian Rohr, 'Leben mit der Flut. Zur Wahrnehmung, Deutung und Bewältigung von Überschwemmungen im niederösterreichischen Raum (13.–16. Jahrhundert)', *Studien und Forschungen aus dem Niederösterreichischen Institut für Landeskunde* 46 (2007), 63–114; Frank Oberholzner, 'From an Act of God to an Insurable Risk. The Change in the Perception of Hailstorms and Thunderstorms since the Early Modern Times', *Environment and History* 17 (2011), 133–52.

Only prayer and penitence were seen as acceptable coping strategies,[3] as this was the only way of finding reconciliation with God.[4]

However, there is evidence that these perceptions changed as a result of the Enlightenment – which 'was in part heir to the great "scientific revolution" of the previous century but [was] also a sign of a new cosmopolitanism'[5] – and scientific progress during the eighteenth century. Demystification of the 'wrath of God' resulted. Nonetheless, we cannot tell how quickly the majority of the population was able to adopt this paradigm shift. Yet with the almost complete disappearance of metaphysical ideals, new adaptation strategies had to be found – last but not least, by the early modern state.[6] In German-speaking countries it was the task of the cameralists to discover practical solutions.

This essay therefore examines an economic phenomenon not automatically associated with cameralism: insurance. At first sight this may seem surprising, as insurance is a key element of modern life. However, insurance concepts were already of importance in the early modern period, because – as Keith Thomas rightly pointed out – 'nothing yields greater testimony to the new spirit of self-help than the growth of insurance'.[7] We will here analyse how insurance as a tool for the production of security[8] – or more precisely, as 'measures against misfortune' (*Maasreguln wider die Unglücksfaelle*)[9] supporting the attainment of common and individual happiness (*Glückseligkeit*) – fitted into cameralist thought and policy proposals. Furthermore, we will ask which proposals for the concrete design of such institutions and their use as a political tool can be found in cameralist writings. Given the importance of agriculture during the early modern period we shall focus here on the example of crop insurance.

---

3   I distinguish between short-term coping strategies, which include for example religious acts, and long-term adaptation strategies, which involve a systematic and proactive approach towards catastrophes. See Steven Engler, 'Developing a Historically Based "Famine Vulnerability Analysis Model" (FVAM) – An Interdisciplinary Approach', *Erdkunde* 66 (2012), 157–72.

4   Oberholzner, 'Act of God', pp. 137–42; Frank Oberholzner, *Institutionalisierte Sicherheit im Agrarsektor. Die Entwicklung der Hagelversicherung in Deutschland seit der Frühen Neuzeit* (Berlin, 2015), pp. 96–113.

5   John A. Davis, 'The European Economies in the Eighteenth Century', *An Economic History of Europe. From Expansion to Development*, ed. A. Di Vittorio (London, 2006), p. 97.

6   Oberholzner, *Institutionalisierte Sicherheit*, pp. 113–26.

7   Keith Thomas, *Religion and the Decline of Magic. Studies in Popular Beliefs in Sixteenth-and Seventeenth-Century England* (London, 1991), p. 779.

8   Cornel Zwierlein, 'Insurances as Part of Human Security, their Timescapes, and Spatiality', *Historical Social Research* 35 (2010), 253–74.

9   Johann Heinrich Gottlob von Justi, *Die Grundfeste zu der Macht und Glückseligkeit der Staaten; oder ausführliche Vorstellung der gesamten Policey-Wissenschaft*, vol. 1 (Königsberg, 1760), p. 763.

Principles of insurance

Today, the insurance industry is an institution typical of (post-)modern societies.[10] Every insurance contract delegates[11] a dedicated risk[12] – or, to be precise, its financial consequences – from the individual to a pool of other individuals who are facing at least a similar risk. To participate in this common pool (which is normally managed by an insurance company), a monetary sum, the premium,[13] has to be paid by every customer.[14] These collective amounts are used to cover collective losses. Important in our context is also an understanding of crop insurance. Such a scheme provides compensation for crop damage caused by severe hailstorms or thunderstorms. The calculation of the premium is generally based on long-term experiences regarding local hail risk. Moreover, the vulnerability of the insured crop has to be taken into account. The indemnity is based on the expected yield and market price of the crop. In contrast to other insurance types such as motor insurance, customers cannot influence the probability of damage.[15]

Insurance in the early modern period

Insurance as a whole was not unknown in Germany during the early modern period.[16] Before the Enlightenment it was to some extent provided by the

10   I will not discuss the numerous definitions of 'modernism' and the concept of 'risk societies'. For an overview, see for example Ulrich Beck, *World at Risk* (Cambridge, 2009).
11   Alternatively to risk delegation, the objective of the insurance industry could be described as risk-spreading or risk-transformation. Rob Thoyts, *Insurance Theory and Practice* (London, 2010), pp. 19–20.
12   The term 'risk' can be traced back to the Italian *rischio*, which describes the cause of perils. Two characteristics are most usually associated with risk: uncertainty and the possibility of loss. Thoyts, *Insurance Theory*, p. 4. However from an insurance perspective, a third aspect is essential, which was introduced by Frank Knight for the first time. According to Knight, measurement is the crucial factor for the differentiation between risk and uncertainty. Frank Knight, *Risk, Uncertainty and Profit* (Boston, MA, 1921), pp. 19–20. Furthermore, the extent of loss has to be quantifiable. According to Thoyts, risk from an insurance-industry perspective can be defined as 'the probability of an uncertain event, causative of economic losses'. Thoyts, *Insurance Theory*, p. 5.
13   There are different types of premiums such as flat rate and equitable premiums. However, I will not discuss these aspects in detail.
14   Customers who buy insurance contracts could be risk-averse, risk-neutral or risk-loving.
15   Hans Knoll, *Hagelversicherung* (Wiesbaden, 1964); Franz Büchner, Gerrit Winter, *Grundriß der Individualversicherung* (Karlsruhe, 1986); GDV-Arbeitsgruppe, *Hagelversicherung, Ernte-Mehrgefahrenversicherung in Deutschland. Risikopartnerschaft zwischen Landwirten, Versicherungen und Staat*. Discussion paper, 1 November 2007 (Berlin, 2007).
16   There is an ongoing discussion on the roots of the modern insurance industry. For Germany, the common understanding is that there were two origins: premium-based insurance and guild-administered aid, provided to guild members (and sometimes their families), for example in

churches and guilds. For example, we know that even in the High Middle Ages certain contracts existed, which can be seen as predecessors to crop insurance schemes. In 1316, the monastery of St Gereon in Cologne conceded to their tenants that annual payments would be reduced after a severe hailstorm.[17]

Life, marine and transport insurance schemes[18] also existed. For example, a merchant could insure himself against the perils of losing his goods – or slaves – at sea. However, the calculation of the premium was based more on vague assumptions than on appropriate statistical or mathematical techniques.[19] More important for the development of insurance concepts was the development of fire insurance, which took place around 1680. In Germany, one of the most prominent examples was the 'Hamburger General-Feuer-Cassa', which in 1676 was the first government-founded insurance company in the world. Before that, local fire guilds (*Brandgilden*) had provided assistance after the outbreak of a severe fire.[20] The new institution was based on innovative organisational rules, such as the use of double-entry bookkeeping and the introduction of a rationale for the assessment of insured property. All the same, the Hamburg-based company differed fundamentally from guild-administered assistance, which was offered only on a 'trial-and-error' principle. The 'General Feuer-Cassa' played an essential part in the diffusion of fire insurance throughout the Holy Roman Empire.

The years around 1700 marked the beginning of a new epoch. Security was seen as social normality: everything had to be done to prevent the incidence of harm. This differed fundamentally from previous centuries when uncertainty and resignation to fate were normal.[21] This new attitude is manifested in the spread of insurance, and it was cameralists who provided the greater part of its theoretical foundation.

The concept of cameralism

As has been repeated throughout this volume, cameralism is a combination of economic, cameral, and police sciences directed to a variety of questions relating to government and administration. Cameralists – characterised by

---

case of illness or for covering funeral expenses. Cornel Zwierlein, *Der gezähmte Prometheus. Feuer und Sicherheit zwischen Früher Neuzeit und Moderne* (Göttingen, 2011), pp. 24–39.

17   *Bestand Historisches Archiv Köln 215, Gereon U2/110*. Interestingly, there is no indication how this modus operandi was conformable with the ecclesiastical doctrine of natural hazards as a scourge of God.

18   Davis, 'European Economies', p. 113.

19   Lorraine Daston, *Classical Probability in the Enlightenment* (Princeton, NJ, 1988), pp. 112–87.

20   Paul Moldenhauer, *Das Versicherungswesen, Band 1: Allgemeine Versicherungslehre* (Berlin, 1917), p. 22.

21   Zwierlein, *Prometheus*, passim.

Andre Wakefield as 'utopian pragmatists'[22] – focused on the mastery of both mankind and nature. However, this task had often to be fulfilled against the background of the limited resources of a typical German *Kleinstaat*.[23] Cameralists argued that enlightened political rule – the government of a benevolent prince – should deal with material well-being, the safeguarding of the legal system, and the protection of peace and public order. All subjects should be guided towards their own happiness and satisfaction.[24]

Johann Heinrich Gottlob von Justi's[25] book on the nature and essence of states,[26] published in 1760, exemplifies these concerns. Here the most important tasks of the territorial state (*Endzwecke der Republiken*) concerns the general good and the welfare of every individual and family, aggregated in the common happiness of the whole state.[27] Hence the happiness of the state and that of the subject should coincide. Concrete economic policy measures involved the development of manufacturing, mining and trade, as well as the stimulation of agriculture and the development of agricultural management.[28]

22 Andre Wakefield, 'Cameralism: A German Alternative to Mercantilism', *Mercantilism Reimagined. Political Economy in Early Modern Britain and its Empire*, ed. P. J. Stern and C. Wennerlind (New York, 2014), p. 137.

23 Andre Wakefield characterised the German *Kleinstaaterei* as the 'Galapagos Islands of state building': Andre Wakefield, *The Disordered Police State. German Cameralism as Science and Practice* (Chicago, 2009), p. 24.

24 Sophus A. Reinert, *Translating Empire. Emulation and the Origins of Political Economy* (Cambridge, 2011), pp. 234–8.

25 Horst Dreitzel, 'Justis Beitrag zur Politisierung der deutschen Aufklärung', *Aufklärung als Politisierung – Politisierung der Aufklärung*, ed. H.-E. Bödeker and U. Herrmann (Hamburg, 1987), pp. 158–77; Ulrich Adam, *The Political Economy of J. H. G. Justi* (Oxford, 2006). Justi is regarded as one of the most prominent cameralists, although his role is not undisputed by modern scholars. Even his contemporaries were critical, as the following statement of Friedrich Casimir Medicus, the director of the Lautern Cameral Academy, shows: 'Even worse is the situation in the teaching dedicated to […] police, finance and state administration science. Not one single useful book to teach to, and so no guideline for a professor. No wonder, if one just scribbles like Justi, or wants to scribble like him?' Printed in Heinrich Webler, *Die Kameral-Hohe-Schule zu Lautern (1774–1784). Eine Quellenstudie zur geschichtlichen Entwicklung und theoretischen Fundierung der Sozialökonomik als Universitätswissenschaft* (Speyer, 1927), p. 115. It is not clear how much personal animosity dictated this harsh verdict. When Medicus wrote this Justi had been dead for six years.

26 Johann Heinrich Gottlob von Justi, *Die Natur und das Wesen der Staaten, als die Grundwissenschaft der Staatskunst, der Policey, und aller Regierungswissenschaften, desgleichen als die Quelle aller Gesetze* (Berlin, 1760).

27 Justi, *Natur*, p. 45. The original German text reads as follows: 'Dieser Endzweck [der Republiken] kann kein andrer seyn als das allgemeine Beste, die Wohlfahrt aller und jeder Familien, die sich solchergestalt mit einander vereinigen, kurz, die gemeinschaftliche Glückseligkeit des gesammten Staats.'

28 Keith Tribe, *Governing Economy. The Reformation of German Economic Discourse 1750–1840* (Cambridge, 1988), pp. 19–118; Jörg Cortekar, *Glückskonzepte des Kameralismus und Utilitarismus. Implikationen für die moderne Umweltökonomie und Umweltpolitik* (Marburg, 2007); Lars Magnusson, *The Political Economy of Mercantilism* (London, 2015).

What motivated the cameralists?[29] Not altruism and providential inclinations; the rationale was mostly to do with creating revenue, and so strengthening princely power. Corruption and governmental directive were prevalent.[30] Even contemporaries were aware of the limitations of cameralism, as can be seen in a letter by Friedrich Casimir Medicus,[31] from 1777 Director of the Kameral-Hohe-Schule zu Lautern:

> The first academic chair of cameral science was established in 1727. And nearly every German university has one. However, what has been the benefit for Germany, what influence did it have on the colleges, was it of any benefit to the burghers? On the contrary, it created nit-pickers and projectors.[32]

Cameralism and insurance

Regardless of Medicus' negative judgement, cameralists dealt with a wide variety of subjects, among them insurance. Insurance had hitherto been analysed only from a legal point of view, if at all.[33] The person to whom we owe the first well-founded idea of insurance is Gottfried Wilhelm Leibniz (1646–1716),[34] the German philosopher[35] and 'the greatest polymath since

29   Hermann Rebel, 'Reimagining the Oikos: Austrian Cameralism in its Social Formation', *Golden Ages, Dark Ages. Imagining the Past in Anthropology and History*, ed. J. O'Brien and W. Roseberry (Ithaca, NY, 1994), pp. 48–80; Tribe, *Economy*.
30   Wakefield, *Disordered Police State*. Wakefield understands cameralism as a strategic instrument, which means that cameralist ideas were not intended for the advancement of common happiness, but were instead advanced for selfish reasons. Wakefield argues that, envisaging an ideal and well-ordered territorial state, cameralists promoted their own advancement: Ibid., pp. 134–44. Whether we can blame cameralists in this way is questionable.
31   The academy emerged from the Lautern Physical-Economic and Bee Society (established 1768) in 1774 and moved to Heidelberg University in 1784. Tribe, *Governing Economy*, pp. 97–112; Wakefield, *Disordered Police State*, pp. 114–26. Wakefield argues that it was not primarily educational purposes that motivated the academy's founding (and that of Göttingen's university, too!), but instead the idea of luring wealthy students into the provincial town of Lautern. Ibid., p. 143.
32   Printed in Webler, *Kameral-Hohe-Schule*, p. 115. Medicus became director of the Lautern Physical-Economic and Bee Society in 1770. He persuaded several nobles (among them the Elector of Bavaria) to accept honorary membership, leading to the enhanced prestige of the society. Wakefield, *Disordered Police State*, p. 114.
33   Zwierlein, *Prometheus*, p. 35.
34   Donald Rutherford, *Leibniz and the Rational Order of Nature* (Cambridge, 1995); Eike Christian Hirsch, *Der berühmte Herr Leibniz. Eine Biographie* (München, 2007); Anthony Gottlieb, *The Dream of Enlightenment. The Rise of Modern Philosophy* (London, 2016), pp. 163–95.
35   Gottfried Wilhelm Leibniz, *Hauptschriften zur Versicherungs- und Finanzmathematik*, ed. E. Knobloch and J.-M. Graf von der Schulenburg (Berlin, 2000).

Aristotle'.[36] Interestingly, however, his concept of insurance had little relation to his mathematical and probabilistic thinking – which is surprising in view of his contribution to the development of mathematical methods and statistics.[37] Yet the 'probabilistic revolution' – which in our context means the use of quantitative methods for calculating insurance premiums – was a revolution that was slow to develop and was fraught with difficulties. This will be seen in the development of German crop insurance.

Leibniz mentioned the issue in a report on the improvement of state administration addressed to the Holy Roman Emperor Leopold I in July 1680.[38] Among other issues the text mentioned the 'Hamburger General-Feuer-Cassa' as a model for future insurance companies – perhaps an indication of the success of this institution, since Leibniz was aware of it.[39] Simultaneously with the drafting of the letter to the Emperor[40] he prepared a detailed essay on public insurance companies (*Öffentliche Assekuranzen*) in which he placed the issue in a broader socio-political context.[41] Entirely in line with cameralist thinking, he understood insurance as a tool for increasing princely power and the military force of the state. Any misfortune like fire, flooding, or other natural hazards would weaken the whole population[42] and thus the state's economic power, as well as its defence. Germany would be helpless before the increasing power of its neighbours.[43] Therefore the government should promote insurance institutions, which would provide 'help for self-help' to those subjects affected by these risks.[44]

Leibniz was in favour of insurance companies; as he wrote:

> Such insurance companies would be a magnificent work and be very beneficial to the country in many ways; capital could be raised which could be used by the authorities to aid the subsistence of their subjects in many ways, stand by them in times of need and especially in case of damage caused by fire or water, as well as by increasing prices and any other misfortunes.[45]

---

36 Gottlieb, *Dream*, p. 163. According to Gottlieb, 'there has not been a third person who can stand alongside them [Leibniz and Aristotle]'. Ibid.

37 Ivo Schneider, 'Geschichtlicher Hintergrund und wissenschaftliches Umfeld der Schriften', in Leibniz, *Hauptschriften*, pp. 591–6; Hirsch, *Leibniz*, pp. 84–8; 157–8.

38 However, there is no indication of any practical consequences.

39 Leibniz to the Emperor, very probably at the beginning of July 1680, printed in Leibniz, *Hauptschriften*, p. 9.

40 Leibniz, *Hauptschriften*, p. 3.

41 Zwierlein, *Macht*, pp. 8–9.

42 Öffentliche Assekuranzen, printed in Leibniz, *Hauptschriften*, p. 15 (12–19).

43 Öffentliche Assekuranzen, printed in Leibniz, *Hauptschriften*, p. 12.

44 Öffentliche Assekuranzen, printed in Leibniz, *Hauptschriften*, pp. 12–15.

45 Öffentliche Assekuranzen, printed in Leibniz, *Hauptschriften*, p. 15.

He argued that the government's main task was to protect its citizens from all external and internal enemies. Defence of the country against other nations would be the task of the army, while protecting the domestic population from danger would be the mission of insurance companies.[46] His thinking on insurance involves new and innovative principles for supporting economic growth as well as providing security. While not describing the organisational principles of a soon-to-be-founded insurance company in any detail, Leibniz understood insurance to be very important to a functional state and social connectedness.[47]

Leibniz had already noted the positive impact of insurance companies on individual and public happiness. He should not however be strictly counted as a cameralist, and so his views tell us little about cameralist thinking on the subject. We have to examine the writings of classic cameralists such as Johann Heinrich Gottlob von Justi and Ferdinand Friedrich Pfeiffer to gain an impression of their thinking on this topic.

Justi's first discussion of the idea of insurance arises in the context of improving the life of the labouring class, and was published in 1755.[48] He elaborated on the subject in two of his most famous books, *Staatswirthschaft* from 1755,[49] and the first volume of his *Die Grundfeste zu der Macht und Glückseeligkeit der Staaten*, printed in 1760.[50] Typically for Justi, his later works explored the insurance theme at greater length, and not all his suggestions seem that innovative.[51] Ferdinand Friedrich Pfeiffer's memorandum was published in 1780, and was based on his doctoral thesis.[52]

Justi's basic idea was that all perils and calamities affect the individual as well as the general public. A harmed person would not only be unable to

---

46   Öffentliche Assekuranzen, printed in Leibniz, *Hauptschriften*, p. 15.

47   Zwierlein, *Prometheus*, pp. 229–42.

48   Johann Heinrich Gottlob von Justi, 'Vorschlag zu Assecuranzanstalten gegen die Wasser-Hagel- und andere Schaden an den Feldfrüchten', *Göttingische Policey-Amts Nachrichten auf das Jahr 1755. oder vermischte Abhandlungen zum Vortheil des Nahrungsstandes aus allen Theilen der Oeconomischen Wissenschaften benebst verschiedenen in das Göttingische Policey-Wesen einschlagenden Verordnungen und Nachrichten*. Erster Theil (Göttingen, 1755), pp. 145–7.

49   Johann Heinrich Gottlob von Justi, *Staatswirthschaft oder Systematische Abhandlung aller Oekonomischen und Cameral-Wissenschaften, die zur Regierung eines Landes erfordert werden*. Erster Theil, 2, stark vermehrte Auflage (Leipzig, 1758). The book was published for the first time in 1755.

50   Justi, *Die Grundfeste*, I.

51   Dreitzel, 'Beitrag', p. 159; Wolfgang Burgdorf, 'Johann Heinrich Gottlob von Justi (1720–1771)', *Europahistoriker. Ein biographisches Handbuch*, Band 1, ed. H. Duchhardt, M. Morawiec, W. Schmale and W. Schulze (Göttingen, 2006), pp. 53–4.

52   Ferdinand Friedrich Pfeiffer, *Gedanken über Versicherungs-Anstalten hauptsächlich zum Vorteil der Landwirthschaft entworffen, und in höchster Gegenwart Seiner Herzoglichen Durchlaucht wärend den Akademischen öffentlichen Prüfungen verteidigt* (Stuttgart, 1780).

contribute to society's prosperity, but would also be a burden to his fellow men, in particular for his dependency on charity. Consequently, insurance could be characterised by two central features: it would be on the one hand a tool to increase individual happiness, and on the other hand an important lever for economic growth.[53] Pfeiffer understood insurance from a philosophical perspective, as the manifestation of a social contract: 'And so there is no doubt that the purpose of institutions for insuring property and, to a certain degree, revenues is an expression of the social contract – because it provides greater security of life by securing subsistence.'[54] Furthermore, insurance companies would contribute to the positive development of trade and commerce. Consequently, a watchful and caring (*allfürsorglich*) government should require the establishment of insurance companies.[55]

Apart from crop insurance companies,[56] Justi discusses two other interesting applications of this new institution: marine and fire insurance. The first would protect commerce even if the government was unable to secure sea lanes.[57] The benefits of fire insurance in turn could lie in providing quick and unbureaucratic help in case of fire damage, as both Justi and Pfeiffer emphasised. They were therefore of the view that the government should make such institutions mandatory.[58] All insured individuals would be able to protect their goods and property with relatively small premium payments, and both private and commercial activities would benefit from this innovation as well.[59] Ultimately, to lend assistance to individuals in need, Justi justified the introduction of an insurance system for the following reasons: 'It is therefore very beneficial, if through wise institutions and measures the ruler can on the one hand avert and reduce such misfortunes, but on the other distribute the loss among many, so that one individual is not thereby knocked to the ground.'[60] Here, describing insurance as a means to prevent or alleviate disasters, Justi summarises the cameralist concept of the state: the prime purpose of government activity in these matters is to improve both individual and collective happiness.[61]

Cameralist writers placed great emphasis upon the need to establish insurance companies, arguing that these institutions would satisfy the general need for security. Their suggestions were aimed on the one hand at broadly

53   Justi, 'Vorschlag', p. 145. Similarly, Justi, *Grundfeste*, I, pp. 763–4.
54   Pfeiffer, *Gedanken*, pp. 3–4. Following this paragraph Pfeiffer discusses Rousseau's conception of a social contract.
55   Pfeiffer, *Gedanken*, pp. 1–4.
56   See the following section.
57   Justi, *Grundfeste*, I, pp. 765–6.
58   Justi, *Grundfeste*, I, pp. 767–8, Pfeiffer, *Gedanken*, pp. 13–28.
59   Justi, *Grundfeste*, I, pp. 763–5.
60   Justi, *Staatswirthschaft*, pp. 284–5. See also Justi, *Grundfeste*, I, pp. 764–5.
61   Zwierlein, *Prometheus*, pp. 279–80.

institutionalising the principle of insurance, and on the other hand securing insurability, with as few exceptions as possible. Moreover, by producing security insurance companies would provide a benefit for individuals and for society as a whole, since the general public no longer had to pay for losses suffered by individuals. By endorsing this new form of business the government would also implicitly impose a duty on every peasant – that is, the obligation to purchase insurance coverage.[62]

Cameralist discourse on crop insurance

We have seen that cameralists discussed the concept of insurance, using marine and fire insurance as examples. However, crop insurance played a significant part in cameralist writings and could be seen as 'another connection between cameralist teaching and administrative and economic practices'.[63] Therefore, we have to ask why the cameralists called for the establishment of crop insurance companies. We need to consider two factors: the general economic conditions prevailing in German-speaking countries (which means in this context the Holy Roman Empire), and the role of agriculture in cameralist thinking.

Several factors influenced the German economic situation in the second half of the eighteenth century. There are signs of the positive impact of so-called 'proto-industrialisation'[64] on the German economy before 1800. However, the primary sector was still the driving force behind any economic development, since between 75 and 85% of the working population earned their living in agriculture.[65] The movement of agricultural prices therefore had a significant impact on daily life and the general economic situation of the peasantry. From 1720 onwards agricultural markets improved, gaining even more momentum after 1750.[66] One reason for this was the increase of population after 1750 – it is estimated that between 22 and 26 million people lived in the Holy Roman

62 Cornel Zwierlein, 'Grenzen der Versicherbarkeit als Epochenindikatoren? Von der europäischen Sattelzeit zur Globalisierung des 19. Jahrhunderts', *Geschichte und Gesellschaft* 38 (2012), 444; Zwierlein, *Prometheus*, p. 7; Cornel Zwierlein, 'Sicherheit durch Versicherung: Ein frühneuzeitliches Erfolgserlebnis', *Sicherheit in der Frühen Neuzeit. Norm – Praxis – Repräsentation*, ed. Chr. Kampmann and U. Niggemann (Köln, 2013), p. 391.
63 See Marten Seppel's introductory essay in this volume.
64 Franklin Mendels, 'Proto-industrialization. The First Phase of the Industrialization Process', *Journal of Economic History* 32 (1972), 241–61.
65 Wolfgang Mager, 'Landwirtschaft und ländliche Gesellschaft auf dem Weg in die Moderne', *Deutschland und Frankreich im Zeitalter der Französischen Revolution*, ed. H. Berding, E. François and H.-P. Ullmann (Frankfurt, 1989), pp. 73–4.
66 Wilhelm Abel, 'Landwirtschaft 1648–1800', *Handbuch der Deutschen Wirtschafts- und Sozialgeschichte*, vol. 1 (Stuttgart, 1971), pp. 507–14; Wilhelm Abel, *Agrarkrisen und*

Empire around 1750, and the Empire's population increased to between 25 and 31 million by 1800,[67] simultaneously creating a shortage of agricultural land.[68] The increase in population required a commensurate rise in agricultural production, and new institutions to protect these assets.

In parallel, there was in German-speaking countries a significant increase in the number of tracts and treatises discussing the improvement of agriculture during the second half of the eighteenth century. Not only cameralists dealt with the issue, but also representatives of the Enlightenment. This agricultural enlightenment, or agrarian movement – embodied also in efforts to reform traditional systems of serfdom like *Grundherrschaft* and *Gutsherrschaft* – challenged traditional ways of agricultural life and methods of production, arguing for the adoption of new techniques.[69]

Finally, we need to consider the role of agriculture in cameralist thinking. The primary sector served as a basis for food supply. The nobility also depended on agriculture for the revenues that maintained their livelihood. The agricultural estate was considered, as Peter M. Jones has pointed out, to be 'a gift which the landowner held on trust from the Almighty'.[70] Furthermore, this view of agriculture corresponded with an increasingly prevalent conception of nature as a resource that could be exploited to satisfy human needs.[71]

Let us focus on the position taken by Justi. As might be expected, he is

---

Agrarkonjunktur. Eine Geschichte der Land- und Ernährungswirtschaft Mitteleuropas seit dem hohen Mittelalter (Hamburg, 1978), pp. 196–7.

67 Walter Demel, *Reich, Reformen und sozialer Wandel 1763–1806* (Stuttgart, 2005), p. 80. However, there is no consensus on these numbers. For example, Hans-Ulrich Wehler assumes that the population of the Holy Roman Empire was between 16 and 18 million in 1750, and between 23 and 24 million in 1800: Hans-Ulrich Wehler, *Deutsche Gesellschaftsgeschichte. Vom Feudalismus des Alten Reiches bis zur Defensiven Modernisierung der Reformära 1700–1815* (München, 2006), pp. 69–70. John A. Davis suggests that 20.7 million people lived in the German states around 1800: Davis, *European Economies*, p. 106. The reason for this growth was less the improvement of medical and sanitary conditions than interdependencies between the growth of agricultural markets and of the population. However, it is not possible to determine which factors were the driving force behind this development. Davis, *European Economies*, pp. 106–7; Wehler, *Gesellschaftsgeschichte*, p. 70.

68 Friedrich-Wilhelm Henning, *Das vorindustrielle Deutschland 800 bis 1800* (Paderborn, 1994), p. 248.

69 Peter M. Jones, *Agricultural Enlightenment. Knowledge, Technology, and Nature, 1750–1840* (Oxford, 2016), pp. 14–17.

70 Jones, *Agricultural Enlightenment*, p. 20.

71 Günter Bayerl, 'Prolegomenon der "Großen Industrie". Der technisch-ökonomische Blick auf die Natur im 18. Jahrhundert', *Umweltgeschichte. Umweltverträgliches Wirtschaften in historischer Perspektive*, ed. W. Abelshauser (Göttingen, 1994), pp. 29–56; Torsten Meyer and Marcus Popplow, '"To employ each of Nature's products in the most favorable way possible" – Nature as a Commodity in Eighteenth-Century German Economic Discourse', *Historical Social Research* 29 (2004), 4–40; Oberholzner, *Institutionalisierte Sicherheit*, pp. 158–64.

convinced that a state will prosper only if its agricultural sector is flourishing.[72] To achieve this, he advocates reforming the traditional agrarian
order. He criticises farmland fragmentation and recommends the abolition of
collective land use, as well as any compulsory labour and other services.[73] In
a thoroughly enlightened tradition, the ultimate goal of these reforms would
be the abolition of serfdom and the transfer of property to the peasants,
which would benefit the whole of society: 'In any case, it must be considered
a great obstacle to the most complete cultivation of the land and to agricultural prosperity when a peasant lives under oppression[.] The class of people
who engage in the agriculture on which [...] the power and happiness of the
state – yes, one can say, the welfare of all other ranks and classes of people –
so much depends, deserves neither oppression nor disrespect.'[74] It is because
of this thinking that Horst Dreitzel attributes to Justi an important role in the
process described as 'politicisation of the Enlightenment'.[75] Justi, however,
not only argued in favour of reforms, but also criticised the peasantry,
repeating contemporary clichés about their alleged laziness and carelessness.
He saw this attitude as a major obstacle to progress in agriculture, besides the
archaic social structure mentioned above.[76]

Concepts of crop insurance in cameralist discourse

As far as we know, crop insurance was first discussed in a short piece in the
Oeconomische Nachrichten, published in Leipzig in 1749.[77] The note was
submitted anonymously and the editors of the *Oeconomische Nachrichten*
were not able to identify the author.[78] Nonetheless, they decided to publish it
because all members of the editorial board were convinced of the importance
of the new institution of crop insurance – although they were also sceptical
about whether such an enterprise could ever be realised.[79] Many cameralist
writers cited the note, and so it is worth discussing in some detail.

   According to the author, hazards to crops such as hail and locusts should
be covered by insurance. However, malformation of crops should be excluded,
since insuring this would make the peasants lazy. From an organisational

72   Johann Heinrich Gottlob von Justi, *Abhandlungen von der Vollkommenheit der
Landwirthschaft und der höchsten Cultur der Länder* (Ulm/Leipzig, 1761), pp. 1–3.
73   Justi, *Abhandlungen*, pp. 4–10, 17–18, 24–8.
74   Justi, *Abhandlungen*, p. 28.
75   Dreitzel, 'Beitrag'.
76   Justi, *Abhandlungen*, pp. 29–30.
77   Anon., 'Ohnmaßgeblicher General-Entwurf zu Einrichtung einer Wetter-Casse',
Oeconomische Nachrichten 8 (1749), 570–83.
78   Anon., 'General-Entwurf', p. 569.
79   Anon., 'General-Entwurf', p. 570.

perspective, crop insurance ought to be modelled along the lines of fire insurance companies, and it was suggested that every district or principality should have such a company.[80] A board of directors would be responsible for the operation of the business.[81]

Technical details were also dealt with. While the level of premiums to be paid was not elaborated, they were to be collected exclusively as payments in kind, in the hope that this would encourage greater participation among farmers. Compensation would also be given in kind. The author argued that peasants would be more inclined to pay more to the insurance company if paying in kind rather than in cash. Only the owners of fields could be insured, as they were the ultimate beneficiaries of the insurance scheme. In conclusion, the utility of crop insurance for both individual peasant and society as a whole was discussed. The benefits were obvious for everyone; crop insurance would enable the insured to protect their fields from natural hazards. Furthermore, negative phenomena such as 'pleading hail'[82] (*Hagelbettelei*) would vanish.[83]

The proposal had no immediate impact. However, the idea was taken up several years later by various cameralists, including Justi and Pfeiffer. The concept turned up in a similar form in many of Justi's writings, appearing for the first time in 1755 in the *Göttingische Policey-Amts-Nachrichten*,[84] and later in his book *Die Grundfeste zu der Macht und Glückseeligkeit der Staaten*.[85] In general, he saw crop insurance as a chance for implementing the cameralist programme:

> These same reasons and causes that have induced us to create similar insurance institutions to deal with the fearsome misfortune of fire, should also move us to establish insurance institutes to deal with losses from water and hail, locusts, and other misfortunes pertaining to field crops. The detrimental consequences of these misfortunes for private persons and the general labouring class are no less important and apparent.[86]

Furthermore, he saw the opportunity for doing away with the tax remissions that the state often granted after a severe hailstorm, since the insurance company would cover the losses.[87]

It is clear from this quotation that some of Justi's provisions were borrowed wholesale from the 1749 proposal, for example repeating the suggestion

---

80 Unfortunately, it is unclear what territorial entity is meant by 'district'.
81 Anon., 'General-Entwurf', pp. 570–2.
82 Oberholzner, *Institutionalisierte Sicherheit*, pp. 90–1.
83 Anon., 'General-Entwurf', pp. 572–83.
84 Justi, 'Vorschlag', pp. 145–7.
85 Justi, *Grundfeste*, I, pp. 769–71.
86 Justi, 'Vorschlag', p. 146.
87 Justi, 'Vorschlag', p. 146.

that the area of operation of each insurance company should be a district or principality, without specifying what a district was.[88] Among several new suggestions was one to classify fields into three categories (good, mediocre and bad) so as to estimate the value of their crops. Justi believed that it would be simply to make such a classification on the basis of the so-called *Contributionsfuß* (standard contribution), the tax estimate for the property. Furthermore, the calculation of premium and of loss should be based upon the way in which fields were divided up. The authorities should examine the extent of damage and specify the amount of compensation. Justi suggested three rates of payment: one third, one half or a total loss.[89]

Unlike the anonymous author in 1749, Justi argued for monetary payments rather than payments in kind. He countered the idea that insurance premiums would represent a new burden for farmers by referring to the personal and social advantages of the project.[90] He did not, however, fully trust farmers to recognise the positive effects of agricultural insurance and thus argued for mandatory insurance: 'If benefaction is ever to be forced upon the people then it must be done by the institutions of government. The ruler, as a wise and benevolent father of his people, should not be deterred if the medicine he gives tastes somewhat bitter to […] his children.'[91]

Two other cameralists, Johann Friedrich von Pfeiffer and Ferdinand Friedrich Pfeiffer, also discussed the concept of crop insurance in their writings. Analysis of their two proposals leads to the conclusion that Johann Friedrich and Ferdinand Friedrich must have read the article that appeared in the *Oeconomische Nachrichten* of 1749, as well as Justi's writings on the subject.

Johann Friedrich von Pfeiffer gave a brief synopsis of his ideas in his textbook on police science. Again, he presented crop insurance as an essential tool for improving the condition of the labouring class (*Nahrungsstand*). Similar to Justi and the anonymous author of the 1749 article, Pfeiffer regarded floods, locusts, and hailstorms as the greatest perils for agriculture. Pfeiffer proposed to classify the fields into different categories in order to calculate premium and compensation.[92]

His namesake Ferdinand Friedrich Pfeiffer discussed the topic in more detail. Interestingly, he proposed that specialised insurance companies be established for each hazard. Specifically, he argued for livestock insurance as well as special companies for the protection of vines. The latter idea is

---

88   Justi, *Grundfeste*, I, p. 769.

89   Justi, 'Vorschlag', pp. 146–7.

90   Justi, *Grundfeste*, I, pp. 769–71.

91   Justi, *Grundfeste*, I, p. 771.

92   Johann Friedrich Pfeiffer, *Natürliche aus dem Endzweck der Gesellschaft entstehende Allgemeine Policeiwissenschaft*. Erster Theil (Frankfurt, 1779), pp. 338–40.

probably owed to the fact that Pfeiffer was a native of Württemberg, an important wine-producing region in the southwest of the Holy Roman Empire.[93] Crop insurance in the proper sense – Pfeiffer called it 'insurance for arable land'[94] ('*Versicherung des Ackerfelds*') – was the final step in protecting the peasant's property. Since fire insurance would secure the farm buildings and livestock insurance would cover the death of animals, the new institution could insure crop yields.[95]

Pfeiffer also notes that one condition for success with insurance is to provide cover for a sufficiently large area, although he is not specific about size. He also considers that detailed knowledge of the land to be insured is very important, a knowledge that can be obtained from tax records and tithe registers. Official registers could also be supplemented with data collected by the newly established crop insurance companies.[96] After a hailstorm, officials and reliable third parties should assess the damage. Compensation should only be monetary, as in-kind transfers would be too costly, and payments were to be calculated based on the regional market prices of the affected crops.[97] Like Justi before him, Pfeiffer saw the creation of crop insurance companies as an instrument for the relief of public finance.[98]

Not all cameralists were as positive about the project of crop insurance as Justi or Pfeiffer. Johann Heinrich Jung, also known as Jung-Stilling, deals with the issue in his textbook *Lehrbuch der Staats-Polizey-Wissenschaft*, published in Leipzig in 1788. In contrast to Justi and Pfeiffer, he suggests providing insurance against weather events within the framework of a general insurance company, to be established for every principality. He argued that a crop insurance company could be successful only in bigger states. In smaller territories there would be few who remained unaffected by a disaster, and so the one territory would bear the whole weight of the loss. Jung-Stilling also points to potential problems in calculating adequate and equitable premiums, which may occur owing to regional differences in hailstorm risk.[99] He also adds the following argument against crop insurance: 'Ultimately, this kind of support [from insurance companies] can make a peasant indolent, so that he will not try to prevent poor plant growth with hard work and fertiliser. In this way one would ultimately have to give every buyer coverage against his own private misfortune, and that would be almost the same as holding all goods collectively, as the first Christians or the Jesuits in Paraguay did.'[100]

93   Pfeiffer, *Gedanken*, pp. 28–46, 64–76.
94   Pfeiffer, *Gedanken*, p. 46.
95   Pfeiffer, *Gedanken*, p. 55.
96   Pfeiffer, *Gedanken*, pp. 48–50.
97   Pfeiffer, *Gedanken*, pp. 59–63.
98   Pfeiffer, *Gedanken*, p. 93.
99   Johann Heinrich Jung, *Lehrbuch der Staats-Polizey-Wissenschaft* (Leipzig, 1788), p. 398.
100 Jung, *Lehrbuch*, pp. 398–9.

Nevertheless, Jung-Stilling was in a minority among the cameralists, as an overview of the literature shows. The majority of his colleagues favoured the establishment of crop insurance.

To briefly summarise: crop insurance was seen as an institution that could stimulate the agricultural sector and satisfy peasants' need for security, based on firm rules regarding the transfer of risk from the insured to the insurer. Moreover, the new type of insurance would enable difficulties with tax remissions to be overcome, since the insured would sign an explicit insurance contract and would not need any governmental support in case of a severe hailstorm. In addition to this, Johann Friedrich von Pfeiffer's idea of introducing comprehensive insurance for agricultural hazards is still of relevance today, since the modern insurance industry offers such schemes.

However, it should be clear from the above that the cameralists' suggestions had shortcomings as well. In particular, they often involved an arbitrary calculation of premiums, without a sound empirical basis.[101] All in all, though, the cameralist proposals paved the way for the introduction of long-term strategies for dealing with risks to crops through the establishment of crop insurance companies.

From theory to practice: German crop insurance in the late eighteenth century

The first efforts towards the realisation of cameralists' proposals were initiated by the state some years later.[102] In 1770 the government of the principality of Ansbach-Bayreuth (part of contemporary Bavaria) planned a new institution of this kind. As cameralists had proposed, the company was to be organised along the lines of fire insurance and was to be a state-owned enterprise. The calculation of the premium was to be based on the local incidence of hailstorms, although there was a lack of precise data, and because of this the idea came to nothing. Nonetheless, most of the officials involved were positive about the necessity and the urgency of the project. The government by contrast was more cautious, owing to its lack of experience with this new type of insurance.[103]

---

101   Even contemporaries like Carl Theodor Beck mentioned this important fact: Carl Theodor Beck, 'Ueber HagelSchadens-AssekuranzGesellschaften', *Allgemeine deutsche Justiz- und Polizey Fama* 40 (1804), 341–50.
102   See Oberholzner, *Institutionalisierte Sicherheit*, pp. 172–82 for a detailed analysis.
103   *Das bayerische Hagelversicherungsgesetz vom 13. Februar 1884/4. April 1910 in der Fassung der Bekanntmachung vom 23. April 1910. 2. Auflage*, ed. H. Ritter von Haag (München, 1910), pp. 6–7; Bayerische Versicherungskammer, *Bayerische Landeshagelversicherungsanstalt 1884–1984* (München, 1984), p. 7.

Some years later, in 1774, the governor of the Prussian province of Magdeburg initiated a similar scheme. As in Ansbach-Bayreuth, the new company was to be organised on the model of fire insurance. Only the dependant peasants of the province were to be forced to join the new institution. Premiums were to be paid in cash only, and were to be based on the incidence of local hailstorms. Frederick II of Prussia himself took an interest, and although he was convinced of the usefulness of the new institution, he rejected the plan because the financial burden would have been too high for the peasants who already had to pay for fire insurance. Frederick argued against statutory insurance, but at the same time he realised that the time was not right for a voluntary scheme.[104]

Finally, in 1791, the first company opened for business in the principality of Brunswick, in northwest Germany. This enterprise was founded by private landowners and organised as a local co-operative. Only peasants who owned more than 100 Morgen (about 2,500 square metres) could become members of the new scheme; small landowners were not accepted. Again, rates were based on the local incidence of hailstorms.[105] However, the company was dissolved in 1794 due to the small number of customers and faulty calculations.[106] After these more or less unsuccessful initial efforts several new companies were founded around 1800 and the real development of the business began, leading to functional risk management in modern agriculture.[107]

Conclusion

This essay has examined cameralist discourse on insurance, and especially crop insurance. Most cameralists viewed insurance as an effective 'measure against misfortune' or *Maasreguln wider die Unglücksfaelle*. As the discussion of the proposals by Justi as well as Johann Friedrich and Ferdinand Friedrich Pfeiffer showed, the idea of insurance fitted in with cameralist thinking in several ways. Both individual and common happiness would be enhanced given the increased security, as well as making a contribution to overall economic progress. Gottfried Wilhelm Leibniz had argued along the same lines in his writings several decades previously.

Most cameralists also supported the introduction of crop insurance. Justi, the two Pfeiffers as well as the anonymous author of 1749 believed

---

104   Bernhard Rosenmöller, 'Versuche zur Gründung einer Hagelversicherungsanstalt in den Jahren 1774 und 1793', *Zeitschrift für die gesamte Versicherungs-Wissenschaft* 12 (1912), 590–7.
105   Niedersächsisches Landesarchiv 40 Slg 13052; 23 Neu FB. 1 Nr. 1585.
106   Hans Schmitt-Lermann, *Der Hagel und die Hagelversicherung in der Kulturgeschichte* (München, 1984), pp. 246–7.
107   Oberholzner, *Institutionalisierte Sicherheit*, pp. 182–219.

that crop insurance would contribute to the prosperity of the agrarian sector, and thus to overall economic development. Furthermore, they argued that crop insurance would improve state finances by removing traditional support payments. The first proposal published in 1749 in the *Oeconomische Nachrichten* was further developed over the following years, and new aspects like the classification of the fields into three categories in order to estimate the value of their crops, the preference for cash payments and the consideration of regional market prices of the affected crops were introduced. Ferdinand Friedrich Pfeiffer even argued for the establishment of specialised insurance companies for each agricultural risk.

However, not all cameralists were positive about crop insurance. Johann Heinrich Jung pointed to several problematic aspects, such as the inadequate calculation of a premium due to the lack of precise data, or the fact that too small a geographical area of operations would cause severe problems for the business. Interestingly, most of these issues did arise during the last few decades of the eighteenth century, with the development of several projects for crop insurance. However, neither the project in Ansbach-Bayreuth nor that in Magdeburg could be brought into operation. Finally, in 1791, the first crop insurance company was successfully founded in Brunswick, but it lasted only a few years. It took until the beginning of the nineteenth century before crop insurance became attractive for a more broadly based market. However, cameralism laid the foundation for the transfer and reduction of risk, and today's agricultural sector would be unimaginable without insurance as a means for protecting the fields against natural hazards.

11

The Decline of Cameralism in Germany at the Turn of the Nineteenth Century

HANS FRAMBACH

Introduction

In the early nineteenth century a fundamental transformation in the established German system of governance occurred; at the same time, *Kameralwissenschaft* went into decline. These two events have been linked, and several explanations advanced for this linkage, but none is convincing in detail. The decline of cameralism has often been treated as a result of the 'rise of liberalism' and the diffusion of English political economy, especially in the wake of Adam Smith's *Wealth of Nations*. Unfortunately, this argument – like others along similar lines – is simply incorrect. On the one hand, the influence on contemporary German economic thought that some theorists assign to the *Wealth of Nations* is exaggerated; and on the other, cameralism continued to play a substantial role in German offices and administrations, even though its theoretical presence had altered and it was progressively replaced by *Nationalökonomie* in German universities.

A central focus of this chapter will be the development of cameralism as a university discipline and its divorce from administrative practice. Keith Tribe has argued that the pedagogical and philosophical influence of late cameralism should not be underestimated, suggesting a closer analysis of the changing philosophical foundations of university scholarship and training during the nineteenth century, when the idea of happiness as the goal and purpose of the state was increasingly replaced by that of the state providing the conditions for autonomous personal development. Insight can also be derived from Andre Wakefield's critical view of the authenticity of the ideas and teaching of many cameralists, especially regarding their personal credibility and professional ambitions. Finally, arguments for the decline of cameralism at the turn of the nineteenth century can be described by the idea that 'cameralism becomes more legally minded'. Here I will highlight the impact of alterations to the financial support of the court household that led the activities of the *Kammern* to be transferred into the sphere of constitutional law.

The development of cameralism as a science and its perception in theory

From the mid-eighteenth century a new curricular structure emerged in German universities including disciplines such as natural law, constitutional law and, of course, the theory and practice of cameralism [*Kameralwissenschaft*]. Cameralism offered the prospect of telescoping the related subjects of law, history, politics and economy into a single system without rejecting the old teaching tradition of the *philosophia practica*. It was formally introduced into the Germany university curriculum with the foundation of two chairs for *Oeconomie, Policey und Cammersachen* and *Kameral-, Oeconomie- und Polizeiwissenschaft* at the universities of Halle and Frankfurt on the Oder (the 'Viadrina') in 1727 by Friedrich Wilhelm I (1688–1740). Justus Christoph Dithmar (1678–1737), appointed to the chair at the Viadrina, defined the new science as follows:

> Cameralist science teaches how a ruler can increase his revenues, improve them over time and employ them to maintain the common weal [*gemeines Wesen*] in such a way that every year a surplus remains.[1]

Other universities followed suit – Rinteln in 1730, Vienna in 1752, Göttingen in 1755, Prague and Leipzig in 1763, Würzburg in 1764, Freiburg, Klagenfurt and Innsbruck in 1768, Gießen in 1777, and Ingolstadt in 1780 – primarily in order to fill an existing gap in economic teaching for the education of future state officials. Cameralism and *Polizei* became firmly established in Faculties of Philosophy, the most general of the four faculties of Philosophy, Law, Medicine and Theology.[2]

A lasting impact on the systematisation and dissemination of cameralism and *Polizeiwissenschaft* was made by the writings of major cameralists like

---

1 Justus Christoph Dithmar, *Einleitung in die Oeconomische Policei- und Cameral-Wissenschaften*, repr. rev. edn 1745, 1st edn 1731 (Glashütten im Taunus, 1971), p. 225.
2 Wilhelm Bleek, *Von der Kameralausbildung zum Juristenprivileg. Studium, Prüfung und Ausbildung der höheren Beamten des allgemeinen Verwaltungsdienstes in Deutschland im 18. und 19. Jahrhundert* (Berlin, 1972), pp. 64–5; Hans Maier, 'Die Lehre von der Politik an den deutschen Universitäten vornehmlich vom 16. bis 18. Jahrhundert', *Wissenschaftliche Politik. Eine Einführung in Grundfragen ihrer Tradition und Theorie*, ed. D. Oberndörfer (Freiburg im Breisgau, 1962), pp. 96–7; Wilhelm Stieda, *Die Nationalökonomie als Universitätswissenschaft*, repr. (1st edn 1906; Vaduz, 1978), pp. 17–38.

Johann Heinrich Gottlob von Justi (1717/20?–1771) – *Staatswirtschaft oder systematische Abhandlung aller ökonomischen und Cameralwissenschaft* (1755), and his *Grundriss einer guten Regierung* (1759) – as well as by the three volumes of Joseph von Sonnenfels' (1732/33–1817) *Grundsätze der Policey, Handlung und Finanz*, which began publication in 1765 as *Sätze aus der Polizey, Handlungs- und Finanzwissenschaft*. These works circulated widely in several editions over the following decades. Justi's *Staatswirtschaft* presented the first comprehensive and structured version of *Kameralwissenschaft*, and was in the past treated as the first German work of economic theory.[3] He distinguished between *Polizei- and Kameralwissenschaft* (literally 'police science', or what we would call the administration of public order) and cameralism. Sonnenfels followed Justi's systematisation, distinguishing between *Polizeiwissenschaft*, dealing with the inner security of the state (public order); *Handlungswissenschaft*, dealing with the economic provisioning of the people; and *Finanzwissenschaft*, dealing with the improvement of state revenues.[4] While in later writings *Finanzwissenschaft* was often described as cameralism in a narrower sense, Sonnenfels emphasised that German authors subsumed *Polizei-, Handlungs-* and *Finanzwissenschaft* under the heading of *Staatswirthschaft* or *oekonomische Wissenschaft*; whereas *Handlungs-* and *Finanzwissenschaft* came under the heading of the *Kameralwissenschaften*.[5] Nevertheless, the three fields contained material relating to administrative law as well as to economic theory and policy.

In his seminal book, *Die alten deutschen Kameralisten. Ein Beitrag zur Geschichte der Nationalökonomie und zum Problem des Merkantilismus*, Kurt Zielenziger distinguished between the officials, counsellors and secretaries whose daily task was administration, and those leading officials among them who had access to their rulers, consulted with them, worked out their own ideas and plans, and wrote texts. Albion Small distinguished between 'cameralists of the bureaus' or 'fiscalists', and 'cameralists of the books'; Zielenziger treated the latter as the true cameralists (or 'cameralists proper' as Andre Wakefield calls them).[6] Zielenziger questioned the distribution of material between *Polizei* and *Kameralwissenschaften*, favouring

3 John Kells Ingram, *A History of Political Economy*, repr. edn 1915 (New York, 1967), p. 78; Justus Remer, *Johann Heinrich Gottlob Justi. Ein deutscher Volkswirt des 18. Jahrhunderts* (Stuttgart/Berlin, 1938), pp. 26–7; Gerhard Stavenhagen, *Geschichte der Wirtschaftstheorie*, 2nd edn (Göttingen, 1957), pp. 24–5.
4 Erhard Dittrich, *Die deutschen und die österreichischen Kameralisten* (Darmstadt, 1974), p. 111.
5 Joseph von Sonnenfels, *Grundsätze der Polizey, Handlung und Finanz*, vol. I, 5th edn (Vienna, 1787, orig. 1765), pp. 20–1.
6 Albion W. Small, *The Cameralists. The Pioneers of German Social Polity*, repr. 1st edn 1909 (New York, 1962), p. 6; Andre Wakefield, *The Disordered Police State. German Cameralism as Science and Practice* (Chicago/London, 2009), p. 4; Kurt Zielenziger, *Die alten deutschen*

the assignment of *Polizei* to cameralism, and then treating these two areas as *Staatswissenschaften*.[7]

Wakefield remarks on the fact that Keith Tribe, in his important book *Governing Economy*, treated the teaching of the *Kameralwissenschaften* entirely separately from the context of state administration.[8] This is however something of a misapprehension: *Governing Economy* is quite explicitly a study of evolving university practices that present themselves as a pedagogy for administrators.[9] Whether this pedagogy had any real practical impact or relevance is not something that the literature of the *Kameralwissenschaften* itself reveals, or could reveal. The *Kameralwissenschaften* functioned quite autonomously from administrative practice in the *Kammer*, and Tribe, naturally enough, found no evidence for any direct transfer of the academic findings of cameralism to the administration of state offices, at least for the eighteenth century. He does not deny any impact on the education of many state officials, rather that evidence for the 'real practicality' of this teaching cannot be found in the teaching itself, since *claims* to be 'practical' are not self-confirming. This is a principle that is as relevant today when discussing vocational education as it is for the eighteenth century.

In his book *The Disordered Police State* Wakefield lists, among other things, the shifting perception of cameralism as 'a disembodied collection of economic principles, academic sciences, and bureaucratic practices'.[10] Cameralists themselves have been seen both as mere money-grubbers and as selfless supporters of the state. Wakefield presents the darker side of the cameralists, lending insight into character. The leading claim of his book 'is not about how knowledge changed the world; it is about how the world changed knowledge. ... the cameral sciences, which purported to speak publicly about the most secret affairs of the prince, were deeply dishonest.'[11]

James Sheehan, in his *German History 1770–1866*, described cameralism as 'the science of political management'.[12] Reviewing the relationship between the theoretical formulations of cameralism and the practical problems of state-building, he listed a number of cameralists who in their treatises on politics made reasonable suggestions for bureaucratic improvement, seeking to promote general welfare and happiness while also taking account of the

---

Kameralisten. Ein Beitrag zur Geschichte der Nationalökonomie und zum Problem des Merkantilismus (Jena, 1914), pp. 86–7.

7   Zielenziger, *Die alten*, p. 101.
8   Wakefield, *The Disordered*, p. 4.
9   Keith Tribe, *Governing Economy. The Reformation of German Economic Discourse, 1750–1840* (Cambridge, 1988), pp. 10–11.
10   Wakefield, *The Disordered*, p. 5.
11   Wakefield, *The Disordered*, p. 25.
12   James J. Sheehan, *German History 1770–1866* (Oxford, 1989), p. 194.

state's well-being – but always, furthermore, keeping in mind their own career and individual well-being.[13] For, as Wakefield observes:

> Cameralism did not simply reflect administrative practice in well-disciplined German principalities, nor was it wholly unrelated to fiscal administration. Rather, cameralists *created* the well-ordered police state through their ordinances, books, and treatises. But behind these well-ordered visions lurked a disordered world of fear and frustrations. ... Cameralists were fiscal propagandists.[14]

Wakefield demonstrates, in fact, that 'cameralists were not what they seemed to be';[15] they often did the opposite of what they urged in theory (many examples are given).[16] His book concludes with the words 'We have trusted them all too much. ... It is strange that we have believed them.'[17]

Given these different perspectives, how might we approach any explanation of the demise of cameralism? Here it is taken for granted that we cannot treat cameralism as belonging to some 'non-scientific' period of economics, prior to the work of Adam Smith, a position shared both by Wilhelm Roscher's *Geschichte der National-Oekonomik in Deutschland* and, to a lesser extent, Joseph Schumpeter's *History of Economic Analysis*.[18] Commenting on the common view of the distinction between the new (Smithian) political economy and cameralism, in which the former is responsible for the decline of the latter, Keith Tribe observes that: 'While there is a rough correspondence between the rates at which Smithian ideas became popular and the older doctrines declined, it is dangerous to suppose that this coincidence indicates that the demise of the one is entirely the result of the rise of the other.'[19] Tribe argues convincingly that the putative decline of cameralism during the early decades of the nineteenth century should not be interpreted simply as a result of the *Wealth of Nations*, and this for various reasons.[20] On the one hand he reveals inconsistencies and omissions in the reception of the *Wealth of Nations* in the German economic literature of the day.[21] On

13 Sheehan, *German History*, pp. 194–5.

14 Wakefield, *The Disordered*, p. 142.

15 Wakefield, *The Disordered*, p. 143.

16 Wakefield, *The Disordered*, pp. 91–110.

17 Wakefield, *The Disordered*, pp. 142–3.

18 Wilhelm Roscher, *Geschichte der National-Oekonomik in Deutschland* (München, 1874), pp. 231, 473, 533, 536, 593–4, 635, 843; Joseph Aloys Schumpeter, *Geschichte der ökonomischen Analyse*, vol. 1 (Göttingen, 1965), pp. 229–33.

19 Keith Tribe, 'Cameralism and the Science of Government', *Journal of Modern History* 56 (1984), 278.

20 See Tribe, 'Cameralism', pp. 277–84.

21 For example, the arbitrary reception of Smith by Christian J. Kraus and Johann Georg Büsch with reference to Gottlieb Hufeland's *Neue Grundlegung der Staatswirthschaftskunst*,

the other hand he pinpoints some misconceptions in the relevant literature, ranging from early works such as Friedrich Benedict Weber's *Handbuch der Staatswirthschaft* (1804) to Hans Maier's *Habilitation* (post-doctoral treatise) *Die ältere deutsche Staats- und Verwaltungslehre*, as well as other unfounded arguments.[22] One could also mention others such as Adam Müller, Friedrich List, Bruno Hildebrand and Karl Knies, all of whom had a critical distance from Smith, and no commitment to the older issues of cameralism.

However, these thoughts will not be pursued any further here. Attention will be drawn only to one aspect of the relationship between the cameralist literature of the time and Smith's *Wealth of Nations*: one not only of contradiction but also of convergence, with some cameralists definitely sharing certain 'modern' positions. For example, Sonnenfels had already described the main principle of the 'promotion of general happiness' to be true, albeit not as a principle;[23] and Justi certainly does not see wealth as synonymous with the content of the royal treasury, as is all too often assumed in writings on cameralism. On the contrary: 'Anything which lies idle in the treasure-chamber of the monarch or in the hands of private persons is *not* wealth of the nation. … The wealth [inherent] in the trades is the only true wealth of the nation' (my italics).[24] While the wealth of a nation comprises a greater or lesser abundance of material goods,[25] the term *assets* covers much more than material goods; it also includes members of society and their abilities and knowledge: 'Human capacity is to be understood as anything humans are capable of demonstrating they can do. However, anything they are capable of doing is called assets.'[26] Justi even considered general happiness the ultimate

vol. 1 (1807), Georg Friedrich Sartorius' *Handbuch der Staatswirthschaft* with reference to Roscher's *Geschichte der National-Oekonomik in Deutschland*, and August Ferdinand Lueder's *Ueber Nationalindustrie und Staatswirthschaft. Nach Adam Smith bearbeitet* (1800).

22   Tribe, 'Cameralism', pp. 278–83 referring to Melchior Palyi's 'The Introduction of Adam Smith on the Continent', in *Adam Smith 1776–1926* (Chicago, 1928), pp. 180–233, and Carl William Hasek, *The Introduction of Adam Smith's Doctrines into Germany* (New York, 1925); Tribe, *Governing Economy*, ch. 7, pp. 147–8.

23   Sonnenfels, *Grundsätze*, vol. I, pp. 22–32, esp. pp. 24, 27.

24   Johann Heinrich Gottlob von Justi, *Gesammlete Politische und Finanzschriften über wichtige Gegenstände der Staatskunst, der Kriegswissenschaften und des Kameral- und Finanzwesens*, vol. I (3 vols), repr. edn 1791 (1st edn 1761; Aalen, 1970), p. 524; see also Johann Heinrich Gottlob von Justi, *Die Grundfeste zu der Macht und Glückseeligkeit der Staaten; oder ausführliche Vorstellung der gesamten Policey-Wissenschaft*, 2 vols (Königsberg/Leipzig, 1760–61), I , pp. 701–2.

25   Johann Heinrich Gottlob von Justi, *Staatswirthschaft oder systematische Abhandlung aller Oekonomischen und Cameralwissenschaften, die zur Regierung eines Landes erfordert werden*, vol. I (2 vols), repr. 2nd edn 1758 (1st edn 1755; Aalen, 1963), pp. 152–6.

26   Johann Heinrich Gottlob von Justi, *System des Finanzwesens. Nach vernünftigen, aus dem Endzweck der bürgerlichen Gesellschaften und aus der Natur aller Quellen der Einkünfte des Staats hergeleiteten Grundsätze und Regeln abgehandelt*, repr. 1st edn 1766 (Aalen, 1969), p. 3, see also p. 5.

objective of civil society, describing the welfare of all members of society in the sense of the common good. This includes material comfort, and a high level of freedom. Such a 'comfortable life' should, among other things, enable the individual to make the required contribution to the public good.[27] Another example of convergence between cameralism and political economy lies in the conception of the task of government to be the securing of a framework involving 'legislation for the welfare of the state', intervening only when the interests of the common good, and thus also the economic capacity of a society, are in danger. 'Accordingly, the freedom of commerce and industry is the unlimited ability of the industrious to undertake everything they consider advantageous for themselves, insofar as this does not harm the common good and the welfare of the state.'[28]

One way of explaining the decline of cameralism can be traced back to Pierangelo Schiera's *Il cameralismo e l'assolutismo Tedesco. Dell'arte di governo alle scienze dello stato*. This treats the economics of Prussian absolutism as reflected in the economic writings of the time, concluding that with Napoleon's triumphal progress, the defeat of Prussia and its administration would naturally bring about the demise of the related literature. Tribe questioned Schiera's thesis, because the political transformations Schiera described do not fit with the reality in the universities. Despite changes in the political framework, waves of reforms, and university teaching, 'the daily business of office and ministry remained much the same'.[29]

The idea of happiness and welfare as the ultimate objective

I have already touched on the importance of welfare in the early development of political economy and cameralism. The new *Nationalökonomie* stressed the importance of human needs and interests, focusing on regularities that were no longer the product of regulation but the result of a self-generating order. This is a manifestation of a more general development, away from courtly absolutism through forms of 'enlightened absolutism'[30] to German Idealism: a development that redefined the relationship between people and

27   Justi, *Staatswirthschaft*, p. 66; Justi, *Gesammlete Politische*, p. 523.
28   Justi, *Die Grundfeste*, I, p. 699.
29   Tribe, *Governing Economy*, p. 11; Rüdiger vom Bruch, 'Wissenschaftliche, institutionelle oder politische Innovation? Kameralwissenschaft – Polizeiwissenschaft – Wirtschaftswissenschaft im 18. Jahrhundert im Spiegel der Forschungsgeschichte', *Die Institutionalisierung der Nationalökonomie an deutschen Universitäten. Zur Erinnerung an Klaus Hinrich Hennings (1937–1986)*, ed. N. Waszek (St Katharinen, 1988), pp. 106–8; Maier, 'Die Lehre', pp. 96–7.
30   The concept of enlightened absolutism was introduced by Wilhelm Roscher in his *Umrissen zur Naturlehre der drei Staatsformen* in 1847, Angela Borgstedt, *Das Zeitalter der Aufklärung* (Darmstadt, 2004), p. 21, but it is also mentioned in Roscher's *Geschichte*, pp. 380–1, 448.

state, individual and government. Happiness remained the proper concern of government; but no longer to be achieved by the ruler acting alone; it was now to originate in good government using the means of *Staatswissenschaft*.

The philosopher Christian Wolff (1679–1754) had defined welfare as the highest good, the progress from one perfect state to the next, and he saw this as directly connected with happiness. To attain happiness a well-ordered state is required. General welfare, safety and security were declared to be the supreme laws of the community and the basis of any decision made within it: 'Do what promotes general welfare and maintains general safety. By contrast, desist from anything that impedes general welfare or is counter to general safety.'[31] Hence those rulers who seek to promote general welfare enhanced the happiness of their subjects, and Wolff declared that type of community to be the best that did the most to foster general welfare and safety, where the majority of people are able to live in happiness together.[32] Improvement of general welfare itself depended on the reason and virtue of its subjects.[33] However, the members of the community should (still) always align their actions with the promotion of general welfare and preservation of internal and external security (general welfare is prior to particular or individual welfare).[34]

Cameralism built these ideas into a comprehensive list of requirements for the state, connecting political doctrine with the dynamics of life in individual principalities and territories. Ulrich Engelhardt has remarked that cameralism can be seen as a prime indicator for the general secularisation of perceptions of life and state purpose in the Age of Enlightenment, and for the growth of state competence with respect to general welfare within the political system of enlightened absolutism.[35]

Johann Gottlieb Fichte (1762–1814) in *Zurückforderung der Denkfreiheit von dem Fürsten Europens* (1793) criticised 'that poisonous source of all our misery', meaning the destiny and calling of the prince to keep watch over the happiness of his people. Shortly before this, the young Wilhelm von Humboldt (1767–1835), in a letter to Friedrich von Gentz of August 1791, had condemned the 'principle that the government has to provide for the happiness and well-being of the nation', as the 'most terrible and severest

---

31   Christian Wolff, *Vernünfftige Gedancken von dem gesellschaftlichen Leben der Menschen und insonderheit dem gemeinen Wesen zu Beförderung der Glückseeligkeit des menschlichen Geschlechtes den Liebhabern der Wahrheit mitgetheilet*, repr. 1st edn 1721 (Frankfurt a.M., 1971), p. 158, §215, see also p. 7, §11.
32   Wolff, *Vernünfftige Gedancken*, p. 3, §3, pp. 160–1, §223, pp. 177–8, §245, see also the foreword.
33   Wolff, *Vernünfftige Gedancken*, pp. 175–6, §§242–3.
34   Wolff, *Vernünfftige Gedancken*, p. 159, §218, see also p. 6, §10, pp. 454–5, §433.
35   Ulrich Engelhardt, 'Zum Begriff der Glückseligkeit in der kameralistischen Staatslehre des 18. Jahrhunderts (J. H. G. v. Justi)', *Zeitschrift für historische Forschung* 8 (1981), 43–4.

despotism'.[36] Against this, Humboldt proposed an idealistic conception of a state that is to provide its citizens only with freedom for the attainment of their purposes. The state ensures this provision by protecting the individual and his (or her) properties against internal and external dangers.[37] Humboldt, who considered *Bildung* to be the supreme social purpose, wanted people to achieve the highest *Bildung* of which their creative energies are capable, and such creative energy grows best in a climate of freedom. The state had to support this. Thus it is no surprise that Humboldt is regarded as a progenitor of German liberalism, a position diametrically opposed to the conservative monarchical forces in the state of Prussia which he served as a leading diplomat:

> The true end of Man, or that which is prescribed by the eternal and immutable dictates of reason, and not suggested by vague and transient desires, is the highest and most harmonious development of his powers to a complete and consistent whole. Freedom is the first and indispensable condition which the possibility of such a development presupposes.[38]

Under the condition that 'no one can at any time, or in any way, obtain a right to dispose of the powers or goods of another without his consent or against his will',[39] Humboldt laid down the following principle for the practical application of his theory, thereby at the same time explaining the relationship of state, people and freedom:

> With regard to the limits of its activity, the State should endeavour to bring the actual condition of things as close to those prescribed by the true and just theory as is possible, and in so far as it is not opposed to reasons of real necessity. Now, the possibility consists in this, that men are ready to receive the freedom which theory always approves, and that this freedom can succeed in producing those salutary consequences which always accompany its unhindered operation. The reasons of necessity which may oppose this are: that freedom, once granted, is not calculated to destroy those conditions, without which not only all further progress, but even existence itself, is endangered. In both of these cases the statesman's judgement must be formed from a careful comparison between the present state of things, and the contemplated change, and between their respective consequences.[40]

36 Engelhardt, 'Zum Begriff der Glückseligkeit', pp. 74–5.
37 Wilhelm von Humboldt, *The Limits of State Action* (London/New York, 1969), p. 43, *The Limits* is the translation of *Ideen zu einem Versuch, die Grenzen der Wirksamkeit des Staates zu bestimmen*, repr. 1st edn 1851, written in 1792 (Leipzig, 1945).
38 Humboldt, *The Limits*, p. 16; Humboldt, *Ideen zu*, p. 12.
39 Humboldt, *The Limits*, p. 137.
40 Humboldt, *The Limits*, pp. 137–8; Humboldt, *Ideen zu*, pp. 198–9.

Some remarks on Immanuel Kant (1724–1804) may be appropriate here in connection with the relationship of happiness, the individual, the state and freedom. According to Kant, happiness is the 'epitome of all purposes of men, rendered possible by nature both apart from and in man' – i.e. to a bare and changeable idea.[41] Kant described happiness [*Glückseligkeit*] as secure well-being, enjoyable life and complete contentment with one's situation [*beständiges Wohlergehen, vergnügtes Leben, völlige Zufriedenheit mit seinem Zustand*];[42] it is an aim people set for themselves and which they strive to attain, not a state of nature, nor simply a given condition. People can only ever hope to *attain* the state of happiness, which they will do only if they prove themselves worthy [*würdig*]. *Reason* takes on the function of enabling people to make themselves worthy, because reason supports the genesis of good will.[43]

In his 'Idee zu einer allgemeinen Geschichte weltbürgerlicher Absicht' (1784) Kant made a plea for properly constituted civil society as well as for freedom. He explains, among other things, that people who live in 'wild freedom' cannot exist together for any length of time. The ideal condition is civil unification, civil society, which imposes limits on the individual, limits under which man, however, with all his inclinations, can develop to the greatest degree: just as trees in a forest, by always striving to take the air and sun away from each other, eventually stand tall and straight. If their branches grew randomly, with untrammelled freedom, – they would become crippled, crooked and twisted.[44] The history of the human species can therefore be considered as the fulfilment of a hidden plan of nature to create a perfect national constitution.[45] Kant wrote in similar vein in his essay 'Beantwortung der Frage: Was ist Aufklärung?' (1784) that enlightenment arises from freedom, and freedom means making use of reason in the public sphere. The prerequisite for this is an independent intellect that has escaped the bonds of immaturity.[46]

Ultimately the idea of happiness as the final aim and purpose of state policy and as an immutable general law became inappropriate, and the task of the state could only be the direct realisation of the legal premises on which it stood: that one man's freedom does not impair another's. Thus the state's guarantee to provide the conditions for autonomous personal development

41   Immanuel Kant, *Kritik der Urteilskraft*, Akademie Ausgabe vol. V, repr. edn 1908/13 (1st edn 1790; Berlin, 1968), pp. 429–34, see esp. p. 431, §83.
42   Immanuel Kant, *Metaphysik der Sitten*, Akademie Ausgabe vol. VI, repr. edn 1907/14 (1st edn 1797; Berlin, 1968), p. 480.
43   Kant, *Metaphysik der Sitten*, pp. 480–2; Immanuel Kant, *Grundlegung zur Metaphysik der Sitten*, Akademie Ausgabe vol. IV, repr. edn 1903/11, 1st edn 1785 (Berlin, 1978), pp. 395–6.
44   Immanuel Kant, *Idee zu einer allgemeinen Geschichte weltbürgerlicher Absicht*, Akademie Ausgabe vol. VIII, repr. edn 1912/23, 1st edn 1784 (Berlin, 1971), pp. 21–3.
45   Kant, *Idee zu einer allgemeinen Geschichte*, pp. 26–8.
46   Immanuel Kant, *Beantwortung der Frage: Was ist Aufklärung?*, Akademie Ausgabe vol. VIII, repr. edn 1912/23, 1st edn 1784 (Berlin, 1971), p. 36.

replaced happiness as the state purpose – as the only way to a self-determining, individual life full of good fortune and to the general happiness of society; the older positions of Justi and Sonnenfels, involving the priority of the state over economy and society, the vision of state machine seamlessly processing and achieving the envisaged objective of welfare – this no longer retained force and plausibility. It was then only a small step to an economically orientated liberalism organised through civil law, with the free play of resources and the concomitant renunciation of the idea of 'independent, territorially based economic welfare supervision'.[47] As Tribe put it:

> It was the emergence of this tripartite relation of economy, civil society, and state at the end of the eighteenth century that brought about the dissolution of Cameralistic orthodoxy; and in this process, it was the initial separation of the spheres of state and of civil society that opened up the space for a redefinition of economic life and for a series of related conceptual changes.[48]

The ideas of state and civil society, perceived to be identical during the eighteenth century, ceased in the nineteenth century to be synonymous. This argument can be taken as an indication for the detachment of 'police science' (public order) from economics, and hence for the fragmentation of cameralism as a coherent approach. Following the political upheaval in the early nineteenth century, concepts of governance changed their perspective from interior to exterior affairs, from issues of welfare and law to those of power, shifting the typical areas of responsibility of cameralism out of the main political focus. There was an intellectual move away from the police state and the old normative state doctrine to a concept of policy understood as the result of economic, historical and geographical conditions.[49] Political culture developed to the disadvantage of cameralism.

Cameralists in practice

To shed some light on the relationship between the *Kameralwissenschaften* and administrative practice, Andre Wakefield laid emphasis upon the strategic moment between them. He concluded that academic discourse and that of the *Kammer* were 'distinct but interrelated, separate but independent',[50]

---

47   Engelhardt, 'Zum Begriff', p. 75.
48   Tribe, *Governing Economy*, pp. 152–3, with reference to Reinhart Koselleck's term *Sattelzeit*, p. 153, fn. 7.
49   Maier, 'Die Lehre', pp. 102–3.
50   Wakefield, *The Disordered*, p. 137.

agreeing with Keith Tribe's observation that 'cameralist textbooks could not resolve this question, no matter how many of them you read', asserting simply 'Keith Tribe was right about that.'[51] He went on to suggest that the *Kameralwissenschaften* 'lived parasitically from the status and secrecy of the Kammer. That is what made them so popular, elegant, and fashionable. ... the Kammer benefited from the image fostered by the cameral sciences.'[52] Wakefield depicts cameralists as not always noble and virtuous men: some of them 'lied, connived, cheated, and embezzled'; they were able to cope with life, were efficient, power-conscious and aware of their career.[53] Some cameralists were simply projectors [*Projektemacher*] and state adventurers [*Staatsabenteuerer*], and some were imprisoned following accusations of embezzlement – Erik Reinert mentions Georg Heinrich Zincke (1692–1796), Johann Heinrich Gottlob von Justi, and Johann Friedrich von Pfeiffer (1718–87) in this connection.[54] Cameralists promoted the well-ordered police state, promoting an idealised image of the fiscal-police state: 'they *created* the good cameralist', but always bearing in mind their own interests by justifying their influence and conduct and securing their own positions in office and university.[55] In this respect the cameral sciences were *strategic*.

Wakefield's observations correspond to the insights of Max Weber, who distinguished between politicians living *for* politics and those living *from* politics. As a rule, Weber maintained, the cameralists united both aspects. They developed projects and strove at the same time for a durable source of income.[56] This assessment fits with James Sheehan's assessment that in state and administration:

> custody over the state's information became a full-time task, carried out by those who devoted themselves to its acquisition and accumulation. Just as this information was meant to enhance the state's power over society, so its guardians used it to enhance their own position within the ruling councils of the state.[57]

Marc Raeff, in his essay 'The Well-Ordered Police State and the Development of Modernity in Seventeenth- and Eighteenth-Century Europe', indicated that German universities proclaimed individual responsibility and collective

---

51   Wakefield, *The Disordered*, p. 138, with ref. to Tribe, *Governing Economy*, pp. 10–11.
52   Wakefield, *The Disordered*, p. 137.
53   Wakefield, *The Disordered*, p. 141.
54   Erik S. Reinert, 'Jacob Bielfeld's "On the Decline of States" (1760) and its Relevance for Today', *Great Nations at Peril*, ed. J. G. Backhaus (London, 2015), pp. 135–6.
55   Wakefield, *The Disordered*, pp. 137–8.
56   Max Weber, *Wirtschaft und Gesellschaft. Grundriss der verstehenden Soziologie*, 5th rev. edn (Tübingen, 1972), p. 829.
57   Sheehan, *German History*, p. 35.

THE DECLINE OF CAMERALISM IN GERMANY

obligation, but that in practice just the opposite occurred: in the daily business of government actions were undertaken that led to the disruption of group solidarities and the emergence of the selfish, interest-oriented individual.[58] Following Max Weber, who remarked on the increasing inconsistency between the bureaucratic reason [*bürokratischer Vernunft*] of the modern institutional state [*Anstaltsstaat*] as operated by cameralists, and the domestic ceremonial science [*Zeremonialwissenschaft*] of the courts,[59] the conclusion can be drawn that with the erosion of the patrimonially and governmentally organised administration the life of court ceremonial and the livelihood of the cameralists dependent upon it gradually lost their basis.[60]

Wakefield has shed valuable light on the background of some cameralists and their practical as well as academic behaviour, but the negative features and characteristics he observes are also true of other great scientists across all the disciplines, even today. The viability of any theory does not depend a great deal on the integrity of its leading proponents; what is important is truth and trustworthiness, however that is constructed. Posturing, exaggeration, embellishment will all eventually lead to discredit and disrepute. The story does not end here, but for the moment it can be said that Wakefield is surely right in his assertion that some commentaries upon the *Kameralwissenschaften* are overdone or embellished.

For the cameralist in practice a major task was to cope with that what Volker Bauer called the *communicative challenge*.[61] In order to win support, cameralists had to transmit their ideas about the court economy – which were rooted in bureaucratic principles and a specific style of work – to rulers committed to court life and to an old-fashioned ideal of power. If cameralists wanted their recommendations to become reality, they had to rely on their practical experience at court, where insufficient communicative virtuosity could have a devastating effect.[62] Besides their financial competence, cameralists had to be able to communicate, because as public servants they were always dependent on the goodwill of the princes and courts. The highly paid

---

58   Marc Raeff, 'The Well-Ordered Police State and the Development of Modernity in Seventeenth- and Eighteenth-Century Europe: An Attempt at a Comparative Approach', *American Historical Review* 80 (1975), 1241; Marc Raeff, *The Well-Ordered Police-State: Social and Institutional Change through Law in the Germanies and Russia 1600–1800* (New Haven, CT, 1983).

59   Ultimately both were embedded in a patrimonial and governmentally organised administration [patrimonial-staatliche Verwaltung], i.e. the prince organised his political power over his subjects in the same way as he exercised his domestic authority within the court [*Ausübung seiner Hausgewalt*].

60   Weber, *Wirtschaft und Gesellschaft*, pp. 580–624, see esp. p. 585.

61   Volker Bauer, *Hofökonomie. Der Diskurs über den Fürstenhof in Zeremonialwissenschaft, Hausväterliteratur und Kameralismus* (Wien, 1997), p. 222.

62   Bauer, *Hofökonomie*, p. 223.

leading positions they coveted were in the prince's gift; they, like other public employees, depended on the favour and patronage of the court. Consequently, they subscribed to the basic legitimacy of the state and formulated reform proposals primarily in conformity with the system.

Criticism of the financial and economic situation of courts had always existed, of course, but it became a major public issue in the final decades of the eighteenth century. Criticism is commonly found in contemporary publications – not however in the books of cameralists who were dependent on their respective sovereigns. Hard-hitting criticism came primarily from Physiocracy. First and foremost, Johann August Schlettwein, the leading representative of Physiocracy in Germany, denounced the excessive costs of the courts.[63] In his treatise *Historisch-Moralische Schilderung des Einflusses der Hofhaltungen auf das Verderben der Staaten* ('An historical and moral depiction of the impact of the maintenance of courts on the ruination of states') the cameralist August Hennings (1746–1826), a high civil servant in Denmark and Schleswig-Holstein, presented a comprehensive and sweeping criticism of the courts, but at the same time expressed sympathy for the difficult and complex situation of the ruler. He demanded that the principle that a ruler cannot treat the national revenue as his own be regarded as incontrovertible.[64] He stated that 'true monarchy is democratic'[65] and argued in favour of recognising true merits and capabilities instead of privileging the nobility.[66] Describing central elements of that what was called the civil list [*Zivilliste*], Hennings clearly distinguished between the court as the household of the sovereign and the household of the state, noting that the two are not identical.[67]

The introduction of the *Zivilliste* created an institution that separated the incomes of the prince and of the state, making the sovereign subject to budgetary discipline. The conception of the *Zivilliste* is based on a clear separation between princely and state property, in which the property of the ruling princes was paramount. Princely domains, formerly in the possession

---

63   Johann August Schlettwein, *Archiv für den Menschen und Bürger in allen Verhältnissen oder Sammlung von Abhandlungen, Vorschlägen, Planen, Veruschen, Rechungen, Begebenheiten, Thaten, Anstalten, Verfassungen, Gesetzen, Ordnungen, Länder- Aemter- und Ortsbeschreibungen, Bücheranzeigen und Kritiken welche das Wohl und Wehe der Menschheit und der Staaten angehen* (Leipzig, 1780); see chap. VIII, *Anmerkungen über die Badische Cammer-Ordnung in Absicht auf die Fundamental-Grundsätze der Staatswirthschaft, auf die Staats-Bedürfnisse und auf das Staats-Tabellenwerk*, pp. 142–5, 150–2 (141–185), chap. XVIII, *Von Aufhebung der Gemeinschaften der Länder, besonders im deutschen Reiche*, pp. 399–402 (377–429).

64   August Hennings, *Historisch-Moralische Schilderung des Einflusses der Hofhaltungen auf das Verderben der Staaten* (Altona, 1782), p. 389.

65   Hennings, *Historisch-Moralische Schilderung*, p. 41.

66   Hennings, *Historisch-Moralische Schilderung*, p. 46.

67   Hennings, *Historisch-Moralische Schilderung*, p. 5.

of the various royal houses under private law, were officially converted in new constitutions into the property of the state, and as such contributed to the public budget. In return, the ruling princes received the right to a constitutionally guaranteed income, a fixed amount for their personal needs and those of their families and courts.[68] Jung-Stilling described court expenditure as the salary of the monarch, providing him with a life befitting his social standing and education, and adequate to care for his family.[69] By the beginning of the nineteenth century the civil list was no longer a salary or pension, but instead a substitute for domain revenues which had been transferred to the state.[70]

While in the older theories of cameralism only expenditure covered by ordinary income was regarded as legitimate, the later cameralists – for instance, Johann Heinrich Jung-Stilling, Theodor Schmalz and Karl Heinrich Ludwig Pölitz[71] – reverted to the principle of calculating state revenues by the level of expenditure the state needed for the execution of its tasks. From the end of the eighteenth century cameralistic *Finanzwissenschaft* assumed that the various tasks of the state required a corresponding financial coverage which its earnings had to produce. The *Finanzwissenschaft* of later cameralism had, in other words, undergone a fundamental conceptual change, at whose end-point the civil list appeared.[72]

With this radical change in the relationship of revenues and expenditures, financial policy and administration changed. Whereas in the past expected annual earnings had to be estimated, it was now only necessary to determine expenses for the financial year. While the earlier task had primarily required the expert financial knowledge of the cameralists, which therefore assumed a key role, this knowledge became less central, since budgetary planning was reduced to filling given heads of expenditure. In this regard, financial policy became a political rather than cameralistic issue.[73] *Kameralwissenschaft* as a system for financial policy therefore lost its significance and migrated to the fields of administration and jurisprudence – an observation supported by the

68   Bauer, *Hofökonomie*, pp. 267–8; for more details to the civil list, see e.g. Friedrich Wilhelm Rudolf Zimmermann, *Die Zivilliste in den deutschen Staaten* (Stuttgart, 1919), pp. 48–60.

69   Johann Heinrich Jung(-Stilling), *Lehrbuch der Finanz-Wissenschaft* (Leipzig, 1789), p. 18, §32.

70   Heinrich Matthias Zoepfl, *Grundsätze des gemeinen deutschen Staatsrechts mit besonderer Rücksicht auf das allgemeine Staatsrecht und auf die neuesten Zeitverhältnisse*, vol. 2, 5th edn, 1st edn 1841 (Leipzig, Heidelberg, 1863), p. 690.

71   Jung(-Stilling), *Lehrbuch der Finanz*, pp. 20–1; Theodor Anton Heinrich Schmalz, *Staatswirthschaftslehre in Briefen an einen teutschen Erbprinzen*, part 2, 2nd edn, 1st edn 1818 (Berlin, 1869), pp. 152–4; Karl Heinrich Ludwig Pölitz, *Grundriß für encyklopädische Vorträge über die gesammten Staatswissenschaften* (Leipzig, 1825), p. 129; Karl Heinrich Ludwig Pölitz, *Volkswirthschaftslehre; Staatswirthschaftslehre und Finanzwissenschaft, und Polizeiwissenschaft*, 2nd edn (Leipzig, 1827), pp. 282–3.

72   Bauer, *Hofökonomie*, pp. 266–7.

73   Bauer, *Hofökonomie*, p. 267.

fact that the civil list became part of constitutional law [*Staatsrecht*]. During the Napoleonic era this was the case in two of Napoleon's model states, the Kingdom of Westphalia and the Grand Duchy of Frankfurt, as well as in some other member states of the Confederation of the Rhine. After the Congress of Vienna the civil list was gradually established as an element of constitutional law in every member state of the German Alliance, a process that began in 1818 with Baden. The civil list thus clearly reflects the close connection of financial and constitutional questions at a time when the early modern structures of the princely state were being dissolved and a profound process of modernisation was in progress, increasing the efficiency of the state in many ways. Financial administration was being bureaucratised and liberated from its patrimonial qualities; a parliamentary process in political life was emerging.

Cameralism becomes more legally minded

With the introduction of the civil list as a conclusive institutional settlement the sovereign could no longer decide alone on the use of public funds. In addition, discussion of the court economy in general and the civil list in particular was no longer seen as an economic problem but, in the context of national law, as a political problem. This is also suggested by the fact that the relevant nineteenth-century texts contain nothing about the economic and financial nature of courtly consumption, but deal instead with the legal and constitutional implications of the civil list.[74] Hence the work of the *Kammer* shifted its focus from economy to law, moving into the orbit of lawyers, and that region of the *Staatswissenschaften* dominated by law. As the civil list, and with it the viability of the *Kammern*, became part of *Staatsrecht*, cameralism also lost its economic significance and passed increasingly into the area of jurisprudence. It is, therefore, no surprise that late cameralists were often professors of law – for example Joachim Georg Darjes (1714–91), initially professor of moral philosophy and law at Jena, later privy counsellor, and from 1772 president of the University of Frankfurt on the Oder, professor in the faculty of law, and first professor of law. Darjes' classification of the cameralistic disciplines became generally accepted in the later eighteenth century.[75] Karl Gottlob Rössig (1760–1806), initially professor of philosophy and from 1793 professor of natural and international law in Leipzig, was already influenced by the Physiocrats and Adam Smith, as well as by Theodor

74   Bauer, *Hofökonomie*, p. 271.
75   Thomas Simon, *"Gute Policey". Ordnungsleitbilder und Zielvorstellungen politischen Handelns in der Frühen Neuzeit* (Frankfurt a.M., 2004), p. 446; Dittrich, *Die deutschen*, pp. 93–4.

Anton Heinrich Schmalz (1760–1831). Schmalz, who had studied law in Göttingen, was from 1787 professor of law; he then moved to teach law in Berlin with the foundation of the University in 1810. He was the first Rector of the university and also occupied high positions in state administration.[76]

Who actually were the decision-makers in administration and government? Among them would have been many law graduates, cameralists and economists, regardless of whether they had attended lectures in police or financial studies, in *Staatswirtschaftlehre* or *Nationalökonomie*. Most leading officials in public administration had a legal training of some kind. Most of them were thoroughly experienced in cameralist methods from their work as state administrators; they were were probably well versed in cameralist principles, less so in those of political economy. Some notable political figures are known to have attended lectures and courses in cameralism and to have encountered the work of Smith during their legal studies: Heinrich Friedrich Karl vom Stein, Wilhelm von Humboldt, Karl August von Hardenberg, Hans von Bülow, Friedrich von Motz, Ludwig von Vincke and others. It could be that they did to some extent assimilate something of the new spirit of English political economy.

The example of the University of Göttingen is particularly interesting in this context for at least two reasons. First, it was one of the most modern and prestigious universities in Germany at the turn of the nineteenth century;[77] and secondly, Göttingen has been described as an 'intermediary of an English state attitude on the continent'[78] or even as 'England itself'.[79] Johann Stephan Pütter (1725–1807), professor of constitutional law, has been said to have radiated the spirit of English liberalism. Justi had taught in Göttingen in mid-century, but by its later decades any cameralist influence was waning. The last really traditional cameralist treatise began publication in 1796 as *Handbuch der allgemeinen Staatswissenschaft nach Schlözers Grundriß*. As well as a general introduction, it included a philosophical history of the state and of constitutional law. By 1802 five further volumes had followed, devoted to the fields of *Staatswirtschaftslehre*, *Politik*, and the history and literature of the *Staatswissenschaften*. The author, Christian Daniel Voß (1761–1821) first taught philosophy, and later *Staatsrecht* and *Kameralwissenschaften* in Halle. Voß's *Handbuch*, which listed new developments in German and European theory, especially those of constitutionalism and of Adam Smith, is the most important systematic treatment of the theories of natural law,

---

76 Dittrich, *Die deutschen*, pp. 93–4, 119–20.
77 Lothar Gall, *Wilhelm von Humboldt. Ein Preuße von Welt* (Berlin, 2011), p. 29.
78 Franz Schnabel, *Deutsche Geschichte im neunzehnten Jahrhundert*, vol. 1, repr. 1st edn 1927 (Munich, 1987), p. 321.
79 Heinz Durchhardt, *Der Wiener Kongress: Die Neugestaltung Europas 1814/15* (Munich, 2013), p. 48.

economics and administration at the end of the eighteenth century.[80] Voß
dedicated his book to August Ludwig Schlözer (1735–1809), professor of
law in Göttingen; the *Staatswissenschaften* and their associated fields of
philosophy, history, and, of course, jurisprudence gained in importance.
Schlözer had built a concept of the sciences of state on Gottfried Achenwall's
(1719–72) conception of a science of politics, criticising overlapping terms
such as *Kameralwissenschaften* and *Polizeiwissenschaft* and replacing
them with compounds of the word *state* – thus cameralism became *state
administration*.[81]

In 1798 Carl Heinrich Daniel Bensen (1761–1805), newly appointed
professor of *Kameralwissenschaften* and philosophy and extraordinary
professor of law at the University of Erlangen, wrote *Versuch eines systematischen Grundrisses der reinen und angewandten Staatslehre für Kameralisten*
for his students, whom he called 'locally-studying cameralists'.[82] He divided
his book into three approximately equal parts. The first part comprised
pure state theory [*reine Staatslehre*] and some aspects of applied state
theory [*angewandte Staatstheorie*], especially national constitutional theory
[*Staatsverfassungslehre*] and elements of public administration theory
[*Staatsverwaltungslehre*]. The second part comprised *Polizeilehre* and theory
of public education [*Lehre von der öffentlichen Erziehung*]; and the third was
cameralistic or financial studies proper [*eigentliche Kameralwissenschaften/
Staatswirthschaftlehre*]. Even though Bensen's work refers at many points
to various writings of Justi, there is a progressive distinction made between
fields of study. Ludwig Heinrich von Jakob's (1759–1827) *Grundsätze der
National-Oekonomie oder National-Wirthschaftslehre* of 1805 also demonstrates a development of related distinctions, although in this case Jakob was
channelling Jean-Baptiste Say's *Traité d'économie politique* (1803), a direct
translation of which he then published in 1807. Jakob considered an examination of the causes of the wealth of nations to be a prerequisite for *Policey-*
and *Finanzlehre*. He consistently sought to reduce these questions to what
he called the 'pure problem' – i.e. to their economic essence – pinpointing

---

80   Jörn Garber, 'Spätaufklärerischer Konstitutionalismus und ökonomischer Frühliberalismus.
Das Staats- und Industriebürgerkonzept der postabsolutistischen Staats-, Kameral- und
Polizeiwissenschaft (Chr. D. Voss)', *Spätabsolutismus und bürgerliche Gesellschaft. Studien zur
deutschen Staats- und Gesellschaftstheorie im Übergang zur Moderne*, ed. J. Garber (Frankfurt
a.M., 1992), p. 106; Axel Rüdiger, *Staatslehre und Staatsbildung. Die Staatswissenschaft an der
Universität Halle im 18. Jahrhundert* (Tübingen, 2005), pp. 298, 309; Markus Sandl, *Ökonomie
des Raumes. Der kameralwissenschaftliche Entwurf der Staatswirtschaft im 18. Jahrhundert*
(Köln/Weimar/Wien, 1999), pp. 375, 429–32.

81   David F. Lindenfeld, *The Practical Imagination. The German Sciences of State in the
Nineteenth Century* (Chicago/London, 1997), p. 43.

82   Carl Heinrich Daniel Bensen, *Versuch eines systematischen Grundrisses der reinen und
angewandten Staatslehre für Kameralisten* (Erlangen, 1798), p. vi.

the causal factors underlying the increase, distribution and consumption of the wealth of a nation (Say's tripartite distinction), and determining the laws governing these processes. Investigations of *Polizei* and finance were explicitly exempted.[83]

The separation of cameralism from *Nationalökonomie* was in any case by this time fully in progress. The subject matter of *Staatswirtschaft* and *Nationalökonomie* increasingly parted company: whereas the former was reduced to the theory of finance and *Polizey*, the latter was concerned with question of wealth. Jakob drew up a list of definitions that included *Staatsverfassungslehre*, judicial legislation, *Policey* legislation and financial science or *Staatswirthschaftlehre*. Later, Gottlieb Hufeland suggested that it would be better to replace the term *National-Oeconomie* or *National-Wirthschaftlehre* with *Volkswirthschaft* – the contrast to *Staatswirtschaft* would then emerge much more clearly.[84] No further or more detailed discussion of the terminology will be undertaken here. It is sufficient for the present argument to have noted the increasing differentiation in the teaching of cameralism and the assignment of *Staatswirtschaftlehre* to the field of pure jurisprudences.

Cameralist literature of the early nineteenth century focused increasingly on analysis of the legal and constitutional implications of public households, reducing any reflection on the economic and financial results of government expenditure. The civil list disappeared increasingly from economic literature and became part of national law. This is another reason why the significance of cameralism declined in economic theory and increased in jurisprudence. Many aspects of the national budget were assimilated into the legal branch of the political sciences, which – as a conglomeration of administrative sciences, law and economics – began to develop into a discipline with a particular emphasis on administration and law. Hence it can justifiably be said that *Staatswirtschaftslehre* and *Nationalökonomie* existed side by side. A low selectivity between the different economic approaches can be assumed, not least because of the confusion of the Napoleonic wars. In practice, the daily life of universities had to go on. Cameralism had a broad remit: far from being a pure economic theory, it comprised fields of economics, natural science, political science, agriculture, history, philosophy, administrational principles, chemistry, mineralogy, forestry and technology.[85]

83 Ludwig Heinrich von Jakob, *Grundsätze der National-Oekonomie oder National-Wirthschaftslehre* (Halle, 1805), pp. v–vii.
84 Gottlieb Hufeland, *Neue Grundlegung der Staatswirthschaftskunst durch Prüfung und Berichtigung ihrer Hauptbegriffe von Gut, Werth, Preis, Geld und Volksvermögen, mit ununterbrochener Rücksicht auf die bisherigen Systeme*, vol. I (Gießen, 1807), p. 14; for a more detailed discussion, see Tribe, *Governing Economy*, pp. 169–73.
85 For an exemplary shortlist of the wide range of curricula, e.g. at the Cameral Institute in Ingolstadt, see Stieda, *Die Nationalökonomie*, pp. 244–8, and concerning the plan to found

From its breadth and encyclopedic abundance, as well as its openly practical orientation, cameralism drew the reproach of superficiality, to which Jakob and Kraus quickly reacted in their teaching curricula with the separation of *Nationalökonomie* from *Staatswirtschaftlehre*. Anyway, with the increasing penetration of jurisprudence, the number of lectures in cameralism declined. Jakob's warning about disciplinary proliferation went unheard, the superficiality proceeded, and the academic reputation of cameralism fell. The rise of legal studies as the sole academic education of civil servants followed.[86]

There is, however, another important aspect to this process. After the introduction of the Prussian Civil Code [*Allgemeines Landrecht für die Preußischen Staaten*] in 1794, the situation of state servants and officials improved. They were granted a qualified legal right to permanent tenure: royal servants were now servants [*Diener*] and state officials [*Beamte*]. Officials were no longer faced with the threat of arbitrary recall or punishment by the ruler, and members of the civil state bureaucracy now took steps to secure and enhance their established rights [*wohlerworbene Rechte*].[87] Some of these moves can be traced in the various documents and memoranda associated with the so-called Prussian Reforms, which as Ernst Klein made plain are in fact a series of competing bids and projects to redraw boundaries in the face of the pressing need to reorganise state finances.[88] In the *Rigaer Denkschrift* of 1807 the Prussian minister Karl August von Hardenberg (who, incidentally, had also studied law for some semesters in Göttingen and Leipzig) expressed the aspiration that every position in the state without exception might be filled according to ability and without any form of discrimination. In his 'Notice concerning the changed organisation of the highest state authorities' [*Publikandum, betr. die veränderte Verfassung der obersten Staatsbehörden*] of 1808 the whole nation was promised participation in public administration and the civil service, subject only to talent and qualification. Official positions were to be open to everyone, independent of social status – if only in theory.[89]

Although the study of law was not yet required for a career in higher administration, jurisprudence soon moved to the foreground, while cameralism and political sciences were reduced to the communication of administrative technicalities along with practical administrative experience. In 1817 candidates for the higher civil service were expected to have studied law and political sciences, including successful completion of the first state

a Cameral Institute at the University of Halle, see Rüdiger, *Staatslehre und Staatsbildung*, pp. 302–3, 436–9.

86 Bleek, *Von der Kameralausbildung*, pp. 99–101.

87 Hans Rosenberg, *Bureaucracy, Aristocracy and Autocracy. The Prussian Experience 1660–1815* (Cambridge, MA, 1958), pp. 190–1.

88 Ernst Klein, *Von der Reform zur Restauration. Finanzpolitik und Reformgesetzgebung des preußischen Staatskanzlers Karl August von Hardenberg* (Berlin, 1965).

89 Bleek, *Von der Kameralausbildung*, p. 102, see also fn. 45 and 46.

examination in law. Cameralism, which in 1727 had been promoted as the standard academic discipline for training civil servants, now became *de facto* a mere appendix to the study of law, and as such it gradually disappeared from the university and from examination regulations.⁹⁰ Of course, cameralism never was an independent academic discipline, but taught as part of the general programme of Faculties of Philosophy, themselves the most junior of the four faculties. All the same, it should not be forgotten that during the nineteenth century a legal education was extremely important for anyone seeking a higher position in government or public administration. Undoubtedly, administration had become more complex, tasks had grown more demanding, and the importance of jurisprudence had increased. Administration had formally and materially reduced to jurisdiction – not in the sense that administration had in every aspect assumed the character of jurisdiction, but quite the reverse: jurisdiction had taken over the characteristics of administration.⁹¹

What intellectual background was required for a successful career in administration and government? German universities, whether modern ones like Göttingen or long-established institutions like the Viadrina at Frankfurt on the Oder, were primarily intended to train administrators and the clergy. Entry to state service now required a qualification in law, the increase in more highly differentiated tasks making this necessary. The established pathway of learning-by-doing should not however be underestimated, for this remained an important element in the development of a professionalised bureaucracy.

Conclusion

Cameralism had a long tradition and changed in both content and appearance over the decades, beginning with notable authors like Veit Ludwig von Seckendorff (1626–92), Johann Friedrich von Pfeiffer (1717–87), and continuing up to Joseph von Sonnenfels (1733–1817) and Carl Ludwig Pölitz (1772–1838). Despite an emphasis in older commentary on the role of Adam Smith and, more generally, English political economy in displacing cameralistic teaching and argument, it is today evident that only after the latter had begun to decline did Smith begin to have a general impact. By contrast, the international impact of the English political economy of the early nineteenth century has routinely been overestimated, and this is as true for Germany as

90 Bleek, *Von der Kameralausbildung*, pp. 105–7; Klaus Hinrich Hennings, 'Aspekte der Institutionalisierung der Ökonomie an deutschen Universitäten', *Die Institutionalisierung der Nationalökonomie an deutschen Universitäten. Zur Erinnerung an Klaus Hinrich Hennings (1937–1986)*, ed. N. Waszek (St Katharinen, 1988), pp. 46–7.
91 Weber, *Wirtschaft und Gesellschaft*, pp. 485–6.

elsewhere. As Tribe has shown, while Physiocratic teaching did have a delayed impact in the later part of the eighteenth century, it never became part of the standard cameralistic repertoire, circulating mostly outside the university context.

The shift from an older to a new natural law, closely associated with the reception of Critical Philosophy, did have considerable influence on the development of cameralism. The shift from an emphasis on happiness to one upon personal liberty and human needs marked the writings of Jakob, Hufeland and their contemporaries. The primacy of the state in securing popular welfare retreated before arguments that it was the actions of economic agents themselves that should be given attention. With this change in perspective the *Kameralwissenschaften* lost their central function; *Polizeiwissenschaft* was increasingly subsumed into administrative theory, losing its economic significance. The once unified *Kameralwissenschaften* fragmented and migrated into the new *Staatswissenschaften*. This process was accompanied on the one hand by a shift of governmental perspective, focusing on external rather than internal security during the Napoleonic wars, and on the other by an increasingly critical attitude on the part of intellectuals to an authoritarian state.

Of course, even in the new social and political context of the constitutional monarchy under the German Alliance after 1815, the mechanisms of the old administration remained remarkably alive. Although political conditions had changed with the great social transformations of the time, with the development both of parliamentary representation and professionalised bureaucracy, the machinery of government continued to turn according to well-established procedures.

Andre Wakefield has written about the contradiction between what cameralists wrote and said and that what they actually did. They talked about the promotion of the common welfare and happiness, but followed their own private interests. It might seem reasonable to conclude therefore that cameralism failed because somehow it lacked authenticity and credibility. In their publications cameralists described circumstances that were unrealisable, depicted an ideal state organisation, creating an image remote from reality.[92] While the human failings identified by Wakefield are undeniable, they are in no respect specific to cameralism. Such problems are commonly encountered throughout academia, political life and administration. Criticism of the budgetary management of royal courts existed throughout the eighteenth century. Given these circumstances, a cameralist who lived for and from the state had to be sensitive to the demands of court life, and be adept at communication.

During the later eighteenth century the increasing separation of court from state finances took place, a new budgetary discipline being imposed on

---

92   Wakefield, *The Disordered*, e.g. p. 142.

the ruler and his retinue. The civil list was established and became an aspect of constitutional law. Here the essential idea was to allocate a fixed sum for the court and the person of the monarch – an annual amount paid by the state treasury to the monarch and his relatives to support a way of life befitting their social standing and court expenditure. With the transformation of fundamental political and administrative principles, a process was set in motion in which financial policy became an aspect of increasing importance for legal and administrative theory, loosening its original proximity to economic issues and moving it towards the political sphere.

In responding to the question concerning who made decisions in administration and government, attention has been paid above to the variety and scope of influences under the general heading of economic theory to which such leading personalities were subjected. Whether educated as lawyers, cameralists or economists, whether followers of cameralism, Physiocracy or political economy, decision-makers had in practice to have basic knowledge of the legal and constitutional implications of public households, and of the functioning of economic and administrative processes. Much of the relevant knowledge was provided by university courses in law, corresponding to changes occurring in distinguishing fields of study. The civil list disappeared from the economic domain and became part of national law. Legal education became a requirement for a position in public service. The old classifications of *Polizei-*, *Handlungs-* and *Finanzwissenschaft*, and of cameralism in a broader sense, *Staatswissenschaft*, *Staatswirtschaft*, political economy, or *Nationalökonomie* – these all changed their meaning over time. In the first decades of the nineteenth century *Nationalökonomie* and *Staatswissenschaft* became widespread disciplines, and together with the notions of *Staatswirtschaft* and *Finanzwissenschaft* they retained much of their substance far into the twentieth century. Although the notion of cameralism lost its importance, much of its material still survived under other headings.

12

Concluding Remarks

KEITH TRIBE

Cameralism in Practice is marked by a deliberate effort to shift our attention away from the work of writers to the activities of those more directly concerned in the daily tasks of economic administration, whether of state properties, royal domains, forests or manufactures. The handbooks and treatises produced in the German-speaking universities of the eighteenth century direct themselves to the organisation of these economic domains, and so they have in the past often been read as in some way reflecting actual administrative activity. There are two linked problems in this. First, as a literature of pedagogy, the burgeoning field of the *Kameralwissenschaften* had a strongly normative cast, rather than a purely descriptive function; second, the dynamics of the production of this literature are related not primarily to the presence or absence or priority of administrative issues, but instead to the institutional demands of teaching. The substance of the *Kameralwissenschaften* thus lends us no direct insight into the work of administration, nor do changes in the rate of production of such texts directly indicate anything about issues of reform or reorganisation in office and treasury.

All the same, it remains true that, as a genre, the *Kameralwissenschaften* had a profile consistently distinct from contemporary economic literature in Britain and France, and to a lesser degree Italy. A body of writing named after the *Kammer* in which court officials oversaw domain economies, and originally a literature of counsel for the best conduct of such economies, in the course of the early eighteenth century this became incorporated into the teaching of universities; and while the idea that this new body of knowledge should become part of the training of state officials, this was always much more aspiration than reality. As a result, the *Kameralwissenschaften* claimed a relationship to administrative practice that only existed insofar as its practitioners, at least in its early years, did have some relevant administrative experience. There was certainly a link to 'practice', but it was more personal than discursive. Nonetheless, this literature is certainly distinctive:

the only distant parallel that can be drawn with contemporary English and French writing is in the agricultural treatises to which I devoted a chapter in *Land, Labour and Economic Discourse*, tracing the development from the English husbandry tracts of the seventeenth century to the systematic surveys of agricultural practice carried out by the Board of Agriculture in the later eighteenth century.[1] A more direct parallel does exist in the work of Jacques Savary's *Le parfait négociant* (1675) and Malachy Postlethwayt's *Universal Dictionary of Trade and Commerce* (1751–), but this commercial literature lacks the normative ordering imperative typical of the Cameralistic literature. And as Christine Théré has shown, while there was a major boom in economic publishing in France beginning in the later 1740s,[2] she nowhere suggests that any of this writing was comparable to the kind of literature we routinely encounter in Northern Europe.

And so we do have a genuine divergence: in Northern Europe a form of economic discourse that directed itself to ordering economic activity, offering at the very least a window into the daily routine of economic administration, a form of writing that is so notably absent elsewhere. And this discourse has a definite geographical basis, which the different contributions to this volume block out in detail: from the territories of Imperial Austria, across Northern Germany and Denmark to the Baltic, and including Central Europe and Russia. The importance of Sweden here is especially emphasised, in the chapters by Magnusson, Tribe and Rydén, while the importance of cameralistic argument to Russian reform is central to Roger Bartlett's chapter. Ingrid Markussen shows, like Göran Rydén and Guillaume Garnier, how basic conceptions of order typically thought to apply to domain administration were also applied in the management of private estates and manufactories. The one contribution that covers a region falling outside this geographical space is Alexandre Mendes Cunha's interesting case-study of the diffusion of cameralist teachings to the Spanish and Portuguese empires. Significant here however is the mechanism of diffusion, for arguments and ideas do not travel by themselves, they require a medium through which they can be transmitted. Moreover, the mere fact of transmission does not imply a reception process that faithfully mirrors the 'source'. The mechanism at work in this particular case was initially one that worked through the movement of individuals; ideas, precepts, texts originating in Austria migrated to Spain, Portugal and their imperial territories in Latin American because of the emergence of a domestic reform process seeking new frameworks, individuals introducing ideas and materials gathered during their travels in Austria with which

1   Keith Tribe, *Land, Labour and Economic Discourse* (London, 1978), ch. 4.
2   See Table 1.2, Five- and ten-yearly movements in economic publications 1550–1789, Christine Théré, 'Economic Publishing and Authors, 1566–1789', *Studies in the History of French Political Economy*, ed. G. Faccarello (London, 1998), p. 13.

these frameworks might be constructed. In the eighteenth-century world the porosity of cultures depended primarily on the movement of persons between them; and any domestic impact required, as Cunha demonstrates, a specific reason to seek new ways of thinking about problems of administration and reorganisation.

And so extending our understanding of cameralism away from the lecture room and into the office reinforces, rather than weakens, the sense in which this is a body of knowledge that fitted together with particular kinds of Northern and Central European states, and which is relatively invisible to those outside their borders, and who do not speak or read their languages. Among the 1,808 publications listed in Hiroshi Mizuta's catalogue of Adam Smith's library, only three are in German: two copies of volume 1 of the first translation (1776) of *Wealth of Nations*, and one of the 1770 translation of *Theory of Moral Sentiments*, all presumably complimentary copies.[3] Smith did not read German. But we could add to this our knowledge that, during the 1740s in Oxford, he plainly read widely in classical and French literature, and so this purely linguistic constraint can be translated into a broader cultural constraint. By contrast, we know that Sir James Steuart began work on his *Principles of Political Oeconomy* (1767) while in exile in Tübingen; and so the echoes of the cameralistic treatment of the household that we find so clearly in the earlier parts of his book can be attributed to this personal connection. Correspondingly, translations of Steuart back into German sold relatively well in Germany, while the first translation of *Wealth of Nations* into German had little impact. It was not until a second translation was made by Christian Garve and August Dörrien and published 1794–96 that *Wealth of Nations* began to be referred to and discussed by writers, and the reason for this lay not in the quality of the translation but in a new cultural context, where Kantian principles were displacing the Wolffian tropes of an older natural law.[4] Here again, the diffusion of ideas and arguments does not take place in a vacuum, there has to be a medium and a receptive context. While the existence of translations into or out of a language is evidence of something, it is not automatically evidence that these works are being read and understood.

The way in which the *Kameralwissenschaften* present themselves as 'practical' and so linked to conceptions more of (state) household management than of commercial enterprise should also alert us to the relative absence of any comparable systematic treatment of economic administration elsewhere in European economic literature, especially in French and English literature. Rather than treat cameralistic discourse as somewhat idiosyncratic, Germanic

3 Hiroshi Mizuta, *Adam Smith's Library. A Catalogue* (Oxford, 2000), items 1546, 1547, 1558.
4 Keith Tribe, *Governing Economy. The Reformation of German Economic Discourse 1750–1830* (Cambridge, 1988), pp. 138ff.

and Northern, might it not be in order to consider why, elsewhere, we find neither a developed literature articulating a conception of economic adminis- tration, nor systematic efforts to develop any vocationally oriented education suited to the work of economic administration? By bringing together these studies of population and labour supply (Bartlett, Seppel), forest management (Warde), manufacture (Garner, Rydén) and insurance (Oberholzner) the question can be raised: what parallels, if any, can be found elsewhere? If not, why not? Rather than treat cameralism as an idiosyncratic Germanic discourse, one can instead use this 'idiosyncracy' to shed light on the Anglo- French literature that is always assumed to be the standard against which all else is to be judged.

To make progress with this idea we also need to move away from the simple contrast of 'theory' and 'practice' built around the contrast of lecture room to office. Andre Wakefield turned our attention to 'practice' – the subtitle to his book is 'German Cameralism as Science and Practice' – but at the cost of persisting with a simple dualism of 'theory' as idea and 'practice' as reality.[5] All 'practical' work of administration is governed by formal and informal procedures learned on the job, with only the most formal elements being written down as axioms; rules of accounting or of reporting could well be transmitted interpersonally as part of an office routine. All the same, any set of formal and informal procedures is given coherence by conceptions of how things are *supposed* to work, a kind of ideological practice that relates in some way to the theoretical practice communicated in the lecture room. 'Theory' itself presumes a degree of coherence and system in particular bodies of thought not typically found in the kind of literature we encounter in the *Kameralwissenschaften* – even in the nineteenth century general works of political economy usually presented themselves as collections of 'principles', or as expository 'treatises' and not as 'theory', whatever the language. Indeed, this brings us to a more general problem in the history of sciences recently highlighted by Roger Chartier.

Reviewing a new three-volume history of the sciences,[6] and making use of distinctions available in the French language, Chartier first questions how the use of *savoir* in the title of the work he is reviewing relates to *savoir faire*, a term that embeds knowledge in practice.[7] He points out how easy it is to slide from distinguishing scientific from other forms of knowledge to the couple intellectual labour/manual labour, and from there to theory/practice. Do we however need to distinguish *les sciences* from *les savoirs*?; is the first simply a class of the second? How in this context do we hold *connaissance*, the

5 Andre Wakefield, *The Disordered Police State. German Cameralism as Science and Practice* (Chicago, 2009).
6 Dominique Pestre (ed.), *Histoires des sciences et des savoirs*, 3 vols (Paris, 2015).
7 Roger Chartier, 'Sciences et savoirs', *Annales* 71 (2016), 451.

symbolic possession of things, apart from *savoir*, knowing about something, or how to do something? Using these distinctions, he points out that we could talk rather of regimes of knowledge, 'économies du savoir';[8] or, alternatively, define "scientific" *savoir* through the instruments or operations of *connaissances spécifiques*.

Whatever choice we make here takes us away from countering 'theory' to 'practice', and into a rather more diverse 'regime of knowledge' that can be differentiated more finely than with the simple binary choice otherwise offered. Paul Warde's account of the gradual construction of *Forstwissenschaft* from *Landesordnungen* going back to the sixteenth century demonstrates how one set of practical rules and procedures can be transformed into a new frame of 'scientific knowledge'; Frank Oberholzner highlights the way in which the chance and risk of crop failure or flood became seen as something that could be calculated, developing from the practice of fire insurance. In turn, this transformation regularised and formalised a new form of knowledge that could be systematically transmitted. On the other hand, there would in both cases be plenty of practices and assumptions that were simply incoherent, which in any process of systematisation could be winnowed out and discarded. What shifts this process in the direction of 'theory' is not however an epistemological question, creating a distinct organisation of thought, but rather the institutional framework within which this occurs. It so happened that in seventeenth- and eighteenth-century Northern Europe the university had become widely established as the central institution for the transmission of vocational knowledge – of theology, of medicine, and of the law. When administrative practice first entered these institutions – in Halle, in Frankfurt an der Oder, in Uppsala, in Lund – it simply translated the management of estates into a new context. Once more or less established, by mid-century, this new discourse simply took on a life of its own, became part of the practice of the institution it served. In the process a gap opened up between the 'theory' of lecture room and the 'practice' of offices, but this gap was created by the differing practices of, respectively, university institution and office administration.

As Hans Frambach suggests, with the development of a new *Nationalökonomie* in the first decades of the nineteenth century cameralistic knowledge was not simply relegated: it was instead displaced, moving into the *Staatswissenschaften* and becoming linked to law. Correspondingly, while royal lands and their revenues were transformed into state property, and court households became dependent instead on fixed payments, the tasks of estate administration altered, but did not disappear. Nor should the failure of a larger ambition, that the *Kameralwissenschaften* provide the curricular core

---

8   Chartier, 'Sciences et savoirs', p. 456.

for the training of state officials, be lent exaggerated importance. Indeed, to base historical assessment of any reform project on simple criteria of 'success' or 'failure' reduces complex processes to a simple scoresheet upon which 'successes' are given a tick and 'failures' a cross. Historical understanding of any phenomenon or process involves more than a retrospective summing of ticks and crosses. Indeed, it could be suggested that the default outcome of any reform project will be some degree of 'failure',[9] but here it is important to consider whether any such later 'failure' is an outcome of intentions, or of process, or of resources, or of context. And in making such an assessment of the practice of cameralism we can move away from a simple contrast of 'theory' and 'practice' into a richer understanding of the way in which, as Max Weber put it, '"ideas" become effective in history'.[10]

9   This point was made by Paul Warde during discussion at a session devoted to the theme of this book at the Annual Conference of the Economic History Society, Robinson College, Cambridge, 1–3 April 2016.
10   Max Weber, *The Protestant Ethic and the 'Spirit' of Capitalism and other Writings*, ed. P. Baehr and G. C. Wells (Harmondsworth, 2002), p. 35.

Bibliography

Anon. [Eli Bertrand], *Elementos da policia geral de hum estado / traduzidos do Francez, que ao senhor Diogo Ignacio de Pina Manique, offereceo Joao Rosado de Villalobos e Vasconcellos (...)* (Lisbon, 1786 [1781]).

Anon. [Gervásio Pires Ferreira], *Resumo das instituições políticas do Barão de Bielfeld, parafraseadas e acomodadas à forma actual do governo do Império do Brasil* ... (Rio de Janeiro, 1823).

Anon. [Friedrich Ludwig Joseph Fischbach], *Historische politisch-geographisch-statistisch- und militärische Beyträge, die Königlich-Preußische und benachbarte Staaten betreffend*, part 2, vol. 1 (Berlin, 1782).

Anon., 'Obsuzhdenie: Istoricheskij kurs "Novaja imperskaja istorija Severnoj Evrazii"', *Ab Imperio* no. 1 (2015), 323–86, no. 2, 253–337.

Abel, Wilhelm, *Agrarkrisen und Agrarkonjunktur. Eine Geschichte der Land- und Ernährungswirtschaft Mitteleuropas seit dem hohen Mittelalter* (Hamburg, 1978).

——, 'Landwirtschaft 1648–1800', *Handbuch der Deutschen Wirtschafts- und Sozialgeschichte*, vol. 1 (Stuttgart, 1971), pp. 495–530.

Adam, Ulrich, 'Justi and the Post-Montesquieu Debate on Commercial Nobility in 1756', *The Beginnings of Political Economy. Johann Heinrich Gottlob von Justi*, ed. J. G. Backhaus (New York, 2009), pp. 75–98.

——, *The Political Economy of J. H. G. Justi* (Oxford, 2006).

Adams, Julia, *The Familial State. Ruling Families and Merchant Capitalism in Early Modern Europe* (Ithaca, NY, 2005).

Albion, Robert Greenhalgh, *Forests and Sea Power. The Timber Problem of the Royal Navy 1652–1862* (Cambridge, MA, 1926).

Alden, Dauril, 'The Population of Brazil in the Late Eighteenth Century: A Preliminary Study', *Hispanic American Historical Review* 43/2 (1963), 173–205.

Alefirenko, Pelageia Kuzminichna, *Krest'ianskoe dvizhenie i krest'ianskii vopros v 30–50 gg. XVIII veka* ([Moscow], 1958).

Alexander, John T., *Bubonic Plague in Early Modern Russia: Public Health and Urban Disaster* (Baltimore/London, 1980, reprint Oxford, 2003).

Allemeyer, Marie Luisa, '"Dass es wohl recht ein Feuer vom Herrn zu nennen gewesen ...". Zur Wahrnehmung, Deutung und Verarbeitung von Stadtbränden in norddeutschen Schriften des 17. Jahrhunderts', *Um*

Himmels Willen. Religion in Katastrophenzeiten, ed. M. Jakubowski-Tiessen and H. Lehmann (Göttingen, 2003), pp. 201–34.

Allmann, Joachim, *Der Wald in der frühen Neuzeit* (Berlin, 1989).

Almeida Santos, Antonio Cesar de, 'Luzes em Portugal: do Terremoto à Inauguração da Estátua Equestre do Reformador', *Topoi* (Rio de Janeiro) 12/22 (2011), 75–95.

Amelung, Friedrich, 'Die Schutzpockenimpfung in Livland im 18. Jahrhundert', *Rigasche Stadtblätter* no. 28 (15 July 1904), 223–7; no. 29 (23 July 1904), 231–5.

Amussen, Susan Dwyer, *An Ordered Society. Gender and Class in Early Modern England* (Oxford, 1988).

Anfält, Thomas, 'Herrgård och bruk. Om livet på Leufsta på 1700-talet', *Vallonerna*, ed. T. Anfält (Skärplinge, 1996), pp. 65–80.

Annerstedt, Claes, *Uppsala Universitets historia*, vol. II (Uppsala, 1908).

Arnberg, Johan Wolter, *Anteckningar om Frihetstidens Politiska Ekonomi* (Uppsala, 1868).

Artem'eva, Tatiana V., 'Adam Smit v Rossii', *Filosofskii Vek* 19 (2002), 39–67.

———, 'Adam Smith in Russian Translations', *A Critical Bibliography of Adam Smith*, ed. K. Tribe (London, 2002), pp. 153–67.

——— (ed.), *Khristian Vol'f i russkoe vol'fianstvo, Filosofskii Vek* 3 (St Petersburg, 1998).

———, 'Wolffianism as a Philosophical Foundation of Encyclopedism in Russia', *Christian Wolff und die europäische Aufklärung*, I (*Christian Wolff, Gesammelte Werke*, III Abt, Bd 101), ed. J. Stolzenberg and O.-P. Rudolph (Hildesheim, 2007), pp. 165–79.

Asche, Matthias, *Neusiedler im verheerten Land. Kriegsfolgenbewältigung, Migrationssteuerung und Konfessionspolitik im Zeichen des Landeswiederaufbaus. Die Mark Brandenburg nach den Kriegen des 17. Jahrhunderts* (Münster, 2006).

———, 'Peuplierung', *Enzyklopädie der Neuzeit*, vol. 9, ed. Fr. Jaeger (Stuttgart/Weimar, 2009), cols. 1042–5.

Astigarraga, Jesús, *Los ilustrados vascos: ideas, instituciones y reformas económicas en España* (Barcelona, 2003).

Åström, Sven-Erik, 'English Timber Imports from Northern Europe in the Eighteenth Century', *Scandinavian Economic History Review* 18/1 (1970), 12–32.

———, *From Tar to Timber. Studies in Northeast European Forest Exploitation and Foreign Trade 1660–1860* (Helsinki, 1988).

Atorf, Lars, *Der König und das Korn. Die Getreidehandelspolitik als Fundament der brandenburg-preussischen Aufstiegs zur europäischen Grossmacht* (Berlin, 1999).

Backhaus, Jürgen G. (ed.), *The Beginnings of Political Economy. Johann Heinrich Gottlob von Justi* (New York, 2009).

———, 'The German Economic Tradition: From Cameralism to the Verein für

Sozialpolitik', *Political Economy and National Realities*, ed. M. Albertone and A. Masoero (Torino, 1994), pp. 329–56.

————, 'Mercantilism and Cameralism: Two Very Different Variations on the Same Theme', *Economic Growth and the Origins of Modern Political Economy. Economic Reasons of State, 1500–2000*, ed. P. R. Rössner (London/New York, 2016), pp. 72–8.

———— (ed.), *Physiocracy, Antiphysiocracy and Pfeiffer* (New York, 2011).

———— (ed.), *The State as Utopia* (New York, 2011).

Bartlett, Roger, 'The Free Economic Society: The Foundation Years and the Prize Essay Competition of 1766 on Peasant Property', *Russland zur Zeit Katharinas II. Absolutismus-Aufklärung-Pragmatismus*, ed. E. Hübner, J. Kusber and P. Nitsche (Köln/Weimar/Wien, 1998), pp. 181–214.

————, 'German Popular Enlightenment in the Russian Empire: Peter Ernst Wilde and Catherine II', *Slavonic and East European Review* 84 (2006), 256–78.

————, *Human Capital. The Settlement of Foreigners in Russia 1762–1804* (Cambridge, 1979).

————, 'J. J. Sievers and the Russian Peasantry under Catherine II', *Jahrbücher für Geschichte Osteuropas* 32 (1984), 16–33.

————, 'Russia in the 18th-Century European Adoption of Inoculation for Smallpox', *Russia and the World of the Eighteenth Century*, ed. R. Bartlett, A. G. Cross and K. Rasmussen (Columbus, OH, 1988), pp. 193–213.

————, 'Russia's First Abolitionist: The Political Philosophy of J. G. Eisen', *Jahrbücher für Geschichte Osteuropas* 39 (1991), 161–76.

————, 'Serfdom and State Power in Imperial Russia', *European History Quarterly* 33/1 (2003), 29–64.

Bartlett, Roger and Erich Donnert (eds), *Johann Georg Eisen. Ausgewählte Schriften. Volksaufklärung und Leibeigenschaft im russischen Reich* (Marburg, 1998).

Bauer, Volker, *Hofökonomie. Der Diskurs über den Fürstenhof in Zeremonialwissenschaft, Hausväterliteratur und Kameralismus* (Vienna, 1997).

Baugh, Daniel A., *British Naval Administration in the Age of Walpole* (Princeton, NJ, 1965).

Bayerl, Günter, 'Prolegomenon der "Großen Industrie". Der technisch-ökonomische Blick auf die Natur im 18. Jahrhundert', *Umweltgeschichte. Umweltverträgliches Wirtschaften in historischer Perspektive*, ed. W. Abelshauser (= *Geschichte und Gesellschaft*, Sonderheft 15, Göttingen, 1994), pp. 29–56.

Becher, Johann Joachim, *Kluge Haus-Vater. Verständige Haus-Mutter* (Leipzig, [1685] 1747).

Beck, Ulrich, *World at Risk* (Cambridge, 2009).

Becker, Hartmuth, 'Justi's Concrete Utopia', *The State as Utopia. Continental Approaches*, ed. J. G. Backhaus (New York, 2011), pp. 41–56.

Beckmann, Johann Gottlieb, *Anweisung zu einer pfleglichen Forstwirthschaft* (Chemnitz, 1759).

——, *Gegründete Versuche und Erfahrungen der zu unsern Zeiten höchst nöthigan Holzsaat, zum allgemeinen Besten* (4th edn, Chemnitz, 1777).

——, *Versuche und Erfahrungen bei der Holzsaat nebst einigen Beiträgen zur Verbesserung der Forstwirthschaft*, 2 parts (Chemnitz, 1756, 1759).

Beheim-Schwarzbach, Max, *Hohenzollernsche Colonisationen. Ein Beitrag zu der Geschichte des preußischen Staates und der Colonisation des östlichen Deutschlands* (Leipzig, 1874).

Bensen, Carl Heinrich Daniel, *Versuch eines systematischen Grundrisses der reinen und angewandten Staatslehre für Kameralisten* (Erlangen, 1798).

Berch, Anders, *Einleitung zur allgemeinen Haushaltung*, ed. D. G. Schreber (Halle, 1763).

——, *Inledning til almänna hushålningen, innefattande grunden til politie, oeconomie och cameral wetenskaperne* (Stockholm, 1747).

——, *Sätt, at igenom politisk arithmetica utröna länders och rikens hushåldning* (Stockholm, 1746).

——, *Tal om den proportion som de studerande ärfodra till de ledige beställ-ningar i riket* (Stockholm, 1749).

Bergakademie, *Festschrift zum hundertjährigen Jubiläum der Königl. sächs. Bergakademie zu Freiberg, am 30. Juli 1866* (Dresden, 1877).

Bernhardt, August, *Geschichte des Waldeigenthums, der Waldwirtschaft und Forstwissenschaft in Deutschland* (Berlin, 1872–75).

Bielfeld, Baron de, *Nastavleniia politicheskie Barona Bil'felda*, 2 vols (Moscow, 1768–75).

Bishop, W. J., 'Thomas Dimsdale, MD, FRS and the Inoculation of Catherine the Great of Russia', *Annals of Medical History* 4 (1932), 321–38.

Bleek, Wilhelm, *Von der Kameralausbildung zum Juristenprivileg. Studium, Prüfung und Ausbildung der höheren Beamten des allgemeinen Verwal-tungsdienstes in Deutschland im 18. und 19. Jahrhundert* (Berlin, 1972).

Blickle, Peter, *Von der Leibeigenschaft zu den Menschenrechten. Eine Geschichte der Freiheit in Deutschland* (München, 2003).

Bödeker, Hans-Erich (ed.), *Strukturen der deutschen Frühaufklärung* (Göttingen, 2008).

Bog, Ingomar, *Der Reichsmerkantilismus. Studien zur Wirtschaftspolitik des Heiligen Römischen Reiches im 17. und 18. Jahrhundert* (Stuttgart, 1959).

Bourde, André J., *The Influence of England on the French Agronomes 1750–1789* (Cambridge, 1953).

Bourdieu, Pierre, 'Quelques propriétés des champs', in Bourdieu, *Questions de sociologie* (Paris, 1984), pp. 113–20.

——, *Sur l'État. Cours au Collège de France 1989–1992* (Paris, 2012).

Braeuer, Walter, 'Kameralismus und Merkantilismus. Ein kritischer Vergleich', *Jahrbuch für Wirtschaftsgeschichte* (1990), 107–11.

Brandes, Detlef, *Von den Zaren adoptiert: die deutschen Kolonisten und die Balkansiedler in Neurussland und Bessarabien 1751–1914* (Munich, 1993).

Brandl, Helmut, *Der Stadtwald von Freiburg* (Freiburg, 1970).

Brandt, Harm-Hinrich, *Wirtschaft und Wirtschaftspolitik im Raum Hanau 1597–1962. Die Geschichte der Industrie- und Handelskammer Hanau-Gelnhausen-Schlüchtern und ihrer Vorläufer* (Hanau, 1963).

Braun, Hans Joachim, 'Economic Theory and Policy in Germany, 1750–1800', *Journal of European Economic History* 4 (1975), 301–22.

Bregnsbo, Michael, *Samfundsordning og statsmagt set fra prædikestolen* (Odense, 1997).

Brown, A. H., 'Adam Smith's first Russian Followers', *Essays on Adam Smith*, ed. A. S. Skinner and T. Wilson (Oxford, 1975), pp. 247–73.

Bruch, Rüdiger vom, 'Wissenschaftliche, institutionelle oder politische Innovation? Kameralwissenschaft – Polizeiwissenschaft – Wirtschaftswissenschaft im 18. Jahrhundert im Spiegel der Forschungsgeschichte', *Die Institutionalisierung der Nationalökonomie an deutschen Universitäten. Zur Erinnerung an Klaus Hinrich Hennings (1937–1986)*, ed. N. Waszek (St Katharinen, 1988), pp. 77–108.

Brunner, Otto, 'Das "ganze Haus" und die alteuropäische "Ökonomik"', *Neue Wege der Verfassungs- und Sozialgeschichte*, 2nd edn (Göttingen, 1968), pp. 103–27.

Büchner, Franz, Gerrit Winter, *Grundriß der Individualversicherung* (Karlsruhe, 1986).

Buchner, Thomas, 'Perceptions of Work in Early Modern Economic Thought: Dutch Mercantilism and Central European Cameralism in Comparative Perspective', *The Idea of Work in Europe from Antiquity to Modern Times*, ed. J. Ehmer and C. Lis (Farnham, 2009), pp. 191–213.

Burgdorf, Wolfgang, 'Johann Heinrich Gottlob von Justi (1720–1771)', *Europahistoriker. Ein biographisches Handbuch*, vol. 1, ed. H. Duchhardt, M. Morawiec, W. Schmale and W. Schulze (Göttingen, 2006), pp. 51–78.

Bush, Michael L., 'Introduction', *Serfdom and Slavery: Studies in Legal Bondage*, ed. M. L. Bush (London/New York, 1996), pp. 1–17.

——, 'Serfdom in Medieval and Modern Europe: A Comparison', *Serfdom and Slavery: Studies in Legal Bondage*, ed. M. L. Bush (London, 1996), pp. 199–224.

Butler, W. E. and V. A. Tomsinov (eds), *The Nakaz of Catherine the Great: Collected Texts* (Clark, NJ, 2010).

Câmara, Manuel Ferreira da, 'Schreiben von Herrn da Camera de Bethencourt an Herrn Hawkins einige Versuche mit dem Obsidiane betreffend', *Bergmannisches Journal* 6/2 (1794), 239–49.

——, 'Über das Verhalten des Obsidians vor dem Löthrohre, von Hr. Da Camera – Aus dem französischen übersetzt', *Bergmannisches Journal* 6/1 (1794), 280–5.

Cardoso, José Luís and Alexandre Mendes Cunha, 'Discurso Econômico e

Política Colonial no Imério Luso-Brasileiro (1750–1808)', *Tempo* 17/31 (2011), pp. 65–88.

———, 'Enlightened Reforms and Economic Discourse in the Portuguese-Brazilian Empire (1750–1808)', *History of Political Economy* 44/4 (2012), 619–41.

Carlowitz, Hans Carl von, *Sylvicultura oeconomica oder haußwirtschaftliche Nachricht und naturmäßige Anweisung zur Wilden Baum-Zucht nebst gründlicher Darstellung wie zu förderst durch göttliches Benedeyen dem attenthalben und insgemein einreissenden grossen Holz-Mangel ...* (Leipzig, 1713).

Carvalho e Melo, Sebastião José de, *Escritos económicos de Londres (1741–1742)*, ed. J. Barreto (Lisbon, 1986).

Certeau, Michel de, *The Practice of Everyday Life* (Berkeley, 1988).

Chaloupek, Günther, 'J. H. G. Justi in Austria: His Writings in the Context of Economic and Industrial Policies of the Habsburg Empire in the 18th Century', *The Beginnings of Political Economy. Johann Heinrich Gottlob von Justi*, ed. J. G. Backhaus (New York, 2009), pp. 147–56.

Chartier, Roger, 'Sciences et savoirs', *Annales* 71/2 (2016), 451–64.

Chechulin, N. D. (ed.), *Nakaz Imperatritsy Ekateriny II, dannyi Kommissii o sochinenii proekta novogo ulozheniia* (St Petersburg, 1907).

Christensen, Dan Ch., 'Physiocracy – the Missing Link?', *Modernisation and Tradition: European Local and Manorial Societies 1500–1900*, ed. K. Sundberg, T. Germundsson and K. Hansen (Lund, 2004), pp. 78–106.

Christensen, René Schrøder, 'Udskiftningen på Brahetrolleborg. Et eksempel på godsejerens store indflydelse på kulturlandskabet', *Fynske Årbøger* (2005), 39–65.

Clark, Christopher, *Iron Kingdom: The Rise and Downfall of Prussia, 1600–1947* (London, 2006).

Clendenning, P. H., 'Dr Thomas Dimsdale and Smallpox Inoculation in Russia', *Journal of the History of Medicine and Allied Sciences* 29 (1974), 399–421.

———, 'Eighteenth-Century Russian Translations of Western Economic Works', *Journal of European Economic History* 1/3 (1972), 745–53.

Coleman, Donald C., *Revisions in Mercantilism* (London, 1969).

Colerus, Johannis, *Oeconomiae oder Hausbuch*, 2 vols (Wittenberg, 1598).

Conze, Werner, *Quellen zur Geschichte der deutschen Bauernbefreiung* (Göttingen, 1957).

Corni, Gustavo, 'Absolutistische Agrarpolitik und Agrargesellschaft in Preussen', *Zeitschrift für Historische Forschung* 13 (1986), 285–313.

———, *Stato assoluto e società agraria in Prussia nell'età di Federico II* (Bologna, 1982).

Correia, Maria Alcina Ribeiro, *Sebastião José de Carvalho e Mello na corte de Viena de Áustria: elementos para o estudo da sua vida pública, 1744–1749* (Lisbon, 1965).

Cortekar, Jörg, *Glückskonzepte des Kameralismus und Utilitarismus:*

Implikationen für die moderne Umweltökonomik und Umweltpolitik (Marburg, 2007).

Cramer, Johann Andreas, *Kurzer Unterricht im Christenthum zum richtigen Verstande des kleinen Catechismus Lutheri, zum allgemeinen Gebrauche in Schleswig und Holstein* (Pinneburg/Ranzau, 1781).

Cross, A. G., 'The Russian *banya* in the Descriptions of Foreign Travellers and the Depictions of Foreign and Russian Artists', *Oxford Slavonic Papers* 24 (1991), 34–59.

Cunha, Alexandre Mendes, 'A Junta da Real Fazenda em Minas Gerais e os projetos de abolição da circulação de outro em pó (1770–1808): limites às reformas econômicas na colônia dentro da administração fazendária portuguesa', *História Econômica & História de Empresas* 15 (2012), 9–46.

——, 'Police Science and Cameralism in Portuguese Enlightened Reformism: Economic Ideas and the Administration of the State during the Second Half of the 18th Century', *European Journal of the History of Economic Thought* 8/1 (2010), 36–47.

——, 'Polizei and the System of Public Finance: Tracing the Impact of Cameralism in Eighteenth-century Portugal', *The Dissemination of Economic Ideas*, ed. H. D. Kurz, T. Nishizawa and K. Tribe (Cheltenham/Northampton, MA, 2011), pp. 65–83.

——, 'A Previously Unnoticed "Swiss Connection" in the Dissemination of Cameralist Ideas during the Second Half of the 18th Century', *History of Political Economy* 49/3 (2017).

d'Auteroche, Chappe, *Voyage en Sibérie, fait par ordre du roi en 1761 […]*, 2 vols (Paris, 1768).

Dahlgren, Erik Wilhelm, *Louis De Geer 1587–1652. Hans lif och verk* (Stockholm, 1923).

Dahlgren, Stellan, 'Ekonomisk politik och teori under Karl XI:s regering', *Karolinska förbundets årsbok* (1998), 47–104.

——, 'Karl XI:s envälde – kameralistik absolutism?', *Makt och vardag: Hur man styrde, levde och tänkte under svensk stormaktstid*, ed. S. Dahlgren, A. Florén and Å. Karlsson (Stockholm, 1993; 3rd edn, 1988), pp. 115–32.

Dähnert, Johann Carl (ed.), *Sammlung gemeiner und besonderer Pommerscher und Rügischer Landes-Urkunden Gesetze, Privilegien, Verträge, Constitutionen und Ordnungen*, vol. 3 (Stralsund, 1769).

Daston, Lorraine, *Classical Probability in the Enlightenment* (Princeton, NJ, 1988).

Davenant, Charles, *Discourses on the Publick Revenue*, vol. 2 (London, 1698).

Davis, John A., 'The European Economies in the Eighteenth Century', *An Economic History of Europe. From Expansion to Development*, ed. A. Di Vittorio (London, 2006), pp. 92–134.

Deane, Phyllis and W. A. Cole, *British Economic Growth, 1688–1955* (London, 1962).

Delhuyar, Fausto, *Indagaciones sobre la amonedacion en Nueva España sistema observado desde su establecimiento, su actual estado y productos ...* (Madrid, 1818).

——, *Memoría sobre el influjo de la minería en la agricultura, industria, problacion y civilizacion de la Nueva-España en sus diferentes épocas ...* (Madrid, 1825).

Demel, Walter, *Reich, Reformen und sozialer Wandel 1763–1806* (= Gebhardt, *Handbuch der Deutschen Geschichte* Bd 12, Stuttgart, 2005).

Dietz, Burkhard, 'Wirtschaftliches Wachstum und Holzmangel im bergisch-märkischen Gewerberaum vor der Industrialisierung', http://www.lrz -muenchen-de/MW/Hardenstein/Dietz.htm.

Dinges, Martin, 'Medicinische Policey zwischen Heilkundigen und "Patienten" (1750–1830)', *Policey und frühneuzeitliche Gesellschaft*, ed. K. Härter (Frankfurt a.M., 2000), pp. 263–95.

Dithmar, Justus Christoph, *Einleitung in die öconomischen, Policey- und cameral-Wissenschaften*, 5th edn (Frankfurt an der Oder, 1755).

Dittrich, Erhard, *Die deutschen und die österreichischen Kameralisten* (Darmstadt, 1974).

Dixon, Simon, *Catherine the Great* (London, 2009).

Dombernovsky, Lotte, *Lensbesidderen som amtmand. Studier i administrationen af fynske grevskaber og baronier 1671–1849* (Copenhagen, 1983).

Donnert, Erich, *Johann Georg Eisen (1717–1779). Ein Vorkämpfer der Bauernbefreiung in Rußland* (Leipzig, 1978).

——, *Politische Ideologie der Russischen Gesellschaft zu Beginn der Regierungszeit Katharinas II. Gesellschaftstheorien und Staatslehren in der Ära des aufgeklärten Absolutismus* (Berlin, 1976).

Drechsler, Wolfgang, 'Christian Wolff (1679–1754): A Biographical Essay', *European Journal of Law and Economics* 4/2 (1997), 111–28.

Dreitzel, Horst, 'Justis Beitrag zur Politisierung der deutschen Aufklärung', in *Aufklärung als Politisierung – Politisierung der Aufklärung*, ed. H.-E. Bödeker and U. Herrmann (Hamburg, 1987), pp. 158–77.

——, 'Universal-Kameral-Wissenschaft als politische Theorie: Johann Friedrich von Pfeiffer (1718–1787)', *Aufklärung als praktische Philosophie. Werner Schneiders zum 65. Geburtstag*, ed. F. Grunert and Fr. Vollhardt (Tübingen, 1998) pp. 149–71.

Dukes, Paul (ed.), *Russia under Catherine the Great*, 2 vols (Newtonville, MA, 1977).

Durchhardt, Heinz, *Der Wiener Kongress: Die Neugestaltung Europas 1814/15* (Munich, 2013).

Eddie, Sean A., *Freedom's Price: Serfdom, Subjection, and Reform in Prussia, 1648–1848* (Oxford, 2013).

Eggers, Carl Leopold, *Ueber die gegenwärtige Beschaffenheit und mögliche Aufhebung der Leibeigenschaft in den Cammergütern des Herzogthums Mecklenburg Schwerin* (Bützow/Schwerin/Wismar, 1784).

Eggert, Oskar, *Die Massnahmen der Preussischen Regierung zur Bauernbe-freiung in Pommern* (Köln/Graz, 1965).

Eibach, Joachim, 'Das offene Haus. Kommunikative Praxis im sozialen Nahraum der europäischen Frühen Neuzeit', *Zeitschrift für Historische Forschung* 38/4 (2011), 621–64.

Eisen, Johann Georg, 'Beweis, daß diejenige Verfassung des Bauern, wenn selbiger seinem Herrn als ein Eigentümer von seinem Bauernhof untertan ist, der einzige Grund sei, worauf alle mögliche Glückseligkeit eines Staats gebauet werden kann; die Leibeigenschaft hingegen für die erste Ursache von aller Unvollkommenheit in derselben gehalten werden könne', *Johann Georg Eisen (1717–1779). Ausgewählte Schriften. Deutsche Volksaufklärung und Leibeigenschaft im Russischen Reich*, ed. R. Bartlett and E. Donnert (Marburg, 1998).

Eklund, Åsa, Chris Evans and Göran Rydén, 'Baltic Iron and the Organisation of the British Iron Market in the Eighteenth Century', *Britain and the Baltic. Studies in Commercial, Political and Cultural Relations 1500–2000*, ed. P. Salmon and T. Barrow (Sunderland, 2003), pp. 203–15.

Eliseeva, I. I., A. L. Timkovskii, S. F. Svin'in, E. A. Ivanova and L. G. Shumeiko (eds), *M. V. Lomonosov i sotrudnichestvo rossiiskikh i nemetskikh uchenykh. Sb. nauchnykh trudov rossiisko-nemetskogo nauchnogo seminara* (St Petersburg, 2012).

Enders, Lieselott, *Die Altmark. Geschichte einer kurmärkischen Landschaft in der Frühneuzeit (Ende des 15. bis Anfang des 19. Jahrhunderts)* (Berlin, 2008).

——, 'Bauern und Feudalherrschaft der Uckermark im absolutistischen Staat', *Jahrbuch für Geschichte des Feudalismus* 13 (1989), 247–83.

——, 'Emanzipation der Agrargesellschaft im 18. Jahrhundert – Trends und Gegentrends in der Mark Brandenburg', *Konflikt und Kontrolle in Gutsherrschaftsgesellschaften. Über Resistenz- und Herrschaftsverhalten in ländlichen Sozialgebilden der Frühen Neuzeit*, ed. J. Peters (Göttingen, 1995) pp. 404–33.

——, 'Die Landgemeinde in Brandenburg. Grundzüge ihrer Funktion und Wirkungsweise vom 13. bis zum 18. Jahrhundert', *Blätter für deutsche Landesgeschichte* 129 (1993), 195–256.

——, *Die Prignitz. Geschichte einer kurmärkischen Landschaft vom 12. bis zum 18. Jahrhundert* (Potsdam, 2000).

——, *Die Uckermark. Geschichte einer kurmärkischen Landschaft vom 12. bis zum 18. Jahrhundert* (Weimar, 1992).

Endres, Rudolf, 'Wirtschaftspolitik in Ansbach-Bayreuth im Zeitalter des Absolutismus', *Jahrbuch für Wirtschaftsgeschichte* 2 (1994), 97–117.

Engelhardt, Ulrich, 'Zum Begriff der Glückseligkeit in der kameralistischen Staatslehre des 18. Jahrhunderts (J. H. G. v. Justi)', *Zeitschrift für historische Forschung* 8 (1981), 37–79.

Engler, Steven, 'Developing a Historically Based "Famine Vulnerability Analysis

Model" (FVAM) – An Interdisciplinary Approach', *Erdkunde* 66 (2012), 157–72.

Epperlein, Siegfried, *Waldnutzung, Waldstreitigkeiten und Waldschutz in Deutschland im hohen Mittelalter. 2. Hälfte 11. Jahrhundert bis ausgehendes 14. Jahrhundert* (Stuttgart, 1993).

Erdmann-Degenhardt, Antje, *Im Dienste Holsteins. Katharina die Große und Caspar von Saldern*, 2nd edn (Rendsburg, 1987).

Ernst, Christoph, 'Neue Zugänge zur historischen Waldentwicklung. Die Auswertung von Forst- und Landrentmeisterrechnungen (Kurtrier, 1759–1792)', *Langer Reihen zur Erforschung von Waldzuständen und Waldentwicklungen*, ed. W. Schenk (Tübingen, 1999), pp. 207–29.

———, *Den Wald entwickeln. Ein Politik- und Konfliktfeld in Hunsrück und Eifel im 18. Jahrhundert* (München, 2000).

Evans, Chris and Göran Rydén, *Baltic Iron in the Atlantic World in the Eighteenth Century* (Leiden, 2007).

Evelyn, John, *Sylva, or, A discourse of forest-trees, and the propagation of timber in His Majesties dominions* (London, 1664).

Facius, Friedrich, *Wirtschaft und Staat. Die Entwicklung der staatlichen Wirtschaftsverwaltung in Deutschland vom 17. Jahrhundert bis 1945* (Boppard am Rhein, 1959).

Fata, Márta, *Migration im kameralistischen Staat Josephs II. Theorie und Praxis der Ansiedlungspolitik in Ungarn, Siebenbürgen, Galizien, und der Bukowina von 1768 bis 1790* (Münster, 2014).

Felgel, Anton Victor, 'Haugwitz, Friedrich Wilhelm', *Allgemeine Deutsche Biographie* 11 (1880), pp. 66–9.

Flakowski, Curt, 'Beiträge zur Geschichte der Erbpacht unter König Friedrich I', Inaugural-Dissertation (Königsberg, 1910).

Florinus, Francis Philipp, *Oeconomus Prudens et Legalis oder allgemeiner kluger und Rechts-verständinger Haus-Vatter* (Nürnberg, [1701] 1750).

Fonvizin, D., *Torguiushchee dvorianstvo protivu polozhennoe dvorianstvu voennomu* (St Petersburg, 1766).

Forberger, Rudolf, *Die Manufaktur in Sachsen vom Ende des 16. bis zum Anfang des 19. Jahrhunderts* (Berlin, 1958).

Forrester, David A. R., 'Rational Administration, Finance and Control Accounting: The Experience of Cameralism', *Critical Perspectives on Accounting* (1990), pp. 285–317.

Fors, Hjalmar, *The Limits of Matter. Chemistry, Mining and Enlightenment* (Chicago, 2015).

Frambach, Hans, 'Cameralism and Labour in von Justi's Economic Thinking', *The Beginnings of Political Economy. Johann Heinrich Gottlob von Justi*, ed. J. G. Backhaus (New York, 2009), pp. 133–45.

Frängsmyr, Tore, 'Christian Wolff's Mathematical Method and its Impact on the Eighteenth Century', *Journal of the History of Ideas* 36/4 (1975), 653–68.

———, 'Den gudomliga ekonomin: Religion och hushållning I 1700-talets Sverige', *Lychnos. Lärdomshistorika samfundets årsbrok* (1971–72), pp. 217–44.

———, *Svensk idéhistoria. Bildning och vetenskap under tusen år*, 1: *1000–1809* (Stockholm, 2000).

———, *Wolffianismens genombrott i Sverige* (Uppsala, 1972).

Franz, Günther (ed.), *Quellen zur Geschichte des deutschen Bauernstandes in der Neuzeit* (Darmstadt, 1963).

Frauendorfer, Sigmund von, *Ideengeschichte der Agrarwirtschaft und Agrarpolitik im deutschen Sprachgebiet*, vol. 1 (Bonn/München/Wien, 1957).

Frederick II, *Refutation of Machiavelli's Prince; or Anti-Machiavel by Frederick of Prussia* (Athens, OH, 1981).

Freeze, Gregory, 'Bringing Order to the Russian Family: Marriage and Divorce in Imperial Russia, 1760–1860', *Journal of Modern History* 62 (1990), 709–46.

Fritsch, Ahasver, *Corpus Iuris Venatorio Forestalis* (Jena, 1676).

Fuhrmann, Martin, *Volksvermehrung als Staatsaufgabe? Bevölkerungs- und Ehepolitik in der deutschen politischen und ökonomischen Theorie des 18. und 19. Jahrhunderts* (Paderborn, 2002).

Furtado, Júnia Ferreira, 'Enlightenment Science and Iconoclasm: The Brazilian Naturalist José Vieira Couto', *Osiris* 25 (2010), 189–212.

Gadebusch, Thomas Heinrich, *Schwedischpommersche Staatskunde*, vol. 1 (Greifswald, 1786).

Gall, Lothar, *Wilhelm von Humboldt. Ein Preuße von Welt* (Berlin, 2011).

Garber, Jörn, 'Spätaufklärerischer Konstitutionalismus und ökonomischer Frühliberalismus. Das Staats- und Industriebürgerkonzept der postabsolutistischen Staats-, Kameral- und Polizeiwissenschaft (Chr. D. Voss)', *Spätabsolutismus und bürgerliche Gesellschaft. Studien zur deutschen Staats- und Gesellschaftstheorie im Übergang zur Moderne*, ed. J. Garber (Frankfurt a.M., 1992), pp. 77–118.

Garner, Guillaume, *État, économie, territoire en Allemagne. L'espace dans le caméralisme et l'économie politique 1740–1820* (Paris, 2005).

Gay I Escoda, Josep Maria, *Treballs sobre cameralisme a Catalunya i a Espanya* (Barcelona, 1992).

Gerentz, Sven, *Kommerskollegiet och näringslivet* (Stockholm, 1951).

Gesemann, Wolfgang, *Die Entdeckung der unteren Volksschichten durch die russische Literatur* (Wiesbaden, 1972).

Gleditsch, Johann Gottlieb, *Systematische Einleitung in die neuere aus ihren eigenthümlichen physikalisch-ökonomischen Gründen hergeleitete Forstwissenschaft*, 2 vols (Berlin, 1774–75).

Gøbel, Erik, *De styrede rigerne. Embedsmændene i den danske civile centraladministration 1660–1814* (Odense, 2000).

Gorißen, Stefan, 'Interessen und ökonomische Funktionen merkantilistischer Privilegienpolitik. Das Herzogtum Berg und seine Textilgewerbe zwischen

16. und 18. Jahrhundert', *Die Ökonomie des Privilegs, Westeuropa 16.–19. Jahrhundert. L'économie du privilège, Europe occidentale XVIe–XIXe siècles*, ed. G. Garner (Frankfurt a.M., 2016), pp. 279–329.

———, *Vom Handelshaus zum Unternehmen. Sozialgeschichte der Firma Harkort im Zeitalter der Protoindustrie (1720–1820)* (Göttingen, 2002).

Gottlieb, Anthony, *The Dream of Enlightenment. The Rise of Modern Philosophy* (London, 2016).

Graefe, Christa, *Forstlete. Von den Anfängen einer Behörde und ihren Beamten Braunschweig-Wolfenbüttel 1530–1607* (Wisebaden, 1989).

Gray, Marion W., 'Kameralismus: Die säkulare Ökonomie und die getrennten Geschlechtersphären', *WerkstattGeschichte* 19 (1998), 41–57.

———, *Productive Men, Reproductive Women. The Agrarian Household and the Emergence of Separate Spheres during the German Enlightenment* (Oxford, 2000).

Grewe, Bernd Stefan, *Der versperrte Wald. Ressourcenmangel in der bayerischen Pfalz (1814–1870)* (Köln, 2004).

Grimm, Jakob, *Weisthümer gesammelt von Jakob Grimm* (Göttingen, 1840–78).

Grober, Ulrich, *Die Entdeckung der Nachhaltigkeit. Kulturgeschichte eines Begriffs* (Munich, 2010).

Harnisch, Hartmut, 'Der preußische Absolutismus und die Bauern. Sozialkonservative Gesellschaftspolitik und Vorleistung zur Modernisierung', *Jahrbuch für Wirtschaftsgeschichte* (1994), 11–32.

Härter, Karl, *Polizey und Strafjustiz in Kurmainz. Gesetzgebung, Normdurchsetzung und Sozialkontolle im frühneuzeitlichen Territorialstaat* (Frankfurt a.M., 2005).

Hartley, Beryl, 'Exploring and Communicating Knowledge of Trees in the Early Royal Society', *Notes and Records of the Royal Society of London* 64/3 (2010), 229–31.

Harvey, Karen, *The Little Republic. Masculinity and Domestic Authority in Eighteenth-Century Britain* (Oxford, 2012).

Hasel, Karl and Ekkehard Schwartz, *Forstgeschichte. Ein Grundriss für Studium und Praxis*, 3rd edn (Kassel, 2006).

Hauff, Dorothea, *Zur Geschichte der Forstgesetzgebung und Forstorganisation des Herzogtums Württemberg im 16. Jahrhundert* (Stuttgart, 1977).

Hauser, Albert, *Wald und Feld in der alten Schweiz* (Zürich, 1972).

Haussherr, Hans, *Verwaltungseinheit und Ressorttrennung vom Ende des 17. bis zum Beginn des 19. Jahrhunderts* (Berlin, 1953).

Heckscher, Eli F., 'The Effect of Foreign Trade on the Distribution of Income', *Readings in the Theory of International Trade*, ed. H. S. Ellis and L. A. Metzler (Philadelphia, 1949), pp. 272–300.

———, *Mercantilism* (London, 1935; 2nd edn in two vols, 1955).

———, *Merkantilisment; ett led I den ekonomiska politikens historia* (Stockholm, 1931).

———, *Der Merkantilismus* (Jena, 1932).

————, *Sveriges Ekonomiska Historia från Gustav Vasa*, two vols in four parts (Stockholm, 1935, 1936, 1949).

————, 'Utrikeshandelns verkan på inkomstfördelningen. Några teoretiska grundlinjer', *Ekonomisk Tidskrift* 21/2 (1919), 1–32.

Henning, Friedrich-Wilhelm, *Handbuch der Wirtschafts- und Sozialgeschichte Deutschlands. Bd. 1: Deutsche Wirtschafts- und Sozialgeschichte im Mittelalter und in der frühen Neuzeit* (Paderborn, 1991).

————, *Herrschaft und Bauernuntertänigkeit. Beiträge zur Geschichte der Herrschaftsverhältnisse in den ländlichen Bereichen Ostpreussens und des Fürstentums Paderborn vor 1800* (Würzburg, 1964).

————, *Das vorindustrielle Deutschland 800 bis 1800* (Paderborn, 1994).

Hennings, Klaus Hinrich, 'Aspekte der Institutionalisierung der Ökonomie an deutschen Universitäten', *Die Institutionalisierung der Nationalökonomie an deutschen Universitäten. Zur Erinnerung an Klaus Hinrich Hennings (1937–1986)*, ed. N. Waszek (St Katharinen, 1988), pp. 43–54.

Henningsen, Peter, *I sansernes vold. Bondekultur og kultursammenstød i enevældens Danmark*, 1–2 (Copenhagen, 2006).

Heresbach, Conrad, *Foure bookes of husbandry, collected by M. Conradus Heresbachius, counseller to the hygh and mighty prince, the Duke of Cleue: conteyning the whole arte and trade of husbandry, vvith the antiquitie, and commendation thereof. Newely Englished, and increased, by Barnabe Googe, Esquire* (London, 1577).

Hildebrand, Bruno, 'Die gegenwärtige Aufgabe der Wissenschaft der Nationalökonomie', *Jahrbücher für Nationalökonomie und Statistik* 1 (1863), 5–25.

Hildebrand, Karl-Gustaf, *Swedish Iron in the Seventeenth and Eighteenth Centuries. Export Industry before the Industrialization* (Stockholm, 1992).

Hintze, Otto, *Regierung und Verwaltung. Gesammelte Abhandlungen zur Staats-, Rechts- und Sozialgeschichte Preussens*, ed. G. Oestreich, 2nd edn (Göttingen, 1967).

Hirsch, Eike Christian, *Der berühmte Herr Leibniz. Eine Biographie* (Munich, 2007).

Hochmuth, Christian, *Globale Güter–lokale Aneignung. Kaffee, Tee, Schokolade und Tabak im frühneuzeitlichen Dresden* (Konstanz, 2008).

Hohberg, Wolf Helmhard von, *Georgica curiosa aucta* (Nürnberg, [1682] 1701).

Holenstein, André, *'Gute Policey' und lokale Gesellschaft im Staat des Ancien Régime. Das Fallbeispiel der Markgrafschaft Baden(-Durlach)* (Epfendorf/Neckar, 2003).

————, 'Introduction: Empowering Interactions: Looking at Statebuilding from Below', *Empowering Interactions: Political Cultures and the Emergence of the State in Europe, 1300–1900*, ed. W. Blockmans, A. Holenstein and J. Mathieu (Farnham, 2009) pp. 1–33.

Holm, Harald, *Kampen om Landboreformerne i Danmark i Slutningen af det 18. Aarhundrede* (Copenhagen, 1888).

Hölzl, Richard, *Umkämpfte Wälder. Die Geschichte einer ökologischen Reform in Deutschland 1760–1860* (Frankfurt, 2010).

Hont, Istvan, *Jealousy of Trade. International Competition and the Nation-State in Historical Perspective* (Cambridge, MA, 2005).

———, 'The Language of Sociability and Commerce: Samuel Pufendorf and the Theoretical Foundations of the "Four Stages Theory"', *The Language of Political Theory in Early Modern Europe*, ed. A. Pagden (Cambridge, 1987), pp. 253–76.

Hoppit, Julian, 'Political Arithmetic in Eighteenth-century England', *Economic History Review* 49/3 (1996), 516–40.

Hosfeld-Guber, Jutta, *Der Merkantilismusbegriff und die Rolle des absolutistischen Staates im vorindustriellen Preussen* (Munich, 1985).

Hughes, Lindsey, *Russia in the Age of Peter the Great* (New Haven, CT, 1998).

Humboldt, Wilhelm von, *The Limits of State Action* (London, 1969).

Humpert, Magdalene, *Bibliographie der Kameralwissenschaften* (Cologne, 1937).

Ibneeva, G. V., *Imperskaia politika Ekateriny II v zerkale ventsenosnykh puteshestvii* (Moscow, 2009).

Imperatritsa Ekaterina Vtoraia, *Nakaz, dannyi Komissii o sochinenii proekta novogo Ulozheniia*, ed. V. A. Tomsinov (Moscow, 2008).

Ingram, John Kells, *A History of Political Economy* (London, 1888).

Ingrao, Charles, *The Habsburg Monarchy, 1618–1815*, 2nd edn (Cambridge, 2000).

Isaacsohn, Siegfried, *Das Preußische Beamtenthum des siebenzehnten Jahrhunderts* (Berlin, 1878).

Isenmann, Moritz (ed.), *Merkantilismus. Wiederaufnahme einer Debatte* (Stuttgart, 2014).

Jakob, Ludwig Heinrich von, *Grundsätze der National-Oekonomie oder National-Wirthschaftslehre* (Halle, 1805).

Jansson, Karin Hassan, 'Haus und Haushalt im früneuzeitlichen Schweden', *Das Haus in der Geschichte Europas*, ed. J. Eibach and I. Schmidt-Voges (Oldenbourg, 2015), pp. 113–29.

Jenetzky, Johannes, *System und Entwicklung des materiellen Steuerrechts in der wissenschaftlichen Literatur des Kameralismus von 1680–1840* (Berlin, 1979).

Johann, Elisabeth, *Geschichte der Waldnutzung in Kärnten unter dem Einfluss der Berg- und Hütten- und Hammerwerke* (Klagenfurt, 1968).

Johannisson, Karin, *Det mätbara samhället. Statistik och samhällsdröm i 1700-talets Europa* (Stockholm, 1988).

Jones, Peter, *Agricultural Enlightenment. Knowledge, Technology, and Nature, 1750–1840* (Oxford, 2016).

Jonsson, Fredrik Albritton, *Enlightenment's Frontier: The Scottish Highlands and the Origins of Environmentalism* (Yale, 2013).

Jung-Stilling, Johann Heinrich, *Lehrbuch der Staats-Polizey-Wissenschaft* (Leipzig, 1788).

————, *Versuch eines Lehrbuchs der Fabrikwissenschaft zum Gebrauch Akademischer Vorlesungen* (Nürnberg, 1785).

Justi, Johann Heinrich Gottlob von, *Abhandlung von denen Manufactur- und Fabriken-Reglements zu Ergänzung seines Werkes von denen Manufacturen und Fabriken* (Berlin/Leipzig, 1762).

————, *Abhandlungen von der Vollkommenheit der Landwirthschaft und der höchsten Cultur der Länder* (Ulm/Leipzig, 1761).

————, *Gesammlete Politische und Finanzschriften über wichtige Gegenstände der Staatskunst, der Kriegswissenschaften und des Cameral- und Finanzwesens*, 3 vols (Copenhagen/Leipzig, 1761–64)

————, *Die Grundfeste zu der Macht und Glückseeligkeit der Staaten; oder ausführliche Vorstellung der gesamten Policey-Wissenschaft*, 2 vols (Königsberg/Leipzig, 1760–61).

————, *Gutachten von dem Vernünftigen Zusammenhange und practischen Vortrage aller Oeconomischen und Cameralwissenschaften wobey zugleich zur Probe die Grundsätze der Policeywissenschaft* (Leipzig, 1754).

————, *Die Natur und das Wesen der Staaten als die Grundwissenschaft der Staatskunst, der Policey, und aller Regierungswissenschaften, desgleichen als die Quelle aller Gesetze* (Berlin, 1760).

————, *Oeconomische Schriften über die wichtigen Gegenstände der Stadt- und Landwirtschaft* (Berlin, 1760).

————, *Osnovanie sily i blagosostoianiia gosudarstv, ili Podrobnoe nachertanie vsekh znanii kasaiushchikhsia do gosudarstvennogo blagochiniia*, 4 parts (Moscow, 1772–78).

————, 'Vorschlag zu Assecuranzanstalten gegen die Wasser- Hagel- und andere Schaden an den Feldfrüchten', *Göttingische Policey-Amts Nachrichten auf das Jahr 1755. oder vermischte Abhandlungen zum Vortheil des Nahrungsstandes aus allen Theilen der Oeconomischen Wissenschaften benebst verschiedenen in das Göttingische Policey-Wesen einschlagenden Verordnungen und Nachrichten. Erster Theil* (Göttingen, 1755), pp. 145–7.

Kalmár, János and János J. Varga (eds), *Einrichtungswerk des Königreichs Hungarn (1688–1690)* (Stuttgart, 2010).

Kant, Immanuel, *Werke*, Akademie Ausgabe, 9 vols (Berlin, 1902–23).

Karataev, Nikolai K., *Ekonomicheskie nauki v Moskovskom universitete (1755–1955)* (Moscow, 1956).

————, *Ocherki po istorii ekonomicheskikh nauk v Rossii XVIII veka* (Moscow, 1960).

Karlsson, Per-Arne, 'Housekeeping Ideology and Equilibrium Policy in Eighteenth-century Sweden', *Scandinavian Economic History Review & Economy and History* 37/2 (1989), 51–77.

Kaufhold, Karl Heinrich, 'Deutschland 1650–1850', *Handbuch der europäischen Wirtschafts- und Sozialgeschichte*, vol. 4, ed. I. Mieck, H. Kellenbenz, W. Fischer and J. A. van Houtte (Stuttgart, 1993), pp. 523–88.

———, 'Einführung', *Wirtschaft, Wissenschaft und Bildung in Preussen: Zur Wirtschafts- und Sozialgeschichte Preussens vom 18. bis zum 20. Jahrhundert*, ed. K. H. Kaufhold and B. Sösemann (Stuttgart, 1998), pp. 9–16.

———, 'Preußische Staatswirtschaft – Konzept und Realität – 1640–1806. Zum Gedenken an Wilhelm Treue', *Jahrbuch für Wirtschaftsgeschichte* (1994), 33–70.

———, '"Wirtschaftswissenschaften" und Wirtschaftspolitik in Preußen von um 1650 bis um 1800', *Wirtschaft, Wissenschaft und Bildung in Preussen: Zur Wirtschafts- und Sozialgeschichte Preussens vom 18. bis zum 20. Jahrhundert*, ed. K. H. Kaufhold and B. Sösemann (Stuttgart, 1998), pp. 51–72.

Keller, Katrin, 'Saxony: *Rétablissement* and Enlightened Absolutism', *German History* 20 (2002), 309–31.

Kern, Arthur, 'Beiträge zur Agrargeschichte Ostpreußens', *Forschungen zur Brandenburgischen und Preußischen Geschichte* 14 (1901), 151–258.

Kerstens, I. Kh., *Nastavleniia i pravila vrachebnye dlia derevenskikh zhitelei, sluzhashchiia k umnozheniiu nedovol'nogo chisla liudei v Rossii* (Moscow, 1769).

Khodnev, A. I., *Istoriia Imperatorskogo Vol'nogo Ekonomicheskogo Obshchestva s 1765 do 1865 goda* (St Petersburg, 1865).

Kinzinger, Lothar K., 'Schweden und Pfalz-Zweibrücken: Probleme einer gegenseitigen Integration. Das Fürstentum Pfalz-Zweibrücken unter schwedischer Fremdherrschaft (1681–1719)', unpublished diss. (Saarbrücken, 1988).

Kirby, David, *Northern Europe in the Early Modern Period. The Baltic World 1492–1772* (London, 1990).

———, 'The Royal Navy's Quest for Pitch and Tar during the Reign of Queen Anne', *Scandinavian Economic History Review* 22/2 (1974), 97–116.

Klein, Ernst, 'Johann Heinrich Justi und die preußische Staatswirtschaft', *Vierteljahrschrift für Sozial- und Wirtschaftsgeschichte* 48 (1961), 145–202.

———, *Von der Reform zur Restauration. Finanzpolitik und Reformgesetzgebung des preußischen Staatskanzlers Karl August von Hardenberg* (Berlin, 1965).

Knap, Isabelle, 'Die Anfänge "wissenschaftlicher" Forstlehre am Beispiel des *Allgemeinen oeconomischen Forst-Magazins (1763–1769)*' *Landschaften agrarisch-ökonomischen Wissens. Strategien innovativer Ressourcennutzung im Zeitschriften und Sozietäten des 18. Jahrhunderts*, ed. M. Popplow (Münster, 2010), pp. 61–78.

Knapp, Georg Friedrich, *Die Bauern-Befreiung und der Ursprung der Landarbeiter in den älteren Theilen Preußens*, 2 vols (Leipzig, 1887).

Knight, Frank, *Risk, Uncertainty and Profit* (Boston, MA, 1921).

Knight, Roger, 'New England Forests and British Seapower: Albion Revised', *The American Neptune* 44/4 (1986), 221–9.

Knoll, Hans, *Hagelversicherung* (Wiesbaden, 1964).

Koch, Hannsjoachim Wolfgang, *History of Prussia* (London, 1987).

Koerner, Lisbet, 'Daedalus Hyperboreus: Baltic Natural History and Mineralogy in the Enlightenment', *The Sciences in Enlightened Europe*, ed. W. Clark, J. Golinski and S. Schaffer (Chicago/London, 1999), pp. 387–422.

——, *Linnaeus: Nature and Nation* (Cambridge, MA, 1999).

Kohnke, Meta, 'Das Edikt von Potsdam. Zu seiner Entstehung, Verbreitung und Überlieferung', *Jahrbuch für Geschichte des Feudalismus* 9 (1985), 241–75.

Kolchin, Peter, 'In Defense of Servitude: American Proslavery and Russian Proserfdom Arguments, 1760–1860', *American Historical Review* 85 (1980), 809–27.

Komissarenko, A. I., *Russkii absoliutizm i dukhovenstvo v XVIII veke* (Moscow, 1990), pp. 135–42.

Komlos, John, 'Institutional Change under Pressure Enlightened Government Policy in the Eighteenth-Century Habsburg Monarchy', *Journal of European Economic History* 15 (1986), 427–82.

Kozlova, N. V., *Pobegi krest'ian v Rossii v pervoi treti XVIII veka: iz istorii sotsial'no-ekonomicheskoi zhizni strany* (Moscow, 1983).

Kraus, Hans-Christof, 'Kriegsfolgenbewältigung und "Peuplierung" im Denken deutscher Kameralisten des 17. und 18. Jahrhunderts', *Krieg, Militär und Migration in der Frühen Neuzeit*, ed. M. Asche, M. Herrmann, U. Ludwig and A. Schindling (Berlin, 2008), pp. 265–79.

Kriedte, Peter, *Taufgesinnte und großes Kapital. Die niederrheinisch-bergischen Mennoniten und der Aufstieg des Krefelder Seidengewerbes* (Göttingen, 2007).

Krüger, Horst, *Zur Geschichte der Manufakturen und der Manufakturarbeiter in Preussen: die mittleren Provinzen in der zweiten Hälfte des 18. Jahrhunderts* (Berlin, 1958).

Krüger, Kersten, *Finanzstaat Hessen 1500–1567. Staatsbildung im Übergang vom Domänstaat zum Steuerstaat* (Marburg, 1980).

Küng, Enn, 'The Timber Trade in Pärnu in the Second Half of the Seventeenth Century', *Ajalooline Ajakiri* 137/138 (2011), 243–63.

Kurz, Heinz-Dieter, Tamotsu Nishizawa and Keith Tribe (eds), *The Dissemination of Economic Ideas* (Cheltenham, 2011).

Laborier, Pascale, Frédéric Audren, Paolo Napoli and Jakob Vogel (eds), *Les sciences camérales. Activités pratiques et histoire des dispositifs publics* (Paris, 2011).

Lamprecht, Georg Friedrich, *Versuch eines vollständigen Systems der Staatslehre mit Inbegriff ihrer beiden wichtigsten Haupttheile der Polizei- und Kameral- oder Finanzwissenschaft. Zum Gebrauch academischer Vorlesungen* (Berlin, 1784).

Landwehr, Achim, *Policey im Alltag: Die Implementation frühneuzeitlicher Policeyordnungen in Leonberg* (Frankfurt a.M., 2000).
———, 'Die Rhetorik der "Guten Policey"', *Zeitschrift für historische Forschung* 30 (2003), 251–87.
Laslett, Peter, *Household and Family in Past Times* (Cambridge, 1972).
Lebeau, Christine, *Aristocrates et grands commis à la Cour de Vienne (1748– 1791). Le modèle français* (Paris, 1996).
———, 'Beispiel eines Kulturtransfers zwischen Frankreich und Sachsen: die neue Regierungskunst in Sachsen zur Zeit des Rétablissements (1762– 1768)', *Von der Elbe bis an die Seine. Kulturtransfer zwischen Sachsen und Frankreich um 18. und 19. Jahrhundert*, ed. M. Espagne and M. Middell (Leipzig, 1999), pp. 121–35.
Leckey, Colum, *Patrons of Enlightenment. The Free Economic Society in Eighteenth-Century Russia* (Newark, DE/Lanham, MD, 2011).
Legnér, Matthias, *Fäderneslandets rätta beskrivning. Mötet mellan antikvarisk forskning och ekonomisk nyttokult i 1700-talets Sverige* (Helsingfors, 2004).
Lehmann, H., H. Wellenreuther and R. Wilson (eds), *In Search of Peace and Prosperity. New German Settlements in Eighteenth-Century Europe and America* (University Park, PA, 2000).
Leibniz, Gottfried Wilhelm, *Hauptschriften zur Versicherungs- und Finanz- mathematik*, ed. E. Knobloch and J.-M. Graf von der Schulenburg (Berlin, 2000).
Lermann, Hans Schmitt, *Der Hagel und die Hagelversicherung in der Kulturgeschichte* (Munich, 1984).
Letiche, J. M. (trans. and ed.) *A History of Russian Economic Thought: Ninth through Eighteenth Centuries* (Berkeley/Los Angeles, 1964).
Liedman, Sven-Eric, *Den osynliga handen. Anders Berch och ekonomiämnena vid 1700-talets svenska universitet* (Värnamo, 1986).
———, *Den synliga handen* (Stockholm, 1986).
Lindenfeld, David F., *The Practical Imagination: the German Sciences of State in the Nineteenth Century* (Chicago, 1997).
Lindqvist, Svante, 'Labs in the Woods: The Quantification of Technology during the Late Enlightenment', *The Quantifying Spirit in the Eighteenth Century*, ed. T. Frängsmyr, J. L. Heilbron and R. E. Rider (Berkeley, 1990), pp. 291–314.
Lindroth, Sren, *Sveriges lärdomshistoria, del II* (Stockholm, 1997).
Linné, Carl von, *Oeconomia naturæ eller Skaparens allvisa inrättning på vår jord, i agttagen vid de skapade tingens betraktande i de tre naturens riken, till deras fortplantning, vidmagthållande och undergång* (Uppsala, 1750).
Lisch, Georg Christian Friedrich, 'Der Kammerpräsident Luben von Wulffen und die Erbverpachtung, ein Beitrag zur Geschichte des Herzogs Carl Leopold von Mecklenburg', *Jahrbücher des Vereins für Mecklenburgische Geschichte und Altertumskunde* 13 (1848), 197–234.

Lluch, Ernest, 'Cameralism beyond the Germanic World: A Note on Tribe', *History of Economic Ideas* 5 (1997), 85–99.

————, 'El cameralismo más allá del mundo germánico', *Revista de economia aplicada* 4 (1996), 163–75.

————, 'El déficit de la hacienda pública española y las propuestas del cameralismo', *II Seminario de Historia de la Real Sociedad Bascongada* (Donostia, 1988).

————, *Las Españas vencidas del siglo XVIII: claroscuros de la Ilustración* (Barcelona, 1999).

————, 'Der Kameralismus, ein vieldimensionales Lehrgebäude: Seine Rezeption bei Adam Smith und im Spanien des 18. Jahrhunderts', *Jahrbuch für Wirtschaftsgeschichte* (2000), 133–54.

————, 'El pensamiento económico en Cataluña entre el Renacimiento económico y la Revolución Industrial: La irrupción de la escuela clásica y la respuesta proteccionista', unpublished Ph.D. diss. (University of Barcelona, 1970).

Loën, Johann Michael von, *Entwurf einer Staats-Kunst, worinn die natürlichste Mittel entdecket werden, ein Land mächtig, reich, und glücklich zu machen*, 2nd edn (Frankfurt/Leipzig, 1750, originally 1747).

Loit, Aleksander, 'Die baltischen Länder im schwedischen Ostseereich', *Die schwedischen Ostseeprovinzen Estland und Livland im 16.-18. Jahrhundert*, ed. A. Loit and H. Piirimäe (Stockholm, 1993), pp. 63–81.

Lomonosov, M. V., *Polnoe sobranie sochinenii*, ed. S. I. Vavilov (Moscow/ Leningrad, 1950–59).

Löwenhielm, Carl Gustaf, *Tal om landt-skötsel, hållit för Kongl. Svenska Vetenskaps academien* (Stockholm, 1751).

Lowood, Henry E. 'The Calculating Forester: Quantification, Cameral Science, and the Emergence of Scientific Forestry Management in Germany', *The Quantifying Spirit in the Eighteenth Century*, ed. T. Frängsmyr, J. L. Heilbron and R. E. Rider (Berkeley, 1990), pp. 315–42.

Lupetti, Monica and Marco Guidi, 'Translation as Import Substitution: The Portuguese Version of Veron de Forbonnais's *Elemens du commerce*', *History of European Ideas* 40/8 (2014), 1151–88.

Lütge, Friedrich, *Deutsche Sozial- und Wirtschaftsgeschichte. Ein Überblick* (Berlin/Göttingen/Heidelberg, 1952).

————, *Geschichte der deutschen Agrarverfassung vom frühen Mittelalter bis zum 19. Jahrhundert* (Stuttgart, 1963).

Madariaga, Isabel de, 'Catherine II and the Serfs: A Reconsideration of Some Problems', *Slavonic and East European Review* 52/126 (1974), 34–62.

————, *Russia in the Age of Catherine the Great* (London, 1981, latest edition 2002).

Mager, Friedrich, *Der Wald in Altpreussen als Wirtschaftsraum* (Cologne, 1960).

Mager, Wolfgang, 'Landwirtschaft und ländliche Gesellschaft auf dem Weg in die Moderne', *Deutschland und Frankreich im Zeitalter der Französischen Revolution*, ed. H. Berding, E. François and H.-P. Ullmann (Frankfurt, 1989), pp. 59–99.

Magnusson, Lars, *Äran Korruptionen och den Borgerliga Ordningen. Essäer från svensk ekonomihistoria* (Stockholm, 2001).

———, 'Corruption and Civic Order – Natural Law and Economic Discourse in Sweden during the Age of Freedom', *Scandinavian Economic History Review* 37/2 (1989) 78–105.

———, 'Eli Heckscher and Mercantilism – An Introduction', in E. F. Heckscher, *Mercantilism*, vol. 1 (London, 1994), pp. x–xxxv.

———, 'Handeln, Näringarna och den Ekonomiska Politiken', *Det svenska urverket. Kommerskollegium 350 år*, ed. B. G. Hall (Stockholm, 2001).

———, 'Is Mercantilism a Useful Concept Still?', *Merkantilismus. Wiederaufnahme einer Debatte*, ed. M. Isenmann (Stuttgart, 2014), pp. 19–38.

———, *Mercantilism. The Shaping of an Economic Language* (London/New York, 1994).

———, 'Physiocracy in Sweden 1760–1780', *La Diffusion Internationale de la Physiocratie*, ed. B. Delmas, T. Demals and Ph. Steiner (Grenoble, 1995), pp. 381–99.

———, *The Political Economy of Mercantilism* (London, 2015).

———, 'The Reception of a Political Economy of Free Trade: The Case of Sweden', *Free Trade and its Reception 1815–1860*, vol. I, ed. A. Marrison (London, 1998), pp. 145–60.

———, *The Tradition of Free Trade* (London, 2004).

———, 'Was Cameralism Really the German Version of Mercantilism?', *Economic Growth and the Origins of Modern Political Economy. Economic Reasons of State, 1500–2000*, ed. P. R. Rössner (London/New York, 2016), pp. 57–71.

Maier, Hans, *Die ältere deutsche Staats- und Verwaltungslehre* (München, 2009; 1st edn, 1966).

———, 'Die Lehre von der Politik an den deutschen Universitäten vornehmlich vom 16. bis 18. Jahrhundert', *Wissenschaftliche Politik. Eine Einführung in Grundfragen ihrer Tradition und Theorie*, ed. D. Oberndörfer (Freiburg im Breisgau, 1962), pp. 59–116.

Maifreda, Germano, *From Oikonomia to Political Economy. Constructing Economic Knowledge from the Renaissance to the Scientific Revolution* (Farnham, 2012).

Maikov, P. M., *Ivan Ivanovich Betskoi. Opyt ego biografii* (St Petersburg, 1904).

Malone, Joseph J., 'England and the Baltic Naval Stores Trade in the Seventeenth and Eighteenth Centuries', *The Mariner's Mirror* 58 (1972), 375–95.

Malthus, Thomas Robert, *An Essay on the Principle of Population; or, a View of its Past and Present Effects on Human Happiness [...] A New Edition, Very Much Enlarged*, 2nd edn (London, 1803).

Mantel, Kurt, *Forstgeschichte des 16. Jahrhunderts unter dem Einfluß der Forstordnungen und Noe Meurers* (Hamburg, 1980).

Marchet, Gustav, *Studien über die Entwickelung der Verwaltungslehre in Deutschland von der zweiten Hälfte des 17. bis zum Ende des 18. Jahrhunderts* (Munich, 1885).

Markussen, Ingrid, 'Hustavlen og Aristoteles – en disciplinerende affære', *ARR. Idehistorisk tidsskrift* 4 (2013).

———, *Sagens sande Beskaffenhed. Skolereformen på Brahetrolleborg 1783 set i lyset af en forældreklage* (forthcoming).

———, *Til Skaberens Ære, Statens Tjeneste og vor egen Nytte. Pietistiske og kameralistiske ideer bag fremvæksten af en obligatorisk skole i landdistrikterne i Danmark* (Odense, 1995).

Matthieson, Kieko, *Forests in Revolutionary France. Conservation, Community and Conflict, 1669–1848* (Cambridge, 2015).

McCaffray, Susan P., 'What Should Russia Be? Patriotism and Political Economy in the Thought of N. S. Mordvinov', *Slavic Review* 59 (2000), 572–96.

McCormick, Ted, 'Population: Modes of Seventeenth-Century Demographic Thought', *Mercantilism Reimagined. Political Economy in Early Modern Britain and Its Empire*, ed. P. J. Stern and C. Wennerlind (Oxford, 2014), pp. 25–45.

McGrew, R. E., 'Dilemmas of Development: Baron Heinrich Friedrich Storch (1766–1835) on the Growth of Imperial Russia', *Jahrbücher für Geschichte Osteuropas* 24 (1976), 31–71.

Medick, Hans, *Weben und Überleben in Laichingen 1650–1900. Lokalgeschichte als Allgemeine Geschichte*, 2nd edn (Göttingen, 1997).

Medushevskii, A. N., *Proekty agrarnykh reform v Rossii XVIII–nachalo XXI veka* (Moscow, 2005).

Melton, James Van Horn, *Absolutism and the Eighteenth-century Origins of Compulsory Schooling in Prussia and Austria* (Cambridge, 1988).

Mendels, Franklin, 'Proto-industrialization. The First Phase of the Industrialization Process', *Journal of Economic History* 32 (1972), 241–61.

Mendonça, Marcos Carneiro de, *A amazônia na era pombalina: correspondência do governador e capitão-general do estado do Grão-Pará e Maranhão Francisco Xavier de Mendonça Furtado: 1751–1759*, 2nd edn (Brasília, 2005).

———, *O Intendente Câmara: Manoel Ferreira da Câmara Bethencourt, e Sá – Intendente Geral das Minas e dos Diamantes (1764–1835)* (Rio de Janeiro, 1933).

Meurer, Noé, *Jag und Forstrecht* (Frankfurt a.M, 1576).

———, *Vom Forstlicher Oberherrligkeit und Gerechtigkeit* (Pforzheim, 1560).

Meyer, Torsten, 'Cultivating the Landscape: The Perception and Description of Work in Sixteenth- to Eighteenth-Century German "Household Literature" (*Hausväterliteratur*)', *The Idea of Work in Europe from Antiquity to Modern Times*, ed. J. Ehmer and C. Lis (Farnham, 2009), pp. 215–44.

————, *Natur, Technik und Wirtschaftswachstum im 18. Jahrhundert. Risikoperzeptionen und Sicherheitsversprechen* (Münster, 1999).

Meyer, Torsten and Marcus Popplow, '"To employ each of Nature's products in the most favorable way possible" – Nature as a Commodity in Eighteenth-Century German Economic Discourse', *Historical Social Research* 29 (2004), 4–40.

Meyssonnier, Simone, *La balance et l'horloge. La genèse de la pensée libérale en France au XVIIIe siècle* (Montreuil, 1989).

Mill, James, *Elements of Political Economy*, in *James Mill. Selected Economic Writings*, ed. D. Winch (Edinburgh, 1966).

Minard, Philippe, 'Facing Uncertainty: Markets, Norms and Conventions in the Eighteenth Century', *Regulating the British Economy 1660–1850*, ed. P. Gauci (Aldershot, 2011), pp. 177–94.

————, 'L'inspection des draps du West Riding of Yorkshire, ou le jeu des normes au XVIIIe siècle', *Fraude, contrefaçon et contrebande de l'Antiquité à nos jours*, ed. G. Béaur, H. Bonin and C. Lemercier (Geneva, 2006), pp. 621–38.

Mironov, Boris N., *Sotsial'naia istoriia Rossii perioda Imperii (XVIII-nach. XX vv.) [...]*, 2 vols (St Petersburg, 1999).

Mitchell, B. R., *British Historical Statistics* (Cambridge, 1988).

Mittenzwei, Ingrid, 'Die Agrarfrage und der Kameralismus', *Deutsche Agrargeschichte des Spätfeudalismus*, ed. H. Harnisch and G. Heitz (Berlin, 1986), pp. 169–80.

————, *Preußen nach dem Siebenjährigen Krieg: Auseinandersetzungen zwischen Bürgertum und Staat um die Wirtschaftspolitik* (Berlin, 1979).

Mizuta, Hiroshi, *Adam Smith's Library. A Catalogue* (Oxford, 2000).

Moeller, Bertha von, 'Luben von Wulffens Reformen, 1700–1710', *Altpreußische Monatsschrift* 55 (1918), 1–49.

Mohnhaupt, Heinz, 'Fabriksprivileg', *Enzyklopädie der Neuzeit*, ed. Fr. Jaeger, vol. 3 (Stuttgart/Weimar, 2006), cols 753–6.

Moldenhauer, Paul, *Das Versicherungswesen, Band 1: Allgemeine Versicherungslehre* (Berlin, 1917).

Möller, Caren, *Medizinalpolizei. Die Theorie des staatlichen Gesundheitswesens im 18. und 19. Jahrhundert* (Frankfurt a.M., 2005).

Monti, Mario, *Der Preis des "weißen Goldes". Preispolitik und -strategie im Merkantilsystem am Beispiel der Porzellanmanufaktur Meißen 1710–1830* (Munich, 2011).

Moon, David, *The Plough that Broke the Steppes. Agriculture and Environment on Russia's Grasslands, 1700–1914* (Oxford, 2013).

————, 'Reassessing Russian Serfdom', *European History Quarterly* 26/4 (1996), 483–526.

Moreira, Alzira Teixeira Leite, *Inventário do Fundo Geral do Erário Régio, Arquivo do Tribunal de Contas* (Lisbon, 1977).

Moser, Wilhelm Gottfrid, *Grundsäze der Forst-Oeconomie* (Frankfurt/Leipzig, 1757).

Munck, Thomas, *The Peasantry and the Early Absolute Monarchy in Denmark 1660–1708* (Copenhagen, 1979).

Napp-Zinn, Anton Felix, *Johann Friedrich von Pfeiffer und die Kameralwissenschaften an der Universität Mainz* (Wiesbaden, 1955).

Neugebauer, Wolfgang, 'Die Leibeigenschaft in der Mark Brandenburg. Eine Enquete in der Kurmark des Jahres 1718', *Brandenburgische Landesgeschichte und Archivwissenschaft. Festschrift für Lieselott Enders zum 70. Geburtstag*, ed. Fr. Beck and K. Neitmann (Weimar, 1997), pp. 225–41.

Nichtweiss, Johannes, *Das Bauernlegen in Mecklenburg. Eine Untersuchung zur Geschichte der Bauernschaft und der zweiten Leibeigenschaft in Mecklenburg bis zum Beginn des 19. Jahrhunderts* (Berlin, 1954).

Niggemann, Ulrich, *Immigrationspolitik zwischen Konflikt und Konsens. Die Hugenottenansiedlung in Deutschland und England (1681–1697)* (Köln/Weimar/Wien, 2008).

———, '"Peuplierung" als merkantilistisches Instrument: Privilegierung von Einwanderern und staatlich gelenkte Ansiedlungen', *Handbuch Staat und Migration in Deutschland seit dem 17. Jahrhundert*, ed. J. Oltmer (Oldenbourg, 2016), pp. 182–97.

Nipperdey, Justus, *Die Erfindung der Bevölkerungspolitik. Staat, politische Theorie und Population in der Frühen Neuzeit* (Göttingen, 2012).

———, 'Die Hugenottenaufnahme als Katalysator der Idee des Populationismus', *Francia: Forschungen zur westeuropäischen Geschichte* 40 (2013), 113–38.

———, 'Regulierung zur Sicherung der Nahrung. Zur Übereinstimmung von Menschenbild und Marktmodell bei Zünften und Kameralisten', *Regulierte Märkte: Zünfte und Kartelle/Marchés régulés: Corporations et cartels*, ed. M. Müller, H. R. Schmidt and L. Tissot (Zürich, 2011), pp. 165–82.

Nokkala, Ere Pertti, 'The Machine of State in Germany – The Case of Johann Heinrich Gottlob von Justi (1717–1771)', *Contributions to the History of Concepts* 5 (2009), 71–93.

North, Michael, *The Baltic. A History* (Cambridge, MA, 2015).

———, 'Die Entstehung der Gutswirtschaft im südlichen Ostseeraum', *Zeitschrift für Historische Forschung* 26/1 (1999), 43–59.

———, 'The Export of Timber and Timber By-products from the Baltic Region to Western Europe, 1575–1775', in Michael North, *From the North Sea to the Baltic, Essays in Commercial, Monetary and Agrarian History, 1500–1800* (Aldershot, 1996), pp. 1–14.

Oberholzner, Frank, 'From an Act of God to an Insurable Risk. The Change in the Perception of Hailstorms and Thunderstorms since the Early Modern Times', *Environment and History* 17 (2011), 133–52.

———, *Institutionalisierte Sicherheit im Agrarsektor. Die Entwicklung der*

Hagelversicherung in Deutschland seit der Frühen Neuzeit (= Schriften zur Wirtschafts- und Sozialgeschichte, Band 87, Berlin 2015), pp. 96–113.

Oestreich, Gerhard, *Geist und Gestalt des frühmodernen Staates* (Berlin, 1969).

Ohlin, Bertil, *Interregional and International Trade* (Cambridge, MA, 1933).

Omel'chenko, O. A., *"Zakonnaia monarkhiia" Ekateriny II. Prosveshchennyi absoliutizm v Rossii* (Moscow, 1993).

Ondrušová, Eva, 'Staatswirtschaftslehre des Kameralismus: Theorie und Praxis am Beispiel von den Kameralherrschaften im Mittelslowakischen Bergbaugebiet. Einführung in das Thema', *Economy and Society in Central and Eastern Europe: Territory, Population, Consumption. Papers of the International Conference Held in Alba Iulia, April 25th–27th 2013*, ed. D. Dumitran and V. Moga (Vienna, 2013), pp. 63–76.

Örnberg, Magnus, *Oeconomisk Beskrifning öfwer Stapel Staden Gefle* (Stockholm, 1755).

Osterloh, Karl-Heinz, *Joseph von Sonnenfels und die österreichische Reformbewegung im Zeitalter des aufgeklärten Absolutismus. Eine Studie zum Zusammenhang von Kameralwissenschaft und Verwaltungspraxis* (Hamburg, 1970).

Otruba, Gustav and Harald Steindl, 'Einleitung', *Österreichische Fabriksprivilegien vom 16. bis zum 18. Jahrhundert und ausgewählte Quellen zur Frühgeschichte der Industrialisierung*, ed. G. Otruba (Graz/Cologne/Vienna, 1981), pp. 11–120.

Overbeek, Johannes, 'Mercantilism, Physiocracy and Population Theory', *The South African Journal of Economics* 41 (1973), 167–74.

Penther, Friedrich, *Praxis geometriae worinnen nicht nur alle bey dem Feld-Messen vorkommende Fälle, mit Stäben, dem Astrolabio, der Boussole, und der Mensul, in Ausmessung eintzeler Linien, Flächen und gantzer Revier, welche, wenn deren etliche angräntzende zusammen genommen, eine Land-Carte ausmachen, auf ebenen Boden und Gebürgen, wie auch die Abnehmung derer Höhen und Wasser-Fälle, nebst beygefügten practischen Hand-Griffen, deutlich erörtert, sondern auch eine gute Ausarbeitung der kleinesten Risse bis zum grösten, mit ihren Neben-Zierathen, treulich communiciret werden* (Augsburg, 1761).

Petander, Karl, *De nationalekonomiska åskådningarna i Sverige sådana de framträda i litteraturen. Del I: 1718–1765* (Stockholm, 1912).

Peters, Jan, 'Die Pommern als neue schwedische Untertanen. Über Ökonomie und patriotische Phraseologie in der 2. Hälfte des 17. Jahrhunderts', *Economy and Culture in the Baltic 1650–1700. Papers of the VIIIth Visby Symposium held at Gotlands Fornsal Gotland's Historical Museum, Visby August 18th–22th, 1986*, ed. S.-O. Lindquist (Visby, 1989), pp. 121–8.

———, 'Schwedische Bauernpolitik in Vorpommern vor 300 Jahren', *Wissenschaftliche Zeitschrift der Ernst-Moritz-Arndt-Universität Greifswald* 9 (1959/60, Gesellschafts- und sprachwissenschaftliche Reihe), no. 2/3, pp. 151–7.

Pfeiffer, Johann Friedrich von, *Der Antiphysiocrat oder umständliche Untersuchung des sogenannten Physiocratischen Systems vermöge welchem eine allgemeine Freiheit, und einzige Auflage, auf den reinen Ertrag der Grundstücke, die Glückseligkeit aller Staaten ausmachen soll. Von dem Verfasser des Lehrbegrifs sämtlicher Oekonomischer- und Cameralwissenschaften* (Frankfurt a.M., 1780).

––––––, *Gedanken über Versicherungs-Anstalten hauptsächlich zum Vorteil der Landwirthschaft entworffen, und in höchster Gegenwart Seiner Herzoglichen Durchlaucht wärend den Akademischen öffentlichen Prüfungen verteidigt* (Stuttgart, 1780).

––––––, *Grundriß der Staatswirthschaft zur Belehrung und Warnung angehender Staatswirte* (Frankfurt a.M., 1782).

––––––, *Grundriß der wahren und falschen Staatskunst*, 2 vols (Berlin, 1778–79).

––––––, *Grundsätze der Universal-Cameral-Wissenschaft* (Frankfurt, 1783).

––––––, *Lehrbegrif sämmtlicher oeconomischer und Cameralwissenschaften* (1st edn, 1764–65; 2nd edn, Mannheim, 1773–78).

––––––, *Die Manufacturen und Fabricken Deutschlands nach ihrer heutigen Lage betrachtet und mit allgemeinen Vorschlägen zu ihren vorzüglichsten Verbesserungs Mitteln begleitet* (Frankfurt a.M., 1780).

––––––, *Natürliche aus dem Endzweck der Gesellschaft allgemeine Policeiwissenschaft* (Frankfurt a.M., 1779).

––––––, *Vermischte Verbeßerungsvorschläge und freie Gedanken über verschiedene, den Nahrungszustand, die Bevölkerung und Staatswirtschaft der Deutschen betreffende Gegenstände* (Frankfurt a.M., 1777).

Pfeisinger, Gerhard, *Arbeitsdisziplinierung und frühe Industrialisierung 1750–1820* (Cologne, 2006).

Philippi, Johann Albrecht, *Die wahren Mittel zur Vergrößerung eines Staats* (Berlin, 1753).

Piasecki, Peter, *Das deutsche Salinwesen 1550–1650* (Idstein, 1987).

Pisarevskii, G. G., *Iz istorii inostrannoi kolonizatsii v Rossii v XVIII veke* (Moscow, 1909).

Plavinskaia, Nadezhda, 'Catherine II (1729–1796)', *Dictionnaire Montesquieu*, dir. C. Volpilhac-Auger (Lyon, 2013).

Pleve, I. R., *Nemetskie kolonii na Volge vo vtoroi polovine XVIII veka*, 2nd edn (Moscow, 2002; American translation 2001).

Pölitz, Karl Heinrich Ludwig, *Grundriß für encyklopädische Vorträge über die gesammten Staatswissenschaften* (Leipzig, 1825).

––––––, *Volkswirthschaftslehre; Staatswirthschaftslehre und Finanzwissenschaft, und Polizeiwissenschaft*, 2nd edn (Leipzig, 1827).

Polonska-Vasylenko, N., 'Manifest 3 serpnia roku 1775 v svitli togochasnykh idei', *Zapiski istoriko-filol. viddilu Ukrains'koi Akad. Nauk* 12 (1927), 165–80.

Poovey, Mary, *A History of the Modern Fact. Problems of Knowledge in the Sciences of Wealth and Society* (Chicago, 1998).

Prange, Wolfgang, *Die Anfänge der großen Agrarreformen in Schleswig-Holstein bis um 1771* (Neumünster, 1971).

Pribram, Karl, *Geschichte der österreichischen Gewerbepolitik von 1740 bis 1860. Auf Grund der Akten*, vol. 1: *1740 bis 1798* (Leipzig, 1907).

Priddat, Birger P., 'Kameralismus als paradoxe Konzeption der gleichzeitigen Stärkung von Markt und Staat. Komplexe Theorielagen im deutschen 18. Jahrhundert', *Berichte zur Wissenschaftsgeschichte* 31 (2008), 249–63.

———, 'Die unbekanntere Seite: Joh. Beckmann als Herausgeber und Kommentator der Von Justi'schen "Policeywissenschaft"', *Johann Beckmann-Journal. Mitteilungen der Johann Beckmann-Gesellschaft e.V.* 4/2 (1990), 23–44.

Rackham, Oliver, *Trees and Woodland in the British Landscape* (London, 2001).

Radkau, Joachim, *Holz – wie ein Nahrstoff Geschichte schreibt* (München, 2007).

Raeff, Marc, 'The Well-Ordered Police State and the Development of Modernity in Seventeenth- and Eighteenth-Century Europe: An Attempt at a Comparative Approach', *American Historical Review* 80 (1975), 1221–43.

———, *The Well-Ordered Police State. Social and Institutional Change through Law in the Germanies and Russia, 1600–1800* (New Haven, CT, 1983).

Ranke, Leopold von, *Neun Bücher Preußischer Geschichte*, vol. 1 (Berlin, 1847).

Ransel, David, *Mothers of Misery. Child Abandonment in Imperial Russia* (Princeton, NJ, 1988; reprint 2014).

Rasmussen, Carsten Porskrog, 'Modern Manors?', *Modernisation and Tradition. European Local and Manorial Societies 1500–1900*, ed. K. Sundberg, T. Germundsson and K. Hansen (Malmö, 2004), pp. 48–77.

———, *Det sønderjyske landbrugs historie 1544–1830* (Åbenrå, 2013).

Rebel, Hermann, 'Reimagining the Oikos: Austrian Cameralism in its Social Formation', *Golden Ages, Dark Ages. Imagining the Past in Anthropology and History*, ed. J. O'Brien and W. Roseberry (Ithaca, NY, 1994), pp. 48–80.

Reinert, Erik S., 'German Economics as Development Economics: From the Thirty Years' War to World War II', *The Origins of Development Economics. How Schools of Economic Thought Have Addressed Development*, ed. K. S. Jomo and E. S. Reinert (London, 2005), pp. 53–9.

———, 'Jacob Bielfeld's "On the Decline of States" (1760) and its Relevance for Today', *Great Nations at Peril*, ed. J. G. Backhaus (London 2015), pp. 133–72.

———, 'Johann Heinrich Gottlob von Justi – The Life and Times of an Economist Adventurer', *The Beginnings of Political Economy. Johann Heinrich Gottlob von Justi*, ed. J. G. Backhaus (New York, 2009), pp. 33–74.

Reinert, Erik S. and Kenneth E. Carpenter, 'German Language Economic Bestsellers before 1850', *Economic Growth and the Origins of Modern Political Economy*, ed. Ph. R. Rössner (London, 2016), pp. 26–53.

Reinert, Erik S. and Hugo Reinert, 'A Bibliography of J. H. G. von Justi', *The Beginnings of Political Economy. Johann Heinrich Gottlob von Justi*, ed. J. G. Backhaus (New York, 2009), pp. 19–31.

Reinert, Sophus A., *Translating Empire. Emulation and the Origins of Political Economy* (Cambridge, MA, 2011).

Remer, Justus, *Johann Heinrich Gottlob Justi. Ein deutscher Volkswirt des 18. Jahrhunderts* (Stuttgart, 1938).

Renner, Andreas, *Russische Autokratie und europäische Medizin. Organisierte Wissenstransfer im 18. Jahrhundert* (Stuttgart, 2010).

Reyscher, A. E., *Vollständige, historisch und kritisch bearbeitete Sammlung der württembergischen Gesetze* (1828–).

Rice, John, 'Patterns of Swedish Foreign Trade in the Late Eighteenth Century', *Geografiska Annaler. Series B, Human Geography* 47/1 (1965), 86–99.

Richter, Susan, 'German "Minor" Thinkers? The Perception of Moser's and Justi's Works in an Enlightened European Context', *Administrative Theory & Praxis* 36 (2014), 51–72.

Rinman, Sven, *Anledning Til Kunskap Om Den gröfre Jern- och Stål-Förädlingen Och des Förbättrande* (Stockholm, 1772).

Roberts, Michael, *The Age of Liberty: Sweden 1719–1772* (Cambridge, 1986).

Rohr, Christian, *Extreme Naturereignisse im Ostalpenraum. Naturerfahrung im Spätmittelalter und am Beginn der Neuzeit* (= Umwelthistorische Forschungen, Band 4, Cologne, 2007).

———, 'Leben mit der Flut. Zur Wahrnehmung, Deutung und Bewältigung von Überschwemmungen im niederösterreichischen Raum (13.–16. Jahrhundert)', *Studien und Forschungen aus dem Niederösterreichischen Institut für Landeskunde* 46 (2007), 63–114.

Rohr, J. B. von, *Compendieuse Haußhaltungs-Bibliothek* (Leipzig, 1716).

Roscher, Wilhelm, *Geschichte der National-Ökonomik in Deutschland* (Munich, 1874).

Rosen, George, 'Cameralism and the Concept of Medical Police', *Bulletin of the History of Medicine* 27 (1953), 21–42.

Rosenberg, Hans, *Bureaucracy, Aristocracy and Autocracy. The Prussian Experience 1660–1815* (Cambridge, MA, 1958).

Rosenmöller, B., 'Versuche zur Gründung einer Hagelversicherungsanstalt in den Jahren 1774 und 1793', *Zeitschrift für die gesamte Versicherungs-Wissenschaft* 12 (1912), 590–7.

Rössig, Carl Gottlob, *Lehrbuch der Polizeywissenschaft* (Jena, 1786).

Rössner, Philipp R. (ed.), *Economic Growth and the Origins of Modern Political Economy. Economic Reasons of State, 1500–2000* (London/New York, 2016).

———, 'Heckscher Reloaded? Mercantilism, the State, and Europe's Transition to Industrialization, 1600–1900', *Historical Journal* 58 (2015), 663–83.

———, 'Kameralismus, Kapitalismus und die Ursprünge des modernen

Wirtschaftswachstums – aus Sicht der Geldtheorie', *Vierteljahrschrift für Sozial- und Wirtschaftsgeschichte* 102 (2015), 437–71.

———, 'New Inroads into Well-known Territory? On the Virtues of Re-discovering Pre-classical Political Economy', *Economic Growth and the Origins of Modern Political Economy. Economic Reasons of State, 1500–2000*, ed. P. R. Rössner (London, 2016), pp. 3–24.

Rüdiger, Axel, *Staatslehre und Staatsbildung. Die Staatswissenschaft an der Universität Halle im 18. Jahrhundert* (Tübingen, 2005).

Runefelt, Leif, *Att hasta mot undergången. Anspråk, flyktighet, föreställning i debatten om konsumtion i Sverige 1730–1830* (Lund, 2015).

———, *Dygden som välståndets grund. Dygd, nytta och egennytta i frihetstidens ekonomiska tänkande* (Stockholm, 2005).

———, *Hushållningens dygder. Affektlära, hushållningslära och ekonomiskt tänkande under svensk stormaktstid* (Stockholm, 2001).

Rutherford, Donald, *Leibniz and the Rational Order of Nature* (Cambridge, 1995).

Rydén, Göran, 'Provincial Cosmopolitanism – An Introduction', *Sweden in the Eighteenth-Century World: Provincial Cosmopolitans*, ed. G. Rydén (Farnham, 2013).

Rydén, Göran and Chris Evans, 'Connecting Labour. Organising Swedish Ironmaking in an Atlantic Context', *Labour, Unions and Politics under the Northern Star. The Nordic Countries, 1700–2000*, ed. M. Hilson, S. Neunsinger and I. Vyff (New York/Oxford, 2017), pp. 71–87.

Sabean, David Warren, *Property, Production, and Family in Neckarhausen, 1700–1870* (Cambridge, 1990).

Sächsische Carlowitz-Gesellschaft (eds), *Die Erfindung der Nachhaltigkeit. Leben, Werk und Wirkung des Hans Carl von Carlowitz* (München, 2013).

Salvius, Lars, *Beskrifning öfver Sveriget, Första Tomen om Upland* (Stockholm, 1741).

Sandl, Markus, *Ökonomie des Raumes. Der kameralwissenschaftliche Entwurf der Staatswirtschaft im 18. Jahrhundert* (Cologne, 1999).

Schäfer, Ingrid, *"Ein Gespenst geht um." Politik mit der Holznot in Lippe 1750–1850. Eine Regionalstudie zur Wlad und Technikgeschichte* (Detmold, 1992).

Schäfer, Rudolf, *Die Förderung von Handel und Wandel in Kurmainz im 18. Jahrhundert* (Frankfurt a.M., 1968).

———, *Die kurmainzische Porzellanmanufaktur zu Höchst a.M. und ihre Mitarbeiter im wirtschaftlichen und sozialen Umbruch ihrer Zeit (1746–1806)* (Frankfurt a.M., 1964).

Scharf, Claus, *Katharina II, Deutschland und die Deutschen* (Mainz, 1996).

Schenk, Winifried, *Waldnutzung, Waldzustand und regionale Entwicklung in vorindustrieller Zeit im mittleren Deutschland* (Stuttgart, 1996).

Schiera, Pierangelo, *Dall' Arte di Governo alle Scienze dello Stato. Il Cameralismo e l'Assolutismo Tedesco* (Milan, 1968).

————, 'Il cameralismo e il pensiero politico tedesco: un "Sonderweg" anticipato!', *Römische historische Mitteilungen* 31 (1989), 299–317.

Schippan, Michael, *Die Aufklärung in Russland im 18. Jahrhundert* (Wiesbaden, 2012).

Schirren, Carl (ed.), *Die Recesse der livländischen Landtage aus den Jahren 1681 bis 1711. Theils im Wortlaute, theils im Auszuge* (Dorpat, 1865).

Schlechte, Horst (ed.), *Die Staatsreform in Kursachsen, 1762–1763: Quellen zum kursächsischen Rétablissement nach dem siebenjährigen Kriege* (Berlin, 1958).

Schlözer, A. L., *Von der Unschädlichkeit der Pocken in Russland und von Russlands Bevölkerung überhaupt* (Göttingen-Gotha, 1768).

Schlumbohm, Jürgen, 'Gesetze, die nicht durchgesetzt waren – ein Struktur-merkmal des frühneuzeitlichen Staates', *Geschichte und Gesellschaft* 23 (1997), 647–63.

Schmalz, Theodor Anton Heinrich, *Staatswirthschaftslehre in Briefen an einen teutschen Erbprinzen* (Berlin, 1869).

Schmidt, Uwe E., *Der Wald in Deutschland im 18. Und 19. Jahrhundert* (Saarbrücken, 2002).

Schmidt am Busch, Hans-Christoph, 'Cameralism as "Political Metaphysics": Human Nature, the State, and Natural Law in the Thought of Johann Heinrich Gottlob von Justi', *European Journal of the History of Economic Thought* 16 (2009), 409–30.

Schmoller, Gustav, *The Mercantile System and its Historical Significance* (New York, 1897).

————, 'Das Merkantilsystem in seiner historischen Bedeutung [1884]', *Umrisse und Untersuchungen zur Verfassungs-, Verwaltungs- und Wirtschafts-geschichte* (Berlin, 1898), pp. 1–60.

Schneider, Ivo, 'Geschichtlicher Hintergrund und wissenschaftliches Umfeld der Schriften', in Gottfried Wilhelm Leibniz, *Hauptschriften zur Versicherungs- und Finanzmathematik*, ed. E. Knobloch and J.-M. Graf von der Schulenburg (Berlin, 2000), pp. 591–623.

Schubert, Ernst, 'Der Wald: wirtschaftliche Grundlage derspätmittelalterlichen Stadt', *Mensch und Umwelt im Mittelalter*, ed. B. Herrmann (Stuttgart, 1987), pp. 257–69.

Schumpeter, Elizabeth Boody, *English Overseas Trade Statistics 1697–1808* (London, 1960).

Scott, H. M. (ed.), *Enlightened Absolutism. Reform and Reformers in Later Eighteenth-Century Europe* (Basingstoke/London, 1990).

————, 'The Rise of the First Minister in Eighteenth-century Europe', *History and Biography: Essays in Honour of Derek Beales*, ed. T. C. W. Blanning and D. Cannadine (Cambridge, 1996), pp. 21–52.

Seelaender, Airton Cerqueira-Leite, *Polizei, Ökonomie und Gesetzgebungslehre: ein Beitrag zur Analyse der portugiesischen Rechtswissenschaft am Ende des 18. Jahrhunderts* (Frankfurt a.M., 2003).

Semevskii, V. I., *Krest'iane v tsarstvovanie Ekateriny II*, 2 vols (St Petersburg, 1901–03).

———, *Krest'ianskii vopros v Rossii v XVIII i pervoi polovine XIX veka*, 2 vols (St Petersburg, 1888, reprint 1971).

Serrão, Joaquim Veríssimo, *A população de Portugal em 1798. O censo de Pina Manique* (Paris, 1970).

Sheehan, James J., *German History 1770–1866* (Oxford, 1989).

Shmidt, Sigurd Ottovich, 'Proekt P. I. Shuvalova 1754 g. "O raznykh gosudarst-vennoi pol'zy sposobakh"', *Istoricheskii arkhiv* 6 (1962), 100–18.

Shpilevskii, M. M., 'Politika narodonaseleniia v tsarstvovanie Ekateriny II', *Zapiski Imperatorskogo Novorosiiskogo Universiteta* (Odessa), VI (1871), 1–178.

Sieferle, Rolf-Peter, *The Subterranean Forest. Energy Systems and the Industrial Revolution* (Cambridge, 2001).

Silva, Andrée Mansuy-Diniz, *Portrait d'un homme d'État: D. Rodrigo de Sousa Coutinho, Comte de Linhares – 1755–1812, Vol. II: L'homme d'État. 1796–1812* (Paris, 2006).

Silva, António Delgado da, *Collecção da Legislação Portugueza desde a ultima compilação das Ordenações* (Lisbon, 1830).

Simon, Thomas, *'Gute Polizey'. Ordnungsleitbilder und Zielvorstellungen politischen Handelns in der frühen Neuzeit* (Frankfurt a.M., 2004).

———, 'Merkantilismus und Kameralismus. Zur Tragfähigkeit des Merkan-tilismusbegriffs und seiner Abgrenzung zum deutschen "Kameralismus"', *Merkantilismus. Wiederaufnahme einer Debatte*, ed. M. Isenmann (Stuttgart, 2014), pp. 65–82.

———, 'Policey im kameralistischen Verwaltungsstaat: Das Beispiel Preußen', *Policey und frühneuzeitliche Gesellschaft*, ed. K. Härter (Frankfurt a.M., 2000), pp. 473–96.

Skalweit, August, *Die ostpreussische Domänenverwaltung unter Friedrich Wilhelm I. und das Retablissement Litauens* (Leipzig, 1906).

Skinner, Quentin, 'The Idea of Negative Liberty: Machiavellian and Modern Perspectives', in Quentin Skinner, *Visions of Politics: Renaissance Virtues* (Cambridge, 2002).

Skrubbeltrang, Fridlev, *Det danske Landbosamfund 1500–1800* (Copenhagen, 1978).

Slack, Paul, *The Invention of Improvement. Information and Material Progress in Seventeenth-Century England* (Oxford, 2015).

Slawinger, Gerhard, *Die Manufaktur in Kurbayern: die Anfänge der großgew-erblichen Entwicklung in der Übergangsepoche vom Merkantilismus zum Liberalismus 1740–1833* (Stuttgart, 1966).

Small, Albion W., *The Cameralists: The Pioneers of German Social Polity* (Chicago, 1909).

Smith, Pamela H., *The Business of Alchemy. Science and Culture in the Holy Roman Empire* (Princeton, NJ, 1994).

Søkilde, N. Rasmussen, *Gamle og nye Minder om Brahetrolleborg og Omegn* (Brahetrolleborgs Folkemindesamling og Øster Hæsinge lokalhistoriske arkiv, 2001).

Sokolov, N. S., *Raskol v Saratovskom krae. Opyt issledovaniia po neizdannym istochnikam* (Saratov, 1888).

Sonnenfels, Joseph von, *Antrittsrede von der Unzulänglichkeit der alleinigen Erfahrung in den Geschäften der Staatswirthschaft* (Vienna, 1764).

———, *Grundsätze der Polizey, Handlung und Finanz*, 3 vols (Vienna, 1765–71).

———, *Nachal'nye osnovaniia politsii ili blagochiniia* (Moscow, 1787).

Spicer, Michael W., 'Cameralist Thought and Public Administration', *Journal of Management History* 4 (1998), 149–59.

Sporhan, Lore and Wolfgang von Stromer, 'Die Nadelholzsaat in den Nürnberger Reichswäldern zwischen 1369 und 1600', *Zeitschrift für Agrargeschichte und Agrarsoziologie* 17 (1969), 79–99.

Stadelmann, Rudolph, *Preussens Könige in ihrer Thätigkeit für die Landeskultur* part 1 and part 4 (Leipzig, 1878 and 1887).

Stanziani, Alessandro, *Bondage: Labor and Rights in Eurasia from the Sixteenth to the Early Twentieth Centuries* (New York/Oxford, 2014).

Stavenhagen, Gerhard, *Geschichte der Wirtschaftstheorie*, 2nd edn (Göttingen, 1957).

Stein, Robert, *Die Umwandlung der Agrarverfassung Ostpreußens durch die Reform des 19. Jahrhunderts*, vol. 1 (Jena, 1918).

Steinsiek, Peter-Michael, *Nachhaltigkeit auf Zeit. Waldschutz in Westharz vor 1800* (Münster, 1999).

Stieda, Wilhelm, *Die Nationalökonomie als Universitätswissenschaft* (Leipzig, 1906).

Stolleis, Michael, 'Was Bedeutet "Normdurchsetzung" bei Policeyordnungen der frühen Neuzeit?', *Grundlagen des Rechts*, ed. R. H. Helmholz (Paderborn, 2000), pp. 740–57.

Storr, Christopher (ed.), *The Fiscal-Military State in Europe in the Long Eighteenth Century. Essays in Honour of P. G. M. Dickson* (Farnham/Burlington, VA, 2009).

Straubel, Rolf, *Kaufleute und Manufakturunternehmer: eine empirische Untersuchung über die sozialen Träger von Handel und Großgewerbe in den mittleren preußischen Provinzen (1763 bis 1815)* (Stuttgart, 1995).

———, 'Preußische Kaufleute und Beamte um 1800. Ausgewählte Aspekte ihrer sozialen, wirtschaftlichen und gesellschaftlichen Lage', *Wirtschaft, Wissenschaft und Bildung in Preussen: Zur Wirtschafts- und Sozialgeschichte Preussens vom 18. bis zum 20. Jahrhundert*, ed. K. H. Kaufhold and B. Sösemann (Stuttgart, 1998), pp. 179–90.

Subtil, José, *O terramoto político (1755–1759): memória e poder* (Lisbon, 2007).

Süßmilch, Johann Peter, *Die göttliche Ordnung in den Veränderungen*

Geschlechts, aus der Geburt, Tod, und Fortpflantzung desselben (Berlin, 1741).

————, *Die göttliche Ordnung in den Veränderungen des menschlichen Geschlechts, aus der Geburt, dem Tode und der Fortpflanzung desselben,* 2nd edn (Berlin, 1762); 3rd edn (Berlin, 1765).

Szabo, Franz, *Kaunitz and Enlightened Absolutism 1753–1780* (Cambridge, 1994).

Tadmor, Naomi, *Family and Friends in Eighteenth-century England: Household, Kinship, and Patronage* (Cambridge, 2001).

Tautscher, Anton, 'Kameralismus', *Handwörterbuch der Sozialwissenschaften,* vol. 5 (Göttingen, 1956), pp. 465–6.

————, *Staatswirtschaftslehre des Kameralismus* (Bern, 1947).

Théré, Christine, 'Economic Publishing and Authors, 1566–1789', *Studies in the History of French Political Economy,* ed. G. Faccarello (London, 1998), pp. 1–56.

Thomas, Keith, *Religion and the Decline of Magic. Studies in Popular Beliefs in Sixteenth- and Seventeenth-Century England* (London, 1991).

Thoyts, Rob, *Insurance Theory and Practice* (London, 2010).

Thünen, Johann Heinrich, *The Isolated State in Relation to Agriculture and Political Economy. Part III: Principles for the Determination of Rent, the Most Advantageous Rotation Period and the Value of Stands of Varying Age in Pinewoods* (Basingstoke, 2009).

Tieck, Klaus-Peter, *Staatsräson und Eigennutz. Drei Studien zur Geschichte des 18. Jahrhunderts* (Berlin, 1998).

Tölle, U., *Rudolph Zacharias Becker. Versuch der Volksaufklärung im 18. Jahrhundert in Deutschland* (Münster/New York, 1994).

Tomaselli, Sylvana, 'Moral Philosophy and Population Questions in Eighteenth-Century Europe', *Population and Development Review* 14 Supplement (1988), 7–29.

Tooke, William, *View of the Russian Empire during the Reign of Catherine the Second and to the Close of the Present Century,* 3 vols (London, 1799).

Tribe, Keith, 'Cameralism and the Sciences of the State', *The Cambridge History of Eighteenth-Century Political Thought,* ed. M. Goldie and R. Wokler (Cambridge, 2006), pp. 528–9.

————, *The Economy of the Word. Language, History, and Economics* (New York, 2015).

————, *Governing Economy. The Reformation of German Economic Discourse 1750–1840* (Cambridge, 1988; 2nd edn, Newbury, 2017).

————, *Land, Labour and Economic Discourse* (London, 1978).

————, 'Mercantilism and the Economics of State Formation', *Mercantilist Economics,* ed. L. Magnusson (Boston, MA, 1993), pp. 175–86.

————, 'Philipp Wilhelm von Hörnigks *Oesterreich über alles*' (Vademecum zu einem Klassiker absolutistischer Wirtschaftspolitik, Düsseldorf, 1997).

————, *Strategies of Economic Order. German Economic Discourse, 1750–1950* (Cambridge, 1995/2007).

Troitzsch, Ulrich, *Ansätze technologischen Denkens bei den Kameralisten des 17. und 18. Jahrhunderts* (Berlin, 1966).

————, 'Manufakturen in Deutschland und ihre theoretische Behandlung in der kameralistischen Literatur. Ansätze zu einem Vergleich', *Wirtschaftskräfte und Wirtschaftswege. Festschrift für Hermann Kellenbenz*, ed. J. Schneider (Stuttgart, 1978), vol. 4, pp. 611–24.

Tuchtenhagen, Ralph, *Zentralstaat und Provinz im frühneuzeitlichen Nordosteuropa* (Wiesbaden, 2008).

Tully, James, *Meaning and Contexts: Quentin Skinner and his Critics* (Oxford, 1988).

Uhr, Isaac Johan, *En Brukspatrons Egenskaper* (Uppsala, 1750).

Upton, Anthony F., *Charles XI and Swedish Absolutism* (Cambridge, 1998).

van Creveld, Martin, *Supplying War. Logistics from Wallenstein to Patten* (Cambridge, 1977).

Vangerow, Hans Heinrich, *Vom Stadtrecht zur Forstordnung. München und der Isarwinkel bis zum Jahr 1569* (München, 1976).

Varela, Alex Gonçalves, 'Atividades Científicas no Império Português: um Estudo da Obra do Metalurgista de Profissão Manuel Ferreira da Câmara (1783–1820)', *História, Ciências, Saúde-Manguinhos* 15 (2008), 1201–8.

————, 'Ciência e Patronagem: análise da trajetória do naturalista e intendente das minas Manuel Ferreira da Câmara (1808–1822)', *Revista do Instituto Histórico e Geographico Brazileiro* 446 (2010), 67–92.

————, 'A trajetória do ilustrado Manuel Ferreira da Câmara em sua 'fase européia' (1783–1800)', *Tempo* 23 (2007), 150–75.

Ventzke, Marcus, *Das Herzogtum Sachsen-Weimar-Eisenach 1775–1783. Ein Modellfall aufgeklärter Herrschaft?* (Cologne, 2004).

Vierhaus, Rudolf (ed.), *Deutsche patriotische und gemeinnützige Gesellschaften* (Munich, 1980).

Vocelka, Karl, 'Enlightenment in the Habsburg Monarchy: History of a Belated and Short-Lived Phenomenon', *Toleration in Enlightenment Europe*, ed. O. P. Grell and R. Porter (Cambridge, 2000), pp. 196–211.

Vogel, Jakob, 'Felder des Bergbaus. Entstehung und Grenzen einer wissenschaftlichen Expertise im späten 18. und 19. Jahrhundert', *Figurationen des Experten: Ambivalenzen der wissenschaftlichen Expertise im ausgehenden 18. und frühen 19. Jahrhundert*, ed. E. J. Engstrom, V. Hess and U. Thoms (Berlin, 2005), pp. 79–100.

Wagner, Richard E., 'The Cameralists: Fertile Sources for a New Science of Public Finance', *Handbook of the History of Economic Thought. Insights on the Founders of Modern Economics*, ed. J. G. Backhaus (New York, 2012), pp. 123–35.

Wakefield, Andre, 'Books, Bureaus, and the Historiography of Cameralism', *European Journal of Law and Economics* 19 (2005), 311–20.

————, 'Cameralism: A German Alternative to Mercantilism', *Mercantilism Reimagined. Political Economy in Early Modern Britain and its Empire*, ed. P. J. Stern and C. Wennerlind (New York, 2014), pp. 134–50.

————, *The Disordered Police State: German Cameralism as Science and Practice* (Chicago/London, 2009).

————, 'The Fiscal Logic of the Enlightened German Science,' *Making Knowledge in Early Modern Europe: Practices, Objects, and Texts, 1400–1800*, ed. P. H. Smith and, B. Schmidt (Chicago, 2007), pp. 273–87.

Walter, Ryan, *A Critical History of the Economy. On the Birth of the National and International Economies* (Abingdon, 2011).

————, 'Slingsby Bethel's Analysis of State Interests', *History of European Ideas* 41 (2015), 489–506.

Walz, Robert, 'Privilegien zum württembergischen Gewerberecht im 18. Jahrhundert', *Das Privileg im europäischen Vergleich*, ed. B. Dölemeyer and H. Mohnhaupt, vol. 1 (Frankfurt a.M., 1997), pp. 419–62.

Warde, Paul, *Ecology, Economy and State Formation in Early Modern Germany* (Cambridge, 2006).

————, 'Imposition, Emulation and Adaptation: Regulatory Regimes in the Commons of Early Modern Germany', *Environment and History* 19 (2013), 313–37.

————, 'The Invention of Sustainability', *Modern Intellectual History* 8 (2011), 153–70.

————, 'Sustainability, Resources and the Destiny of State in German Cameralist Thought', *Nature, Action and the Future: Political Thought and the Environment*, ed. K. Forrester and S. Smith (Cambridge, 2018) (forthcoming).

Weber, Max, *The Protestant Ethic and the 'Spirit' of Capitalism and other Writings*, ed. P. Baehr and G. C. Wells (Harmondsworth, 2002).

————, *Wirtschaft und Gesellschaft. Grundriss der verstehenden Soziologie*, 5th rev. edn (Tübingen, 1972).

Webler, Heinrich, *Die Kameral-Hohe-Schule zu Lautern (1774–1784). Eine Quellenstudie zur geschichtlichen Entwicklung und theoretischen Fundierung der Sozialökonomik als Universitätswissenschaft* (= Mitteilungen des Historischen Vereins der Pfalz, vol. 43) (Speyer, 1927).

Wehler, Hans-Ulrich, *Deutsche Gesellschaftsgeschichte. Vom Feudalismus des Alten Reiches bis zur Defensiven Modernisierung der Reformära 1700–1815* (Munich, 2006).

Weidmann, Marc, 'Un pasteur-naturaliste du XVIIIe siècle: Elie Bertrand (1713–1797)', *Revue historique vaudoise* 94 (1986), 63–108.

Wellmann, I., 'Merkantilistische Vorstellungen im 17. Jahrhundert und Ungarn', *Nouvelles études historiques, I. Publiées à l'occasion du XIIe Congrès International des Sciences Historiques par la Commission Nationale des Historiens Hongrois* (Budapest, 1965), pp. 315–54.

Whelan, Frederick G., 'Population and Ideology in the Enlightenment', *History of Political Thought* 12/1 (1991), 35–72.

Wick, Peter, 'Versuche zur Erbverpachtung und Aufhebung der Leibeigenschaft in Mecklenburg zu Beginn des 18. Jahrhunderts', *Jahrbuch für Wirtschaftsgeschichte* (1961), 45–60.

———, *Versuche zur Errichtung des Absolutismus in Mecklenburg in der ersten Hälfte des 18. Jahrhunderts. Ein Beitrag zur Geschichte des deutschen Territorialabsolutismus* (Berlin, 1964).

Widenmann, Kreisforstrath Wilhelm von, *Geschichtliche Einleitung in die Forstwissenschaft* (Tübingen, 1837).

Willoweit, Dietmar, 'Gewerbeprivileg und "natürliche" Gewerbefreiheit. Strukturen des preußischen Gewerberechts im 18. Jahrhundert', *Vom Gewerbe zum Unternehmen. Studien zum Recht der gewerblichen Wirtschaft im 18. und 19. Jahrhundert*, ed. K. O. Scherner and D. Willoweit (Darmstadt, 1982), pp. 60–111.

Wirtschafter, Elise Kimerling, *Russia's Age of Serfdom (1649–1861)* (Oxford, 2008).

Wischermann, Clemens, *Preußischer Staat und westfälische Unternehmer zwischen Spätmerkantilismus und Liberalismus* (Cologne/Weimar/Vienna, 1992).

Witte, Hans, *Kulturbilder aus Alt-Mecklenburg* (Leipzig, 1911).

Zbroschzyk, Markus, 'Die preußische Peuplierungspolitik in den rheinischen Territorien Kleve, Geldern und Moers im Spannungsfeld von Theorie und räumlicher Umsetzung im 17.–18. Jahrhundert' (Inaugural-Dissertation, Bonn, 2014).

Ziekow, Jan, *Über Freizügigkeit und Aufenthalt. Paradigmatische überlegungen zum grundrechtlichen Freiheitsschutz in historischer und verfassungsrechtlicher Perspektive* (Tübingen, 1997).

Zielenziger, Kurt, *Die alten deutschen Kameralisten. Ein Beitrag zur Geschichte der Nationalökonomie und zum Problem des Merkantilismus* (Jena, 1914).

Zimmermann, Friedrich Wilhelm Rudolf, *Die Zivilliste in den deutschen Staaten* (Stuttgart, 1919).

Zincke, Georg Heinrich, *Anfangsgründe der Cameralwissenschaft worinne dessen Grundriß weiter ausgeführet und verbessert wird. Part II* (Leipzig, 1755).

Zoepfl, Heinrich Matthias, *Grundsätze des gemeinen deutschen Staatsrechts mit besonderer Rücksicht auf das allgemeine Staatsrecht und auf die neuesten Zeitverhältnisse*, 2 vols, 5th edn (Leipzig, 1863).

Zwierlein, Cornel, *Der gezähmte Prometheus. Feuer und Sicherheit zwischen Früher Neuzeit und Moderne* (= Umwelt und Gesellschaft, Band 3, Göttingen, 2011).

———, 'Grenzen der Versicherbarkeit als Epochenindikatoren? Von der europäischen Sattelzeit zur Globalisierung des 19. Jahrhunderts', *Geschichte und Gesellschaft* 38 (2012), 423–52.

————, 'Insurances as Part of Human Security, their Timescapes, and Spatiality', *Historical Social Research* 35 (2010), 253–74.

————, 'Sicherheit durch Versicherung: Ein frühneuzeitliches Erfolgserlebnis', *Sicherheit in der Frühen Neuzeit. Norm – Praxis – Repräsentation*, ed. Chr. Kampmann and U. Niggemann (= Frühneuzeit-Impulse, vol. 2, Cologne, 2013), pp. 381–99.

Index

Abarca de Bolea, Pedro Pablo (Count of
  Aranda) 166
Åbo (Turku), University of 12, 27, 63
Achenwall, Gottfried 256
agricultural production and husbandry
  3, 6, 22, 63–4, 136–7
  Berch 31–2, 33–4, 193
  Denmark 203, 204, 205, 207, 208,
    209–12, 215, 217, 218, 220
  Germany 95, 99, 102, 104, 134, 135,
    230–2
  and population 69–70, 92
  reform and policy 15, 21, 74, 111, 140,
    152, 170, 173, 203, 225
  Russia 74, 84, 86
  serfdom 105, 106, 107
  Smith, Adam 18, 41
  writings and research 18, 24, 26–7,
    28–9, 57, 63, 69–70, 105, 111, 129,
    134, 234, 238, 264
  See also insurance, crop insurance
Albion, Robert Greenhalgh 50, 54
Alexander I, Emperor of Russia 87
Amussen, Susan Dwyer 182, 183, 195
Amvrosii, Archbishop, Russia 78
Andrada, José Bonifácio de 174–5
Anton, Theodor 8
Anton, Wenzel (Prince of Kaunitz-
  Rietberg) 165
Arnim, Bernd von 108
arvefæstereformen (tenure reform),
  Denmark 210–11, 216
Ascheraden, Baron Schoultz von 86
Austria 3, 22, 39, 68, 161–5
  Commission of Police
    (Policeyhofkommission) 162
  Directorium in publicis et cameralibus
    161–2
  War of the Austrian Succession 139
  Zensurkommission 163

Autenrieth, Jakob Friedrich 151
balance of trade 27–8, 35, 38, 42, 44, 134,
  137, 189
Baltic area
  agrarian production 63–4
  'Baltic Cameralism' 12–13, 40, 41
  forestry and timber trade 54–6
  Great Britain and 46–7, 48, 50–4
  industrialisation 56
  long-distance trade 40, 56–7
  products and distribution 50–7
  trade in 39–64
  writings on 56, 57–63
  See also Denmark; Great Britain;
    Heckscher; mercantilism;
    oeconomia
Baumeister, Friedrich-Christian 66
Bavaria 93, 139, 140, 141
  forestry ordinances 115
Beccaria, Cesare 66, 67
Becher, Johann Joachim 5, 8, 31–6, 45,
  46, 105, 119, 194
  influence 30, 35, 46, 69, 143, 168
  writings 9, 32–4, 94, 113, 119
Beckmann, Johann 138
Beckmann, Johann Gottlieb 62, 113, 126,
  128–9
Bensen, Carl Heinrich Daniel 253
Berch, Anders 11, 27, 38, 182, 187–95
  hushållning 194, 197
  writings 14, 17–18, 36, 57–8, 194
Berg, Duchy of 147
Berlin, University of 255
Bertrand, Eli 156
Besold, Christoph 8
Betskoi, Count Ivan 71, 77
Bielfeld, Jacob Friedrich Freiherr von
  66–7, 70, 158, 178, 250
Blackstone, Sir William 67

Boerhaave, Herman   165
Bohemia   162, 171
Bornitz, Jakob   8
Botero, Giovanni   22
Bourdieu, Pierre   148
Boymont, Violante Maria Josepha von
        (Countess of Payrsberg)   164
Bradley, Richard   121
Bragança Sousa Tavares da Silva
        Mascarenhas, D. Pedro de (Duke of
        Lafões)   160
Brahetrolleborg, Denmark
        agricultural reforms   203, 209–10, 212
        as crown fiefdom   218
        economic development   211–14, 216
        history of   208–9
        teacher training college   213, 215
        tenancy arrangements   210–11, 216
        See also Reventlow, Christian Ditlev;
                Reventlow, Johan Ludvig
Brandenburg   94, 101–2
        Ämter of Altmark   102
        Uckermark   101
Brandenburg-Prussia   21, 95, 97, 139
        cloth manufacturing   140
Brazil   167, 168, 170, 171, 173–4
        mining in   175–6, 177
Browne, George, Governor-General   86
bruk
        bruksfolket   196
        brukshushållning   14, 196–7, 199–200
        brukspatron   14, 27, 179–82, 186–7,
                194, 195, 199–200
        Leufsta bruk   179, 180, 181, 182, 194,
                196, 197–8, 200, 201
Buffon, Comte de   127
Bülow, Hans von   255

Câmara, Manuel Ferreira da   174, 175–6
cameralism (Cameralwissenschaft/
        Kameralwissenschaften)   6, 7–8, 19,
        30–1, 57, 63, 107, 111, 116, 127, 129,
        148–9, 156, 230, 239, 241–3, 256, 267
        and administrative practice   8–11, 14,
                28, 107, 111, 129, 148–9, 230, 239,
                242–3, 249–54, 256, 257, 258, 261,
                263, 267
        agriculture   129, 193, 231–2, 257
        book cameralism   111, 114
        and the common good   1, 33, 37, 148,
                207, 245

        and foreign markets   13, 134, 137
        Germany and   11–16, 39, 67, 111–31,
                133–54, 188, 239–61
        historiography   4, 6, 91, 134
        Holy Roman Empire   133, 147, 153,
                230
        in Iberia   157, 158, 159, 264
        impact   3–4, 9–11, 16, 91–2, 153–4
        and jurisprudence   15, 253–4, 257,
                258–9, 260
        and mercantilism   6, 18, 19, 42, 43,
                134, 143, 152, 153, 184, 187–95
        mining and   6, 12, 14, 136, 158, 171
        modern interpretations of   242–3, 245,
                249, 250–1, 265, 266, 268
        policy   138–9, 147–52, 253
        and political economy   5, 11, 18, 124,
                125, 245, 249, 255, 261
        and population   68–9, 92, 93, 105
        Portugal   156, 168, 177
        practice and publication   111, 122–9,
                263–4, 265–6
        and serfdom   91–110, 94, 100–8,
                109–10
        social implications   184–5
        spread of   3–4, 39, 67, 156, 157
        and technology   7, 14, 138, 153, 257
        textile industry   140
        translation   23–5, 66–7, 70, 159, 170,
                178
        as university science   25–8, 39, 113,
                121, 131, 135–6, 149–50, 239, 242,
                255, 258
        writers on cameralism   7, 17–18, 32–6,
                45, 128, 135, 188, 206, 243, 263–4,
                265–6
        See also Becher; Berch; forestry;
                insurance; Justi; mercantilism;
                Russia
Carlowitz, Hans Carl von   13, 59, 113,
        119–21, 122, 128, 130–1
Carvalho e Melo, Sebastião José de (Count
        of Oeiras and Marquis of Pombal). See
        Pombal, Marquis of
Cary, John   25
Catherine I, Empress of Russia   66
Catherine II, Empress, cameralism and
        13, 65–89
Celsius, Anders   27
Chancellery of Guardianship of Foreigners
        80

and children 71–2
Foundling Homes 71–25
interest in ideas 66–8
and medical services 75–9
Nakaz ('Great Instruction') 67, 68, 73–4, 86, 87
patronage 66
and population growth 68, 71, 72–3, 75–84, 87
Provincial Statute 79
and serfdom 85–7
Chappe d'Auteroche, Jean-Baptiste 72
Charles XI of Sweden 20, 97–8
Charles XII of Sweden 20, 99
Christian V of Denmark 218
civil list, development of 252, 253–4, 257, 260–1
Claesson, Johann 98
Coimbra, University of 164, 170, 171, 174
Colbert, Jean-Baptiste 142, 144, 164
Colerus, Johann 117, 118
Colloredo, Count Rudolf, Imperial Vice-Chancellor 164
Commissioners for Trade and Plantations (UK) 51
common good 135, 148, 170, 207, 217–18, 219, 245
Copenhagen, University of 205
Corni, Gustavo 93
Cotta, Heinrich 126
courts, legal 160, 161, 167
courts, royal 46, 159–60, 165, 240, 245, 251–2, 253, 254, 260–1, 263, 267
cameralism 8
development of 5
forestry 117
role of 2
Russia 87
Coutinho, Rodrigo de Sousa, Secretary of the Overseas Affairs 175
Cramer, Johan Andreas 215

Danckelmann, Eberhard von 28
Darjes, Joachim Georg 8, 108, 254
Daun, Count Leopold Joseph von 165
De Geer, Charles 179, 180, 181, 182, 186, 199, 200
De Geer, Jean Jacques 179
De Geer, Louis (the elder) 186
De Geer, Louis (the younger) 179

De La Mare, Nicholas 32
Defoe, Daniel 48
Delhuyar, Fausto 173, 178
Delhuyar, Juan José 173
Denmark 3, 100, 109, 203–20
agricultural reform 215–17
education 214–15
peasants 204–5, 208, 209–10, 214–16
religion and economy 203–4
See also Baltic area, forestry and timber trade; forestry
Dithmar, Justus Christoph 8, 12, 23, 26, 28–31, 32, 35, 38, 105, 113, 240
influence 17, 18, 32, 34, 36–7, 121–2
Döbel, Heinrich Wilhelm 128
Donauer, Christoph 119
du Brillet, Le Cler 32

East Elbian region 93, 94, 100
economic sciences 25, 63–4
Eisen, Johann Georg 72, 86, 106
Elagin, Ivan 72, 85, 86
Eleanore Ernestine, Countess of Daun 164
Elizabeth Petrovna, Empress of Russia 68, 70
'emulation', process of 23, 24, 25, 38, 156
Enlightenment 88, 123, 222, 231
cameralists and 39, 93, 205, 231, 246
Continental 150, 156, 203
politicisation of 135, 232
Russia 65, 66, 68, 75, 88
serfdom 93, 110
Erbpacht (Brandenburg-Prussia) 102, 103, 104
Erlangen, University of 256
Ernst von Gotha, Duke 26
Evelyn, John 120, 121
exports, regulation of 141–2

Felice, Fortuné-Barthélemy De 155–6
Fichte, Johann Gottlieb 246
Finanzwissenschaft and *Finanzlehre* 241, 253, 256, 261
Finland 12, 20
timber trade 55
Flemish Council (*Niederländischen Rates*) 164
'Florinus' (pen name) 113, 119
Fonvizin, Denis 67
forestry 49, 58–63, 111–31

administration   118–19, 124
Baltic   40, 56
and cameralism   13, 26, 58–9, 63,
   122–3, 126–8, 257
Denmark   213, 219
forest ordinances   13, 119, 121–2,
   123–4, 127–8
Forstordnungen, Germany   114–15,
   116, 117
France   120, 126
historical context   114–18
Portugal   167, 177
writings   30, 34, 49, 58–9, 62, 119–21,
   122, 123, 125–7, 130
See also timber
Forstwissenschaft   112, 128, 131, 267
development of   267
forest science and training   63, 131
texts   116
Foundling Homes, Russia   71–2, 88
Fragoso, Joaquim Pedro   174
France   4, 24, 44, 46, 47, 48, 49, 63, 64,
   144, 145, 151, 152, 174, 263, 264
cameralism   4, 138, 157
police   166, 170
See also forestry; Physiocracy
Francis I, Austria   162, 165
Frankfurt, Grand Duchy of   254
Frankfurt an der Oder (Viadrina),
   University of   11, 37, 135, 240, 254,
   259
Frederick I, King of Prussia (Frederick III,
   Great Elector)   21, 25, 96, 101, 102
Frederick II ('the Great')   22, 23, 70, 140,
   150, 158, 237
Frederick William, Elector of Brandenburg
   21, 94–5
Frederick William I, King of Prussia
   9, 22, 96–7, 140, 141, 142
Free Economic Society, Russia   84–5
Freiberg Mining Academy (Bergakademie),
   Saxony   140, 158, 171–5, 177
Freiburg, University of   240
Freire, Pascoal José de Melo   170–1
Fürstenau, Johann Hermann   26–7
Furtado, Francisco Xavier Mendonça   168

Garve, Christian   207
Gasser, Simon Peter   26, 31, 105, 121
Genovesi, Antonio   25, 27
Gentz, Friedrich von   247

German Alliance   254
Germany
agriculture   29, 63, 236–7
and cameralism   3, 4, 11, 22, 30, 46,
   63, 97, 133–54, 226, 239–61, 240
'economic population theory' (ökonomische Bevölkerungstheorie)   94
forestry   59, 62, 111–31
idealism   245–6
industrial development   126, 139,
   140–1, 153
industrial policy   138, 141, 143–7
insurance   15, 223–4, 227, 236–7
and Peuplierung   92–5
Physiocracy   252, 259–60
serfdom   96–7, 231
training of officials   149–50
universities in   26, 39, 63, 135, 136,
   226, 239, 240, 250
See also Bavaria; Brandenburg;
   Brandenburg-Prussia; Frankfurt;
   Holy Roman Empire; insurance;
   Mecklenburg; Pomerania; Prussia;
   Saxony; Westphalia; Württemberg
Gewerbepolicey   133, 136, 152, 153, 154
Gießen, University of   240
Gleditsch, Johann Gottlieb   62
Glückseligkeit. See happiness
Göttingen, University of   205, 240, 255,
   259
Great Britain   19, 25, 44, 45, 46, 106, 117,
   145, 203
and the Baltic   46–50
and cameralism   4, 144
overseas trade   46–50, 64, 183
timber imports   52–3, 120
Great Northern War (1700–21)   20, 22, 51
Greifswald, University of   63
Gustavus III of Sweden   21, 190–1

Habsburg Monarchy   22, 136, 151–2
cameralist state   93, 149
Halle, University of   11, 37, 135, 205, 240
Hamburger General-Feuer-Cassa   224,
   227
Handlungswissenschaft   261
happiness (Glückseligkeit/lycksalighet)
   18, 23, 32, 37, 136, 245–9, 260
Hardenberg, Karl August von   255, 258
Harrach, Count Alois Raymund   165
Hartig, Georg   126

Haugwitz, Count Friedrich Wilhelm von
    161–2, 163
Hausvater literature (*Hausväterliteratur*)
    5, 25, 33, 63, 112, 113, 119, 129, 184,
    190, 194, 196, 200
    Becher   119
    and *hushållning*   192
    origins   117
    Pfeiffer   125
Heckscher, Eli F.   17–18, 43, 134, 188
    influence   33
    Mercantilism   19, 45, 46, 49, 50
    views   19–20, 30, 44–5
Heckscher–Ohlin model of comparative
    advantage   45
Hennings, August   252
Henry VIII of England   117
Heresbach, Conrad von   117
Hermann, Court Counsellor B. F.   83
Hildebrand, Bruno   42–3, 244
Hobbes, Thomas   32, 38
Hohberg, Wolf Helmhard von   59, 113,
    119
Holberg, Ludvig   205
Holstein-Plön, Duchy of   105
Holy Roman Empire   21, 133, 147–8, 153,
    171, 230–1, 235
    agriculture   231
    industrial policy   139
    insurance   224
Hörnigk, Philipp Wilhelm von   8, 45, 46
householding (*hushållning*)   18, 179–201
    analysis of   187, 190, 191, 194–5
    Berch and   190–1, 194, 197
    divine   187, 191, 195, 200
    enskild (individual) householding   18
    establishment of   181
    gender aspects   192
    Haushalten   182
    hierarchical aspects of   200
    private   182, 192, 195, 196, 199, 201
    public   182, 192, 194, 196, 199, 200,
    201
    Rinman   194–5
    Touscher   181, 196–200
    See also bruk
Hufeland, Gottlieb   243, 257, 260
Humboldt, Wilhelm von   246–7, 255
Hume, David   25, 35, 71
Hungary   100, 163, 171

immigration   33, 70, 79, 80, 95, 97
    Catherine the Great and   13, 79–80, 86
Ingolstadt, University of   240
Innsbruck, University of   240
insurance   221–38
    cameralism   222, 224, 226–36
    crop insurance   222, 223, 224, 230–8,
    267
    development   16
    in early modern period   15, 223–4
    Jung-Stilling   235–6
    principles   223
iron making
    in Britain   47
    shipbuilding   56
    in Sweden   14, 20, 24, 27, 39, 125, 176,
    179, 180–1, 182, 186–7, 194, 196–7,
    198–9, 200

Jakob, Ludwig Heinrich von   256–7, 258,
    260
Jesuits   163–4, 235
Joseph II, Emperor   9, 16, 80, 93, 162
Jung-Stilling, Johann Heinrich   7, 8, 65,
    136, 150, 235–6, 253
Justi, Johann Heinrich Gottlob von
    85, 108, 131, 158, 159, 244, 249
    on agriculture   15, 107, 231–2
    on general happiness   244–5
    on industrial policy   143–4, 146,
    148–9, 153
    influence   67–8, 126, 138, 149, 156,
    159, 170, 241, 256
    on insurance   15, 228–9, 233–4, 237
    ironworks at Vietz   125
    and manufacturing   14, 138, 142, 143,
    146
    on police science   138, 170, 171
    on population   65, 69
    role in 'politicisation of the
    Enlightenment'   232
    Russia   67–8
    on serfdom   14, 85, 107, 109
    travels   136, 163
    writings   9, 113, 124–5, 138, 139, 145,
    149, 170, 171, 225, 241
    Zensurkommission   163

Kant, Immanuel   66, 248, 265
Karamzin, Nikolai   88

Karl Leopold, Duke of Mecklenburg
    103–4
Karl Maximilian, Prince of Dietrichstein
    165
Kaufhold, Karl Heinrich   9–10
Kerstens, Dr Johann   72
Khevenhüller-Metsch, Princely family
    165
Kiel, University of   63
King, Gregory   192
Kinsky, Count Philipp Joseph   165
Klagenfurt, University of   240
Klaveren, Jacob van   134
Kling, Peter   126
Klingstedt, Timofei von   86
Klock, Kaspar   8
Knies, Karl   244
Kollonich, Leopold   100
Krafft, Academician Wolfgang Ludwig
    72, 83
Kraus, Hans-Christof   258
Kryger, Johan Fredrik   35–6

Lafões, Duke of. See Bragança Sousa
    Tavares da Silva Mascarenhas, D. Pedro
    de (Duke of Lafões)
Lamprecht, Georg Friedrich   143
Lamy, Pierre and Hugues   94
Lau, Theodor Ludwig   8, 32
Lautern, Kameral-Hohe-Schule zu   226
Lautern Society   150, 225
Lefebure, Jean   196, 199
Leib, Johann Georg   8
Leibniz, Gottfried Wilhelm   15, 226–8,
    237
Leiden, University of   282
Leipzig, University of   150, 205, 240
Leipziger Ökonomische Sozietät   150
Leopold I, Emperor   100, 227
Linnaeus, Carl   27, 191
Lisbon earthquake (1755)   157, 159
    impact of on Portuguese politics   157,
    159–60
Lisch, Georg Christian   104
List, Friedrich   19, 24, 244
Livonia   86, 97–8
Lluch, Ernest   3, 11, 158, 166, 173, 287
Loën, Johann Michael von   105
Lomonosov, Mikhail   70–1, 81
Lorenz, Heinrich Reichard (Count Daun)
    164

Louis XIV of France   120
Löwenhielm, Carl Gustaf   191
Lowood, Henry   113
Luben, Christian Friedrich (von Wulffen)
    101–3

Magnusson, Lars   188, 189, 190
Maier, Hans   244
Maifreda, Germano   192
Mainz, University of   136
Malthus, Thomas Robert   83
manufactories, state-run   133, 135–8,
    141–54, 170, 264
Maria Theresa, Empress   68, 139, 162,
    164, 165
Marperger, Paul Jacob   143
Martini, Karl von   163
masts, ships'   46, 48, 50, 51–5, 56
Mecklenburg   13, 56, 103–4
Medicus, Friedrich Casimir   226
Melon, Jean-François   151
Menshikov, Aleksandr   81
mercantilism   42
    and the all-present divinity   187–95
    and cameralism   6–7, 18, 35, 184
    German theories   19, 42–3, 134
    Germany   138
    Great-Britain   134
    Imperial mercantilism
        (Reichsmerkantilismus)   138
    problem of mercantilism   43–6, 152,
        168
    Russia   66
    Sweden   187–90
    theory of trade   35, 137
Methuen Treaty (UK–Portugal)   45
Meurer, Noé   116
Mexico   173, 178
Meyer, Torsten   184
Mill, James   45
Minas Gerais, Brazil   175
mining   14, 20, 63, 130, 140, 167, 193
    and cameralism   6, 12, 14, 136, 158,
        171
    mining development   194, 225
    mining sciences and the Bergakademie
        171–7
    training   140, 158
    writers and   34, 57, 120, 127
Mirabeau, Count of (Honoré Gabriel
    Riqueti)   21, 69, 124

Moltke, Adam Gottlob 204
Montesquieu 66, 67, 69
Moscow, University of 12, 71, 72, 76
Moser, Johann Jakob 151
Moser, Wilhelm Gottfried 59, 61, 113, 122, 126–8, 131, 151
Motz, Friedrich von 255
Müller, Adam 244

Napoleon Bonaparte 47–8, 245, 254
Nationalökonomie 15, 239, 245, 257, 267
natural rights, concept of 32, 37
Netherlands, The 4, 137, 274
Nystad, Peace of (1721) 20

Obrecht, Georg 8
oeconomia/oeconomie 26, 33, 121, 182–6, 191, 197, 240, 257
Berch on 190, 201
cameralists and 5, 17, 29, 58, 126
literature 14, 200
oeconomia privata 194
oeconomia publica 58, 186, 193, 194
oeconomiae divina, concept of 36, 191
Oeconomische Nachrichten 232, 234, 238
writings on 26, 29, 30, 59, 121
Old Believers, Russia 81
Oriental Academy, Austria 163
Orlov, Count Grigorii 80, 86
Osse, Melchior 8

peasants
Brandenburg-Prussia 95, 96, 97, 98, 101–2, 104
cameralism and 105, 106, 107, 109, 230, 232
Denmark 100, 204–5, 208, 209, 210, 214, 215, 216, 217, 218, 219, 220
forestry and 112, 129
and insurance 229, 232, 233, 235, 236, 237
Russia 13, 72, 73, 74, 78, 80, 81, 83, 84, 85, 86–7, 88, 89
Sweden 20, 21, 186, 189, 197, 199
thinkers and 110, 191
See also serfdom
Peñaflorida, Count of 173
Penther, Friedrich 122
Petander, Karl 188

Peter I the Great, Emperor of Russia 65, 66, 70, 81, 87–8
Peter III, Emperor of Russia 86
Petty, William 169, 192
Pfalz-Zweibrücken, Duchy of 99
Pfeiffer, Ferdinand Friedrich 15, 228
on insurance 228, 229, 233, 234–5, 237
Pfeiffer, Johann Friedrich von 8, 113, 123, 139, 250, 259
writings 125–6, 141, 142
Philippi, Johann Albrecht 107
Physiocracy 4, 125, 252, 261
cameralists and 137, 205, 207
critique of cameralism 252
Denmark 205
influence 46, 260
physiocrats 42, 46, 69, 110, 207, 254
and serfdom 93, 110
Smith, Adam, and 24, 41, 42, 46, 254
views of human world 42
Pina Manique, Diogo Inácio de 155, 166
plague, Russia 78
Poland 24, 45, 47, 81, 96
first partition of 22
police (Polizei, Policey) 14, 16, 68, 112, 116, 206, 240, 241, 251, 256, 257
Berch on 33, 35
and cameralism 18, 135, 151, 156, 183, 206–7, 216, 240, 241–2, 250, 256
commercial police 43
Dithmar on 17, 28–9, 30
forestry 113, 114, 115, 123
Justi on 68, 69, 138, 170, 171, 233
Lieutenancy General of Police, Portugal 160, 162, 166
'medical police' 16, 79
police ordinances (Polizeiordnungen) 95, 109, 113, 114–15, 124, 130, 139, 157, 257
police state 66, 243, 249, 250
Policeyhofkommission 162
in Portugal 155–78
and the Portuguese monarchy 166–71
Pölitz, Karl Heinrich Ludwig 253, 259
Polizeiwissenschaft 33, 57, 67, 116, 135, 138, 156, 170, 173, 178, 189, 205–6, 207, 224, 234, 241, 256
writers on 26, 31, 39, 67, 69, 70, 124, 234, 240, 241
Pombal, Marquis of 159, 160, 163–6, 167, 168, 176, 177

and Austrian reforms   164–6
and Brazil   168
educational reforms   174
and Jesuits   163–4
and Lieutenancy General of Police
   166
Pomerania   98, 102–3
   serfdom in   96–7, 98–9
Pontoppidan, Erik   203–4
populationism in Europe and Russia
   68–75, 168–9
   beliefs and theories, eighteenth-century
   68–9
   fear of overpopulation   69
   impact and significance of   87–9
   population policy (Peuplierungspolitik)
   33, 70, 92–5
Portugal   45, 164, 166, 172
   administration   157–61
   cameralism in   11, 14, 155–78, 156, 159
   Casa dos Contos   160–1
   Council of Finance (Conselho da
   Fazenda)   161
   Directory (regulations)   167, 168,
   169–70
   Lieutenancy General of Police   160,
   167
   'police matters'   155, 158, 167, 170
   Portuguese–Brazilian economic thought
   171
   Royal School for Noblemen (Real
   Colégio dos Nobres)   164
   Royal Treasury (Erário Régio)   160–1,
   163, 176
   Secretariat of the Kingdom's Affairs
   159, 160, 163, 166, 167
   See also forestry; Lisbon earthquake;
   Pombal
Postlethwayt, Malachy   264
Potemkin, Prince Grigorii   80
Potsdam, Edict of (1685)   95
Prague, University of   240
Prussia   13, 19, 20–3, 115, 125, 245
   and cameralism   11, 12, 25–6, 43–4,
   149, 264
   civil service   258–9
   domain management   102–3, 104
   economy   22
   forestry   55, 62, 122
   industry   143, 144, 150
   insurance   237

monopolies   150
peasants   95–6
and Physiocracy   24
Prussian Reforms   258
serfdom   95, 96, 97
silk industry   143
trade   47
universities   25–6
See also Brandenburg-Prussia; forestry
Prussian Civil Code (Allgemeines
   Landrecht für die Preußischen Staaten)
   258
public sphere (Öffentlichkeit)   37, 136,
   199
Pufendorf, Samuel   32, 37
Pugachev, Emel'ian   87
Pushkin, Aleksandr   65
Pütter, Johann Stephan   255

Quesnay, François   41–2

Radishchev, Aleksandr   88
Raeff, Marc   66, 79, 250–1
Rantzau, Christian von   108
Réaumur, René Antoine Ferchault de   120,
   126
Reichswald, Nürnberg   116
Reinert, Sophus A.   7, 25
religion and natural disaster   221–2
Renner, Andreas   75, 76, 78, 79
Reventlow, Christian Ditlev   203, 205,
   207, 212, 216, 220
Reventlow, Johan Ludvig   14–15, 203–20
   agricultural reforms   209–11
   cameralist objectives   212
   and the Crown   218–19
   Lutheran standpoint   216–17
   opposition from tenants   216
   and Physiocrats   207
   and the poor   215
   promoting industry   211–14
   and schooling   214–15
   study   205–6
Ricardo, David   45
Rinman, Sven   182, 194–5
Rinteln, University of   26, 240
Rochow, Friedrich Eberhard von   214–15
Rohr, Christian von   121
Rohr, J. B. von   58, 60, 61
Roscher, Wilhelm   18, 243
Rössig, Carl Gottlob   8, 143, 254

Rostock, University of 63
Royal Basque Society of Friends of the
    Country (Real Sociedad Bascongada de
    Amigos del País) 173
Royal Navy, UK 41, 46, 47, 48, 50, 56
Rügen, Sweden 98, 99
Runefelt, Leif 189, 190
Russia 4, 13, 74–5, 84–5
    cameralism 16, 39, 65–89, 264
    census 81–2
    Commission for the Composition of
        the Project of a New Law Code
        67, 74–5
    Free Economic Society and serfdom
        84–5
    immigration and emigration 79–81
    Justi and 68
    legislative reform 67
    marriage in 83–4
    medical services 75–6
    political theory 65–6, 67, 70
    populationist ideas 68–73, 79–80, 82,
        84, 87–9
    public health 79
    serfdom 13, 84–7, 87–9, 106
    trade 47, 54
    See also Catherine II; serfdom;
        smallpox

Saldern, Caspar von 86
Salvius, Lars 191, 194
Sanches, Dr Antonio (Nunes) Ribeiro
    83, 164, 165
Savary, Jacques 264
Saxony 139–40, 142–3
    Rétablissement 139–40, 142, 151
Say, Jean-Baptiste 256, 257
Schäfer, Ingrid 125
Schimmelmann, Ernst 213–14, 216
Schleswig-Holstein 108, 203, 208
Schlettwein, Johann August 252
Schlözer, August Ludwig 72, 82–3, 256
Schmalz, Heinrich 8
Schmalz, Theodor Anton Heinrich 253,
    254–5
Schmeltz (estate administrator) 213
Schmoller, Gustav 19, 43, 44
Schreber, Daniel Gottfried 150
Schröder, Wilhelm von 5, 8, 30, 45–6,
    105, 162
Schroll, Henning 212

Schumpeter, Elizabeth Boody 51, 52–3,
    54
Schumpeter, Joseph 168, 243
Schytte, Professor Andreas 205–7, 216,
    218, 220
Seckendorff, Veit Ludwig von 5, 8, 105,
    259
    on forestry 118–19
    influence 25–6, 33
    writings 22, 26, 113, 118
Secretariat of the Kingdom's Affairs,
    Portugal 159, 160, 163, 166, 167
serfdom (Leibeigenschaft) 13, 91–110
    abolition of 13, 16, 93, 94, 96, 97, 100,
        110
    Denmark 100
    Germany 13, 95–6, 97, 101, 104, 108,
        207, 231
    as hindrance to peopling 94–100,
        108–9
    Hungary 100
    Justi 13, 85, 107, 232
    opposition to 13, 86, 94, 97, 100–8,
        109
    Pomerania 99, 103
    Russia 84, 85–7, 88, 89
    and state population 94–100, 108
    stavnsbånd system, Denmark 205
    Sweden 97–8
    See also peasants
Seven Years' War (1756–63) 21, 48, 54,
    68, 138, 139, 142, 150, 165
Shcherbatov, Mikhail 72
Shpilevskii, M. M. 87
Shuvalov, Count Petr 70, 71, 81
Sievers, Count Johann Jakob 86
Silesia 22, 139, 162
silk production 20, 139, 140, 143, 144
    and monopolies 146–7
Silva-Tarouca, Duke of. See Teles da Silva
Sinzendorf, Count Philipp Ludwig 165
Skinner, Quentin 23–4
Slack, Paul 10, 16
Small, Albion 6–7, 91, 111
smallpox, Russia 76, 77–8, 83
Smith, Adam 18, 24, 35, 41–2, 43, 45, 46,
    89, 239
    influences 243, 244, 254, 255, 265
Somerwell (estate administrator) 213
Sonderweg 11, 18–19

Sonnenfels, Joseph von   8, 14, 135–6, 139,
    143, 151, 244, 249, 259
  methodology   82
  writings   70, 143, 145, 153, 241
Sorø, Academy of, Denmark   205
Spain   64, 151, 166, 168, 172, 173
  and cameralist theory   158–9, 178, 264
  War of the Spanish Succession   141,
    158
Staatswissenschaften   15, 246, 260, 261,
    261
stamping offices (Beschauanstalten)   144
'state economy' (Staatswirtschaft)   145,
    257, 261
Stein, Heinrich Friedrich Karl vom   255
Steuart, James   151, 265
Stolberg, Louise   207, 208
Storch, Heinrich Friedrich   89
Subtil, José   159
Süßmilch, Johann Peter   33, 70, 106–7
Swebilius, Georg   180
Sweden   20–3, 27–8, 97–8, 99, 179–201
  accounting practices   198, 201
  cameralism   3, 4, 11–12, 31, 39, 46
  Cap Party   20, 21
  economic activity   21, 27, 34, 37, 46,
    47, 49, 54, 55, 56, 182
  economic teaching   27, 31, 35, 46, 188
  Great Northern War and impact
    20, 21, 22
  Hat Party   20, 21, 28, 33
  iron manufacture   14, 20, 24, 27, 47,
    179, 180–2, 186–7, 194–9
  Physiocracy   24
  serfdom   97–9
  See also Berch, hushållning
Swieten, Gerard van   163, 165

tar production   47, 48, 50, 51, 52, 53, 55
Tatishchev, Vasilii   70
Tautscher, Anton   8
Teles da Silva, Manuel (Earl/Duke of Silva-
    Tarouca)   162, 164
textile industry   140, 141, 142
Theresian Military Academy
    (Theresianische Militärakademie,
    Theresianum)   163, 165
Thirty Years' War   21, 118, 129
Thomasius, Christian   37
Thünen, Johann Heinrich von   62
  Thünen model   55

timber   51, 54–5, 57, 115, 116, 120, 130,
    214
  changing uses in   56
  Great Britain trade   39, 40, 41, 46, 52–3
  ships   50–1
  trade   13, 40, 54–6, 62, 63, 111, 126
  See also Baltic area, forestry and timber
    trade; forestry; tar production
Tooke, William   73
Touscher, Eric   179–81, 182, 187, 190
  brukshushållning   196–200
  and Charles De Geer   200
Transylvania   175, 176, 177
Tribe, Keith   8, 12–13, 16, 37, 183–4, 190,
    194, 243, 245
  on cameralism   25, 26, 239, 242, 249,
    250, 260
Trunk, Johann Jakob   131
Tully, James   23

Udolov, Fedot   86
Uhr, Isaac Johan   192, 194, 197
Uppsala, University of   12, 17, 27, 63, 187

Vatican   164
venereal disease, Russia   74, 78
Vergara, Seminary of   173
Viadrina, Frankfurt on the Oder   28, 240,
    259
Vienna, Congress of   254
Vienna, University of   163
Villalobos e Vasconcelos, João Rosado
    de   155
Vincke, Ludwig von   255
Voltaire   65, 66
Voß, Christian Daniel   15, 255–6

Wachenhusen, Johann Georg   106, 109
Wargentin, Pehr   201
Weber, Friedrich Benedict   244
Weber, Max   250, 251
Weidmann, Marc   156
weights and measures   44, 145
  defined   185
  scholarly understandings of   184–6
Werner, Professor Abraham Gottlob   174
Wernigerode   124
Westphalia   115, 144, 145, 254
Westphalia, Peace of (1648)   92, 98
Whelan, Frederick   68
Whig interpretation of history   23

Wick, Peter   104
Widenmann, Kreisforstrath Wilhelm von
   58, 62
Wolff, Christian   27, 35, 37, 65–6, 70, 190
   and happiness   246
Württemberg, Duchy of   115, 123–5, 151
Würzburg, University of   240

Zanthier   122
Zaporozhian Cossack 'host'   73
Zech, Johann Christian von   107–8
Zielenziger, Kurt   7, 91, 241
Zincke, Georg Heinrich   8, 105, 113,
   123–4, 250
Zschackwitz, Johann Ehrenfried   32

PEOPLE, MARKETS, GOODS:
ECONOMIES AND SOCIETIES IN HISTORY

ISSN: 2051-7467

PREVIOUS TITLES

1. *Landlords and Tenants in Britain, 1440–1660:
Tawney's* Agrarian Problem *Revisited*
edited by Jane Whittle, 2013

2. *Child Workers and Industrial Health in Britain, 1780–1850*
Peter Kirby, 2013

3. *Publishing Business in Eighteenth-Century England*
James Raven, 2014

4. *The First Century of Welfare:
Poverty and Poor Relief in Lancashire, 1620–1730*
Jonathan Healey, 2014

5. *Population, Welfare and Economic Change in Britain 1290–1834*
edited by Chris Briggs, P. M. Kitson and S. J. Thompson, 2014

6. *Crises in Economic and Social History: A Comparative Perspective*
edited by A. T. Brown, Andy Burn and Rob Doherty, 2015

7. *Slavery Hinterland: Transatlantic Slavery and
Continental Europe, 1680–1850*
edited by Felix Brahm and Eve Rosenhaft, 2016

8. *Almshouses in Early Modern England:
Charitable Housing in the Mixed Economy of Welfare, 1550–1725*
Angela Nicholls, 2017

9. *People, Places and Business Cultures:
Essays in Honour of Francesca Carnevali*
edited by Paolo Di Martino, Andrew Popp and Peter Scott, 2017

Printed and bound by CPI Group (UK) Ltd, Croydon, CR0 4YY

14/04/2025

14656913-0001